History and Traditions

OF

DARWEN AND ITS PEOPLE

By J. G. SHAW.

COMPRISING

AN HISTORICAL AND TRADITIONAL NARRATIVE

OF THE RISE AND PROGRESS OF THE BOROUGH OF DARWEN,

AND SOME INTERESTING

RECOLLECTIONS OF OLD DARWEN FAMILIES

DICTATED TO THE AUTHOR BY

THE LATE JEREMY HUNT.

"And year by year our memory fades
From all the circle of the hills."
—In Memoriam

BLACKBURN:
J. AND G. TOULMIN, PRINTERS, "THE TIMES" OFFICE.
1889.

DARWEN AND ITS PEOPLE.

FIRST EDITION 1889

LIMITED SECOND EDITION REPRINT

T.H.C.L. BOOKS, BLACKBURN, 1991

LIMITED THIRD EDITION REPRINT

HERITAGE PUBLICATIONS, BLACKBURN, 2012

ISBN 978-1-4710-3290-5

More local history books available from our website:

Heritage Publications

www.HeritagePublications.co.uk

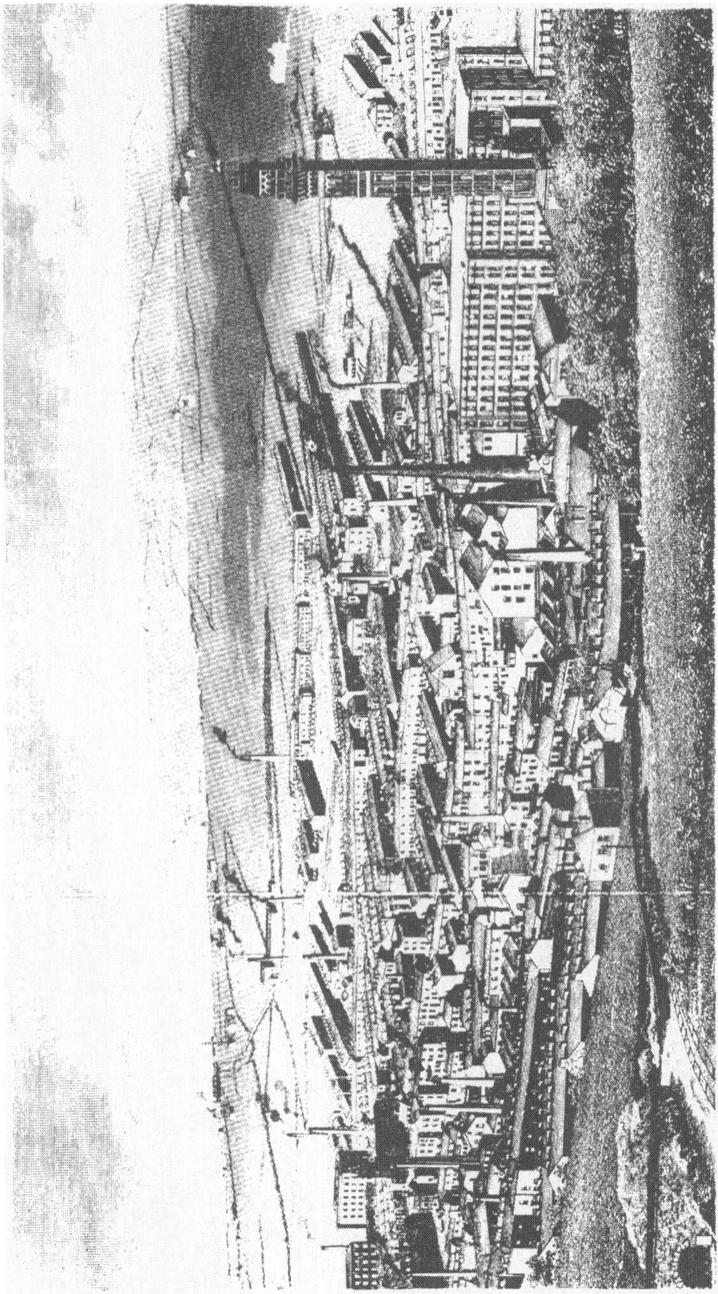

DEDICATED

IN PARTICULAR

TO THE MEMORY OF

MY OLD FRIEND

THE LATE JEREMY HUNT,

AND IN GENERAL

TO THE

PEOPLE OF DARWEN

WHOSE FAMILY HISTORY

IS RECORDED

IN HIS

RECOLLECTIONS.

PREFACE.

THIS unpretentious contribution to local history is submitted to the public in the hope that it will be found not only useful but interesting. I have avoided antiquarian details as much as possible in order to make the book acceptable to the ordinary reader. The special feature of the work is the second portion. I believe that the "Recollections" dictated to me by the late Jeremy Hunt are unique in literature; that they are also intensely interesting to the People of Darwen was proved by the cordial reception given to them when they first appeared in the columns of *The Blackburn Times*. For many years before his death, at the ripe old age of 80 years, I was closely associated with Mr. Hunt, and often listened with pleasure to the treasured traditions which he was continually recalling from the inexhaustible stores of his wonderful memory. During the last five or six years of his life he often expressed a wish to put his Recollections on record, but when, in the year 1884, I offered to take down in shorthand "all he knew," he shrank from the magnitude of the task of collating and dictating, although glad of the opportunity of putting in black and white what he could not write himself. After much consideration he agreed to dictate his "Recollections of Old Darwen Families," and to weave the history and traditions of the town around the genealogies of some twenty families which, he considered, were the original "clans" of the Darwen Valley. After working intermittently for two years or more, we published the first chapter of his Recollections in *The Blackburn Times* in November, 1886, and continued the publication regularly until my colleague's death in July of the following year. His work was then approaching completion, and its publication in book form had been announced. Since then, during the leisure hours of two years, I have written the General History of the town, and though I have felt seriously hampered by the loss of my former colleague, whose extraordinary knowledge of everything that has taken place in Darwen during the last 200 years was invaluable, I have been greatly assisted and encouraged by others, whose many kindnesses I have not space to acknowledge in detail.

My best authority for local tradition since the death of Mr. Hunt has been Mr. Wm. Thos. Ashton, J.P., a gentleman who for forty years has taken a keen interest in the History and Traditions of Darwen and its people, and written several pamphlets thereon, notably "The Heart of Lancashire," "On Some Old Roads and Old Inhabitants of Darwen," "Darwen Valley in the Past," &c. Mr. Ashton has conducted me personally over much historic ground in Darwen, and given me liberty to make free use of his own writings. The Rev. H. H. Moore, M.A., Vicar of St. John's, Darwen, has likewise been one of my best friends. A large portion of the first chapter is from his pen. Mr. J. J. Riley, proprietor of *The Darwen News*, and author of a chronological "History of Darwen," published annually from 1878 to 1884, has not only given me information that cost him much time and money to collect, but lent me engravings to illustrate the work, including a fine copper-plate from which the frontispiece is printed. In preparing the ecclesiastical portion of the book I have had the inestimable advantage of free access to the parochial records of Blackburn, preserved by the Right Rev. Bishop Cramer-Roberts, D.D., who has been most kind in allowing me from time to time the use of his own study at the Vicarage for the purpose of poring over the Coucher Books and other manuscripts. In the Nonconformist section I have had a willing and able helper in the Rev. Benjamin Nightingale, author of a "History of Tockholes Independent Meeting House." To Mr. Charles Costeker, Town Clerk of Darwen; Mr. F. G. Hindle, Clerk to the Darwen Borough Magistrates; and Mr. Joseph Watson, Secretary of the Blackburn Chamber of Commerce, who have furnished me with facts in some cases unobtainable from any other source, I am deeply indebted. My local publishers, Messrs. J. and G. Toulmin, who have printed the work, have also furnished several of the illustrations.

Much research has been spared me by the labours of Whitaker, Baines, Abram, and other historians of high repute. To their works I owe a great deal, and particularly to Mr. Abram's *History of Blackburn*,

While making good use of their books, I have in nearly every instance, where possible, traced their information to its original sources, and thus been able not only to avoid the repetition of errors, but to get the fuller details necessary for a local history. Chief among the valuable public documents which I have consulted are those preserved in the Public Record Office, London, and I am under special obligation to the Chetham Society and the Record Society for the publication of original documents which have saved me the toil of poring over many ancient manuscripts, scarcely legible, and containing only scraps of history concerning Darwen.

JNO. GEO. SHAW.

Lancaster Place,
    Blackburn, August 1st, 1889.

CONTENTS.

	PAGE.
PREFACE	vii-ix
LIST OF ILLUSTRATIONS	xiii-xiv

BOOK I.—GENERAL HISTORY.

CHAPTER I.	PHYSICAL FEATURES AND EARLIEST INHABITANTS	1-20
II.	OLD ROADS	21-32
III.	FROM THE CONQUEST TO THE REVOLUTION	33-70
IV.	ECCLESIASTICAL HISTORY	71-132
V.	THE PROGRESS OF TWO CENTURIES	133-194

BOOK II.—OLD DARWEN FAMILIES.

CHAPTER I.	INTRODUCTORY	1-4
II.	THE AUTHOR'S OWN LIFE	5-13
III.	THE MARSDENS	14-21
IV.	THE HOLDENS	22-32
V.	THE SMALLEYS	33-36
VI.	THE HARWOODS	37-45
VII.	THE PICKUPS	46-47
VIII.	THE ECCLESES	48-58

CONTENTS.

		PAGE.
IX.	THE SHORROCKS	59-62
X.	THE BRIGGSES	63-72
XI.	THE LEACHES	73-78
XII.	THE HINDLES	79-85
XIII.	THE HUNTS	86-94
XIV.	THE JEPSONS	95-101
XV.	THE WATSONS	102-105
XVI.	THE GRIMES	106-112
XVII.	THE WALSHES	113-117
XVIII.	THE FISHES	118-130
XIX.	CONCLUSION	131-132

ADDITIONAL FAMILIES.

XX.	THE ENTWISLES	133-4
XXI.	THE KIRKHAMS	135
XXII.	THE KAYS	136
XXIII.	THE BURYS	136
XXIV.	THE DUXBURYS	137-8
XXV.	THE WALMSLEYS	139
XXVI.	THE LIGHTBOWNS	140-1
XXVII.	THE THOMPSONS	142

LIST OF ILLUSTRATIONS.

CENTRE OF DARWEN - - - - - *frontispiece*
From a copper plate lent by Mr. J. J. Riley.

PORTRAIT OF WILLIAM THOMAS ASHTON, Esq., J.P. *to face page 24*
From a woodcut lent by Mr. J. J. Riley.

UNION STREET BRIDGE - - - - *to face page 26*
From a woodcut lent by Mr. J. J. Riley.

HOLKER HOUSE, Hoddlesden, Built A.D. 1591 - *to face page 45*
Engraved on zinc from a drawing by Mr. Charles Haworth.

WHITE HALL, the Oldest House in Darwen, dated 1557 *to face page 46*
Engraved on zinc from a drawing by Mr. A. G. Grubb.

DARWEN CHAPEL (ST. JAMES'S CHURCH) - - *to face page 86*
From a zinc engraving lent by Messrs. J. and G. Toulmin.

RUINS OF AN OLD NONCONFORMIST MEETING HOUSE
on Pendle Hill - - - - - - *to face page 99*
From a zinc engraving lent by Messrs. J. and G. Toulmin.

LOWER CHAPEL - - - - - - *to face page 111*
From a zinc engraving lent by Messrs. J. and G. Toulmin.

PORTRAIT OF CHARLES PHILIP HUNTINGTON, Esq., J.P. *to face page 161*
From a woodcut lent by Mr. J. J. Riley.

ARMS OF THE BOROUGH OF DARWEN - - - *page 169*
From a woodcut lent by Mr. J. J. Riley.

PORTRAIT OF WILLIAM SNAPE, Esq., J.P. First Mayor
of Over Darwen - - - - - *to face page 171*
From a woodcut lent by Mr. J. J. Riley.

LIST OF ILLUSTRATIONS.

PORTRAIT OF ALEX. T. ECCLES, Esq., Mayor of
Darwen - - - - - . - - *to face page 172*
From a woodcut lent by Mr. J. J. Riley.

DARWEN MARKET HALL AND MUNICIPAL OFFICES *to face page 174*
From a woodcut lent by Messrs. J. and G. Toulmin.

PLAN OF THE PUBLIC FOOTPATHS ON DARWEN MOOR *to face page 178*
Engraved on zinc from a drawing by Mr. W. Stubbs.

FOUNTAIN IN THE WHITEHALL PARK - - - *to face page 178*
From a woodcut lent by Mr. J. J. Riley.

PORTRAIT OF LORD CRANBORNE, M.P. - - *to face page 184*
From a woodcut lent by Mr. J. J. Riley.

MAP OF THE DARWEN DIVISION OF LANCASHIRE *to face page 184*
Engraved on zinc from a drawing.

PORTRAIT OF JOHN GERALD POTTER, Esq., J.P. *to face page 186*
From a woodcut lent by Mr. J. J. Riley.

PORTRAITS OF T. LIGHTBOWN AND GRAHAM FISH,
Esqrs. - - - - - - - *to face page 188*
From Meisenbach engravings lent by Mr. J. J Riley.

PORTRAIT OF THE LATE JEREMY HUNT *frontispiece to Book II.*
Photogravure from a photo by Mr. T. Lindley.

HISTORY AND TRADITIONS

OF

DARWEN AND ITS PEOPLE.

BOOK I.—GENERAL HISTORY.

Chapter 1.—Physical Features and Earliest Inhabitants.

Name of the Borough—The Backbone of England, and its Rossendale Offshoot—The Darwen Valley—Source and Course of the River Darwen—Steep and Rugged Hills—Darwen Moor—Scenery of the Valley—The Lower Coal Measures and the Millstone Grit—Original Swamps of the Darwen District—Upheaval of the Pennine Chain—Climate and Vegetation—Water Supply—Origin of the Local Industries—Quality of Darwen Coal—Formation of Flag Rock—Hoghton Tower Rock—Glaciers—The Old and New Stone ages—Pre-historic Man—Supposed Neolithic Temple on Turton Heights—Celtic Invasion of Britain—Cymric and Gaelic Place Names—The Saxon Invasion—Archæological Remains at Whitehall—Cymric Place-names in Darwen—Abundance of Saxon Names—Evidence of Primeval Forests—Supposed Saxon Burial Grounds—Scandinavian Place-names.

DARWEN is the name given by Act of Parliament, in the year of Jubilee, 1887, to a modern borough situated on the banks of a small Lancashire stream, from which the name is derived. The borough, which is 5,919 acres in extent, embraces the whole of the township of Over Darwen, and portions of the townships of Lower Darwen and Eccleshill. It stands in a peculiar position near the source of the river, and the disposition of its buildings along the course of the stream for upwards of three miles gives it a remarkable, elongated appearance. Its ground plan was laid by the cooling of the earth's crust, ages before the palmy days of the Jews, the Greeks, and the Romans; and the facts given in this chapter will show that the town owes its general appearance, its trade, its development, in fact its very existence, to the physical character and geological structure of the Darwen Valley, whose history takes us back so many thousand years.

When the great ridge of the Pennine chain of hills, forming the backbone of England, was elevated, many transverse ridges were thrown up on each side of it, with their lines of upheaval running at various angles to the principal range. The Darwen and Rivington hills form the western termination of a range of high ground, which is a transverse offshoot from the main Pennine range, and is called by geologists the Rossendale anticlinal. The town of Darwen stretches along the bottom of a deep, narrow valley, lying among these hills, with its mouth opening towards the north into the wider valley which runs westward from Blackburn towards Preston. The Darwen brook rises on the northern side of a watershed of peaty moorland, which on the southern side slopes towards Bolton and Entwistle. At the foot of the moorland slopes the waters of the brook are gathered in Jack Kay's reservoir, from which they flow through the hamlet of Sough and the whole length of the town of Darwen, and unite with the Blakewater at Blackburn. Thence the Darwen turns at a right angle westward, and flows past Hoghton tower and hamlet into the Ribble, between Walton-le-Dale and Preston. The hills which hem in the town on the western side are steep and rugged in most places, and rise to the height of a quarter of a mile at the highest point of Darwen Moor.[1] Cultivation has spread about two-thirds of the distance up their sides, but the upper portion is still undrained, uncultivated moorland, covered with ling and the bilberry or whinberry plant. The hills on the eastern side of the town are not so high and rugged, but rise with a more gradual, easy slope, and with a more even surface, and are consequently cultivated to the summit of the ridge. The town has therefore a natural tendency to extend more up the wider, easier slopes on the eastern side of the valley, than up the steeper heights on the west. The scenery of the valley presents a bare, bleak aspect. Excepting in the narrow dingles which mark the steep, winding course of two or three brooks down the western hill-side, there is an almost utter absence of wood. Wide bare slopes of grass, divided by stone walls, with clusters and rows of stone houses scattered irregularly about, and the dark, rugged moors overlooking the valley on the west and south, combine to produce an impression of sternness and untidiness. The view of Darwen Moor, however, with its bold outline and steep, rugged slopes, as seen from the east side of the valley, is not without beauty, especially in summer. The summit of Darwen Moor (which is the first hill from the sea), and the numerous walks lately constructed over it, offer facilities for far-reaching and interesting views, extending the whole length of Morecambe Bay

---

[1].—The highest point of Darwen Moor, according to the Ordnance Survey, is 1,319½ feet.

to Black Combe, and embracing the Bollandshire Fells, Ingleborough, Pendle, and the flat country north and south of the Ribble estuary. On the northern base of Darwen Moor the short, pretty, wooded valley of Sunnyhurst runs into the main valley of the Darwen; and at its north-western base is the narrow, winding valley of the Roddlesworth, which runs along a wooded and, in places, rocky bottom to join the Darwen at Feniscowles Hall. In the first part of its course this brook is connected with and forms part of the series of reservoirs which end in the large Rivington and Horwich lakes, and supply Liverpool with part of its water.

The physical aspect of the country around Darwen is explained by its geological structure. The two strata which come to the surface are the Lower Coal Measures and the Millstone Grit. The Yoredale Shales, which form the stratum next below the Millstone Grit, crop up in the Mellor and Pendle range of hills, and the Carboniferous or Mountain Limestone, underlying the Yoredale Shales, is exposed at Clitheroe and Chatburn. We find the Middle Coal Measures, which come next above the Lower Coal Measures, by going south from Darwen to Bolton, which lies just on the northern edge of the strip of country consisting of that stratum. The Lower Coal Measures form the cap of Darwen Moor, Cranberry Moss, Turton Heights, Winter Hill (between Darwen and Tockholes), and all the Blacksnape ridge and slopes forming the eastern boundary of the Darwen valley, and they extend north and north-east to Lower Darwen, Blackburn, Accrington, Clayton-le-Moors, and Oswaldtwistle. Originally this district was a continuous level swamp of Lower Coal Measures' vegetation, but when the upheaval of the Pennine Range occurred, a great fracture in the strata took place along the line now forming the Darwen valley, whereby the Darwen Moor, on the west side of this line, was elevated, and the land on the east side of the line was depressed. Consequently the Lower Coal Measures, which are found as a capping on the elevated summit of Darwen Moor, on the western side of the valley, are, on the eastern side, found at a level several hundred feet lower[1]. By the elevation of the Western side the Millstone Grit rocks, underlying the capping of the Lower Coal Measures, have been exposed to view, and they form the base and slopes of Darwen Moor along the Darwen, Sunnyhurst, Roddlesworth, and Yarnsdale Valleys. The line of this fault follows very closely the line of the highway from Bull Hill, where it commences, to Ewood, near Blackburn. It will be easily understood how water and other natural agencies would inevitably operate to scoop out a deep

1. The throw of the fault in a line with Holy Trinity Church is estimated at not less than 400 yards.

trough or valley along such a line of weakness and irregularity of surface. Wherever the soft shales of the Lower Coal Measures or Millstone Grit occur we find straight slopes, but where the harder rock strata of the Millstone Grit come to the surface, we find steep edges, lines of cliff, or bold projecting terraces. To these are due the sharp ridge of the Billinge and Revidge Heights, Blackburn; the cliffs in Yarnsdale, and the projecting terrace running along the hill-side on the west of Darwen, in which quarries are worked at Bull Hill, Radford Head, and Woodside. Owing to the presence of stiff, close clays, the Lower Coal Measures generally form a surface of damp, cold soil, which naturally produces only a coarse vegetation, even grass growing in it only when it is well drained. This damp, sterile character is of course still more intensified when these strata occupy an elevated position on the top of high hills and plateaux. In such positions then as the hill-tops on the west and south of Darwen, we naturally find wastes of boggy moorland, producing a vegetation whose characteristic is few species, many individuals,—consisting only of the common ling, whinberry, and coarse sedges and mosses. The Millstone Grit formation, when occupying elevated positions, is marked by the same characteristics, as in Winter Hill (Rivington Range), and the adjoining heights of the Rivington Range, and in Pickup Bank Moss and the moors towards Musbury.

The coldness and dampness of the climate of Darwen are a necessary consequence of its natural conditions and surroundings. The soil is cold and damp. An extensive range of lofty, swampy, moorland hills extends west and south-west of it, and being the first elevation from the sea intercepts and condenses the moisture-laden winds from the Atlantic. The valley itself lies open to the north and under the shade of hills on the south and west; all which circumstances, of course, have one and the same tendency, in lowering the temperature and saturating the air with moisture. Such climatic conditions, while bracing and invigorating to the strong and healthy, are very unfavourable for those who have a predisposition to rheumatism and lung and bronchial affections. In other respects the physical formation of the valley favours sanitation. There is abundance of pure, fresh air from the neighbouring moorland hills and not distant sea. The rapid declivities of the hill-sides and the regular fall of the valley bottom favour the quick removal of the sewage by gravitation. The water supply, also on the gravitation principle, is easily and abundantly obtained. It needs care in its use for drinking purposes, however, for, like all water collected from a gathering ground of peaty moorlands, it contains an abundance of humic and other acids produced by the decomposed vegetable matter; and owing to this circumstance, combined with its softness, it readily absorbs lead. It is therefore a necessary precaution not to use for drinking and culinary purposes water which has been standing in lead pipes or lead cisterns. Owing to its complete deficiency in mineral elements, as lime and silex, it is also unfavourable to the formation and preservation of the teeth, and it is important that oatmeal porridge and oatcake should form a large element in the daily dietary of growing children; and that limewater should be mixed with the milk they drink, if their teeth and bones are to be fully supplied with the elements necessary for their composition.

Not only the scenery, the soil and its products, the climate, and the sanitary conditions of the district, but also its industrial occupations and interests are directly dependent on and determined by the geological formation. The abundant water-supply to be found in this valley was the cause of the original introduction of the cotton manufactures, cotton bleaching, and paper making, and the dampness of the climate is also naturally favourable to cotton weaving and spinning. When steam power was introduced the advantages of the district were still further available, because supplies of coal as well as of water were found close at hand. The rocks of the Millstone Grit strata which are exposed on the eastern and northern flanks of Darwen Moor are largely worked by means of open quarries. The flag rocks of the Lower Coal Measures on the other hand are worked on the eastern side of the fault by means of deep shafts. The coal seams of the capping of Lower Coal Measures which remains on the top of Darwen Moor have been worked chiefly by adits and tunnels in the hill-side, while on the eastern side of the fault they have had to be reached by sinking shafts. Good fire-clay is also found in abundance in connection with the coal-seams of the Lower Coal Measures.[1] Hundreds of men consequently find employment in connection with the quarries, flagpits, collieries, and brick and tile works of the district.

The seams of coal found in the Lower Coal Measures are but few, and generally thin and poor, not at all to be compared with the thicker and richer seams of the Middle Coal Measures of such districts as Wigan; nevertheless, about Burnley they attain a greater thickness and better quality than usual. These Lower Coal Measures' seams are often called the Gannister Beds or Mountain Mines. They frequently crop

---

1. Every coal-seam lies upon a bed of underclay, which is really the fine mud in which the coal plants once grew and rooted themselves. Occasionally the roots of the coal plants are found still imbedded in the clay where they grew. These were once thought to be a distinct kind of plant, and were called *stigmaria*, but are now known to be the roots of *sigillaria*.

out at the surface on the hill-sides and are worked by level drifts into the hills, the mouths of which are called "day-eyes", a name indicating more poetical sentiment than one would expect in colliers. In Darwen there are two of these seams which are principally worked, viz. : (1) The Upper Mountain Mine, called the Yard Seam, because it is about 3ft. thick; and (2) The Gannister Coal or Half-yard Mine, which is from 18 inches to 2 feet thick. This latter lies 70 yards under the former Besides these two principal seams there are two others, thinner,—on. of 12 inches thickness lying 18 yards above the Half-yard Mine, and another 12 yards above the Yard Seam, and only 10 inches thick,—this rests upon a true Gannister floor, and it is well exposed as it crops out in the cutting at the Sough end of the railway tunnel. Above this again are flagstones which are extensively worked by Messrs. Entwisle and Messrs. Lloyd and Millward. The Yard and Half-yard Mines are now entirely exhausted on the western or Darwen Moor side of the valley. In the direction of the Hoddlesden Valley, which is parallel to that of Darwen, about a mile further east, the strata that separate the 10 inch seam and the Yard Seam gradually thin out, and the two seams come so close together as to be worked together at the old Hoddlesden Colliery. In this position they continue for some distance northward, but divide again at Belthorn, where the upper part is called the "Half-yard," and the lower the "Little Coal." The flagstones of Darwen are of an excellent quality and find ready sale for forming the footpaths of the large towns in the neighbourhood. The flag rock was formed by the continuous deposit of successive layers of very fine sand of regular thickness and on the same plane or level, each deposit being hardened by the air and sun, as it lay exposed, between tides, on the sea beach or sand-banks of a river estuary. Mica, felspar, carbon, and other mineral matter suspended in the waters, were also deposited with each layer of sand, and coated its surface, thus operating to make the cleavage of the laminæ more easy and regular. The innumerable fresh layers of sand and mud thus deposited by successive tides were finally depressed and buried under an enormous superincumbent bulk of other deposits, and hardened by pressure into solid rock. Frequently there may be seen in the flag rock the impressions of the ripple-marks of the sea, and indentations made by drops of rain or hail, and even the tracks of worms. Wherever those ripple-marks or worm-tracks are visible, however, the value of the flags is thereby depreciated. Much of the flag rock of Darwen is very micaceous, the surface of the stones when cleaved shining as if coated with silver.

The Hoddlesden Valley has been formed like the Darwen Valley by great fractures of the rock strata. While the Lower Coal Measures have been thrown down on the western side, and form the bed of the valley and its western slopes, the Millstone Grit strata have been upheaved on the eastern side of the valley and form the high ground of the Pickup Bank ridge, and the hills towards Haslingden Grane and Musbury.

The members of the Millstone Grit series of strata found in Darwen are: (*a*) the 1st Grit or Rough Rock, (*b*) Shales, (*c*) the 2nd Grit, (*d*) Shales, (*e*) the 3rd Grit, (*f*) Shales, and (*g*) the 4th or Kinder Scout Grit. The 1st Grit, or Rough Rock, is the uppermost of the series, and on it the base of the Lower Coal Measures rests. It is a coarse, massive conglomerate, full of pebbles of quartz, some of considerable size, which the quarrymen commonly call lumps of suet. It is quarried at Bull Hill, Old Briggs's Waterfall, Smalley Delf, Thorney Height Delf, Knowl Heights, and Lower Wenshead Hey Quarry. Perhaps the finest development of this rock to be found in the North of England is the bluff on which Hoghton Tower is situated, where this rock attains the thickness of 400 feet, and is well exposed in the quarry on the north-east side of the hill. The 2nd Grit is the next lower rock, and is a finer-grained grit, and more flaggy. This is quarried at the back of the Cemetery, at Dole Delf, at Radfield Head Delfs, High Lumb Waterfall Delf, and the quarry below Wood Head. The 3rd Grit is quarried at Dollymoor Delf on the High Lumb Brook, below Punstock. The 4th, or Kinder Scout Grit, the lowest of the series, is not exposed, but lies under the Belgrave Chapel and School. The Millstone Grit rocks are largely quarried for setts for the paving of streets. The stone of which Holy Trinity Church is built is a fine-grained red sandstone, belonging to the Lower Coal Measures, and came from Red Delf, near the top of the north-east end of Darwen Moor.

The last feature of the geology of Darwen to be noticed is the fact that the whole of the surface of the country is covered with deposits of sand and clay left by glaciers, among which are found innumerable specimens of felsites and granites, which have been transported hither from the mountains of Cumberland and Westmorland; and of limestones from the Yorkshire hills. Lumps of both the red and the grey Shap granite are found everywhere in the glacial clay in abundance.

PRE-HISTORIC MAN.

No traces of the first race of men inhabiting our country—the men of the Palæolithic or old stone age—have been found in or near Darwen, nor of the animals which were contemporaneous with men. The Palæolithic men were roaming savages, with no other homes than caves or tree branches, and their relics are chiefly rudely-formed flint weapons and tools. Their successors—the men of the Neolithic or new stone age—had fixed habitations, and definite centres of population. Though, like the Palæolithic men, they lived in some cases in caverns (*e. g.* in the notable case of the Victoria Cave, Settle), yet they had also camps and houses. The great circular rampart found at Amesbury, Wiltshire, with the concentric circles of stones enclosed within it, are thought to have been one of their temples. There are also many smaller circles of stones, in every part of the country, which were once attributed generally to the Druids of the Celtic race, but nine out of ten of them are now believed to be the work of the Neolithic men. If this be so, then there may be a trace of their presence in the neighbourhood of Darwen, for on the top of Turton Moor, south of Entwistle reservoir, and between the Lancashire and Yorkshire railway and the Darwen to Bolton Road, was a circle of small stones of this character, set upright in the ground on an elevated position, and marked as usual in the Ordnance Map as a Druidical Circle. Unfortunately some ignorant farmer removed all the stones to build into a wall. The circle was a very perfect one, but now only one large and two small stones are left standing upright. Of course it cannot be certain whether this circle of stones is the work of the Neolithic men or of their Celtic successors.

THE CELTIC INVASION OF BRITAIN.

The Celtic race moved from its home in Central Asia and invaded or immigrated into Europe in two successive waves or swarms. The Gaels formed the first division, and dispossessed the Neolithic or Euskarian race, pushing them forward into the remoter western and northern corners of Europe and of the British Isles. They were soon followed by their kinsmen—the Cymric division of the Celtic family—who in turn largely dispossessed the Gaels of their territory and drove them on westward and northward. The Gaels found in Britain were driven out into Ireland, into the Scotch Highlands, Wales, Cumberland, Westmorland, and into Devon and Cornwall. In those districts they would find and absorb the remnants of the Neolithic or Euskarian race which they had previously supplanted. Throughout the greater part of Europe and South Britain, the names of the rivers and mountains rarely belong to the Gaelic dialect, but almost always to the Cymric dialect of the Celtic language. The Cymri who settled in Britain are popularly known as the Ancient Britons. Their presence in Darwen is proved by the name itself. It is composed of the Cymric words *Dwr*, meaning "water," and

Gwyn, meaning "clear," "bright," or "sparkling," and thus means "*the clear stream*." The name is thus a misnomer at the present time when the stream is in a state of notorious pollution. The names *Darwen* (Lancashire), *Derwent* (Derbyshire, Yorkshire, Cumberland and Durham), *Darent* (Kent), *Trent* (Notts), *Dart* (Devon) *Derwen* (Denbighshire), are all modifications of the same two roots. So likewise are the *Durance*, in France, and the *Trento*, in Italy. *Sough*, the name of a hamlet forming part of the town of Darwen, is also a Cymric word meaning "drain," "sink." *Pendle Hill* is a very interesting name because it is an accretion of words belonging to different languages and periods of history. The first syllable *Pen* is the Cymric word for "hill" or "mountain." The Anglo-Saxon invaders would hear the hill spoken of by this name among their British captives and serfs, and thinking it a proper name, added a word of their own, *hyl*, meaning "hill." When, by the fusion of the two words into one, the meaning of the Anglo-Saxon termination had been forgotten, the later English word "hill" was added, so that we have in this one name a threefold repetition of words having the same meaning, and when we say "Pendle Hill" we do really say "Hill-hill-hill." But *Pendle* is an interesting name for another reason. The prefix "Pen" is of value as a test word for determining the relative local positions and boundaries of the two divisions of the Celtic race in Britain. "Pen" belongs to the Cymric dialect of the Celtic language, while its equivalent in the Gaelic dialect is "Ben." Wherever we find the form "Pen" existing, we know that the early inhabitants of that district were Cymri; wherever "Ben" prevails, the people were Gaels. Now "Ben" is found as a common prefix to the names of mountains in Ireland and the Scotch Highlands, as *Bunnabeola, Ben Nevis, Ben Lomond*, &c. But in Wales and England, and the eastern half of the Scotch Lowlands, we find "Pen" not "Ben," as *Pendle, Penyghent, Penmaen-Mawr, Penrith*, &c. The termination "pians" in *Grampians*, and the second syllable in *Apennines*, are also from the same root. Thus we know that Darwen and its neighbourhood were occupied by, and received the names of its hills and streams from the Cymri. It is very probable that the word "Bull" in the name *Bull Hill* is a softened form of the Cymric word "Bwlch," which means "gap," or "pass," and which is often found in Wales, as *Tan-y-Bwlch*. The reasonableness of this derivation is shown by the fact that it is just that portion of the range of hills to the west and south of the Darwen valley where there is the deepest depression or gap in the ridge. The approach to the valley from the south, and the exit from it on that side must always have followed that line. If one attempted to cross the ridge either to the west or east of this depression, one would have not only to mount to a much higher part of the ridge, but would also find that the deep hollow of Yarnsdale and the upper part of Cadshaw Brook valley would interpose considerable obstacles to one crossing them at right angles. Whereas, just where the Bull Hill road crosses the ridge, the Cadshaw valley can be crossed at its narrowest and shallowest point, and an easy slope leads down to the more level country about Bolton. Another explanation of the term "Bull Hill" also refers it to the ancient Britons, who may have called it *Pwl* (Pool) Hill. So complete were the subjugation and extermination of the Ancient Britons that their language entered but very slightly into the English which was founded on the Anglo-Saxon of their conquerors. The names of rivers and mountains remain, and have been incorporated in the English tongue, but local place-names of Celtic origin are exceedingly rare in England. There are, however, three or four old names in Darwen in addition to those just mentioned, which appear to date back to a period anterior to the Saxon settlement here. "Drummer Stoops," the name of part of the ridge of Blacksnape, seems to come from the Celtic *drum*, a ridge; and "Pole Lane," a section of the old road leading from the Roman road to the British burial-place at Whitehall, is probably derived from the Celtic *pwl*, a pool or marsh. A row of low, poor cottages, off Pole Lane, bears the singular name of "Hutty Croo." Though we have not the slightest proof that there have been *huts* there since the times of the ancient Britons, it is possible, if not probable, that the name is a corruption of "Huttock Row," and is derived from the Celtic *huddo*, to cover, Anglo-Saxon *hydan*, the origin of our English *hut*. In "Cadshaw" and "Catleach" the first syllable may be from the Celtic *coed*, a wood, or it may refer to the wild cat which was once plentiful in the district. "Shaw" and "leach" are Saxon, the former meaning a wood or shady place, Anglo-Saxon *sceaga*, and the latter a lake or pool, Anglo-Saxon *lac*, corrupted to *lache* and *leach*. Two little streams in Darwen, bearing the name of Earnsdale have had their nomenclature attributed to the Celtic period,[1] but the second portion of the word, "dale," is clearly Anglo-Saxon, or Danish, and I shall show anon that the name is probably a Saxon one.

[1] Mr. W. T. Ashton, J.P., in a lecture on "Darwen Valley in the Past," delivered in Belgrave School, on December 21st, 1887, says:—"I shall now direct myself to showing the past appearance of the township and valley of Darwen from its present names, which are mostly Saxon, with one or two rather important exceptions. One of these is the name Earnsdale. There are two Earnsdales—one which comes down below Sunnyhurst Wood and flows into the River Darwen at Hollins Grove, and the other which is located in the lower part of the Cadshaw Valley. The Cadshaw Brook takes two or three names. In the upper part it is known as the Green Lowe Brook; at another point it is called the Cadshaw Brook; and at another the Earnsdale Brook. There is a singularity about this, showing that in addition to the names Darwen, Ribble and Pendle, there appears to be a British or Gaelic origin to the word Earnsdale. Consulting the "Gaelic Topography of Scotland," written by

BRITISH BURIAL GROUND AT WHITEHALL.

But the names of the natural features of the country around Darwen are not the only proofs of the residence of the Cymri here in very early times, for those people have also left archæological remains behind them in the Darwen Valley. In October, 1864, excavations were being made by Mr. William Shorrock Ashton for the foundations of the house called "Ashleigh," at the south end of Darwen, on a low mound near Whitehall. The mound was about 30 yards in diameter, and rose gradually to the height of about 12 feet above the surrounding land. On a careful examination traces of 10 distinct interments were found there. One of them was simply a heap of burnt bones, without any cist or urn; others were enclosed in urns, only one of which was found in an inverted position. On the top of each of the cinerary urns was a rough flat stone, and each urn was surrounded and covered with small stones carefully piled up. Two of the cinerary urns were in a tolerably perfect state; the others were very much broken. Two small vessels called *incense-cups* were found within the urns. The most perfect of the urns was one 12 inches in height and 10 inches in diameter at the top. It narrowed to the base and was ornamented in its upper part with dotted indentations, evidently made with the point of a stick before the clay was baked. No coins or flint implements were found, but with the burnt bones was a bronze dagger or spearhead, $7\frac{1}{2}$ inches long, 3 inches wide at the thickest part, and $\frac{3}{8}$ths of an inch thick. Some account of these remains has been given in Whitaker's *History of Whalley*, Mr. Abram's *History of Blackburn*, *The Preston Guardian*, and in a paper by Mr. Llewellyn Jewitt in *The Reliquary*.[1] The consensus of opinion is that they are to be attributed to the period of the Roman occupation, as they are evidently the rude work of the Ancient Britons, who learnt the art of pottery from the Romans and adopted the system of cremation, instead of burial, in imitation of the Romans. The pottery of the Romans and the Saxons gives evidence of better workmanship than that of the Ancient Britons, and cremation was abandoned when the Saxons succeeded the Celts as the inhabitants of this island. The vessels containing the burnt bones, the bronze spearhead, and the coins, were given to the Historical Society of Lancashire and Cheshire, and are now de-

Col. Jas. A. Robinson, F.S.A., I find that the word "Earn," and the River Earn in Perthshire, mean *the east-flowing river*. Col. Robinson gives the word as *Ea-an*, signifying in the Gaelic 'the east-flowing river.' Now, it is a remarkable fact that these two streams do flow east. The Earnsdale Brook is as near due east as it could possibly be. The other Earnsdale from one or two points of view —the stream is a little tortuous in its upper part—is almost due east."—Mr. Ashton's careful research and ingenious reasoning carry great weight, and I quote his opinion here while preferring to classify the name Earnsdale as a Saxon one (see after). It will be observed that he traces it to the Gaelic not the Cymric branch of the Celtic race.

posited in the Public Free Museum at Liverpool. This fact must suggest the need for Darwen to have a good Museum of its own, for want of which any local antiquities or geological specimens that may be found in the neighbourhood are liable to be scattered about the country, out of reach of the very persons most interested in and most entitled to their possession.

The Romans never settled in the Darwen valley, so far as I can ascertain, but merely passed it by in their highland marches between Manchester and Ribchester. Of this I shall have something to say in the chapter on old roads. During the Roman period the Darwen valley was occupied by the Celts, as shown by the discoveries at Whitehall, and the Celts were eventually driven out by the Saxons, as will now be shown.

PREPONDERANCE OF SAXON PLACE-NAMES.

Place-names afford a valuable clue to the original condition of a quiet country district like Darwen, and they are of all the more importance here, because being out of the track of kings and their armies, and almost out of the reach of priests and monks, Darwen has no written history, except of a very fragmentary character, prior to the seventeenth century, when it became the home of persecuted Nonconformist congregations, who worshipped God amid the wild solitudes of its moors and in the shady nooks of its secluded glens. Without placing too much reliance on etymological theories we may safely conclude that the Ancient Britons dwelt in this district and gave the name *Dwr-gwyn* (clear water) to the river which flows through the Darwen valley, that the Norsemen or Danes penetrated into its fastnesses, and that the Saxons eventually formed settlements on the river banks, retaining but little of the ancient nomenclature and naming every object in the landscape after their own fashion. The Celtic and Scandinavian place-names preserved to the present day are exceedingly rare, but the name of the river stands out pre-eminent as the oldest and most important name in the neighbourhood. It is without doubt Celtic, and was given to the clear stream which is now so muddy by those Ancient Britons who named most of the other principal rivers of Lancashire and some of the hills.[1] The Saxon conquerors afterwards settled on the stream at Over and Lower Darwen, and so completely exterminated the aborigines that scarcely a trace of them is left. There is not a scrap of written history to be found referring to Darwen before the time of the Norman Conquest, but the name *Derewenta*, which we find applied to

[1] Sir James Mackintosh in his *History of England* says :—" The only tie between the Britons and the modern English is the unaltered names of the grander masses of earth and water."

Over and Lower Darwen, shortly after this event, is a Saxon modification of the original Celtic name.

Saxon is such a common element in our language that I do not wish to lay too much stress on the ancient origin of the Saxon place-names which occur so abundantly in the Darwen valley. Some of them may be comparatively modern, but I would point out that the names of the hills and the dales, the woods and the streams, like that of the township, are likely to have existed, with slight variation, from very early times, and that the fact of these being Saxon shows that Darwen was an important Saxon settlement long before the days of the Conqueror. A host of names of this class can be adduced to prove that Darwen was originally a forest abounding in clumps of timber, stretches of wild moorland, and numerous pretty *denes* or cloughs.[1] There were also patches of fertile meadow and pasture land, and the inhabitants dwelt in folds and hamlets scattered about the landscape. One acquainted with the present aspect of the townships of the Darwen valley will have no difficulty in picturing the state of the Saxon settlements in those primitive days, and we need not rely too implicitly on the derivation of words for proof of this early condition, because many discoveries have been made justifying the names given to places which they do not now describe, and the memory of man confirms the accuracy of the description in several important cases.

Pickup Bank, formerly Piccop, or Piccope, Bank, appears to be derived from the Anglo-Saxon words accurately describing the landscape —*pic*, a peak or point; *copp* or *cope*, a cap or head (equivalent to the Latin *caput*); and *banc*, a mound or ridge. The "Pike" in Rivington Pike is also from Anglo-Saxon *pic*.[2] Blacksnape is the bleak snape or ridge, Anglo-saxon *blac* or *blæc*, cold, open, exposed, dreary; and Anglo-Saxon *cnæp*, the smoothed summit of rising ground, or of a ridge of hill. Knowl Heights, like Pendle Hill or Pickup Bank, are doubly described, the derivation evidently being from Anglo-Saxon *cnoll*, a knoll or hill-top, and *heahtho*, or *heatho*, from *heah*, high, an elevation. Another common description of hills in Darwen is "lowe," as in Little Lowe,

---

[1] The Rev. Isaac Taylor, the eminent philologist, writes thus about the probability of Lancashire generally having been originally thickly wooded:—"Lancashire, which is now such a busy hive of workers, was one of the most desolate and thinly peopled parts of England before coal was found underlying her barren moorlands and thick forests. An analysis of the local names will enable us to make a rough comparison of the area anciently under cultivation with that which was unreclaimed. Throughout Lancashire we find very few names ending in *borough*, *by*, or *thorpe*, and hence we conclude that the number of villages and towns was small. There is a fair sprinkling of names in *ham*, *worth*, and *cote*, suffixes which would denote detached homesteads; while the very large number of names which are compounded with the words *shaw*, *holt*, *ley*, *hill*, and *mere*, prove that the greater portion of the country consisted only of woodland or wild moor."

[2] Cf. the name *Pic du Midi*, a summit of the Pyrenees in the extreme south-west of France.

Great Lowe, High Lowe, and Green Lowe; also, Hoglowe, on the way to Haslingden. "Lowe," from the Saxon *hlæow*, or *hleow*, means a hill, or, more particularly, a mound or tumulus, and wherever the name occurs it is supposed that it indicates a tribal burial place of the Saxons who founded the settlements of Over and Lower Darwen. "Hill" is pure Saxon, and Eccleshill is probably a Saxon name because the syllables *les* (lea) and *hill* both come from the Anglo-Saxon tongue and both describe the nature of the land in the township.[1]

The common names of the valleys around Darwen, like those of the hills, are also Anglo-Saxon, for instance the "den" in Hoddlesden, Lyon's Den, &c., comes from Anglo-Saxon *dene*, *dæn*, a deep wooded valley; "hurst," in Sunnyhurst, Oakenhurst, &c., is from Anglo-Saxon *hyrst*, a clump of trees, a thick wood. "Bottoms," meaning a dale or valley, is given by Dr. Angus as one of the few words that have come down intact to us from the Ancient Britons, but it is generally derived from the Anglo-Saxon *botm*, to which it is allied. "Shaw" is a shady place, such as a wooded clough, Anglo-Saxon *sceaga*; it is a common termination of Darwen place-names, as Cadshaw, Dugshaw, Langshaw, and Hawkshaw. Many of these names imply the abundance of trees and woods, and the nature of these woods is more particularised in such names as Sunnyhurst, Oakenhurst, Fearnhurst (fern hurst), Greenhurst, Hollins Grove, Hawkshaw or Oakshaw, Thorney Height, Birch Hall, Hill Wood, Lower Wood, and Woodhead. There are two Woodheads, one in the Darwen Valley and the other at Pickup Bank, beyond Hoddlesden, and Jeremy Hunt has handed down a tradition that there was "once upon a time" a great wood extending from the one Woodhead to the other. Heys Lane, Hey Fold, Sunnyhurst Hey, The Hag, &c., indicate the presence of hawthorn trees, the derivation being from Anglo-Saxon *haga*, a hedge, and the thorn with which hedges are commonly made. This root occurs frequently in place-names in the forms hey, hay, haw, and haigh. Ewood means the wood by the river, from Anglo-Saxon *ea*, water or stream, and wood.

Tracts of land were also named by the Saxons, for we have lea and croft, moor and moss, the Green, and the Holmes, all pure Saxon words. The "les" in Eccleshill and the "ley" in Astley have been attributed to the Saxons, but with regard to the latter it should be known that it is not an old local name but was imported from Astley Bridge, by Richard Kershaw Smalley, who built Astley Bank House in the early

[1] Three local antiquaries whom I have consulted prefer to think that Eccleshill means the "church hill," from the Latin *ecclesia*, a church. (Cf. the Welch *egluys*). But there is no reason to suspect the existence of any early church in that township, and Darwen Chapel, which is near, did not exist before the Reformation.

part of this century, and named it in honour of his wife, who came from Astley Bridge. There was a family in Darwen of the name of Astley in the time of Charles I., but the principal place-name Astley is Astley Bank. The Lea (commonly spelled Lee) is the name of a district near the centre of Darwen which is peculiar to the town, and its etymology is hidden in its incorrect spelling. There are the Lee School and the Lee Foundry, both taking their name from that which described the tract of hill-side where they are situated before it was covered with buildings The words "lea," "leigh," and "ley," are derived from the Anglo-Saxon *leah* or *legh*, which again comes from Anglo-Saxon *liegan*, to lie down. The Lea therefore is the place where cattle would pasture and subsequently repose. Croft, in Turncroft, Earcroft, &c., both ancient names of districts, is an Anglo-Saxon word meaning an enclosed field; and the numerous folds in Darwen were named by the Saxons because they were enclosures made of *felled* trees. Earcroft, from Anglo-Saxon *ear*, to plough, means the ploughed field, and such a field would be noticeable because the soil and climate of Darwen are too damp and cold to favour corn-growing. As a rule, therefore, every field is a pasture or a meadow, though corn used to be grown at Chapels, and the name Earcroft would indicate that the soil was tilled in that neighbourhood also. The first syllable in Turncroft comes from the old Norse word *tiorn*, a small tarn. Moor and Moss are common Saxon names of tracts of swampy land, and there is one place now called Moss Bridge, which before there was any bridge there was simply called "The Moss," without any distinguishing adjective as in Cranberry Moss, Hoddlesden Moss, and Darwen Moor. The Holmes, from which Holmes Mill is named, comes from Anglo-Saxon *holm*, a river isle, or a low flat tract of rich land on the banks of a river. The Green is the last place-name describing a district or tract of country that I shall consider. It is the name of a hill-side slope touching the centre of modern Darwen, and, by analogy with "The Lea," "The Holmes," "The Moss," and other peculiar Darwen names, it means simply "The Green," or the Village Green. It would originally be a green field with a few folds and farms around it, and would be used as the playground of village children, the place where the May-pole was erected, and the market where stalls and booths were put up at fair times. This would imply that The Green was of old, as it is at present, the centre of Darwen, whereas history shows that the district called Chapels must have been the centre of population three hundred years or more ago. But there is evidence that there were several hamlets about the Darwen hills and valleys in early times and that one of the most important of these was situated on

Darwen Green. It would be to a great extent cut off from Chapels before the days of bridges, by the floods of the River Darwen, and would be of sufficient importance to have a village green of its own.

Some authorities think that Hollinshead should not be confounded with Hollins Grove. The latter means a grove of holly bushes (Anglo-Saxon *holi* or *holegn*, the holly tree); the former may be the house of the Hollings, from Anglo-Saxon *hedern* and *heder*, a house, and *Hollings*, a common Anglo-Saxon patronymic.[1] Barton House, cottage, row, and pits, and the old Darwen family Barton, take their name from Anglo-Saxon *bear*, the crop; and *tun*, *ton*, or *town*, an enclosure. Barton, from these roots, meaning a rickyard. The Bent is from Anglo-Saxon *bent*, meaning coarse grass, such as grows on cold, wet land. Mucky Stones is from Anglo-Saxon *meox*, dirt, involving the idea of moisture. High Lumb is apparently derived from Anglo-Saxon *lam*, which means loam and also clay. The Saxon word "twistle" in Entwistle, means a boundary or division, as in Oswaldtwistle, Tintwistle, Extwistle, &c. Dr. March suggests that the first syllable in Entwistle may be from *Endr*, a man's name, as in Enderby. In Roddlesworth the first part of the word comes from red, the colour, and the last is Anglo-Saxon *worth*, a fenced field or farm.[2] The first syllable in Hoglowe, Hoghton, &c., is derived from Anglo-Saxon *heah*, *hoh*, high, and while the former means the high mound, the latter signifies the high town or enclosure. Punstock was probably the ancient pinfold of the Saxons, the word being formed from Anglo-Saxon *pyndan*, to impound, and *stoec*, a stake, from which we get stock, stoke, and stockade. The important place-names Earnsdale and Yarnsdale both seem to be formed from a contraction of the name of the heron, and *dale*, a valley. An old proverb describes an ignorant man by saying that "he does not know a hawk from a hand-saw," the latter word being a corruption of "heron-

[1] Mr. W. T. Ashton regards Hollinshead (Tockholes), Hollins Grove or Hollin Grove (Darwen), and Hollin Bank (Blackburn), as all springing from the same root, and being derived from the name of the holly tree. He observes that Hollinshead is pronounced Hollinhead by old Darwen people, and, placing great reliance on tradition, he thinks this is the correct name, especially as Mr. Abram, the historian of Blackburn, has found the spelling Hollinhead in a deed 500 years old.

[2] The Rev. Robert Allan, formerly Minister of Tockholes Congregational Church, says, in a letter to a friend:—"I used to amuse myself, when at Tockholes, tracing out the meaning of the names of some of the places. Thus Winter Hill is simply 'win-dar' (or 'der') hill, and 'win-der' is just 'Dar-wen,' the clear water. Here you have Celtic and Saxon again. And so with Hollinshead. 'Holl' is just *holl* or hill, and 'win,' water—or the hill-water-head. James Worsley's farm you may remember is called Winshead. The water rises at the hill head and gives its name to Hollinshead Hall. Take Roddlesworth: here, too, we have three words. It is 'roth-wells-worth,' or the red-well-enclosure, 'worth' meaning enclosure."—Wenshead or Winshead is believed by Mr. Ashton to come from the whins or furze which covered the head or hill, and he believes Winter Hill to be named from the same thing, having ascertained from families who cleared it that it was once covered with whins. There is a great deal of uncertainty about such etymological theories, unless facts clearly bearing upon the subject can be adduced as evidence.

shaw" or "hearnshaw," a young heron. Or the first syllable may be the Anglo-Saxon *earn*, the eagle. Both the wooded dales mentioned above would be likely haunts either of the heron or of the eagle in olden times, when they were more secluded and remote from the population. This etymology seems to me to be more probable than that which traces the word to the Gaelic *ea-an*, an east-flowing river.[1] In the neighbourhood of Earnsdale there is the place-name Hawkshaw, which probably means the wood where hawks abound, although by some it is supposed to be a corruption of Oakshaw.

There is a tradition sometimes quoted that the name Stepback originated with Oliver Cromwell, who said to his men—though perhaps not in so many words—"Step back! Go no further." I believe, however, that there is no foundation for this tradition, and the best explanation I can find of the word is, *steep-beck*, "beck" being a well-known Lancashire word for a mountain stream. The gorge of Stepback is a veritable gate of the hills. Its western side is very steep and well planted with trees, and, from the high moor above, the brook dashes down in a rapid succession of tiny cascades.

Mr. W. T. Ashton, J.P., in his lecture on "Darwen Valley in the Past," already referred to, adduced a good deal of evidence in support of his explanation of various local place-names. The following abstract of a portion of his lecture is made with the object of preserving the evidence that he brought forward:—Bury Fold Lane takes its name from the Bury family. It was once a thickly-wooded lane, as an incident related to me by the late Mr. James Grime will show. He stated that a man once met with an accident at Grainings Brook, and it was necessary for him to be conveyed to Blackburn to receive the attendance of a doctor. A covered cart, or caravan, was obtained to convey the injured man to Blackburn. At that time Bolton Road did not exist, and the road from Grainings Brook went pretty nigh by Whitehall, Printshop, down Bury Fold Lane, along what is now called the Old Lane, and then off the corner of where Hope Mill at present stands, past an old corn mill which stood somewhere about the site of the existing offices at Hope Mill. To obtain a passage for the cart men had to go with "bills" to lop off the branches of the overhanging trees. Thorney Height formerly extended from the top of Astley Bank right down to the River Darwen. If I recollect aright, the names of the fields about Astley Bank refer to their thorny nature, and I believe, speaking from old tradition, that the whole of the slope from the top of Thorney Height to the River Darwen was a mass of thorns, brambles, and trees. A little below, on the other side of the river, were the Holmes, where Mr. John Walmsley's mill has been erected. The Holmes mean a rich tract of land, or pasture, beside a river, and there are residents of Darwen who can well remember the time when there were rich, beautiful meadows there, well deserving the name of the Holmes. The name Astley Bank was given by the late Richard Kershaw Smalley in honour of his wife, whom he brought from Astley Bridge. Mr. Smalley built a house there and called it Astley Bank. Passing along Thorney Height we come to the Higher and Lower Trees Farms, the names indicating that the country was thickly

[1] But see footnote on pp. 10-11.

wooded. Some years ago I had a conversation with the tenant of the Lower Trees Farm—whose name I regret I did not make a note of—and he told me that in his father's time there was a great row of beeches extending right away to High Lumb. The same tenant also told me that in digging drains, and sometimes in deepening ditches, he had come upon a good many buried trees. He had come across hazel trees, he said, with the nuts upon them, laid four and five feet deep in the ground. At that time High Lumb Wood was much more covered with trees—and very fine ones too—than it is now. The late Joshua Baron told me that, when he commenced business at Dob Meadows, he wanted sycamores of a very large size for certain rollers, and Mr. Joseph Bentley, a wheelwright and timber merchant in the town, was requested to search the country for them. In his journeyings Mr. Bentley went as far as the Lake District, but he found that the largest sycamores were to be had just below the present High Lumb Reservoir. Thirty-eight or thirty-nine years ago the Lea (or Lee) as I remember it, was a very beautiful place. It was entered not very far from Messrs. Shorrocks' foundry, and the walk wound round Prospect Hill and Lower Sunnyhurst. Often have I met the herds belonging to Mr. Nicholas Holden coming and going, in the morning and evening, from the rich pastures and meadows, irresistibly calling to mind the lines in Grey's "Elegy,":—

> The curfew tolls the knell of parting day;
> The lowing herds wind slowly o'er the lea.

In ancient times this lea ran through a deep wood, called the Hag. This is a name which is seldom mentioned now, but when I was young, and lived at Prospect Hill, it was a common thing for young people to say, "We'll go and have a walk through the Hag." Sir Walter Scott describes a hag as an oak-wood, so dark and impenetrable that sunlight could scarcely penetrate the branches. The objection has been taken that not many oaks were likely to have grown in Darwen, but I can remember them being a conspicuous sight. In my younger days I used to take frequent walks, turning off from Brookside Mill, opposite Mr. Walmsley's present mill, Vale Street, until I got on the Lea, and at one point, when the trees were in full leaf, looking in the direction of Earnsdale and Darwen Bank, the hedgerow was so filled with oaks that it presented the appearance of a dense wood. Your chairman [Alderman Henry Green] whom I often met, can bear me out in this. The fields were small in extent, and in addition to the oaks in the hedgerows there were isolated oaks in the open meadows. Turning this dark wood and going round the shoulder of the hill we are able to appreciate the meaning of the names Lower and Higher Sunnyhurst—"hurst" being Saxon for a wood. In making the Sunnyhurst Hey Reservoir the workmen found hundreds of oak and birch trees several feet below the surface of the ground—but not very large ones, as may be imagined, at an elevation of 900 feet above the level of the sea.[1] The name of Dob Meadows indicates a strong loamy clay. Mr. Joshua Baron informed me that the name originated from the following circumstance. The old footpath from Tockholes to Darwen crossed the Earnsdale Brook, and crossed these meadows behind Darwen Bank, in the direction of Livesey Fold. In wet weather the ground there was so soft that the stiff clay adhering to the feet made walking difficult. To avoid this, stepping stones or "dobs" were placed on the footpath, and that incident was the origin of the name Dob (or Daub) Meadows. Land so stiff as that was capable of sustaining oaks.

---

[1] It is a common thing to find birch and oak trees buried a few feet below the surface of mossy land, and they are not, as a rule, to be taken as evidence of the former state of the country thereabouts, because geologists believe them to have been deposited in these swamps when the country was under water in pre-glacial times.

The Danes over-ran Britain in the tenth century and probably crossed the Darwen Valley to get inland from the sea coast on the west. One of the best explanations of the name of Tockholes tends to show that it is of Danish origin,[1] and the slight Scandinavian element of the ancient population of Darwen is to be traced in names like Grimehills, from Grim, one of the names of the God Odin, and a common name of Danish chieftains; Dob Meadows, which may be from the Old Norse *diup*, depth, a deep hole in a river, or a deep pond;[2] Grainings and Haslingden Grane from Old Norse *grein*, a division or cleft; and Turncroft, from Old Norse *tiorn*, a small tarn.

A curious example of the formation of modern place-names may be given here. Situated in a depression of the moor near the source of the Earnsdale Brook is a little farm called Lyon's Den. The curious name of this farm originated as follows. About 100 years ago it became known to some of the farmers in the valley that a stranger named Lyon had bought and settled upon a piece of land in the middle of the moor. As he never came down to the village and did not appear to be building a house, some interest was felt in his mode of life, and one Sunday morning, three men from Sough, Andrew Duxbury, William Shorrock,

[1] The following are the spellings, with their dates, which I have noticed: Tokholes, 1227; Tocholes, 1292; Tockhols, 1294; Tockhole, 1311; Tokeholes, 1500; Tockhooles, 1650; Tockholls, 1663; Tockley, 1672. It will be seen from this that the present form of the word is but very little removed from its earliest form. In *Mamecestre* the following definition of the name is given: Tockholes is "from *Tohaccan* (Anglo-Saxon), to hack in two, to cut down, and *Hol* (Anglo-Saxon) a hole or bottom. The cut or hacked hollows." The Rev. Jonathan Shortt, vicar of Hoghton, has very kindly supplied me with another, though it is only proper to say that he puts it forth doubtfully. I give it as likely to interest my readers. "Tockholes," he says, "is Toadscholes, the toad-wood; scholes being equivalent to shaw,"—the shady place. A much more interesting explanation of the name than either of the foregoing is one supplied by Dr. March, of Rochdale. I give in full his statement: "It has been suggested," says he, "that inasmuch as there are two farms, with names associated with the word Stockclough, in the neighbourhood of Tockholes, the latter is a corruption of *Stockholes*. I do not think that this is admissible. There is a place in Hauxhead Parish, Furness, called Tockhowe, 1597, and Tockhowe, 1642. This fixes the first syllable as a *personal name*. How is a funeral mound, and Tóki was a common old Danish personal name. Tockhow,=the tumulus of Tóki. In the Whalley Coucher Book occurs the following: 'The said bek under the Toghes stone,' 1457, and the reference is to a place in Great Harwood. 'Toghes Stone' means, as I take it, Tókis Stone. In Old Norse, hóll means a hill or mound, and is a common suffix in place-names. Tockholes I take to be the hills or mounds of Tóki. The final *s* may have *intruded*, as is often the case, and it *may* formerly have been Tók hóll." If this be the true meaning of the name, it takes us back to a date much anterior to that of any document known to us in which the name of Tockholes appears. During the ninth and tenth centuries the north-western coasts of England were repeatedly ravaged by Danes and Northmen. The kingdom of Northumbria, which included Lancashire, and was bounded by the Mersey, fell into their hands. Tockholes, therefore, at that time would be in the hands of the Danes, and may have then got its name. And if, as the explanation above given would suggest, it has been the residence of some famous old Danish warrior, who was accustomed to fire homesteads, slay men, drive women to slavery and shame, toss children on pikes, and whose remains now lie mouldering beneath one of its hills, the village will henceforth appear different from what it has usually seemed. Dr. March's explanation of the name is certainly very interesting, and will no doubt be preferred by many of my readers.—*History Old Independ. Ch., Tockholes.* pp. 10-12.

[2] But see the evidence of Mr. W. T. Ashton, in the lecture just quoted.

and Ralph Almond, went to look him up. For a long time after arriving on the land they could discover no traces of the stranger, but at last the sound of their voices attracted his attention, and as he issued out of a small sod hut, "on all fours," one of the farmers caught sight of him, and said to his companions, "Lyon is coming out of his den." John Lyon, who thus made his first appearance before the natives of Darwen, came from Westhoughton, and appears to have been as remarkable for his strength as for his mode of life. An aged man, who knew him, once described him to Mr. W. T. Ashton, as about six feet in height, 12 score in weight, big-boned, with a head like a "cush," and one of the strongest men in England. He kept no beast of burden, and it was his habit to fetch all his supplies from Preston on his back. It appears to have been a common occurrence to him to fetch a load of meal, or a sack of potatoes from Preston to his farm. On one occasion when walking from Preston, with a load of meal on his back, he was accosted in front of the "Hare and Hounds" at Wood's Fold, by William Wood, the farmer, who wished to know the news from Preston. As Wood's enquiries were more than usually numerous, and the conversation had lasted a long time, Lyon said, "As you want to know so much, I think I had better put this load of meal on the wall for a time, for I have a long way to go yet." Lyon sold his farm to Henry Shuttleworth, farmer, from Grimehills, who also bought the adjoining piece of land called Higher Sides, now known as "Old Lyon's."

Chapter 2.—Old Roads.

Darwen a Roadside Town—The Oldest Memorial of the Work of Man—Marches of the Romans through Darwen—Description of the Road through Blacksnape—An Old Saxon Bridle Road—The "Limersgate"—Holker House, Hoddlesden, 1591—The Slack—Pole Lane Graveyard—Sough—Whitehall, 1557—Among the Mansions—Printshop—Bury Fold—Radfield Fold—Bold Venture Reservoir—The Pinfold—Tockholes Road.

ROADS, ancient and modern, furnish us with one of the most interesting chapters of the History of Darwen. When England formed part of the great Roman Empire, at the beginning of the Christian era, there was a great road running through the district now called Darwen, from north to south, and this old Roman road is in existence at the present day, with a modern highway, a railway, and a steam tramway, running parallel to it. Darwen, in fact, is a roadside town, its chief communications being with Manchester on the south and Blackburn on the north. The Roman road is the oldest memorial of the work of man in the town, yet, considering its age, its remains are in a remarkable state of preservation, and they furnish a lasting testimony to the power which the Romans possessed and exercised.

When the Romans conquered Britain thay found in this northern part of the island a very powerful tribe, or perhaps, more probably, confederacy of tribes, belonging to the Cymri, or Ancient Britons, and called the Brigantes. The Brigantes occupied the whole of the district included in the modern Lowlands of Scotland, and the English counties of Northumberland, Durham, Yorkshire, Cumberland, Westmoreland, and Lancashire; in fact the whole of the country from the Mersey and Humber on the south, to the Caledonian Forest on the North. The Britons forming one of the subject or confederate tribes were called the Seganti or Segantes, and they inhabited the district now called Lancashire. Although the invasion of Britain by Julius Cæsar took place in B.C. 55, it was not until A.D. 79 that the Roman armies and power penetrated as far as Lancashire. In the year of our Lord 79, Julius Agricola concentrated at Chester a large army of 30,000 foot and 6000 cavalry, and then, crossing the Mersey, subdued the whole of the Brigantes, and made himself master of their territory. The Roman occupation of this part of the country lasted about 369 years, from Agricola's attack on the Brigantes, A.D. 79, to the final withdrawal of the Romans about the year 448, when the Britons, now effeminate, were left a prey to the attacks of the Picts and Scots in the north, of the Angles and Saxons on the south, and of the Norse on the north-west coast. Their weakened state after the Romans had vacated the island, and their inability to defend themselves from their numerous enemies led to the Anglo-Saxon conquest and occupation of South Britain, and the Cymri or Ancient Britons who escaped death or slavery took refuge in Wales, Devon, and Cornwall, and the mountainous parts of Cumberland (Cymri-land), Westmoreland, Yorkshire, and Lancashire. The Romans did not quit Britain, however, without leaving many marks of their long occupation of it in every part of the country. During the greater part of the Roman occupation of Britain, the 20th Legion, one of the most renowned regiments of the Roman army, consisting chiefly of Sarmatians, a people something like the Russian Cossacks, from the eastern plains of Europe, had its head-quarters at Chester, and furnished the garrisons of the forts and military stations in Lancashire. A detachment of them was regularly encamped at Ribchester. There are clear traces of their passage through Darwen. The road that runs along the Blacksnape ridge of the hill bounding the east side of the valley is their work. It was a very important military road which they made as a direct communication between Manchester and Ribchester, two of their most noted military stations in Lancashire. From the highest part of Blacksnape heights, near what is called the Temple, this road may be seen extending in a straight line for many miles—northwards past Higher Chapel, Eccleshill, and Lower Darwen to Blackburn; and southwards, beyond Edgeworth to Offside in the direction of Radcliffe and Prestwich.

THE ROMAN ROAD.

The section of this great Roman military road running through Darwen exhibits in a remarkable manner the two main features which characterised those old highways for it is perfectly straight and it is a highland road. Neither boggy marshes nor steep hills were suffered to stand in the way of the Roman army. They went straight from one camp to another, building bridges, filling up bogs, and laying their hard pavement, without regarding the difficulties of the way. While marching along the ridge of Blacksnape the generals would keep the country all around in view, and have perfect command of their army, though it might be miles in length. In this way they would be secure against surprise by the wild tribes who dwelt among the hills, and their commanding position on the hill tops would amply repay them for the toil of their arduous marches. Whenever the Roman surveyors diverged from the straight line they did it on the top of a hill, as being the safest point at which to do so. In the road from Manchester to Ribchester there are two angles of this kind, one, a very slight one, on the highest point of the Blacksnape ridge, in Darwen, and the other, a more pronounced angle, on the top of Hunt's Bank, just as the road leaves Manchester. This road was not merely a highway between Manchester and Ribchester, but a continuation in a straight line of the road coming into Lancashire on the south and running beyond Ribchester in a straight line to the top of Longridge Fell, where it takes a sudden turn towards Yorkshire. It is generally believed to be the veritable "10th Iter" of Antoninus, although some authorities claim that honour for a lowland road running through Wigan and Walton-le-Dale. The road was formed of a hard, well-pressed, gravelly substratum, with a surface of large stone "setts" or, in some cases, squared flags. Many interesting remains have been discovered along the route.[1]

From the top of Blacksnape we can see the line of the road southward over Offside, where it bears the name of Watling Street, and northward through Black-a-Moor. On the hill tops the line of the Romans has been preserved, and the modern road coincides with the old one, but as the old road fell out of repair, after the withdrawal of the Romans, the pack-horses of the Saxons and their successors preferred circuitous routes, for the purpose of crossing streams in the valleys and avoiding slippery banks and treacherous ground.

Mr. John Just, an eminent antiquary, after making an exhaustive survey of the road, read a paper on the subject before the Manchester Literary and Philosophical Society on March 22nd, 1842. Referring to the section through Darwen, he says:—

From the highest part of the road at Blacksnape we see the dense smoke of Blackburn in the low ground directly before us. The line of the Roman road here is

[1] "A farmer at Spen Moor told two gentlemen and myself when examining the line for the Ordnance Survey, now carrying on within the county, that in draining he frequently had to cut through the substratum of the road. When asked to show us in what direction the line of road ran, he led us to a field below the farm house, where he pointed out to us, across the field where this substratum was found, the very line of the road; told us moreover that the hard gravelly bed was about seven or eight yards broad, about half a yard thick, and about a foot below the surface of the soil, just beneath the reach of the plough. He pointed out to us the course of this line across other fields belonging to his farm, and, when asked if he ever heard aught about what it was, he instantly replied, 'It was an old road that the devil made, called the devil's way by old people still.'"— J. Just, *Memoirs Manchr. Lit. and Phil. Socy.*, (N.S.), vol. vii, pp. 5-6.

on the left hand side of the public road, and very distinct remains may be observed as we pass along in a continuous ridge, running between the houses of the village, many of which stand on classical ground. A house falling to ruins here shews the remarkable feature of having a part of its foundation laid across the very summit of the Roman road, which in its full characters it preserves. Descending from Blacksnape, the line of Roman road is left in the fields, where it is scarcely distinguishable, until we come nearly opposite Ellison Fold, where it again approaches the public road, and is visible as a slightly elevated ridge and white line, till it crosses the road ; and continues as an intercepted white line through the fields, here and there a little elevated, until it passes Harwood Fold, below which it falls in with a footpath and fence, and proceeds along with them nearly to where it again crosses the public road. A small rill of water follows the line of the fence and the road. Cutting off a small corner of the field, after crossing the public road, it falls in with the garden and farm yard of Davy Field, where are very marked remains. Indeed the most convincing remains are generally about farmsteads and houses, for there cultivation cannot be carried on. At Davy Field the line falls in again with the modern road. We here learned from the farmer, who was very civil and communicative when he learned our business, that the present road was very difficult to keep in repair ; that notwithstanding all their attempts to improve it they had failed ; because the old road, which we were inquiring about was underneath it, as far as the first turn, and being paved with large rough stones, the broken stones laid upon them were soon ground to pieces by the wheels of the vehicles which passed over the road, and until lately the reason was not known ; but being threatened with an indictment, they had dug down to see what the road ailed and thus ascertained the fact he mentioned. At the turn in the road the Roman road keeps to the right, and forms a strong line across the fields to the River Darwen. Again, beyond the river, it falls in with the modern road, showing traces at the fence, and with slight deviations from the line of the modern road, which is here nearly perfectly straight, it passes through Lower Darwen, where, close by the houses, as at Blacksnape, its remains are very conspicuous, and continues coinciding with the modern road to the next turn, This straight portion of the road is very evident from the high ground at Blacksnape, corresponding exactly with the line, as in the instance before mentioned. At the angle in the road, the Roman road continues straight forward through the fields to the right, showing a moderate elevation, and where drains had been recently cut through it, exhibiting its gravelly substratum in strong contrast with the clayey soil on each side of it. In other fields the levelling was going on at the time of our survey ; modern improvements not yet being satisfied with what fourteen centuries have done to obliterate it. The line now crosses the quarries near the Blackburn and Bury road, and intersects Blackburn about forty yards to the east of St. John's Church.[1]

I subjoin Mr. Wm. Thos. Ashton's description of the state of the country about Blacksnape twenty years ago. In a paper " On some Old Roads and Old Inhabitants of Darwen " read before the members of the Discussion and Elocution Class of the Darwen Mechanics' Institute, on February 25th, 1868, he says :—

What may have been the appearance of the country about Grimehills when the Romans first bridged its stream would now be difficult to realise, but it is probable that less change has taken place hereabouts than on any other part of the road. The

[1] *Memoirs Manchr. Lit. and Phil. Socy.* (N.S.), vol. vii, pp. 10-13.

W. T. ASHTON, Esq., J.P.

cultivated part of the land is bleak and of limited extent, while tracts of moss extend on every side. The brook which forms the boundary of the township is also used as a road to farms bordering on Aushaw Moss. Although frequently used, this road is very difficult, for the brook flows over a rocky bed, and instances have been known of saddle horses losing three shoes in traversing half-a-mile. On the lower part of the stream, in a sheltered hollow, lies Whittlestonehead, a quiet hamlet of great antiquity. At both sides of the bridge are cottages in all shapes of ruin. Roofless, windowless, doorless, their decaying walls covered with moss and lichens, they present an appearance of desolation it is almost impossible to exaggerate. I only noticed one inhabited house, the "Crown and Thistle," occupied by John Yates. He ought to be naturally of a cheerful disposition to withstand the depressing influences by which he is surrounded. When the long Winter sets in, and the brook becomes a torrent, and the uplands are shrouded in drizzling rain or swirling sleet, this lonely inn must be a dismal abode except there is within the warmth and sunshine of domestic life. Ascending from the bottom, we pass Grimehill School, on the edge of the moor of that name. This school, once in connection with Holy Trinity Church, but now in the new parish of St. John's, stands invitingly near the road, the chain of its little bell hanging down in the highway with quaint simplicity. Steadily rising, and never deviating more than a few yards from the Roman line, we reach Drummer's Stoops, at an elevation of 1,024 feet, when the view changes as if by magic, and we see the Valley of Darwen lying at our feet, and a wide extent of country which must have reminded the ancient legionaries of the lower ranges of the Jura. From no other point can such a complete view of our valley be obtained, and I have often been truck with its great extent, as seen from this point, compared with its apparent narrowness as viewed from the lower road. Although the hill on which we stand is, in words of an old Lancashire song, "Wild and bare," the evidences of higher cultivation are before us, and lower down there are some charming meadows, fringed with extensive woodlands. Passing by Rushton Heights and Baron's, we rapidly descend through Blacksnape, in the days of hand-loom weaving a populous and thriving hamlet, the abode of many respectable families, but now showing on all sides evidence of decay. For nearly half-a-mile the road is bordered with houses, some roofless, others neat and tidy as of old, and mostly occupied by a hardy race, who linger on "the tops," and love their keen breezes more than the shelter of the valley. Amongst this population the dialect is preserved it its most racy forms, and stories of the past linger long,—how famous wrestlers went forth to challenge the champions of other townships; how football matches had been played for generations with the men of Offiside and Tottington,—said matches nearly always ending in fights which called out the manhood of half-a-dozen valleys; and how young men had gone forth and won glory on nobler fields, marching beneath the banners of England thro' the long Peninsular War, assisting to overthrow the Great Emperor at Waterloo, and following him to his grave beneath the willows of St. Helena.[1]

AN OLD SAXON BRIDLE ROAD.

Tradition and observation both point to the conclusion that there was once an important road for horses and cattle passing through Darwen from east to west, and crossing the old Roman road at right angles. The remains of this road are sufficiently distinct to prove its importance,

[1] For traditions of these wrestlers, footballers and soldiers, see "Jeremy Hunt's Recollections of Old Darwen Families," which form the second part of this history.

for we find the oldest houses of the town built upon it, and its winding course, avoiding difficulties of bog and river, show that it was a great highway in times when highways were merely cross-country tracks. Whether it dates back to Saxon times is a matter more of conjecture than anything else, but we frequently meet with Saxon names along its course, and there can be little doubt that it was the road used by our Saxon forefathers.[1] Along the old Roman road running through the township there are no remains to compare with those found on this road, and the pack-horse road through Chapels, Darwen Green, and Sough from Blackburn to Bolton has not the same evidence of antiquity about it as has the ancient road now under notice. For instance, the pack-horse road from Blackburn to Bolton crossed the river Darwen at the spot where Union-street Bridge now stands, and, as anyone acquainted with the depth and impetuosity of the river will know, it was quite impassable there in flood times [2] until bridges came into vogue. On the other hand, the great road from east to west, which I will henceforth call the old Saxon road, can be traversed on horseback in the worst seasons of the year, and, although now as green in some parts as the fields around it, it has been sunk six, eight, ten and even fifteen feet below the adjacent land by the mere trampling of horses and cattle in centuries past.

Under the guidance of Mr. Wm. Thos. Ashton, J.P., who is familiar with every road and lane in the township by reason of his habit of riding and walking along them, I have carefully traced this old road from its entry into Darwen over the Pickup Bank brook to its exit on the western side along the embankment of Dean Reservoir. It has to this day several very marked distinguishing features which indicate its antiquity. Instead of crossing the township direct through Chapels it skirts it towards the southern side until Darwen Moor is reached, then striking across the spurs of the moor northwards, it eventually turns northwest, and lastly due west, leaving the township in the direction in which it entered. In every instance where it crosses a large stream the crossing place is chosen where two streams join, so that each can be forded separately, and crossed even in flood times, when to attempt the passage twenty yards lower down might prove fatal to both horse and rider, and to cross higher up would be out of the track, which evidently required the road to run from east to west. Along its whole course it avoids the boggy or swampy pitfalls which are to be found on the

[1] A gentleman who has made local history a study suggests to me that this road may have been originated by the Danes who landed at the mouth of the Ribble, and made incursions into Lancashire and Yorkshire.

[2] See anecdote of the drowning of Mrs. Bowden, given in a subsequent chapter.

UNION STREET BRIDGE.

Near the centre of Darwen. Width 13ft. 2in. 2,388 foot passengers and 242 conveyances passed over this Bridge on October 31st, 1878, between 8 a.m. and 6 p.m., as recorded in Mr. Riley's chronological *History of Darwen*. The Bridge was shortly afterwards re-built and widened.

moors, neither river nor swamp blocking it at any point. Among the old homesteads which stand upon it are two Elizabethan mansions, which are, without doubt, the oldest buildings of any kind in Darwen, namely, Whitehall, dated 1557, and Holker House, dated 1591, besides other ancient folds and residences of scarcely less importance, Bury Fold, the Pinfold, and others being amongst the number. It is probably a portion of the "Limersgate" passing through Lancashire and Yorkshire, and deriving its name from the fact that it was constantly traversed by strings of "lime-gals" carrying lime in sacks or panniers slung across their backs.

Mr. W. T. Ashton, lecturing in 1868, said :—" Almost at right angles with the Roman road, and therefore crossing our township from east to west, there is an ancient bridle road of unknown age, but of undoubted antiquity, probably coeval with the Saxon occupation of this country. Tradition says it was once the only road across this part of the country from Preston to Haslingden, and it is most likely a portion of that old pack-horse road called the 'Limersgate,' which traverses the northerly side of the Forest of Rossendale, and it is said to have been at one time the principal means of communication between the west of Lancashire and the easterly side of the kingdom."

The "Limersgate" approaches Darwen from Rossendale by a sheer descent over Pickup Bank Heights, close by Pickup Bank Chapel, and crosses the brook into the township of Over Darwen at a wild but charming spot near the village of Hoddlesden. The first building of interest on the route is Holker House, which stands at a sharp turn in the road, shortly after its entry into the township of Darwen. Thence it passes Langshaw Head, where a cottage bears the inscription, "John and Mary Hindle, A.D. 1790," and descends rapidly into a picturesque clough—the long shaw. The stream at the bottom is crossed by a narrow footbridge, and cattle have to ford it. Ascending the steep bank on the other side to a farm called Stand we find the track as green as the adjacent fields. No one can contemplate the old road at this spot without being struck with its antiquity. Except by the occupants of a small row of cottages in the "Slack" and those of the two folds of Langshaw Head and Stand, it would appear that the road is now rarely used, yet there is an old well by the wayside, and the broad grass-grown track has in ages past been trodden so much that it is deeply sunk below the level of the adjoining fields. Along Heyes Lane the road is modernised, being much used as a thoroughfare between Hoddlesden and Blacksnape. But the late Seth Harwood, an old inhabitant of Hoddlesden, remembered this neatly-walled modern lane being simply a hoof-track through a wood. The adjacent land is now bleak and bare.

On reaching the Roman road at Blacksnape our path turns at right angles to the north, and coincides with the Roman road for a few hundred yards. In this short section we pass the cottages of a hardy hilltop race, whose isolation helps them to preserve their peculiarities of speech and manner. We also notice a considerable quantity of ruined stone property, the very stones themselves crumbling to dust, and an interesting roadside Sunday school with an inscription showing that it was built in 1824, principally through the exertions of one man—a member of the renowned Harwood family. Before reaching the modern end of Pole Lane we find a footpath on our left which will take us to the point where Pole Lane shows evidence of having been lengthened. It was extended in the direction of Hoddlesden in consequence of the great amount of cart traffic between Darwen and Hoddlesden, and that portion of the old road joining Pole Lane to Blacksnape has fallen into disuse. This little section has been blocked by a low stone wall of recent erection, with an opening wide enough for foot passengers but not for horses. Although the track is of ample width, and evidently more than a mere footpath, a horseman would have to divert his course here and traverse the modern portion of Pole Lane. From Pole Lane there is a good view of " Princes," an isolated but historic fold on the summit of the hill dividing Darwen from Hoddlesden. On every hand there are old coal-pit shafts, flag-pits, and fire-clay works, showing what an important mining district this has once been, and, in some respects, still is.

Pole Lane Chapel, built by a party of seceders from Lower Chapel in 1792, is now no more. The graveyard is walled round and deserted, and only the foundations of the old chapel are visible in one corner. The gateway is blocked up, and the only way in and out of the old burial ground is over the high wall which encloses it. A few stunted trees and six tombstones are all the enclosure contains on the surface. On one of my rambles in this neighbourhood I copied the inscriptions on the tombstones, and here I append them :—

(1) Sacred to the memory of Wm. Leach, late of March House, who, during a long life, checquered with various afflictions, maintained a constant walk with God, and, in the good hope of a glorious resurrection, died on the fifth of Feby., 1817, in the 70th year of his age.

Mary, his wife, died Jany. 6th, 1825, in the 81st year of her age.

(2) Dedicated by filial affection to the memory of Nicholas Fish, who departed this life July 29th, 1809, in the 59th year of his age; also of Catherine, his wife, who departed this life Nov. 13th, 1797, in the 44th year of her age.

Dear friends, farewell ! we meet no more
Till you arrive on Canaan's shore,
There in united strains to tell,
Our Saviour has done all things well.

(3) In memory of Thomas Hindle. He died May 2nd, 1854, aged 70 years.

(4) x 1847
*Willi*A*M*te*A
*M*AN *Wood*
cock

(5) Sacred to the memory of James Green, late of Darwen Chapels, a man whose character was eminently distinguished by unaffected piety, a meek and quiet spirit, and unlimited exertions for the spread of vital religion, especially in the congregation of which he was a member, whose transit from weak and frail state to endless joy and rest was easy and happy. He was born Nov. 1st, 1754, he died Sep. 30th, 1808, aged 53.

(6) This stone is erected here to the memory of John, the son of Joseph and Peggy Walmsley, who died 9th April, 1795, aged 3 years; likewise Isaac, their son, who died 31st of January, 1804, aged 6 months; also Hannah, their daughter, who departed this life 3:th of July, 1816, aged 19 years.

Fond parents, she cry's, my spirit's at rest
Where I with my Saviour shall ever be blest.
Your mourning give o'er, pray weep not for
My sorrows are past in every degree; [me,
Prepare for God's glory which now I possess,
That we all together our Saviour may bless.

Also Peggy, the wife of Joseph Walmsley, and mother of the above children, who departed this life June 7th, 1839, aged 73 years; also of Joseph Walmsley, her husband, who departed this life July 8th, 1849, aged 82 years.

The first three of the stones are ordinary flat stones, the fourth is a little loose flag measuring about 18in. by 10in., and the fifth and sixth are raised stones, the former standing on four pillars, and the latter on four slabs.

Pole Lane School belongs now to a man named Ralph King. It is an upper room adjoining the old burial ground and is approached by a flight of dilapidated stone steps and a wide wooden staircase with a rude and narrow door. At the head of the staircase there is a little window containing four tiny panes of glass. On entering the old school-room, which is now unoccupied, we find that it was evidently adapted for the purposes of a school, and that originally it was really two or more rooms. The ceiling is open to the slates, which, together with the timbers supporting them, are whitewashed. In the centre of the room there is a small iron pillar supporting the roof. At one end there is an old kitchen fire range, and at the other a chimney breast with the fire-place bricked up. The room is dimly lighted by two small windows overlooking Pole Lane. Near the middle of the floor there is a trap door. On opening this we find that it covers a narrow wooden staircase leading down to one of the cottages below, and we were informed that this was formerly used by the schoolmaster, who lived below. An exciting scene occured in Pole Lane Chapel in the year of Jeremy Hunt's birth, and Jeremy has dictated to me the full history of it, but the particulars given below by Mr. Ashton are sufficient to place on record.

This little chapel and graveyard, now so quiet was once the scene of active religious labours and exciting events. On the first Sunday of August, 1806, the then minister ascended his pulpit stairs for the lrst time. Two stern deacons, who deemed him unworthy of his office, seized him and forced him into his pew, and afterwards locked the chapel against him. His alleged fault was one that has often vexed humanity.

In the hamlet of Sough, which is cut in two by the railway, one of the most interesting buildings is the residence of "Old James Pickup, of Sough," formerly a dwelling and handloom weaving shop, now an office. The railway, a little to the south of this, runs under Cranberry Moss, through Sough Tunnel. Many old inhabitants remember stage coaches running from Sough to Bolton before Sough Tunnel was made. Passengers would come from Blackburn by train, and continue their journey by coach. The old Sough Station was a miserable little hut on the southerly side of the present bridge, carrying the highway over the rails. In wet weather passengers used to shelter under the single arch of this bridge, and the accommodation at the station was so wretched that this arch was called by way of a joke the "first-class waiting-room."

Watery Lane, on the westerly side of the railway, is the continuation of our old road which the railway has cut in two. In this lane the old Saxon road, and an old pack-horse road from Blackburn to Bolton were identical, They cross the river Darwen now by a bridge at a point where two considerable streams unite, and in flood times each stream would without doubt be forded separately. Crossing Bolton Road near the Tramway terminus our old road, which is slightly diverted hereabouts, takes us past Whitehall—the oldest house in Darwen, dated 1557. We now enter the lovliest part of the road, and find ourselves among the mansions of the Darwen gentry. The road leads in rapid succession to the Woodlands, occupied by Mr. W. B. Huntington, J.P.; Spring Bank; Ashleigh, where the British urns were unearthed in 1864; Low Hill, built and formerly occupied by Mr. Samuel Crompton, inventor of the spinning mule, and afterwards sold to Mr. Eccles Shorrock, the eminent cotton spinner and merchant; Ashdale, built and occupied by Mr. W. T. Ashton, J.P.; Astley Bank, built by Mr. Richard Kershaw Smalley, and now accupied by Mr. C. P. Huntington, J.P.; Thorncliffe, the residence of Mr. F. G. Hindle; and many others, each with an interesting history.

Two very rapid mountain becks have to be crossed at Print Shop, and the old road, which again shows traces of its primitive state, crosses each stream separately just above their confluence. One of these streams a few years ago tore away immense blocks of rock by its violence, and put Mr. Eccles Shorrock to considerable expense in widening its course and making repairs. The scenery here is very fine, the road is steep and tortuous and sunk about 12 feet below the level of the adjacent land. The remains of a range of old sycamores fringe the road on the left, exposed to the prevailing winds, yet as straight and sturdy as ever. Our road takes us past Print Shop and through Bury Fold. This fold is one of the most interesting in Darwen, and the old house which stands in the midst of more modern buildings shows by the style of its masonry that it is of great antiquity. Where the date stone should be over the front door there is a slab devoid of inscription, but it is believed that the Burys have lived in this fold since the times of Elizabeth, if not longer. One writer[1] asserts that the house in Bury Fold was the identical house of William and Henry Berry, licensed as a Nonconformist Meeting place in 1672, but my own investigations have led me to conclude that William and Henry Berry lived in Bury Court, at the opposite end of the town, close to the Lower Chapel. Radfield Fold is another noteworthy enclosure through which the old road passes. It is striking without being beautiful, and very remarkable for its situation. Mr. Ashton says:—

> Here is obtained the best view possible of the large campanile which forms the chimney of India Mill. This noble structure is one of the finest towers in the world, and will, in all likelihood, survive the cotton trade of this country. Its massive base is just visible among the many mills and buildings in the valley, whilst its summit rises past us into the midst of "the sailing birds and the silent air."

Bold Venture Reservoir next blocks our path. During a fearful storm on August 23rd, 1843, the torrent coming down Bold Venture from the lofty moorland swept away a portion of the embankment of the reservoir, and the flood rushed madly down to the centre of Darwen, drowning twelve persons and doing great damage to property. Crossing the glen in which the Bold Venture Reservoir lies, we begin to ascend the moor rapidly. Just beyond Pinfold, where stray sheep and cattle used to be penned, the road strikes off to the west. It is wide and clearly marked by the remains of ancient scraggy-looking hedges on each side, but almost impassable despite its width, and on one side deeply sunk below the level of the adjacent land. This was once the only road for horse or cow from Darwen to Tockholes, except by going round the Golden Cup, and it is to-day the only direct public road to Tockholes. The thoroughfare known as "Tockholes road" is a private one, which was made by Mr. Eccles Shorrock, nearly forty years ago, at a cost of £2,000. His tenants, and those of Mr. Duckworth, lord of the manor, are allowed the free use of it, but the general public are subjected to a toll charge which they gladly pay in preference to going round by the Golden Cup, or along the neglected bridle road of their forefathers. At

[1] Rev. R. Nicholls, in the *Manchester Congregational Magazine*.

a point just above Higher Sunnyhurst the old bridle road from Rossendale, the course of which we have been tracing, is intersected by another ancient bridle road, which can be seen striking up the moor towards the south. This road comes up from the Blackburn and Bolton highway at Hollins Grove, past Earnsdale, over Prospect Hill, past Lower Sunnyhurst and Higher Sunnyhurst, and crossing the Rossendale Road mounts still higher and follows the edge of the Darwen Moor by Dugshaw, Lord's Hall, Wheathead, and Cadshaw, to Turton and Bolton. This was one of the ancient pack-horse roads between Blackburn and Bolton, used before the construction of the present highway. Intersecting the moorland track to Bolton the old Saxon road continues westward after a modern diversion, and finally leaves the township of Darwen, along the bank of the Dean Reservoir. The diversion has been made by a Sunnyhurst farmer, who has blocked the road with a stile and wicket-gate, making it passable only by foot-passengers, just as has been done on the Blacksnape side of the town, as noticed above. Such encroachments tend to effectually destroy all traces of the interesting old road, and in the present case must cause a serious inconvenience to horsemen by compelling them to go out of their track, up hill and down dale, and along a bit of the moorland road to Bolton as shockingly dilapidated as any road can be without being absolutely useless.

Chapter 3.

From the Conquest to the Revolution.

Feudalism—First Mention of Darwen, *circa* 1130—A House in Darwen, 1280—The Great De Lacy Inquisition, 1311—Manor of Over Darwen—Atonement for Murder - Disputed Title to the Lordship of Over Darwen, 1556—Darwynd Hall—The Pinfold—Lord's Hall—Manor of Nether Darwen—Fernehurst, 1528—The Reputed Manor of Eccleshill—Yate-and-Pickup Bank—Some Old Inhabitants—The Earliest Inhabitant—Darwen Freeholders of Henry VII's time—Military Musters -Domiciles and other Buildings in Queen Elizabeth's reign—Place Names—Camden's Notice of the River Darwen—Inhabitants of Darwen in the time of Queen Elizabeth—A Murderer Discovered through a Dream—Inhabitants of Darwen in the time of James I.—Inhabitants of Darwen in the time of Charles I. Inquisitions *post mortem*—King James's Visit to Hoghton Tower—The De Hoghton Family—The Civil War—Hoghton Tower Blown Up—Battle of the Ribble and Darwen Bridges—Seizure of Lands by the Commonwealth—Population and Assessment of Darwen in the time of the Commonwealth—The Revolution.

FEUDALISM, which still leaves traces of its influence in the laws and customs of land tenure, was in its prime at the time the first mention of Darwen now extant was made in written history. Either the last of the Normans (Stephen) or the first of the Plantagenets (Henry II.) was on the throne—authorities disagree on the subject;—and under him Henry de Lacy, the great northern earl, held the royal manor of Walton, which included and still nominally includes the smaller manors or townships of *Heccleshull* and the *two Derewents*. This manor, which is mentioned in *Domesday Book*, was granted by de Lacy to Robert Banastre, by a deed hereafter to be quoted. It may be useful to note, before proceeding to trace the land tenure of Darwen from the time of the Conqueror down to the present day, that the leading feature of feudalism was that all land was under a military tenure, the tenant paying a nominal rent in corn, cattle, or money, and holding himself in readiness to fight under his lord's banner, without any pay, when called to arms. The very word "feudalism" is derived from *feod* or *feud*, a piece of land. The obligation to military service was divided and subdivided with the land. "The king owned all land; he allotted large districts to the nobles; they subdivided these among the gentry (the Saxon *thanes*, called by the Normans franklins); these again sub-let their land to their vassals,—in every case the higher requiring from the lower service in war." References to this system of military service, which in course of time became obsolete, is found running through all the documents bearing on the relation of the landlord to the tenant. Gilbert de Lacy, Earl of Pontefract, a knight who came over with the Conqueror, was the first to drive the Saxons out of the Ribble Valley. He built Clitheroe Castle to guard the pass into Lancashire from the north, and another castle was built at Penwortham, in succession to a fortress that had existed there in Saxon times. Walton, as already stated, was claimed by the King himself. The Manor of Walton extended as far east as Eccleshill, and embraced the hill of Hoghton, on the south bank of the Darwen, on the crest of which was afterwards built Hoghton Tower, a castelet of less importance than the fortresses abovementioned, and intended more for the protection of private interests than as a national stronghold. It is often stated that Roger de Poictou, a Norman earl, had the lordship of Lancashire, including this district, conferred upon him about two years after the Conquest, and that he placed at Walton a Norman baron named Warin Banastre. No evidence has been found in support of this, but there is a distinct record of Walton having come into the possession of the Banastres by deed granted by Henry de Lacy, as lord of the Honor of Clitheroe, in the reign of Henry II. De Lacy's charter conveys to Robert Banastre —"Walatun cum pertinentiis Melver [Mellor], et Heccleshull [Eccleshill], et Haravuda [Little Harwood], et duas Derewentas [the two Derwents],"[1] for the service of one knight. This Robert Banastre was the son of a Robert Banastre who came over the with the Conqueror and built at Englefield in North Wales, a tower, which was destroyed in 1167, when a brave Welshman, Owen Gwynedd, drove out the English and recovered his lands, Immediately after that event Robert Banastre the second brought all his people into Lancashire, and took possession of his lands between the Ribble and the Mersey, including the Manor of Walton. The *Liber Feodorum* compiled by Ralph de Nevill in the reign of Henry III. shows that the heir of Robt. Banastre then held "one knight's fee in Waleton and Blakeburnscire of the fee of the Earl of Lincoln, and he in chief of the lord the king." About the year 1280, Roger, son of Henry de Whalley, gave by deed to the Abbot and Convent of Stanlaw "three perches of my land in *Superiore Derwent*, in length from the messuage on the east that John, son of Bibby, held of Richard de Alffton, unto the road on the west that leads to the house of Alexander de Keuerdale, and two perches in

[1] This charter is said by some antiquaries to have been granted in the reign of Henry II., who ascended the throne in 1154, and by others to have been made "about 1130."

breadth, for the site of one barn, with the house on that land built, for their tenth sheaf (tithe) of the said vill." Some twenty years later (temp. Edward I.) Hoddlesdene is mentioned in the Duchy records among the possessions of Henry de Lacy, Earl of Lincoln. An heiress of the Banastres, by marriage with John, son of Robert de Langton, brought the manor of Walton into the possession of the Langtons, of Leicestershire, about the end of the 13th century. Two parcels of the manor, both including land in Over Darwen, passed shortly afterwards into the possession of the heirs of Samlesbury and of Cuerdale, but a portion of the manor remained in the hands of the Langtons for 400 years, when it was conveyed to the Hoghtons. The great De Lacy Inquisition, made in 1311, shows that Nether Darwen was still in the possession of the Banastres, but that Over Darwen had changed hands. "Sir Adam Banestre holds 2 carucates of land in Nether Derwent, and paid yearly ij^s· x^d·;" but "The heirs of Samlesbury and of Keuersdale hold one carucate in Oudrewent, by the service of $\frac{1}{8}$ Knight's fee and suit of the Court of Clyderhou." From a quotation given above, it would appear that Alexander de Keuerdale had a house in or near Over Darwen.

OVER DARWEN.

Sir Robert de Holland, Knt., is the heir of Salmesbury alluded to in the De Lacy Inquisition. By homage and fealty to Ralph de Langton, he had come into possession of land in the manor of Walton, and when he died in 1373, Matilda, daughter of his eldest son, inherited some of his estates, but John Holland, his younger son, was found to be heir to the lands in tail male, which included "one fourth part of Over Derwent." John de Holland died in 1451, and by inquisition taken the following year he was found to hold "one bovate of land in Over Derwent, of Henry Langton." Upon the death of John de Holland the estate appears to have passed into the possession of the "high and myghty prynce Henry the duc of Excestre and Anne his wyeffe," for Canon Raines notes that on the 7th of March, 30 Henry VI., the Duke of Exeter leased to Peter Legh, "O'ia maner: terr: ten : redd : et servic : cu o'ibz suis p'tinentiis in villis de Haydocke Newton Harewode Brightmede *Overderwyne and Netherderwyne* que nuper descenderunt eidem duci jure hereditar: post portem Joh 'is Holand militis," &c. Seven years later these estates of the duke and duchess are described as "their lordshippes and manours of Haydokke, Newton-in-Makerfield and Lauton, Bryghtmede, Harwode and Over Derwynde." The successive lords of Samlesbury held this portion of the Darwen manor, and in the 15th century it is found in the possession of the Southworths of Samlesbury Hall.

The heir of Cuerdale mentioned in the De Lacy Inquisition as holding a moiety of the manor of Over Darwen was Adam de Keuerdale, whose heiress, Jane de Keuerdale, carried it over to her husband, Thos. Molineux. Katherine, grand-daughter of Thomas Molineux, and heiress of Cuerdale, became the wife of Alexander Osbaldestone, and so this portion of the manor of Over Darwen came into the possession of the Osbaldestones.

In the 17th century several farms and tenements in Over Darwen are found to be held under the Hoghton family in socage, the Hoghtons claiming their lordship over these lands as part of the manor of Walton. A curious tradition of the circumstances under which the Hoghtons came into possession of the manor will be found given hereafter. Briefly, it is stated that Thomas Hoghton was killed by Thomas Langton, lord of the manor of Walton, in 1589, and being arrested for the offence, secured an "amicable settlement" by presenting the manor of Walton to Hoghton's widow.

> In 1589 he [Langton] and a number of his dependants were engaged in a fray with his neighbour, Mr. Thomas Hoghton, of Lea, with whom he was remotely connected by marriage, which resulted in the death of the latter. For this he was indicted before a special magisterial assize at Preston, but was eventually permitted to compromise the offence by the surrender of the valuable estate and manor of Walton-le-Dale to the heir of the deceased gentleman as Frumgeld—the old Saxon payment to the kindred of the slain as a sort of atonement for murder—his escape from the more serious consequences being mainly due to the friendly offices of his kinsmen, Henry, Earl of Derby, and Lord Strange.[1]

The Osbaldestons and the Southworths had a serious family feud for generations concerning their respective rights of common on Darwen Moor, which ended in a suit in the Duchy Court in 1556. A dozen old inhabitants gave evidence in this suit, some stating that John Osbaldeston, of Osbaldeston, son of Sir Alexander Osbaldeston, was the sole lord of the manor of Over Darwen, and others that Sir John Southworth was joint lord. Sir John was summoned before the Duchy Court for turning his beasts and cattle to graze on Darwen Moor, and for carrying away over 1,000 loads of turf. Osbaldeston disputed the title deeds that Sir John held concerning the lordship of the estate, and proved that he alone had the right to hold a Court Leet, to appoint constables, to enclose waste, and to make use of the grass, the turf, and minerals on Darwen Moor. It was deposed that the Pinfold belonged to Osbaldeston, and that he and his ancestors had always used and

[1] *History of Samlesbury*, p. 47.

occupied the chief house and Mansion Place of Over Darwynd, commonly called "Darwynd Hall." Mr. Abram, who copied the depositions in this suit from the records of the Chancery Court of Lancaster, states that the award does not appear, but that the omission of all mention of the manorial estate of Over Darwen in the category of the estates of Sir John Southworth, who died in 1595, indicates that the Southworths had before then ceased to exercise manorial rights in the township. The Osbaldestons held the manor certainly for eighty years after this trial, and possibly for the greater part of two centuries.

In 1766 and again in 1799 the manor was offered for sale by public auction and acquired by John Trafford. The advertisement which appeared in the Manchester newspapers on the latter occasion is worth quoting on account of the information it gives concerning the manorial rights and privileges and the value of the estate.

To be sold by auction, either together or in lots as shall be agreed upon at the time and place of sale, at the house of Mr. Samuel Barton, innkeeper, at Over Darwen, in the county of Lancaster, on the 2nd and 3rd days of June, 1779, subject to such conditions as will be then and there produced (unless disposed of in the meantime by private contract) the Manor and Lordship of Over Darwen with the Court Leet, Court Baron, and extensive Royalties of the said Manor, and also fee simple and inheritance of sundry messuages, farms, tenements, and hereditaments situate in Over Darwen aforesaid, now let at about £260 per annum, and also several fee farm rents, issuing and payable from messuages, lands, and hereditaments within Over Darwen aforesaid, amounting to upwards of £64 a year, clear of all taxes and reprizes. N.B.—Sundry other farms in Over Darwen, worth about the same yearly sum as the above premises, but now in lease for lives, subject to the payment of small reserved yearly rents, will be sold at the same time and place above-mentioned, if the purchaser, or any other person, shall be desirous of purchasing the same, subject to conditions to be then produced, if not sold along with the above premises by private contract in the meantime. The lordship of Over Darwen is situate in a pleasant and populous part of the county of Lancaster, between the two great trading towns of Blackburn and Bolton. The Royalty of Over Darwen includes some thousand acres, in which there is great plenty of grouse, partridge, and other game. There are also coal mines under most part of the lordship, and extensive commons conveniently situated for the occupation of the several farms, with almost every requisite for producing beneficial and lasting improvements for the several estates at an easy expense. The premises may be viewed by applying to Mr. Roger Aspinall, in Over Darwen, and for particulars of the several estates apply to Messrs. James Greenway, Messrs. Elk. Hoyle, James Hoyle, and Jonathan Wheelwright, of Ripponden, near Halifax, or Mr. Watson, attorney, Stockport, Cheshire.

A detailed description of the Manorial estate of Over Darwen as defined in the year 1799 was printed in *The Preston Guardian* of Feb. 7, 1880. It shows that the lands let in farms on yearly tenancies and on leases measured 845a. 2r. 31p.; lands in the holding of Mr. Trafford, lord of the manor, 416a. 2r. 7p.; waste or unimproved lands, 94a.

2r. 30p.; plantations, 12a. 0r. 36p.; total acreage of the manor, 1,369a. 0r. 24p.; total acreage of the township of Over Darwen, 5,134a. Forty-two tenants held parcels of the estate for 9,999 years, paying chief rent to the lord of the manor amounting in the aggregate to £54 14s. 6d.

There is no trace left of the old manor house of Over Darwen, and its situation is a matter merely of conjecture. Lord's Hall, a farm house overlooking the entrance to the Dogshaw Clough, was built as a manor house about the end of last century by Mr. Trafford, the new lord of the manor. When he first came to settle in Darwen he wished to build his house on the Higher Side Farm in a field between Fickle Hall and Dogshaw Clough, but his tenant, James Briggs, who had a life lease, positively refused his consent. It is said that Briggs, who lived to be nearly 90, only paid 19s. 9d. per annum for the farm, and was offered all the land on the other side of the brook for ever, if he would let Mr. Trafford build where he wished. Finding his tenant immovable, Mr. Trafford chose the wild and inaccessible site occupied by an old thatched farmhouse called Smooth Barn, and there built Lord's Hall. As the road from Bury Fold did not then exist, all the materials had to be carted under the moor and past Wheathead Farm. The right to make and use the present road was subsequently acquired from the owners of the Bury Fold estate. Trafford did not long remain here. If he liked it little, his wife is said to have loved it less; and at the beginning of this century the manor of Over Darwen again changed hands and was purchased by the Duckworths, a family who came from the adjoining township of Musbury. Since then Lord's Hall has been occupied alternately as a beershop, a farm house, a keeper's lodge, and again as a farm house. Facing the east, about 1,200 feet above the sea level, the house stands upon a projecting spur of the hill, without a wall, or bush, or tree, to shelter it. Behind it the moorland stretches with few interruptions to Rivington Pike. Below lies the valley of Darwen; afar off the countless hills of East Lancashire and Yorkshire extend to the horison.[1]

The Duckworths of Musbury trace their ancestors back to the time of Henry VIII. Several members of the family have been Greaves of the Forest of Rossendale. George Duckworth, Esq., who purchased Over Darwen estate, in 1810, died in 1815. The present lord of the manor, the Rev. William Arthur Duckworth, of Beechwood Forest, Hampshire, was born on March 17th, 1829.

By favour of Mr. Henry John Robinson, steward of the manor, I have

[1] *The Heart of Lancashire*, by W. T. Ashton, ch. v.

examined the records of the "Darwen Manor Court" from 1811 to the present day. The Court is held annually at the New Inn, and it is described as the "Court Leet and View of Frankpledge of our sovereign lady the Queen, and Court Baron of the Rev. Wm. Arthur Duckworth, clerk, lord of the manor of Over Darwen." The list of those owing suit and service at the Court in the year 1888 comprises the names of 132 persons or firms, of whom 17 are farm tenants, and 115 freeholders paying chief rents. The steward, as representative of lord of the manor, presides over the Court, twelve jurors are sworn, and by them the following officers are appointed:—Bellman, constable, market looker, three affearers, five moss lookers, five fence lookers, five watercourse lookers, five inspectors of weights and measures, one pounder, five moor lookers, and 12 special constables. In 1811 the Court was held at the Red Lion Inn; in 1812 it was transferred to the Waggon and Horses; in 1820 to the Commercial Inn; and in 1829 to the New Inn, where it is held to this day. Mr. Robert Kay was the first steward under the Duckworths; Mr. Dixon Robinson succeeded him in 1830; and Mr. H. J. Robinson received his appointment in 1879. For the last forty years the business of the Court has been more a matter of form than anything else, officers being appointed, but no presentments being made, and no fines imposed except the regulation fine of 1s. each upon tenants and others who fail to appear at the Court and acknowledge the suit and service owing to their lord. Prior to 1847 presentments were frequently made regarding the obstruction of highways and watercourses, the neglect of fences, and the committal of nuisances. Fines varying in amount from 10s. to £20 were imposed upon offendors, who, however, had generally a fortnight or a month allowed to repair their neglect, or remove the nuisance or obstruction complained of, and so escape the penalty. After each Court the steward would call the attention of the constable to the presentments made at the Court, and require him to summon the offendors before the affearers, in order that the penalty imposed by the jury might be affeared.[1] The last fine on record is one of £2 10s. imposed on a person charged with laying rubbish in Foundry Street, in the year 1847. After this the duty of keeping highways in repair and removing nuisances appears to have been left to the modern authorities. It is recorded that a discussion took place at the Court held in May, 1865, respecting the powers and duties of the "pounder," also touching trespasses on the Moor, imperfect fences, &c., but that no formal presentments were made. The powers of the Court have, in fact, to a large extent become obsolete.

[1] Settled or moderated.

NETHER DARWEN.

Lower Darwen, formerly called Nether Darwen, was one of the "two Derewents" granted by Henry de Lacy to Robert Banastre in the time of Henry II.[1] Nearly two centuries later the township is found in possession of the same family, for the De Lacy Inquisition shows that Sir Adam Banastre paid 2s. 10d. yearly and suit to the Clitheroe Court for the two carucates of land he held in Nether Darwen. By the marriage of Alice Banastre to Sir John de Langton, Nether Darwen, as part of the manor of Walton, became the property of the Langtons, and it was still in possession of the Langton family in 1569, although portions of it had been sold or given to other families such as the Arderns, the Bradshaws, and the Talbots. In 1392 it was found by inquisition *post mortem* that John de Ardern, son of Sir Thomas de Ardern, Knight, had died possessed of "16 messuages, one mill, 200 acres of land, 200 acres of meadow, 1,000 acres of pasture, and 20 acres of wood, parcel of the manor of Nether Derwynd," his widowed mother enjoying the profits thereof for the rest of her life, which was extended by more than 30 years after this date. De Ardern held his freehold *in capite* of John of Gaunt, Duke of Lancaster. Two of John de Ardern's daughters married respectively Hugh and John de Bradshaw, and the descendants of one or other of them inherited a portion of the Nether Darwen estate. In Henry VIII.'s time (1511) William Bradshaw was found to possess three-fourths of the whole township of Lower Darwen, namely, 500 acres of land, 100 acres of meadow, 200 acres of pasture, and 1,000 acres of moor and moss. His estate had 30 messuages built upon it, and he held it as the ninth part of a Knight's fee. In 1542 John Bradshaw possessed "12 messuages, the 4th part of a fulling-mill, 67 acres of land, 67 acres of meadow, 330 acres of pasture, and 6 acres of woodland, in Nether Derwynt, parcel of the manor of Nether Derwynt." His son John, who succeeded him possessed also the manor of Bradshaw, near Bolton.

A third daughter of John de Ardern, Anne, became the mother of Sir Thomas Talbot, of Bashall, Knt., who in 1499 was found to hold "Nether Derwynd Manor by 2s. 6d. rent." The Talbots held the lordship of Lower Darwen Manor for several generations, but let the manor house, "Fernehurst," to tenants, among whom were Gilbert Talbot, uncle of the lord of the manor, Sir Thomas; and several members of the Livesey family. Gilbert died at Fernehurst in 1547. William Clayton, clerk, and Alexander Clayton claimed

---

[1] In 1291-2 John de Blackburn claimed two parts of the manor of Nethirderwent, as held by his father, but failed in his suit.

the right to occupy this house in the time of Henry VIII., and lodged a complaint in the Duchy Court against James and Thos. Livesey and 19 other persons, who on the 20th of April, 1528, had forcibly taken the possession of the manor, and held it by threatening with "long bowes, bylles, and other unlawful weapons," all who attempted to drive them out. The manor and manor house were sold by the Talbots in the closing years of the 16th century to Sir Thomas Walmesley, Knight, in whose possession the "manor of Netherdarwynd, alias Lowerdarwent," is found in 13th Charles I. (1637). From Sir Thomas Walmesley the manor passed to the family of Lord Petre.

ECCLESHILL.

Eccleshill, in conjunction with Mellor, is mentioned as a member of the Walton Manor as early as 1130, as already recorded, although the two townships are not geographically connected in any way. Early in the next century a family of De Eccleshull is heard of, and in the latter half of the same century Robert de Eccleshull gave a perch of land in his vill of Eccleshill to the Abbot and Monks of Stanlaw for the site of a barn. The situation of this plot of land is described as on the "west side of Bruderndyng, between Hoddisdenebrok and the Mill of Eccleshull." The township is called "Ocleshill" in the escheat of Henry de Lacy, 4 Edw. II. (1311). A carucate of land in Melling (Mellor) and Eccleshill formed part of the possessions of the Langtons of Walton, by knight service rendered to the lord of the Honor of Clitheroe. In 1377-8 the lordship of Eccleshill was claimed by Thomas Molineux, in the right of his wife, who was a grand-daughter of Geoffrey de Kuerdale, but at the same time manorial rights in Eccleshill were exercised by the Grymesheys of Clayton.

About 1276, Rd. de Grymeshagh, evidently the successor of the de Eccleshulls, gave half-an-acre of the vill of Eccleshill to the monks of Stanlaw. The Grimshaws are supposed to have lived at a tenement called Grymeshaw, near the spot where Grimshaw Bridge now spans the brook in Eccleshill, but subsequently they occupied Clayton Hall, which came to Adam de Grymeshaw on his marriage with Cecilia, daughter and heir of John de Clayton. The Eccleshill estate was owned by the Grimshaws until the time of the Commonwealth, when it was confiscated for recusancy, as will be shown hereafter. The Eccleshill estate belonged in the first half of the present century to Thos. Wilson, of Preston, who had purchased it from the Claytons of Adlington, but in 1848 the "reputed manor or lordship of Eccleshill" was sold to James Hodgson, of Liverpool, since deceased. The land where Eccleshill,

Pickup Bank, and Over Darwen meet has served a large tract of Lancashire with coal for 300 years, but the coal measures are now exhausted.

YATE-AND-PICKUP BANK.

This township in the Darwen chapelry forms the western extremity of the ancient Forest of Rossendale. The chief of the early copyholders were the Yates or Yateses, and the Holdens. Greaves of the Forest have often been chosen from among the yeomen of Yate-and-Pickup Bank and Hoddlesden. Hoddlesden is mentioned in the Chancery Rolls of 2 Edward IV. as a vaccary in the Forest of Rossendale. Yate-and-Pickup Bank is a small township deriving its names from the lofty banks or hills, which are its chief topographical feature. Its chief centre of population is the hill-top village of Belthorn, in an isolated portion of the Forest. In the 1835 edition of the *History of Lancashire* it was included in the parochial chapelry of Church, and stated to be partly in Over Darwen, in the parish of Blackburn, and partly in the township of Oswaldtwistle. The census returns formerly gave it as part of the parish of Whalley, but now they include it in the parish of Blackburn. Mr. Harland, in his edition of the *History of Lancashire*, after investigating its correct position, declares that it is extra-parochial. The Ecclesiastical Survey of 1650 shows that it was reckoned part of the chapelry of Over Darwen and of the rectory of Blackburn in the time of the Commonwealth,[1] and it is intimately connected with Darwen in many ways. The principal glebe lands of the Darwen Chapel are situated in this township, just below Belthorn. In Pickup Bank there is a small family burial ground of the Yateses containing about forty graves.

TRADITION OF A SERPENT AT PICKUP BANK.

I am informed by some persons, who had it by tradition from ancient people, that formerly there was in this country a monstrous serpent of four or five yards long, and thicker than a common [wooden] axle-tree of a cart, and very mischievous, preying upon lambs, &c. Its chief residence was in a wood, near Pickup Bank, a few miles from Blackburn, in Lancashire, called Ouse Castle, wherein there is yet a little spot of ground called Griom's Ark, which is a deep cavern, situated among rocks in a wood, from whence it was seen to come out and bask itself upon a sunny bank. The picture of this serpent is drawn with wings, two legs, and talons like an eagle, which is seen in some ancient houses (and particularly at Clayton Hall, near Dunkinhall), by which it appears to be very large and furious. It is said one Grimshaw, esq., proprietor of that hall, shot the monster with arrows, and had an estate offered him for that good service done to his country, which he generously refused, and only desired

---

[1] But in the assessment of the Blackburn Hundred, made by the Commonwealth in 1654, the township of Yate-and-Pickup Bank is not mentioned.

that he might have a passage through that wood to a township he had on the other side of it, which was granted, the title of which is found in ancient writings. "It is observable," says my author, "that in the front of Clayton Hall are two figures drawn in plaister in the form of a coat of arms; on the right side of the escutcheon is a figure with wings, four feet, and a tail twisted in the form of a serpent. The like figure is drawn in plaister in several antient houses in that neighbourhood, which go under the name of the Griffin's Picture, and the sign is used at publick-houses. There is a place in that wood called Griffin's Ark."[1]

SOME OLD INHABITANTS.

Most of the family names of the older inhabitants, like the old place-names of the Darwen townships, are pure Saxon, and documentary evidence proves that the names still common among the people of Darwen are identical with those of the gentry and yeomen who farmed the district during the medieval period of English history. Except on the basis of "Jeremy Hunt's Recollections of Old Darwen Families," I have not attempted to make this book a family history. Many years ago the Deputy Keeper of the Public Records observed that "the documents now opened afford untouched mines of information relating to the private history of persons and families. . . . . . There are manors or townships through which the history of the lord and the tenant, the hirer and the servant, the landlord and the labourer, may be pursued accurately and amply, for all practical purposes, from the Conquest to our living times. The public records have been searched and catalogued to a very considerable extent since these sentences were penned in 1859, and this gives increased force to them. My own object in consulting these public records has not been to search for "the private history of persons and families" but rather to ascertain the general condition of the inhabitants and the townships of the Darwen valley during the period covered by these scraps of documentary history. So far as the inhabitants are concerned I have endeavoured to make a list of the principal householders and heads of families during the century extending from the accession of Queen Elizabeth to the institution of the Commonwealth. The earliest inhabitant I have seen mentioned is "John, son of Bibby," who in the year 1280 was the tenant of a messuage in Superiore Derwent, under Richard de Alffton. It would appear from the wording of a deed of this date that Alexander de Keuerdale had also a house in Darwen, and Adam de Grymeshaw is supposed to have been resident lord of the manor of Eccleshill.

Some family names still common in the Darwen and Hoddlesden valleys appear among the oldest Darwen names on record. These are found in a Subsidy Roll showing the amount of the levies made by

[1] *Natural History of Serpents*, 1742, p. 144.

Henry VII. upon his subjects in the years 1523-4. The list given below[1] contains the names of the principal inhabitants of this neighbourhood in the time of Henry VII., and it shows that Lower Darwen was then a more important residental district than Over Darwen. Almost every name is a common patronymic in Darwen to-day. The particulars given show the worth of the principal inhabitants in land and goods and amount they were assessed to pay to the King under the subsidy :—

DERWYND SUPERIOR—	VALUE.	LEVY.	DERWYND INFERIOR (contd.)—	VALUE.	LEVY.
Rychard Crosse, in landes	40s.	2s.	Peter Haworth, in goodes	£4	2s.
William Berre, in landes..	20s.	12d.	Edmond Harwood, in goodes	40s.	12d.
Rauf Hey, in goodes	£4	2s.	Richard Haworth, in goodes	40s.	12d.
DERWYND INFERIOR—			HODILSDEN —		
James Lyvesey [Fernehurst] in landes	£3	3s.	William Yate, in goodes..	£3	18d.
William Mersden, in landes	20s.	12d.	Robert Fyshe, in goodes..	40s.	12d.
Rauf Waddington, in goodes	£4	2s.	Robert Baron, in goodes..	40s.	12d.
Edmond Haworth, in goodes	£4	2s.			

The lords of the manors of Over Darwen and Lower Darwen did not reside in the townships at this period, so their names do not appear in the list, but Gilbert Talbot, uncle of Sir Thomas Talbot, shortly afterwards lived at Fernehurst, and died there in 1547. Eccleshill was linked with Mellor ("Mellor-cum-Eckells"). The Rychard Crosse mentioned in the list may be the same man as the Rychard Crosse who was a trustee of the Earl of Derby's Chantry in Blackburn Parish Church, founded in the year 1514. James Livesey, of Lower Darwen, was accused in 1529 of forcible entry and tortious possession of lands in Fernehurst manor, and in 1536 James Lyvesey, who held a lease at Lower Darwen under Abbot Paslew, of Whalley, went to law against Richard Wamborsley and others respecting a disputed title to tythe corn and other tythes of Blackburn parsonage and Whalley Abbey in Livesey, Tockholes, and Fernehurst.[2]

Lancashire men took an important part in the victorious battle of Flodden, and doubtless there were some sturdy country youths from Darwen in the wing that was led by Sir Marmaduke Constable and Sir Edward Stanley, for the ballad minstrel of the period, singing the praises of the Lancashire men, included the

> lustie ladds, liver and light,
> From Blackborne and Bolton in the Moores.

There were frequent levies of armed men made upon Lancashire, and the country generally, for the foreign wars that commenced in

---

[1] Copied from the Subsidy Roll in the Public Record Office by Mr. Abram, the historian of Blackburn.

[2] *History of Blackburn*, p. 483.

HOLKER HOUSE, HODDLESDEN, BUILT A.D. 1591.

Queen Mary's reign. In the first muster (1553) Blackburn Hundred was ordered to raise 400 armed men, and towards these Nether Darwen contributed three, Eccleshill (with Mellor) five, and Over Darwen five. In a trial concerning manorial rights in Over Darwen, in the 3rd and 4th years of the reign of Philip and Mary (1556), it was deposed that John Osbaldeston, lord of the manor, and his ancestors, had always occupied "Darwynd Hall," which is described as the "chief house and mansion place of Over Darwynd." The Darwen men who appeared as witnesses in this suit were—Lawrence Pycop, of Lower Darwynd, tenant to Richard Livesey, gentleman, aged 72; John Crosse, of Over Darwynd, 66; John Pyllyn, of Over Darwynd, 63; and Edmonde Barton, of Over Darwynd—all tenants of John Osbaldeston; William Yate, of Eccleshill, aged 70, tenant to Rauf Holden, Esq.; William Shorrock, of Eccleshill, 66; Edward Baron, of Eccleshill, 50, tenant to Richard Grimshaw, gentleman; William Fysshe, of Lower Darwynd, 72, and George Aspeden, of Lower Darwynd, 76, tenants of Sir Thomas Talbot, Knight. There was at that time a pinfold in Darwen, in all probability on the same site as the one still standing on the edge of Darwen Moor, and it was the custom to impound the cattle and beasts of strangers dwelling out of the lordship of Over Darwen which were found straying on Darwen Moor.

Of the Elizabethan period there are several interesting historical relics. Two unpretentious mansions and a still less pretentious little chapel mark the site of similar buildings that existed in the days of Queen Elizabeth, and one of these buildings—Holker House, Hoddlesden—stands to-day pretty much as it was erected in 1591. It is built of local stone at a bend in an old Saxon road just within the eastern boundary of the township of Over Darwen. It is now a simple farmhouse, but bears signs of having been the residence of an influential gentleman. It is at present associated with the name of the Hindles, an old Darwen family of note, descended from one Christopher Hindle, of Holker House, who occupied the dwelling in the early part of the last century. But its original owner was probably an Entwistle, of Entwistle, judging by the letters R.E.I. over the door. Mr. Ashton's description, quoted below, applies almost equally well in the present year as it did in the year 1868, when it was written.

> Holker House bears unmistakable evidence of having once been the abode of some family of note. Facing the south, with the remains of its pleasaunce occupying the space between the front and the road, this old homestead attracts irresistibly the thoughtful passer-by. The porch, the ponderous lintel, and well-hewn corner stones, the recessed windows, and the one old but well-designed chimney, tell, after the lapse of many generations, that its owner was a man of taste and means.

Approaching nearer we can discern a stone on which are sculptured the letters R.E.I. between two arrowets, a griffin, the owner's crest, and the date 1591. Who owned this old house in the days of Queen Elizabeth I cannot at present ascertain, but the subject is worth inquiry.

Whitehall, the oldest house in Darwen, is now occupied by R. T. Gillibrand, Esq., J.P. Being anxious to ascertain its exact date, I examined it, in 1888, in company with Mr. W. T. Ashton and Mr. Gillibrand, and, after careful scrutiny, we agreed that the inscription on an old stone chimney-piece in a disused portion of the house is "R.H. 1557." The two last figures are very indistinct, but we satisfied ourselves by close inspection that the inscription is as I have now given it. Whitehall is an Elizabethan mansion, standing on a flat well-wooded piece of ground, with neatly-kept walks, fences, and gardens. One of the most remarkable features of the house is a tiny oak tree of great antiquity growing out of the wall above one of the bedroom windows in the older portion. It has shown leaf every Spring for years, and there is not another oak about the place, though the ash, the elm, and the sycamore are to be found in abundance. This oak is called the "Fairy Tree," and to this day the people of the neighbourhood cherish a tradition that if it is cut down at night it will grow again by next morning. Various alterations have been made in the house of late years to adapt it to modern requirements.

Darwen Chapel will be found fully dealt with in the next chapter. The Osbaldestons, lords of the manor of Over Darwen, had a mill in the township at this period, and they used Darwen Moor as a sheep run.

The subjoined list of inhabitants during the reign of Queen Elizabeth is chiefly compiled from the Wills and Inventories preserved at Chester, and the Subsidy Roll of 1570. The men assessed to the Subsidy would be the principal settlers, for these subsidies, granted by Parliament, and levied by the Monarch, were the taxes which were utilised for warfare, for the carrying on of the affairs of the nation, and for the expenditure of the royal household. Richard Livesey, of Fernhurst, and Nicholas Grimshaw, of Oakenhurst, are the only Darwen freeholders of the year 1600 mentioned in the list of "Libere tenentes infra Hundred' de Blakeburne," preserved in the Harleian MSS., No. 2,042. William Crosse, who was assessed to the Subsidy of 1570, was probably the William Cross who held the position of a Governor of the Blackburn Grammar School. It is a matter of surmise, and yet of probability, that William Berye, who contributed to the last Subsidy of Elizabeth's reign, lived at Bury Fold, an enclosure of great antiquity on the slope of Darwen Moor near Whitehall. The Barons were an important family, for they gave

WHITE HALL.
THE OLDEST HOUSE IN DARWEN, DATED 1557.

their name to a plot of land, afterwards known as "Baron's oulde land." Nicholas Grymshaw, gentleman, who resided at Oakenhurst, Lower Darwen, was undoubtedly a member of the de Grymshaw family which succeeded the de Eccleshulls as lords of the manor of Eccleshill about the year 1276-7. Grimshaw Bridge, over the Grimshaw Brook, is a place-name derived from their tenure of the land in that neighbourhood. Lawrence Haworth, of Nether Darwyn, and Nicholas Haworth, who seems to have lived at Hoddlesden, were Governors of the Blackburn Grammar School, which was founded in Elizabeth's reign. Among the names of the original Governors of the School appears that of Richard Heyworth, who has been supposed to be of the same stock as the Haworths of Nether Darwen. The Haworths were a numerous and important family of yeomen and gentlemen having residences at Highercroft, Newfield, Hoddlesden, and other places in the neighbourhood. Hindle was a name which had not become common in Darwen so early as Elizabeth's reign, but it is curious that Henry Hindle, of Eccleshill, in his will dated 1578, describes himself as a "clerk." The Holdens of Pickup Bank, were related to the Holdens of Holden Hall, Haslingden, and we are not surprised, therefore, to find Robert Holden of Picope Bank holding the office of Greave of Rossendale Forrest, in 1591. The family was well connected, having marriage ties with the Haworths of Highercroft. An old house at Pickup Bank, bearing the initials "G.H." and the date "1602," still stands to testify to the social position of this old Darwen family, which at the present time is one of the most numerous families in the town. There were several Marsdens in the neighbourhood, particularly about Livesey and Tockholes, but the only two Darwen Marsdens I have met with belonging to the Elizabethan period are those of Henry Mersden, who was nominated one of the original Governors of the Blackburn Grammar School in 1567, and Christopher Mersden, a landowner of Lower Darwen, who was assessed to the Subsidy of 1570. The Yates of Yate Bank were a numerous and wealthy family, and spread over a considerable portion of the Hoddlesden valley and the adjacent "banks." George Yate, of Yate Bank, yeoman, by his will about 1590, gave 6s. 8d. to the Blackburn Grammar School. In 1595 nearly 2,000 men were mustered for military purposes in the Hundred of Blackburn, Over Darwen supplying five, Nether Darwen 22, and Mellor-cum-Eccleshill 16. Among the noteworthy place-names occurring in documents of the time of Elizabeth I notice Highercroft, Okenhurst, Fearnehurst, Grimeshaw Bridge, Walsh Fold, Newfield, Earnsden, Darwen Croft, Darwen Hey, and Soughe; besides Eccleshill Yatebank, Picop Bank, Hoddlesden, Over and Lower Darwen, &c.

The Elizabethan antiquary, Camden, noted the river Darwen on his second tour through Lancashire. He says[1] :—

Below it [Preston] the Ribell receives the Derwen, a small river. which first waters Blackborne, a noted market town ; which formerly belonged to the Lacies, and gave to the tract adjacent the name of Blackburnshire. Thence it passes by Houghton Tower, which gave name to a famous family that long resided at it ; and Waleton, which William, lord of Lancaster, son of King Stephen, gave to Walter de Waleton, but it afterwards belonged to the famous family of the Langtons, which derive themselves from the Waltons.

INHABITANTS OF DARWEN, *TEMPUS* QUEEN ELIZABETH.[2]

Aspinall, Lawrence, of Nether Darwen... ....W	1603
Aspinall, Thos., of Nthr. Darwen.S	1570
Aspinall, Lawrence,of N. Darwen d	1600
Banester, of Derwen	1567
Berye, Wm., of Darwyn Superior S	1570
Baron, Richard, of Over Darwen.	1562
Baron, William, of Over Darwen.	1565
Baron, Edmund, of Over Darwen.S	1570
Crosse, William, of Over Darwen.S	1570
Cooper, Roger, of Over Darwen, yeoman.....................	1602
Fish, William, of Eccleshill ......W	
ffishe, Lawrence, of Darwen ......d	1603
ffishe, Ralph, of Soughe, Over Darwen......................	1588
Grymshawe, Nicholas, of Nether Darwen, gent...............	1578
Grimshaw, Rd., of Nether Darwen........................Inv.	1602
Grymshawe, Nichus, de Okenhurst, gent.	1600
Grymshaw, John, of Eccleshill...Inq.	1587
Haworth, Lettice, daugh. of Lawrence, of Lower Darwen ....W	1603
Haworth, Nicholas, of Hod'l'sden.	1588
Haworth, Rd., of Lower Darwen.W	1603
Haworth, Wm., of Over Darwen.W	1598
Haworth, Lawrence, of Nether Darwyn	1585
Haworth, Peter, of Nthr. Darwyn.S	1570
Haworth, Piers, of Highercroft, Lower Darwen.............d	1600
Haworth, Rd., of Lower Darwen, gent. ....d	1603
Haworth, Giles, of Newfield, Lower Darwen ....d	1590
Haworthe, Nycholas ....d	1597
Holme, Edward, of Hoddlesden ....W	1597
Horridge, James, of Over Darwen. Inv.	1603
Hindle, Henry, of Eccleshill, clerk ....W	1578
Holden, George, of Picop Bank..Inv.	1602
Holden, Robert, of Picope Bank, Rossendale ....W	1597
Holden. Robert, of Picope Bank, Greave of Rossendale......	1591
Holden, Thos., of Hoddlesden, co. Lancaster ....W	1593
Lyvesaye, Rd., of Nether Darwen [de Fernyhurst, gent.] ....S	1570
Livsaye, Ricus, de fearnehurst, gent............................	1600
Lommas, Rd., of Lower Darwen.	1562
Mersden, Henry [of Okenhurst ?]	1567
Mersden, Christopher, of Lower Darwen ....S	1570
Piccop, James, of Nether Darwen.Inv.	1592
Piccop, Robt., of Nether Darwen.W	1593
Pycoppe, Edward, of Lower Darwen	1560
Piccope, Robt., of Nether Darwyn, yeoman ....Inq.	1603
Piccope, James, of Nthr. Darwen.	1603
Pyccope, Robt., of Earnsden, Netherdarwyne ....d	1603
Sharp, Wm., of Hoddleston......W	1594
Shorrock, Thos., of Eccleshill ...Inv.	1573
Shorrock, Wm., of Eccleshill ...S	1570
Waddington, Ralph, of Nether Darwen ....d	1597
Yate, Hy., of Yatebank ....W	1603
Yate, Jas., of Lower Darwen, yeoman......................W	1599
Yate, John, of Yatebank ....W	1588
Yate, Robt., of Yatebank ....W	1598
Yate, Wm., of Yatebank, yeoman (son of John)	1588
Yate, Geo., of Yatebank, yeoman.W	1590
Yate, Robt., of Yatebank ....m	1602

1 Gough's *Camden*, vol. iii., p. 379.

2 In the lists of names here given the letter W prefixed to the date, shows that the figures give the date of a will ; S means assessed to the Subsidy ; Inv. inventory ; Inq. inquisition ; m. married ; d. died.

Little need be said concerning the inhabitants of Darwen during the reign of James I. The Aspinalls are numerous, particularly in Lower Darwen, and one of them holds the office of constable. The Barons remain on the "oulde land" of their fathers, and a Berye is to be found at Bury Fold. Estates like Turncroft and Oakenhurst have come into the possession of the Crosses. The Fishes appear in a shoal, and one of them, in his will dated 1617, informs us that the district now called "Chapels" was known as "The Chapel" when only one place of worship existed, and it follows that the old place-name simply took the plural number when the Nonconformists erected the Lower Chapel. At Lower Darwen, the Harwoods and the Haworths appear in strong force, and in the former family we read of a man who became an eminent divine, while the Newfield branch of the latter family has its escutcheon blotted with the story of a horrible murder. The Rev. Edward Welshe, who retired to his country house at Walsh Fold, on The Green, Over Darwen, in 1606, was a Vicar of Blackburn, who was suspended for Nonformity, and it is probable that the Walshes of Darwen, high and low, rich and poor, are mostly related to him. The Yates or Yateses continue to thrive. One of them is named as residing at "the Water" in Eccleshill, which will mean Waterside, and another, who lived at Woodhead in Hoddlesden, was a Greave of Rossendale Forest, of which this hamlet is the western extremity. Some of the old names drop out and new ones appear. Among the new ones is the name of William Dewhurst, who was living in Over Darwyn in 1619, aged 90 years. Another place-name appears in this list, namely, "The Hollins in Lower Darwen," and Eccleshill is again mentioned in conjunction with township of Mellor.

The story of Giles Haworth, who was outlawed for murder, contains many points of public interest. Giles appears to have been a younger son of "Gyles Haworth, of Newfielde," who died in 1590, and to have been a minor at the time of his father's death. His elder brother Ralph succeeded to the property, but apparently died without issue, leaving Giles in possession. Giles was a married man, but became entangled with the wife of a man named Waters, and murdered him. This occurred in 1604. I have found records of four Inquisitions touching this matter, the object being to find out, on behalf of the King, whether the Newfield estate did not become forfeited to the Crown on account of its owner being attainted of murder and outlawed. A great deal appeared to depend on whether the property was held of the King in chief (*in capite*) or of the King in his capacity as Duke of Lancaster. The first inquisition was held at Blackburn in January, 1607, and showed that the property of Giles Haworth, deceased (the murderer's father), was held of Thomas Walmsley, Knight. A second was held the same year, when it was declared that Haworth held his estate of the King, as of his Duchy of Lancaster, by knight's service. At the third, conducted at Preston in 1610, it was stated that the land was held of the King *in capite*, in free and common socage, and was forfeited by reason of the attainder of murder. A fourth inquiry was demanded, and held at Wigan in 1611, when it was proved that the estate was not held by knight's service, nor of the King in chief, but by free and common socage (probably a rent charge) of the King as Duke of Lancaster. Under these circumstances it was not forfeited, but handed over to Edmund Haworth, a brother or son of the murderer, whose wife had died in 1608. An Edmund Haworth, who is believed to be the same man, became a warden at the Blackburn Parish Church in 1634. I give below a summary of the Inquisitions relating to the case:—

Inq. taken at Wigan, 24 September, 1607, by a writ[1] of melius inquirendo. Giles Haworth, who died 7 December, 1590, was seized of a messuage, a garden, an orchard, 6 acres of land, 4 of meadow, and 6 of pasture, in Netherdarwen, held of the late Queen and now of the King, as of the Duchy of Lancaster, by the 200th part of a knight's fee, and worth per annum 10/-. So seized, by his Will bearing date 2 November, 32 Eliz. [1590], he devised a moiety of the premises to his wife, Alice, for her life, as dower, and the other moiety to her until his heir male should arrive at full age, the reversion thereof being to Ralph, his son, and heirs of his body, with remainder to the next heir male of his own body begotten and the issue of such heir; in default to John Haworth, brother of Giles, in tail male with remainder further to his own right heirs for ever. Alice, his wife, survives at Nether Darwyn. Ralph, his son and heir, is aged 21 years.

Inq. taken at Preston, 19 April, 1610, before Edward Rigby, Esq., Escheator, and Henry Sothworth, gentleman, Feodary of the county, concerning the lands, tenements, goods and chattels, which escheated, or ought to escheat, to the King, by reason of an attainder of murder lately committed by Giles Haworth, of Nether-darwinde. The jury say that Giles Haworth, at the time of his attainder, was seized in fee of 2 messuages with the appurtenances, 10 acres of land, 6 acres of meadow, and 10 acres of pasture with common of pasture for all manner of cattle in Nether-derwyn; which messuages, &c., held of the King *in capite*, in free and common socage, and worth per annum 10/- in all issues beyond reprises, ought to revert to the King as his escheats for the reason aforesaid.

Inq. taken at Wigan 27 March, 1611, before Edward Rigbye, Esq., Escheator, and Henry Southworth, gentleman, Feodary of the county. The jury on oath say:—Whereas by a certain Inquisition taken before the same Escheator and Feodary at Preston, 19 April last, it is found that Giles Haworth, of Nether Derwyn, at the time of his attainder of a murder committed by him, was seized in fee of 2 messuages with

---

[1] The annexed writ refers to an Inquisition taken at Blackburne, 10 January, 1606-7, by which it is found that the lands, &c., of Giles Haworth were said to be held of Thomas Walmysley, Knt., in free socage,, but are now understood to be held of the King *in capite*. Hence the necessity for further inquiry.

the appurtenances, 10 acres of land, 6 of meadow, 10 of pasture, and common of pasture for all manner of his cattle in Nether Derwyn, which were then held of the King in free and common socage and not *in capite*—the Jurors now say that the messuages, &c., are and were held of the King in free and common socage, AS OF HIS DUCHY OF LANCASTER, and not *in capite*.

The discovery of the murder was attended by very curious circumstances, and witchcraft was suspected. Sir Richard Baker, commenting on it in 1670, observed—" And now what hope can murtherers have of being concealed, when they are subjected to be discovered by a man's dream ?" Dr. Webster, the annalist, a native of Clitheroe, gives the following account of it :—

In the second year of the reign of King James of famous memory, a strange accident happened here, to the terror of all bloody murtherers, which was this, as it was taken from the mouths of Thomas Haworth's wife, her husband being the dreamer and discoverer, and from his son, together with many more, who both remember and can affirm every particular thereof. The narrative was taken April the 7th, 1663, and is this[1] :—In the year above said [2 James I, 1604], John Waters, of Lower Darwen, in the County of Lancaster, gardiner, by reason of his calling was much absent from his family, in which his absence, his wife (not without cause) was suspected of incontinency with one Gyles Haworth, of the same town; this Gyles Haworth and Waters' wife conspired and contrived the death of Waters in this manner. As soon as Waters came home and went to his bed, Gyles Haworth and Waters' wife conducted the hired executioner to the said Waters. Who seeing him so innocently laid betwixt his two small children in bed, repented of his enterprise, and totally refused to kill him. Gyles Haworth, displeased with the faint-heartedness of Ribchester, takes the Axe into his hand, and dashed out his brains ; the murderers buried him in a cowhouse. Waters being long missing, the neighbours asked his wife for him ; she denied that she knew where he was. Thereupon public search was made for him in all pits round about, lest he should casually have fallen into any of them. One Thomas Haworth, of the said town, yeoman, was for many nights much troubled with broken sleep and dreams of the murder ; he revealed his dreams to his wife, but she laboured the concealment of them a long time. This Thomas Haworth had occasion to pass by the house every day where the murder was done, and did call and inquire for Waters as often as he went near the house. One day he went into the house to ask for him, and there was a neighbour, who said to Thomas Haworth, It's said that Waters lies under this stone (pointing to the hearth-stone), to which Thomas Haworth replied, And I have dreamed that he is under a stone not far distant. The constable of the said town being accidentally in the said house (his name Myles Aspinall), urged Thomas Haworth to make known more at large what he had dreamed, which he relateth thus. I have (quoth he) many a time within this eight weeks (for so long it was since the murder) dreamed very restlessly, that Waters was murdered and buried under a stone in the cowhouse ; I have told my troubled dreams to my wife alone, but she refuses to let me make it known ; but I am not able to conceal my dreams any longer, my sleep departs from me, I am pressed and troubled with fearful dreams, which I cannot bear any longer, and they increase upon me. The constable hearing this made search immediately upon it, and found, as he

[1] *The Display of Supposed Witchcraft*, by John Webster, Practitioner in Physic, ch. xvi. p. 297.

had dreamed, the murdered body eight weeks buried under a flat stone in the cowhouse. Ribchester and Gyles Haworth fled and never came again. Anne Waters (for so was Water's wife's name), being apprehended, confessed the murder, and was burned.

INHABITANTS OF DARWEN, *TEMP.* JAMES I.

Alman, John, of Upper Darwen..W	1605	Grimshaw, Ralph, of L. Darwen Inv,	1623
Aspinall, Giles, of Lower Darwen.W	1606	Harwood, Edmund, of L. Darwen Inv.	1616
Aspinall, Miles, of Over Darwen.W	1618	Harwood, Edmund, of Netherderwen........Inq.	1616
Aspinall, Thos., of Nthr. Darwen.W	1609		
Aspinall, Lawrence, of Nether Darwen......d	1604	Harwood, Margaret, of Netherderwen........Inq.	1618
Aspinall, Myles, of L. Darwen, constable......	1604	Harwood, Edward, of N. Darwin S	1611
		Harwood, Edmond, of N. Darwen S	1611
Aspinall, Thos., of Nthr. Darwen.	1618	Harwood, Richard, of L. Darwen	1625
Aspinall, Robt., of Nthr. Darwen.	1618	Haworth, Alice, of Newfield, in Nether Darwen, widow...W	1608
Aspinall, John, of Netherdarwyne Inq.	1620		
Aspinall, Thos., of Netherdarwyne......	1620	Haworth, John, of Lower Eccleshill........W	1618
Barker, John, of Nether Darwen.Inv.	1618	Haworth, Lawrence, of O. Darwen W	1617
Baron, James, of Overderwine....Inv.	1619	Haworth, Lawrence, of N. Darwen S	1611
Baron, John, of Overderwine, [yeoman]......W	1611	Haworth, Lawrence, of Hurcrofte, Netherderwen, gentleman.Inq.	1618
Baron, John, of Overderwent, gentleman ......Inq.	1611	Haworth, Giles, of Netherdarwinde (attainted of murder)Inq.	1610
Baron, John (Heirs of), Upper Darwin......S	1611	Haworth, Edmond, of Netherdarwinde......	1611
Berye, Wm., of Over Darwen ...m	1625	Haydock, Oliver, of Over Darwen W	1624
Birkenhead, John, of Over Darwen......W	1623	Heap, John, of Nether Darwen .W	1613
		Hey, George, of Mellor-cum-Eccleshill........S	1611
Crosse, John, of [Turncroft] Upper Darwin [gentleman]S	1611	Horwich, John, of Over Darwen.W	1622
Crosse, Henrie, of Nether Darwin S	1611	Hindle, Wm., of Overderwen ...Inq.	1617
Crosse, Hy., of Okenhead [Oakenhurst]	1616	Hulton, John, of Overderwine ...Inq.	1606
		Ireland, Richard, of Mellor-cum-Eccleshill........S	1611
Dewhurst,'Wm., of Overdarwyne, living, aged 90 years	1619	Kirkham, John, of Darwen ......W	1611
Ellison, Jennett, of the Hollins in Lower Darwen, widow ...W	1614	Lightowler, Robt., of Wyndybank W	1620
Ellison, Wm., of Over Darwen...W/	1618	Livesey, Roger, of Darwen ......W	1620
Ellison, Wm., of Overdarwyne...Inq.	1619	Livesey, Henrie, of Upper Darwin S	1611
Entwistle, Hy., of Over Darwen.W	1606	Livesey, Hy., of Nether Darwen.	1611
Fish, John, of Eccleshill...........Inv.	1609	Livesey, Henry, of Over Darwen Inv.	1622
Fish, Ralph, of Nether Darwen...W	1618	Marsden, Rd., of Nether Darwen W	1620
Fish, Thos., of the Chapel, in Over Darwen ......W	1617	Marsden, Hy., of Netherdarwyne Inq.	1620
		Marsden, Christopher, of Netherdarwyne	1620
Fish, Thos., of Over Darwen ...W	1617	Mawdsley, Hy., of Overdarwyn...Inq.	1607
Fish, Wm., of Over Darwen......Inv.	1616	Morris, Geo., of Nether Darwen.Inv.	1619
Fish, Wm., of Overderwen, yeoman......Inq.	1616	Pomfret, Thos., of ["Pomfret's"] Nether Darwen	1618
Fish, Ralph, of Overderwen......Inq.	1623	Pomfret, Rd., of ["Pomfret's"] Nether Darwen	1618
Fishe, Margaret, of Overderwen.W	1623		
Fishe, Ralph, of Eccleshill ......W	1621	Piccop, John, of Eccleshill ......Inv.	1623
Fishe, Ralph, of Eccleshill, gentleman......Inq	1623	Piccoppe, John, of Eccleshill ...d	1623
		Pyccope, Robert, of Earnsden, Netherdarwyne, yeoman ......Inq.	1620
ffishe, Rauf, of Mellei-cum-Eccleshill......S	1611	Pyccope, Jas., of Nether Darwen	1620
Gelybrande, of Mellor-cum-Eccleshill......S	1611	Sharrock, Rd., of Eccleshill ......Inv.	1606
Gregson, John, of Lower Darwen W	1624	Shorrock, Thos., of Mellor-cum-Eccleshill ......S	1611

Waddington, Margaret, of Over Darwen ....W	1616	Yate, Jennet, of Yatebank, par. of Blackburn ....W		1613
Walmsley, Rd., of Mellor-cum-Eccleshill ....S	1611	Yate, John, of the Water, in Eccleshill ....Inv.		1609
Walmisley, Christopher, of Nether Darwine	1622	Yate, Lawrence, of Eccleshill ...Inv.		1619
Walmisley, William, of Nether Darwine, gentleman ...Inq.	1622-3	Yate, Lawrence, of Nthr. Darwen. W		1606
Ward, Jas., of Mellor-cum-Eccleshill ....S	1611	Yate, Robt., of Yatebank ....W		1607
Welch, John, of Over Darwen...W	1606	Yates, Wm., of Yate Bank, in Hoddlesden...............W		1617
Welch, Mr., lecturer de Darwen..	1622	Yates, Robert, of Yate Bank......m		1624
Welsh, John, of Over Darwen ...W	1612	Yate, William, of Yate Bank, yeoman.................d		1617
Welsh, Thos, of Over Darwen ...W	1608	Yate, Rd., of Yate Bank		1611
Welshe, Edward, of Walsh Fold, O. Darwen (a suspended Vicar of Blackburn)		Yate, Thos., of Yate Bank ......d		1623
		Yate, Wm., of Yate Bank.........m		1617
		Yate, John, of Yate Bank.........m		1623
Walsh, Lawrence, of O. Darwen .W	1625	Yate, Geo., de Windie Bank......m		1617
Yate, Geo., of Yatebank ....W	1619	Yate, Jas., of Woodhead, Hoddlesden, Greave of Rossendale.		1608
Yate, Giles, of Yatebank, co. Lancaster........ ......W	1609	Yate, Lawrence, of Netherdarwen, yeoman............Inq.		1606

NOTE ON THE REV. EDWARD WELSHE.

The Rev. Edward Welshe, of Walsh Fold, Darwen, was Vicar of Blackburn in 1590, when he and 16 other Lancashire "preachers" signed a petition concerning "The Manifolde Enormities of the Ecclesiasticall state in most partes of the Countie of Lancaster." Among the things complained about were the "Manifolde Popishe Superstitions used in the Burial of the Dead"—such as garnishing the corpse with crosses and candles, neglecting the prescribed service, praying for departed souls, and banqueting in the alehouse after the funeral. Six years later Mr. Welshe was cited before the Commissioners at Chester and charged with refusing to wear his surplice. His reply was "that he neither did nor would refuse to wear the surplice if the same was fit and tendered to him in good sort." He was "enjoyned to wear it hereafter," but appears to have persisted in his nonconformity, for in 1604 he again appeared at Chester, and was "required" by the Bishop to subscribe to the three articles in the 36th Canon of 1603. In 1605 he was deprived of his Vicarage, when he retired to Walsh Fold, on Darwen Green, where he lived for 20 years. It is probable that he continued to preach after his deposition, as I have noted elsewhere. He died at Walsh Fold in April, 1628.

Our third list of names indicates who were the principal inhabitants of Darwen in the reign of Charles I., and brings us down to the time of the Commonwealth. It contains a few features worthy of special mention, such as the introduction of the place-names Soonehurst, Brocklehead, &c., and the mention of the trade of a mason. The Thomas Lomas, husbandman, mentioned was one of the earliest known contributors to the endowment of Darwen Chapel, his gift being £10. He resided in Over Darwen, but was probably related to the Lomases of Lower Darwen, one of whom, Ralph Lommas, appears in the Elizabethan list (1562). Thomas Fishe, of Eccleshill, who was elected a Governor of the Blackburn Grammar School in 1635, was a prominent member of a numerous local family. He married Elizabeth, daughter of Richard Hoghton, of Red Lee, Tockholes, gent., and their initials appear over the doorway of Eccleshill Fold—"T.E.F., 1641,"—which they built for a residence. Under an old statute, believed to date from Edward the First's time, squires and gentlemen who were knighted by the King were allowed to buy themselves off by payment of a fine. At first every landowner with £20 a year was liable to be summoned to accept the Order of Knighthood, then the qualifying income was raised to £40, and eventually the holders of lands otherwise than by knights' fees were included, so long as they had the requisite annual income. One Darwen gentleman, the representative of an old local family, is named among those who paid the fine for declining the honour of knighthood in 1631. This was John Crosse, of Over Darwen, who paid the sum of x$^{li.}$ at Blackburn on the 15th of September, in the seventh year of Charles I. It does not, however, follow that at that time the King desired the services of John Crosse as a knight, for it was notorious that the knighting of his subjects had become one of the various means of raising money, and that he wanted the fines, not the men. The event which caused John Crosse to be summoned to the service of his King was the coronation of that monarch, which had been delayed for several years. The incident is interesting as showing the status of Crosse in the township and in the country.[1]

INHABITANTS OF DARWEN, *TEMP.* CHARLES I.

Aspinall, Wm., of Nether Darwen	W 1640	Foole, John, of Eccleshill .... W	1631
Aspinall, Thos., of Lower Darwen	Inv. 1638	Grymshawe, Nicholas, of Nether Darwyne .... d	1642
Aspinall, Thos., of Lower Darwen	Inq. 1633	Haddock, John, of N. Darwen... W	1634
Astley, Ralph, of Over Darwen	Inq. 1642	Haddock, Thurstan, of Eccleshill W	1631
Astley, Randle, of Eccleshill, yeoman .... W	1641	Haworth, Thos., of Waterside, yeoman .... W	1638
Astley, Thomas, of Eccleshill, yeoman .... W	1649	Haworth, Thos., of Lwr. Darw'n d	1637
Baron, Wm., of Over Darwen, husbandman .... W	1635	Holden, Ellen, of Piccope Bank, W	1640
Broughton, Frances, of Nether Darwen, widow .... W	1636	Holden, Geo., of Pickop Bank ... Inv.	1633
Crosse, Hy., of Lower Darwen... Inv.	1630	Holden, Geo., of Piccope Bank, parish of Blackburn......... W	1626
Crosse, John, of Upper Darwen, gentleman.	1631	Holden, Robt., of Lower Eccleshill, parish of Blackburn... W	1638
Crosse, John, of Upper Darwen . Inv.	1641	Holden, Thos., of Hoddlesden, yeoman .... W	1647
Dewhurst, Wm., of Over Darwen, yeoman .... d	1634	Holden, Thomas, of Holdesten, co. Lancaster .... W	1649
Fish, James, of the Hill in Lower Darwen................. Inv.	1632	Horwich, Jas., of Over Darwen . Inv.	1632
		Holden, Geo., of Pickup Bank ...	1626
Fish, James, of Nether Darwen, husbandman .... W	1640	Holden, Geo, jun., Pickup Bank d	1626
		Holden, Thos., of Pickup Bank .	1626
Fish, Wm., of Lower Darwen ... W	1639	Holden, Ellen, of Pickup Bank, widow .... W	1637
Fish, John, of Over Darwen ...... m	1632		
Fishe, Thos., of Over Darwen ... Inq.	1631	Holden, James, of Pickup Bank, Greave of Rossendale	1644
Fishe, Thos., of Eccleshill	1635		

[1] Oliver Cromwell is recorded to have refused knighthood and paid the fine in 1631.

Livesey, Thos., of Nether Darwen	1628	Proctor, Christopher, of Lower Darwen ....W	1638
Lomax, Thos., of Over Darwen, parish of Blackburn.........W	1641	Smalley, Rd., of Nether Darwen, mason ....W	1638
Lomas, Thos., of Over Darwen, husbandman...................	1641	Waddington, Ralph, of the Soonehurst, in Ov.Darwen.W	1635
Lomas, John, of Nether Darwen.Inq.	1641	Walley, John, of Lower Darwen.Inv.	1628
Leaver, Robt., of Lower Darwen, husband man.................W	1637	Walsh, Edward, of Ov. Darwen. W	1628
Marsden, Christopher, of Lower Darwen.......................Inv.	1630	Walsh, Ralph, of Lower Darwen, husbandman..................W	1633
Marsden, Hy., of Ov. Darwen, parish of Blackburn ...W	1635	Whalley, Jas., of Lower Darwen, yeoman.........................W	1633
Marsden, Hy., of Ov. Darwen ...Inq.	1637	Yate, John, of Woodhead, in Yatebank, parish of Black-	
Marsden, Ralph, of Ov. Darwen.W	1627	bank ....W	1636
Marsden, Christopher, of Lower Darwen ....Inq.	1631	Yate, John, of Yate Bank, yeoman.........................W	1632
Marsden, Hy., of Lower Darwen.	1631	Yate, Wm., of Eccleshill ....W	1627
Marsden, James, of L. Darwen..Inq.	1630	Yate, James, of Yate Bank .... d	1641
Marsden, Christopher, of Okenhurst, yeoman	1630	Yate, James, of Yate Bank	1640
Marsden, James, of Okenhurst...Inq.	1637	Yate, Robt., of Woodhead, Hoddlesden ....m	1629
Piccope, John, of Nthr. Darwen.Inv.	1633	Yates, Rd., of Yate Bank	1638
Pollard, Mary, of Brockholehead, in Eccleshill, widow......W	1630		

I will not pursue this collection of names further, though many more belonging to the seventeenth century have come under my notice, but under the head of Ecclesiastical History will be found a list of persons who contributed to the fund for the rebuilding of Darwen Chapel, about the end of the century, and for more recent history than that the reader is referred to the "Recollections" of Mr. Jeremy Hunt.

INQUISITIONS *POST MORTEM.*

Among the most valuable sources of information relating to family history are the Inquisitions *post mortem* instituted on behalf of the monarch. Mr. J. Paul Rylands, who has translated and compiled for the Record Society three volumes of Lancashire Inquisitions, observes that :[1]—

The *Inquisition,* or *Inquest of Office,* was an inquiry made by the King's Officer (his Sheriff, Coroner, or Escheator) by virtue of his office, or by Writ sent to him, or by Commissioners specially appointed, concerning any matter that entitled the King to lands or tenements, goods or chattels. This was done by a Jury of no fixed number. .... Their business was to inquire, firstly, whether the King's Tenant died seised of property of which the reversion accrued to the King ; secondly, whether A, who held immediately of the Crown, died without heirs, in which case the lands became the King's by escheat ; thirdly, whether B be attainted of treason, whereby his estate is forfeited to the Crown ; fourthly, whether C, who has purchased lands, be an Alien, another cause of forfeiture ; fifthly, whether D be an idiot from birth, and therefore, together with his lands, falls to the custody of the King ; and other questions of the like import regarding the circumstances of the Tenant, and the value, &c., of the lands. On the death of any of the King's Tenants, an Inquest of

[1] Lancashire Inquisitions, Part I., pp. v., vi.

Office was held, called an *Inquisition post mortem*, to inquire of what lands he died seised, who was his heir and of what age, in order to ascertain whether the King was entitled to his Marriage, Wardship, Relief, Primer, Seisin, or other advantages.

The information contained in these records is most valuable, as it consists of sworn testimony, verified by the production of original documents. The name and age of the heir is given, together with a pretty full description of the property he inherits. Most of the Inquisitions are inquisitions *post mortem*, but there are exceptions to the rule, as in the case of Giles Haworth, of Newfield, when the property which formed the subject of the inquiry belonged to an outlaw.

These inquisitions show that the great landowners of the Darwen district were—the King, both in his capacity as monarch and in his capacity as Duke of Lancaster; the Langtons and the Hoghtons, who held by knight service the ancient Royal manor of Walton, extending over the Darwen Valley; the Osbaldestons, lords of the manor of Over Darwen, and the Grimshaws, lords of Eccleshill. The most common titles to the property were military service to the King and fealty to the lord of the manor.

Subjoined are some inquisitions of James the First's time given in a summary form, but showing the principal points of public interest:—

1606. JOHN HULTON, OF OVERDERWINE.

Inquisition taken at Bolton-on-the-Moors, 18 Oct., 1606. John Hulton, who died at Blackburne, 21 July, 1606, was seised (among other things) of one messuage and 26 acres of m. and p. land in Overderwine, *alias* Overderwentt, held of Rd. Houghton, Knt. in free socage by fealty and worth per ann. 9s. John Hulton, his son and heir, is aged 13 years.

1606. LAWRENCE YATE, OF NETHERDARWEN.

Inquisition taken at Blakeborne, 20 Dec., 1606. Lawrence Yate, of Netherdarwen, yeoman, who died 24 Sep., 1606, was seised in fee of two-thirds of a messuage, a garden, an orchard, 12 ac. of land, 4 ac. of meadow and 8 ac. of pasture, in Netherdarwen, held of the King, as of his Duchy of Lancaster *in capite*, by knight service, and worth per ann. 30s. Alice Yate, his widow, is dowered with one-third for life, William, his son and heir, is aged 4 years.

1607. HENRY MAWDESLEY, OF OVERDARWYN.

Inquisition taken at Bolton, 8 Jan., 1607-8. Henry Mawdesley, of Blackborne, yeoman (*sic*) who died 2 Dec., 1607, was seised of two messuages, 20 ac. of land, 6 of meadow, and 10 of pasture, in Overdarwyn, and of 13 acres in Clitheroe, the former held of Richard Houghton, Knt., in socage by fealty only, and worth per ann. 13s. 4d. Elizabeth Mawdesley, his widow, is alive at Bolton. Thurstan, his son and heir, is aged 13 years.

1613. SIR THOMAS WALMYSLEY, LORD OF NETHERDARWEN.

Inquisition taken at Blackburne, 23 Aug., 1613. Thos. Walmysley, Knight, and Justice of Common Pleas, died at Dunkenhalghe, 26 Nov., 1612, seised (among other things) of a moiety of the manor or lordship of Netherdarwen, held of the King, as of his Duchy, by the eighth part of a knight's fee, and worth per ann. clear £5. Thomas Walmysley, Esq., his son and heir, is aged 38 years.

1610-19. BARON, OF OVERDERWENT.

Inquisition taken at Preston, 4 April, 1611. John Baron, of Overderwent, gentleman, died 6 Sept. 1610, seised of 2 messuages, 30 ac. of land, 10 of meadow, 10 of pasture, and 3 of wood in Overderwent, called "Baron's ould land;" 4 messuages, 20 ac. of land, 6 of meadow and 6 of pasture, lately purchased of Edward Osbaldeston, Esq., and situate in Overderwent; 12 ac. of meadow and pasture land and the 20th part of an acre (late parcel of waste in Eccleshill),—"Baron's ould land" being held of Edward Osbaldeston, Esq., as of his manor of Overderwent in socage by fealty and 12d. rent, and worth per annum 20s.; the four messuages, &c., held of the King, as of his Duchy, by the 20th part of a knight's fee, and worth per annum 20s.; the lands in Eccleshill, held of the King, as of his Duchy, by the 100th part of a knight's fee, and worth per annum 6s. 8d. James Baron, his son and heir, is aged 14 years.

Inquisition taken at Blackeborne, 6 Ap., 1619. James Baron, who died 26 Jan, 1618-19, was seised in fee of 5 messuages, 10 gardens, 1 orchard, 20 acres of land, 12 ac. of meadow, 12 ac ot pasture, and 10 ac. of heath and briar in Overderwine, and of 10 ac. of land, 10 ac. of meadow and 6 ac. of pasture in Eckleshill; the former held of Edward Osbaldeston, Knt., in free and common socage by fealty and 12d. rent, and worth per ann. 40s.; the latter held of Nicholas Grimshawe, Esq, in free and common socage by fealty and 10d. rent, and worth per ann. 10s. His daughter Alice, aged 3½ yrs., and his daughter, Elizabeth, aged 4 mos., are his co-heirs.

1616. EDMUND HARWOOD, OF NETHERDERWEN.

Inquisition taken at Blackburn, 4 Oct., 14 James [1616]. Edmund Harwood, of Netherderwen, was seised in fee of 2 messuages, 3 gardens, 16 acres of land, 6 acres of meadow and 6 acres of pasture, in Netherderwen, which are held of the King, as of his Duchy of Lancaster, by the 60th part of a knight's fee, and are worth per ann. (clear) 20s. Edmund Harwood died 24 July last past [1616], Margaret, his late wife, yet surviving in Netherderwen, and Richard Harwood, his son and heir, aged 24 yrs.

1616. WILLIAM FISH, OF OVERDERWEN.

Inquisition taken at Chorley, 9 Jan., 1616-17. William Fish, yeoman, who died 21 June, 1616, was seised in fee of 1 messuage, 1 garden, and 20 acres of meadow and pasture land, at Overderwen, held of Richard Houghton, Knt. and Bart., in free socage by fealty and 1d. rent, and worth per ann. 5s. Ellen, his widow, survives. James, his son and heir, is aged 1 year.

1617. WILLIAM HINDLE, OF OVERDERWEN.

Inquisition taken at Preston, 7 April, 1617. William Hindle, who died at Church, 22 Dec., 1616, having kinsfolk at Harwood and Church, was seised in fee (among other property) of the messuage and 18 acres of meadow and pasture land in Overderwen. He devised the aforesaid messuage and other premises in Overderwen to Thos. Hindle, his eldest brother, for life, &c. The messuage and other premises in Overderwen are held of Richard Houghton, Knt. and Bart., as of his manor of Walton, in free socage, and are worth per ann. 40s. John Hindle, son of Michael the brother of William, is his heir, and is 44 years of age.

1618. LAWRENCE HAWORTH, OF HURCROFTE.

Inquisition taken at Blackeburne, 14 April, 1618. Lawrence Haworth, gentleman, who died 2 March, 1617-18, was seized in fee of the messuage called Hurcrofte, and 20 acres of land, 6 acres of meadow, and 20 acres of pasture in Netherderwen, of one other messuage in Netherderwyn in the tenure of Richard Pomfrett, together with 6 acres of land, 4 of meadow, and 10 of pasture; held of the king *in capite* by the 50th part of a knight's fee, and worth per annum 30s. Peter Haworth, his son and heir, is aged 26 years.

1618-20. ASPINALL, OF NETHERDARWEN.

Inquisition taken at Preston, 1618-19. Lawrence Aspinall, who died at Netherdarwen 1 April, 1604, was seised in fee of the reversion of 5 messuages, 56 acres of land, meadow and pasture, in Netherdarwen, held of the King, as of his Duchy of Lancaster, by the 100th part of a knight's fee, and worth per annum (clear) 10s. Thos. Aspinall, grandson, aged 40 years, is his heir. Robert Aspinall also survives at Netherdarwen.

Inquisition taken at Blackburn, 14 September, 1620. John Aspinall, of Netherdarwyne, yeoman, died on the last day of March, 1620, seised in fee of 1 messuage in Netherdarwyne, and of 5 acres of land, 2 acres of meadow, 1 acre of wood, and of the 5th part of the moor in Netherdarwyne, in 69 parts divided, held of the king *in capite* by military service, and worth per annum 4s. Thomas, his son and heir, is aged 40 years.

1619. WILLIAM ELLISON, OF OVERDARWYNE.

Inquisition taken at Chorley, 29 July, 1619. William Ellison, who died 12 Aug., 1618, was seised of 1 messuage, 15 acres of meadow and pasture land in Overdarwyne, held of the heirs of Thomas Langton, Knt., of the manor of Walton, in free socage, and worth per annum 10s. William Dewhurst, his kinsman and heir, is aged 90 years 3 months and 10 days.

1620. ROBERT PYCCOPE, OF NETHERDARWYNE.

Inquisition taken at Blackeburne, 14 September, 1620. Robert Pyccope (or Piccope), of Netherdarwyne, yeoman, died 26 March, 1603, seised in fee of the 4th part of the messuage in Netherdarwyne, parcel of Earnsden; and of 3 acres of land, 2 acres of meadow, 1 acre of wood, and 6 acres of moor, in Netherderwyne, held of the king *in capite* by military service, and 2d. rent, and worth per annum (clear), 2s. 8d. James, his son and heir, is aged 35 years.

1620. HENRY MARSDEN, OF NETHERDARWYNE.

Inquisition taken at Blackburne, 14 September, 1620. Henry Marsden, of Netherdarwyne, who died 12 April, 1619, was seised in fee of one moiety of 1 messuage, 10 acres of land, 2 acres of meadow, 10 acres of pasture, 5 acres of wood, 40 acres of moor, moss, heath, and briar, in Netherdarwyne; and he and his wife were seised of the other moiety; held of the king *in capite* by military service and 5d. rent, and worth per annum 15s. Christopher, his son and heir, is aged 40 years. Alice, his widow, survives.

1622-3. ALEXANDER WADDINGTON, OF THE STREET, GENTLEMAN.

Inquisition at Chorley, 10 Jan., 20 James I. Alexander Waddington died seised in fee (among other estates) of "12 acres of land, 2 acres of meadow, 5 acres of pasture, 200 acres of moor, moss, and turbary in Eccles-hill." . . . . "All his lands, &c., in Heathchernoke, Rivington, and Eccles-hill, and elsewhere, he gave to Lawrence Waddington, his son, and his heirs for ever." Henry Waddington, of Daviefield, was desired to be one of the two overseers of his will. "The lands, tenements, and other premises in Eccles-hill are held of Nicholas Grymshawe, gent., in free socage, namely by fealty and the yearly rent of ½d., and are worth per ann. (clear) 13s. 4d."

1622-3. WILLIAM WALMISLEY, OF NETHER DARWEN, GENTLEMAN.

Inquisition at Blackburn, 26 Feb., 20 James I. William Walmisley, late of Netherdarwine, who died 5 April last past [1622[, was "seised in fee of 1 messuage, 1 garden, 1 orchard, and 24 acres of land, meadow and pasture, in Netherdarwine which are held of the King, as of his Duchy of Lancaster, *in capite* by military service, and 2d. rent, and are worth per ann. (clear) 10s." Christopher Walmisley, his son and heir, is aged 54 years.

1623. RALPH FISHE, OF ECCLESHILL, GENTLEMAN.

Inquisition at Blackburn, 8 April, 21 James I. Ralph Fishe, late of Eccleshill, gentleman, died "seised in fee of 1 messuage, 1 garden, 10 acres of land, 5 acres of meadow, 5 acres of pasture, and 4 acres of moss in Overdarwine. So seised, by deed dated 10 October, 2 James [1604] he enfeoffed John Crosse and James Cunliffe of the said premises to the use of Randal Astley and Margery his wife and their heirs; and in default to the use of Margery and her heirs, and in default to the use of the right heirs of himself the said Ralph Fishe for ever. Margery died at Overdarwine 19 November 16 James [1618]. The premises in Overdarwine are held of William Cokaine, knt., as of his manor of Walton in le Dale in free and common socage by fealty, and are worth per annum (clear) 10s. [The date of the death of Ralphe Fishe is not given.] Randal Astley survives at Blackburne, and Agnes Cunliffe, wife of James Cunliffe, and Thomas Astley, son of the said Randal and Margery, are co-heirs of Ralph Fishe." Agnes is aged 40 years; Thomas Astley "5 years and 12 months."

1623. THOMAS ASTLEY, OF STAKES, GENTLEMAN.

Inquisition at Bolton, 31 July, 21 James I. Thomas Astley, of "le Hall of Stakes," Livesaie, died 20 June, 1623, at Livesaie, possessed of the freehold of land in Witton and Livesey, and also of "1 messuage, 10 acres of land, 4 acres of meadow, and 10 acres of pasture in Netherdarwine." Thomas Astley, his heir, is aged 9 years. "The messuage and other the premises in Netherdarwine are held of the king *in capite* by knight service, viz., by the 100th part of a knight's fee, and are worth per annum (clear) 10s.

HOGHTON TOWER.

Hoghton Tower, a picturesque fortress crowning a wooded hill on the south-west bank of the river Darwen, is the seat of the lords of Walton, an ancient royal manor including lands in Over Darwen, Lower Darwen, and Eccleshill. It is a stronghold built rather for the protection of private interests than as a national fortress, but it played an important part in the Civil War of the seventeenth century, when its central tower, containing a hundred hostile soldiers, was blown up. Dr. Whitaker describes it as the only specimen in the neighbourhood of a true baronial residence, with two courts crowning the summit of an elevated ridge [rather knoll], and appearing at a distance like a fortified town. Thomas Hoghton, Esq., who succeeded his father, Sir Richard, in 1588, built Hoghton Tower in 1563, to replace the manor house which stood in Hoghton Bottoms. His initials "T. H." and a faint fragment of the date "1565" are still to be seen above the gateway on the inner wall of the courtyard. The principal feature of the mansion has been described by one who knew it, as "a very tall strong tower or gatehouse," situated "betwixt the inward square court and the second," but this was blown up in 1643, and has never been rebuilt. Mr. Chas. Cattermole, R.I., painter of an historical picture representing the pageant of King James I. at Hoghton Tower in 1617, has depicted this central tower as a massive square building, harmonising in style and appearance with the principal gateway, but standing about one-third higher. The mansion presents a majestic frontage to the south-west, consisting of an embattled wall with three large towers, the central tower having below it a depressed Tudor arch, which forms the principal gateway. Quadrangular in plan, the buildings embrace an inner and an outer court, the former being about 70 feet square. A bronze statue of William, Prince of Orange, 6ft. high, stands in the centre of the court, on a stone pedestal. Among the principal "sights" shown to strangers are the Royal Banqueting Hall, the King's Room, the King's Bedroom, the King's Staircase, and the King's Stables. The large bay windows, mullioned and transomed, and each bay forming five sides of an octagon, are a prominent feature; the doorways are low and square-headed. The whole place had fallen into a sad state of decay, but it has recently been extensively renovated, and is at present occupied by Sir Chas. de Hoghton, Bart.

In his "Royal Progress" from Scotland to London, in 1617, James I. spent four eventful days at Hoghton Tower, attended by a powerful retinue of nobles, knights, baronets, and squires. Six years before, the merry monarch had created the new order of Baronet, and Richard Hoghton was one of the first batch of gentry on whom the title was conferred. Sir Richard spared no expense in his entertainment of the Royal Party, and it is reported that the avenue leading up the hill to the Tower was carpeted with velvet. Sir Richard met the King at Myerscough, and on August 15th the King and Court advanced through Preston over the Ribble and Darwen bridges to Hoghton Tower. The central tower was then standing. It is recorded that the Royal Party alighted from their equipages at the foot of the hill and proceeded on foot along the grand avenue; but Mr. Cattermole's picture, which is accepted as an authority, represents the party riding up. The neighbouring squires and the tenantry of the Hoghtons, wearing the Hoghton "livery cloaks," are assembled to do homage to the King. Preceded by his drummer and his trumpeter, James rides up the avenue on a black horse, attended by Sir Richard Hoghton and Sir Gilbert Hoghton, and followed by a long train of celebrated courtiers, foremost among whom comes the notorious Villiers, Earl of Buckingham. Although considerable time had been spent during the day in riding from Myerscough and feasting at Preston, the Royal Party hunted and killed a stag in Hoghton Park before dining and retiring for the night. Of the next day, Nicholas Assheton records in his *Journal*[1], "Aug. 16, Hoghton. The King hunting; a great companie. Killed affore dinner a brace of staggs. Verie hott; soe hee went in to dinner. Wee attend the lord's table; and about 4 o'clock the King went downe to the Allome mynes [Alum Scar, on the right bank of the river Darwen], and was ther an hower, and viewed them preciselie, and then went and shott at a stagg, and missed. Then my Lord Compton had lodged two brace. The King shott again, and brake the thigh-bone. A dogg long in coming, and my Lord Compton shott again and killed him. Late in to supper." Of the third day, which was Sunday, the journalist records :—"Aug. 17, Hoghton. We served the lords with biskett, wyne, and jellie. The Bushopp of Chester, Dr. Morton, preached before the King. To dinner. About four o'clock ther was a rushbearing, and pipeing afore them, affore the King in the middle court; then to supp. Then, about ten or eleven o'clock, a maske of noblemen, knights, gentlemen, and courtiers, afore the King, in the middle round, in the garden. Some speeches; of the rest dancing the Huckler, Tom Bedlo, and the Cowp Justice of the Peace." This gay Sabbath was the precursor of the infamous "Book of Sports" which was published in the following year. The peasantry presented the King with a petition protesting against the restrictions which Queen Elizabeth had placed upon sportiveness on the Sunday, and praying for liberty to enjoy themselves after Evening [afternoon] Prayer. The petition of the "good people" was granted, and next year the King issued his "Book of Sports[2]." On the fourth day, Monday, Aug. 18th, the King breakfasted at Hoghton, and then departed for the Earl of Derby's seat at Lathom. There were fifty-five dishes, prepared by fourteen cooks, served up for the Sunday's dinner, and tradition says that here the King knighted the loin of beef—

Henceforth it shall be *Sir-Loin*, an' see ye ca' it sae.

The de Hoghtons are an old and important Lancashire family, whose history, which has been often written, is too long to be given here. The first Adam de Hocton, a Knight of the time of Henry II., was probably a descendant of Hamo Pincerna, who in the time of William Rufus received the estates of Hocton and Eccleston as a marriage portion with his wife, who was the daughter of Warin Bussel, Baron of Penwortham. Eccleshill was mentioned in 1377 as one of the manors

---

[1] Page 40.
[2] This "Book of Sports," as republished by Charles I. in 1633, was in 1643 ordered by Parliament to be burnt by the common hangman.

in the possession of Sir Richard de Hoghton. In 1468, Henry Hoghton, Esq., who succeeded to the estate, obtained a Bull from the Pope to make legitimate the offspring of his mistress Helen Mosson. A herald who visited Lancashire in 1533 met with a rebuff at the residence of the Hoghtons, and made the following curious but inaccurate record :—

Sr Ric Houghton Knight did mary [marry] Alice, daughter and one of the heyres to Sr. Thoms of Asheton Knight, and they have yssue : Katherine, who is married to Sr. Thoms Gerard Knight. The said Sr. Ric. hath putt away his lady and wife, and kepeth a concobyne in his house, by whom he hath divers children, and by the lady he hath Ley Hall ; which armes he beareth quartered with his in the first quarter, he sahs that Mr. Garter licensed him so to doe. and he gave Mr. Garter an angle noble, but he gave me nothing nor made me no good chere, but gave me proude woords.[1]

As a matter of fact, the Sir Richard here mentioned was seventh in descent from the Sir Richard de Hoghton who married the heiress of Lea. His son, Thomas Hoghton, Esq., who married Katherine, daughter of Sir Thomas Gerard, built Hoghton Tower, in the early years of Elizabeth's reign, but being denounced as a Catholic he was banished to the Continent four years after the completion of his stately mansion. He died at Liege in 1580, and was succeeded first by his brother Alexander, and then by his half-brother, Thomas. The last-named Thomas Hoghton was killed in an armed encounter between his retainers and those of a neighbouring squire, Thomas Langton, in 1589. A dispute took place as to the possession of certain cattle that were pasturing on Thomas Hoghton's land at Lea, near Preston, and which were claimed by a widow named Singleton. Squire Langton took the Widow Singleton's part, and, attended by 80 retainers, armed to the teeth, went to the farm near Lea Hall to drive off the cattle in the dead of the night. But Thomas Hoghton had been warned of the raid, and he lay in ambush with 30 armed men, awaiting the threatened visit. A serious conflict occurred about one o'clock in the morning of November 20th. Hoghton and one of his followers were killed, and Langton was severely wounded. The latter was arrested, but no satisfactory verdict could be obtained, and it is stated that an amicable settlement was ultimately arrived at, Langton presenting to Hoghton's widow the manor of Walton as a peace-offering. Since that time the manor of Walton-le-Dale has been held by the Hoghton family.[2]

THE CIVIL WAR.

The connection of Darwen with the great Civil War of the years 1641-51 centres round the stronghold at Hoghton on the banks of the River Darwen, and the Bridge over the Darwen at Walton which formed

1. *Visitation of Lancashire* (Chet. Socy.), p. 48.   2 See *ante*, p. 36.

one of the defences of Preston and an important obstacle on the main road from North to South. Lancashire was essentially Puritan and Parliamentarian, but Sir Gilbert Hoghton was a staunch Royalist, and his naturally fortified position was a "standing menace" to the unprotected town of Blackburn. The only other strongholds in this part of Lancashire were Clitheroe Castle and the town of Preston, the former garrisoned by the Roundheads and the latter by the Royalists. Early in the war Parliament disarmed the Papists in East Lancashire and stored the spoil in Whalley Abbey, under the protection of the garrison at Clitheroe. With the view of seizing these, Sir Gilbert lit a beacon on Hoghton Tower and rallied the Royalists around him. A Puritan writer of the period, Thomas Jesland, writes :—

> For the last Weeke Sir Gilbert Hoghton set his Beacon on fire, which stood upon the top of Hoghton Tower, and was the signal to the Countrey for the Papists and Malignants to arise in the Field [Fylde] and in Lealand Hundred; whereupon great multitudes accordingly resorted to him to Preston in Andernesse, and ran to Blackburn, and so through the Countrey, disarming all and pillaging some, which Master Shuttleworth, a Parliament man, and Master Starkie hearing off, presently had gotten together out of the places formerly mentioned about 8000 men, met with Sir Gilbert and his Catholique Malignants at Hinfield [Enfield] Moor, put them to flight, tooke away many of their armes, and pursued Sir Gilbert so hotly that he quit his Horse, leaped into a field, and by the comming on of the night escaped through fur bushes and by-wayes to Preston, and there makes great defence by chaining up the Ribble Bridge.[1]

In December of the same year (1642), a Parliamentary garrison having been quartered at Blackburn, Sir Gilbert laid siege to the town. A quaint chronicler in his *Discourse of the Warr*[2] says :—

> Sir Gilbert "marched forward from Preston the twenty fourth daye of December, being Christmas time, up the way to Mellor loan head, soe vpon the North syd of Blackburne; set downe most of his forces about and near the house of . . . . . a husbandman by a bye name called Duke of the Banke, and having a small piece of Ordnance plaid most of that night and the day folowing against the Towne, the greatest execution that it did, as was hard of, a bullet shot out of it entered into a house upon the South syde of the Church Yard and burst out the bottom of a fryen pan. There was noe nearer assault to the Towne than a quarter of a Mile. They wear afraid of comming near one another, The Souldiers within the Towne went out of it and dischardged there muskets towards them at randome, for any thing was knowne there was not a man sleyne or hurt. Vpon Christmas Day at night Sir Gilbert withdrew his forces being weary of his Siege, and his Soldiers and Clubmen were glad of it that they might eate their Christmas pyes at home. But they did the good man about whose house they lay much harme not only in eating his provision of Meale and Beeffe and the like, as also in burninge his barne doors with his Carts, wheels, and other usbandry stuff. This was all the expedition of Sir Gilbert Houghton against Blackburne."

[1] *Civil War Tracts*, pp. 65-6. [2] Ib. pp. 21-2.

In February of the following year the Roundheads, under Sir John Seaton, captured the bridges over the Darwen and the Ribble at Walton and Preston from the Royalists after two hours' severe fighting. Many of the King's officers were killed or taken prisoners, but Sir Gilbert Hoghton escaped to Wigan. Following up the Preston victory three companies of East Lancashire soldiers drew up before the gates of Hoghton Tower and demanded its surrender. The small garrison left there by the fugitive Royalists at once opened the gates and laid down their arms, but the prize was dearly bought, for the conquerors had no sooner gained admission than the central tower was blown up, either by accident or design, killing Captain Starkie and over a hundred of his men. A tract dated February 14, 1642-3, contains "a punctuall relation of" . . . "the taking of Houghton Tower by the Parliament's Forces, and the perfidious treachery of the Papists, who, after they had upon quarter yielded up the Tower, treacherously set fire to a traine of powder and blew up Captaine Starkey with above a hundred men." The writer says :—

Upon Tuesday, being the 14th of this instant, there was sent from Preston three Captaines and their Companies, to the number of about three hundred, the most of Blackeborne men, to take a castle called Haughton Tower (belonging to Sir Gilbert Haughton) which lies between Preston and Blackeborne, and was fortified with three great pieces of ordnance, and some say with betwixt thirty and forty musqueteers, and some say more. Our men approaching near the said Tower first shot against it to summon it, whereupon they in the Tower desired half an houre's time to consider what they should doe, which was granted unto them accordingly, after which the result of the parley was that they would deliver up the Tower to our men upon quarter, which was by our men granted unto them as they desired, whereupon our men (thinking all had beene as was pretended by them) entered the Tower ; and Captain Starkey of Blackeborne, a worthy gentleman, and his Company, were the first that entered into the said Tower, and in the same found good store of armes and powder strewed upon the stairs, wherefore he with his Company going into the upper rooms of the said Tower to search for more, were most treacherously and perfidiously blown up by two of them to whom they had before given quarter, who had a traine of powder laide, and when Captain Starkey and his men, to the number of above one hundred, were above in the House, gave fire to the said traine, and blew both him and all his men, with the top of the House up, threescore whereof were afterwards found, some without armes and some without legges, and others fearefull spectacles to looke upon. Six of them whom they had given quarter to they had in hold, the rest got away before, but our men have the Tower and three pieces of great Ordnance that were cast besides divers Armes.[1]

Another contemporary writer attributes the blowing up of the Tower to accident, or rather to the careless use of matches and lighted pipes by the Parliamentary soldiers, who were great smokers. He says :—

[1] *C. W. Tracts*, pp. 79-81.

Our men were going down to take the Tower, and finding it prepared for entrance, possessed themselves of it, till being burdened with the weight of their swearing. drunkenness, plundering, and wilfull waste at Preston, it dispossessed them by the help of Powder to which their disorders laid a Train fired by their neglected Matches, or by that great Soldier's Idoll, Tobacco.[1]

Some description of the Tower which was blown up has already been given.[2]

BATTLE OF THE RIBBLE AND DARWEN BRIDGES.

The Battle of Preston, on August 17th, 1648, which was the death-knell of Charles I, and the turning point in the great Civil War, is everlastingly connected with the History of Darwen by one line of the immortal Puritan Poet, Milton—

> Darwen stream with blood of Scots imbued.

Two bridges formed the keystones of the Royalist position, one over the Ribble and the other over the Darwen, and it was the knowledge which Cromwell's Lancashire troops possessed of the character of the ground that enabled the great General to gain both bridges and drive the entrapped Royalists at "push of pike" into the swollen river Darwen, which was reddened with blood and strewn with corpes. The Royalists, under the Duke of Hamilton, held Preston and Walton, being posted strongly on both bridges ready to dispute the passage of Cromwell's army southward. As Cromwell came from Skipton through Clitheroe, on the south side of the Ribble, he could have evaded the main army, but as a matter of military tactics it was better for him to keep the enemy before him, and not give them a chance of coming up in the rear. He therefore crossed the Ribble at Clitheroe, held a Council of War on the old Hodder Bridge near Stonyhurst, and spent the night of August 16th at Mr. Sherburne's house preparing for an attack on Preston. Having fought his way through Preston on the morning of the 17th, he boldly attacked the Ribble Bridge, which was vainly defended at "push of pike" in the face of Cromwell's sharpshooters, who occupied commanding heights on the Preston side. The bridge once gained, Cromwell's Lancashire troops rushed over it, and ignoring the flying foe, made straight for the bridge over the Darwen, which lay a very short distance ahead. Another fight took place on the Darwen Bridge, which was likewise won by the Parliamentary army. The Duke's troops were scattered in all directions. Those between the two rivers were either killed or captured; the stragglers in Preston flew to the

---

[1] *Lancashire's Valley of Achor*, Civil War Tracts, p. 128.   [2] See *ante*, pp. 55-60.
[3] While Darwen stream with blood of Scots imbued
And Dunbar field resound thy praises loud.
—*Sonnet to Cromwell.*

north, and the remnant of the Royalist forces retreated precipitately to the south. Cromwell held the position, and the same day he wrote to "The Honourable Committee of Lancashire, sitting at Manchester," in the following terms[1] :—" The principal part whereof [of the enemy], with Duke Hambleton, is on the south side Ribble and Darwain Bridge, and we lying with the greatest part of the Army close to them, nothing hindring the ruine of that part of the enemie's army but the night ; it will be our care that they shall not pass any ford beneath the Bridge to goe northward, or to come betwixt us and Whalley." Three days later, writing from Warrington to the Speaker of the House of Commons, Cromwell gave a minute description of the battle, in which the following passage occurs :—

Col. Deans and Col. Prides outwinging the enemy, could not come to so much share of the action ; the Enemy shaging down towards the Bridge, and keeping almost all in reserve, that so he might bring fresh bands often to fight, which we not knowing, but lest we should be outwinged, placed those two Regiments to enlarge our Right Wing, which was the cause they had not at that time so great a share in the action ; at the last the Enemy was put into disorder, many men slain, many prisoners taken, the Duke with most of the Scots horse and foot retreated over the Bridge, where after a very hot dispute betwixt the Lancashire Regiments, part of my Lord Generals and them being at push of Pike, they [the enemy] were beaten from the Bridge, and our horse and foot following them, killed many, and took divers prisoners ; and we possessed the bridge over the Darwent and a few houses there, the Enemy being driven up within musket shot of us where we lay that night, we not being able to attempt further upon the Enemy, the night preventing us. In this position did the Enemy and we lie the most part of that night.[2]

An officer of the victorious army writes :—

Abundance were killed in the feildes on the East syd of Preston, and so did drive them doune towards Ribble Bridge. The Duke with his forces and carriages being passed over before, having Barocaded up the bridge, stood at resistance. It was reported that when word came to the Duke that Generall Cromwell was in the reare of Sir Marmaduke Langden's Army fighting and killing them his answer was, " Let them alone,—the English dogs are but killing one another," So little regard had he of them. At the Bridge they had a great Dispute for a long time, but at last Cromwell's Army did beat them off and they fled over Darwen Bridge, and soe up that hill above Walton Toune. In the feilde upon the east of the way they maid Cabbins and lodged there that night. Where the Duke quartered I hard not. So night comming the Armies guarded both Bridges ; and Generall Cromwell returned to Preston and there quartered, giving orders to our Lancashire forces there to abide.[3]

We have also "an impartial relation of the late fight at Preston," in a letter by Sir Marmaduke Langdale, a Royalist General, dated 26 August, 1648. He says[4] :—

[1] *Civil War Tracts*, p. 257. [2] Ibid, p. 262. [3] *Discourse of the Warr*, p. 65.
[4] *Civil War Tracts*, p. 269.

The Scots continue their march over the River, and did not secure a Lane near the Bridge, whereby the Parliament Forces came on my flanks; neither did the Forces that were left for my supply come to my relief, but continued in the Reare of mine, nor did they ever face the enemy, but in bringing up the Reare. When most part of the Scots were drawn over the Bridge, the Parliament Forces pressed hard upon me in the Van and the Flanks, and so drive me into the Towne, where the Duke was in person with some few horse; but, all being lost, Retreated over a foord to his Foote. After my forces were beaten the Parliament Forces beat the Scots from the Bridge presently, and so came over into all the lanes, that we could not joyne with the Foote, but were forced to Charlow [Chorley], where we found Lieut.-General Middleton ready to advance towards Preston towards the Foote, which he did; but, not finding them there, returned to Wiggan, where the Duke was with his Foote (mine totally lost).

The Darwen Bridge referred to in these papers exists no longer, but traces of its foundations may be seen on the banks of the river a few yards higher up the stream than the modern bridge. The "rapid Darwent" hereabouts is deep and sluggish, and after the heavy rains which preceded the Battle of Preston it would be impassable except by the bridge. The Civil War in which Darwen Bridge played such an important part is the only "systematic or continuous warfare known to have existed in Lancashire."

SEIZURE OF LANDS BY THE COMMONWEALTH.

Charles I. having been beheaded, Parliament began to punish the landowners who had supported the Royalist cause by seizing their property, in whole or in part. It was chiefly the Roman Catholics that were plundered in this way, and East Lancashire, being decidedly Puritan, was not much affected. But in the Royalist Composition Papers preserved at the Record Office I find an account of the sequestration of an estate at Eccleshill and Yatebank, including a valuable coal-mine, for the recusancy of John Grimshaw and Elinor his mother. Since this period the Grimshaws of Eccleshill, after holding land there for four hundred years, have been lost sight of, and the proceedings reported in connection with the sequestration by the Commonwealth furnish a probable explanation of their loss of land in this neighbourhood. The accounts transcribed below show that two-thirds of the estate were taken in the first instance, and that the other was swallowed up in making repairs which the Commissioners authorised to be made and charged upon the third part of the estate.

PETITION OF NICHOLAS ASSHETON, 21ST JANUARY, 1650.

To the Right Hon. the Commissioners for Compounding with Delinquents. The humble petition of Nicholas Assheton sheweth that the estate of John Grimshawe, in the County of Lancaster, situate and beinge in Clayton, *Eccleshill*,

Burneley, *Yatebank*, and Preston, in ye said county, are sequestered for ye recusancie of the sayd John Grimshawe, and for ye recusancie of Elinor Grimshawe, his mother, whoe houldeth parte of his estate for her lyfe for her joynture, and ye sayd John Grimshawe and his sayd mother have a third parte allowed, accordinge to ye late ordinance for ye mayntenance of them, theire children, and families, in which sayd sequestered lands there are certaine collieries of good value, which, for want of repayres are almost utterly lost, the sayd premises consistinge much of colemines, and ye same will require at ye least £500 to put them into good repayre and made usefull for ye comonwealth, and those to whome ye Commissioners in ye contie doe lett the same premyses from yeare to yeare will not bestowe the charges which will be required in doeinge of soe greate a work. whereby ye sayd colemines will be totally lost if ye same be not timely prevented. Wherefore, your petitoner, haveinge a mind to imploy his endevors in ye effectinge of soe good a work for ye comonwealth, humbly prayeth your honnrs. wilbee pleased to lett all the sayd sequestered premises to yoe. petitione. for ye tearme of seaven years under a valuable rent, to ye intent your petitione. repayre, sett on foote, and maintayne the sayd colemynes, which, otherwayes, wilbee totally lost. And your petitione. shall ever pray, &c.,

NICHOLAS ASSHETON.

21st January, 1650.

(Referred to ye Commissioners for Sequestrations for Lancashire to certifie the value.)[1]

Grimshaw, after this, found that the Commissioners were managing the residue of his estate without any regard for his interests, and presented a petition for a hearing. This "humble petition of John Grimshaw of Clayton, in the county of Lancaster, gentleman," dated, 3rd January, 1653, sheweth "that there are several examinations taken and returned . . . . concerning a coal mine in Eccleshill and a watercourse in Burnley," and humbly prayeth that he may have a hearing, and that the agents should forbear to destroy "your petitioner's goods."[2] Another petition is dated 31st January, 1653, and a third, quoted hereunder, was presented in the following July :—

The petition (to the Commissioners for Compounding to Delinquents) of John Grimshaw, of Clayton, dated 12th July, 1653, sheweth—That your petitioner being possessed of a coal mine in Eccleshill, and two parts of the profits being sequestered for his delinquency, and the late Committee for the County being informed that the profits thereof would be utterly lost to the Commonwealth for want of a sough or watercourse for drying or draining of the coals in the said mines, because the same was old and decayed, and in many places fallen down and obstructed that it would not long be reparable as it stood then, the said Committee thereupon referred the truth of the information to Colonel Richard Shuttleworth and Colonel John Starkie to examine and certify, who, having caused the decay of the said sough and watercourse to be viewed, did certify that the information aforesaid was true, whereupon it was ordered that the profits of the coal mines should be taken and appended towards the making of a new sough or watercourse, yet, notwithstanding, the honourable Commissioners for Sequestration in the said county have caused their agents to seize

[1] Royalist Composition Papers, vol. 4, p. 325.   [2] Ibid, vol. 79, p. 404.

the goods of the petitioner and of other men for two parts of the said profits, and yet have not heard or admitted the workmen to bring in their accounts, which they would have tendered, and will be yet ready to do the same, upon their oaths, but the Commissioners do refuse to allow of the same, and to take off the said seizure without your order . . . . . humbly prayeth the Commissioners that the Committee of Lancashire may be ordered to discharge your petitioner's and other the goods from the said seizure; to testify what they know; and to examine witnesses; that your petitioner may have relief.

(Signed), JOHN GRYMSHAWE.

(Referred to the Committee in Lancashire to examine and certify.)[1]

A Report, dated 20th April, 1654, and signed "Jo' Bradsnge," gives the following information concerning the estate and its management :—

"According to your order of the 12 of July, 1653, and 31 of January, 1653, upon the petition of John Grimshaw, desiring allowance of the profits of certain coal mines which were formerly allowed him by the late Committee of Lancaster for repairing the said coal mines, and also desiring that the seizure made by the Commissioners of his goods may be discharged, I find [recites the last document of Grimshaw's, and then proceeds :—] And whereas the petitioner, being seized of some lands in Burnley in the said county, which, being subject to decay by the irruption and breaking forth of the water from the same, and moving you for allowance towards reparations of such decay, you did order on 12 January, 1650, that the said Committee should proportion unto the petitioner a third part of his estate in specie, and to keep the other two-third parts for the use of the Commonwealth, and take care that the two-third parts did not suffer prejudice by the overflow or breaking in of the water, but the bounds be maintained in good repair, yet, nevertheless, the agent of the Committee hath seized the petitioner's goods for the reparation of the decay of the said two third parts, which he is not liable to contribute . . , ... the Committee did order and appoint that the rents and profits arising since the said order out of the said coal mine shall be allowed for and towards the making of a new watercourse for drying of the said coal mine, and the agent John Howard to see the work forwarded, and thus to continue from time to time until the same be made." The Commissioners [now] transmit an account of the profits of the coal mine from February, 1649, till October, 1652, amounting to £24 5s.; also account of the money disbursed since February, 1649, for making a sough, which amounted to £27 12s. 11d.; and another account showing that the profits of the coal mine amounted to £24 16s. They ordered that the said John Grimshaw shall pay for the use of the state two full third parts of the said £24 16s., or, in default thereof, the agent to levy distress. The evidence collected on the subject is summarised as follows : —"Thos. ffish deposed that the said coal mine was in the year 1649 mightily decayed and ruined for want of a sough or watercourse so that he believes half or all the profits would have been lost and is lost for want of a sough. And the like is deposed by John Lilego, and the said Thomas ffish deposeth that about the same time he petitioned the then Committee on behalf of the said John Grimshaw for repair thereof, whereupon there was a reference to Colonel Shuttleworth and Colonel Starkie, two of the Committee, to examine the truth thereof, who thereupon made an order for the clearing, opening, and repairing of the said coal mine and sough, And Thomas Duckworth deposeth to the same effect. On the 12th July, 1650, you order the Committee

[1] Ibid, vol. 79, p. 412.

of Lancaster to proportion out to John Grimshaw one-third part of the estate in specie, and to keep the other two parts to the use of the Commonwealth, and to take special care that those two parts, in their occupation or possession, did not suffer prejudice by the overflowing or breaking in of the said river, but that the banks and fences for preservation of the same be maintained in good repair, and ordered their agent to view the damage at Burnley. George Hindle deposed that the deponent and one of the Commissioners caused the same to be repaired accordingly, but that the Commissioners, nor the deponent, did ever repair any of the third set out for the recusant to the deponent's knowledge, and that since the two sequestered parts were repaired he destrained the goods of Mr. Grimshaw for part of the charges disbursed in repair of the said two parts, according to the order of the 2 May, 1652, made by the then Commissioners for Sequestrations in that county."[1]

The record of the case here breaks off, the fate of the unfortunate recusant's property being left in obscurity.

THE REVOLUTION.

From the time of the Commonwealth to that of the Revolution the chief interest in Darwen centres round the old Elizabethan chapel. An inquisition taken at Blackburn of June 25, 1650, states that the chapelry of Over Darwen contained 400 families. An assessment of the county for public taxation was made in 1654, when it was set forth that when the total contributions of the Hundred of Blackburn should make £47 1s. 7d., the amount due from Over Darwyne should be 14s., from Mellor-cum-Eccleshill 12s., and from Nether Darwyne 10s. 4d., and so on in proportion, according to the rise and fall of taxation[2] A Presbyterian minister, Joshua Barnard, occupied the pulpit at Darwen Chapel in 1649-50, and the people of Darwen became imbued with a spirit of Independency which culminated in 1687 in the seizure of the chapel-of-ease and its restoration by weak James II. to the Vicar of Blackburn. A full account of these stirring events is reserved for the next chapter. The weakness and vacillation of James II., whose character is strikingly exemplified by the Darwen incident, led to the "Glorious Revolution," which took place in the following year; James abdicated and absconded, and William Prince of Orange ascended the English throne.

[1] Royalist Composition Papers, vol. 79, p. 411. [2] *Preston Guardian*, November 6 1880.

Chapter 4.—Ecclesiastical History.

Origin of the place-name "Chapels"—Darwen Chapel in 1577—A Chapel-of-ease in Darwen, 1616—Lecturer of Darwen in 1622—Endowment of Darwen Chapel in 1638—Endowment in 1685 for the use of "an orthodox minister" -Joshua Barnard, Presbyterian Minister, 1649-50—A Curate from Blackburn, 1683—Darwen Chapel seized by the Congregationalists, July, 1687—Restored to the Vicar of Blackburn, Oct., 1687 -Activity of the Churchmen, 1688— Names of Prominent Churchmen in Darwen, circa 1700—Darwen Chapel Re-built, 1723—Description of the Fabric—Its Endowments—List of Curates and Incumbents—Modern Churches—Nonconformity—Two Sects within the Church—The Act of Uniformity, 1662—Two Thousand Ministers Ejected—Presbyterianism—Nonconformist Services in Darwen Chapel—The House of William and Henry Berry—Congregationalism Acknowledged by James II., 1687—Claims of the Nonconformists to Darwen Chapel—The Chapel Seized—Bottoms—"Our Fathers Worshipped in this Mountain"—Jollie's Chapel on Pendle—Biography of Charles Sagar—Mr. Griffith and the Churchmen—Tramping from Haslingden to Darwen Chapels—The Present Lower Chapel Built, 1719—Mr. Griffith and his Wig -The Rev. Robert Smalley—Drowning of his Child—Formation of Chapel Street Congregational Church, Blackburn—Statistics—Drowning of a Minister's Wife, 1804— Religious Revival—Yates's Chapel—The Pole Lane Secession—Origin of Duckworth-street Chapel—Extraordinary Burial Dispute—Modern Nonconformist and Roman Catholic Places of Worship —Religious Census—Day and Sunday Schools.

CHAPELS, the name of a district in Darwen, owes its origin to the stirring ecclesiastical events that have taken place there, and we do not turn in vain to that neighbourhood in our research for the earliest ecclesiastical history of the town. It was formerly called "The Chapel," when there was only one place of worship there, as I have shown in the previous chapter by quoting the will of "Thomas Fish, of the Chapel, in Over Darwen," dated 1617. There are still standing on the brow of the little hill near the north-eastern boundary of the borough the Higher and the Lower Chapels, which, at the beginning of last century, gave the plural name "Chapels" to the neighbourhood. The oldest portions of these buildings date respectively from 1723 and 1719. A third ecclesiastical building, within a hundred yards of Lower Chapel, is a block of dwellings having some architectural features in common with it. This was formerly called "Yates's Chapel," and it dates back to 1723-4. The "Higher Chapel," referred to above, is now called St. James's Church. It stands, within a few feet, on the exact site of the original Church of Darwen, which always bore the simple name of "Darwen Chapel," or "Upper Darwen Chapel."

The Roman Catholics, whose history is often linked with that of parish churches and old parochial chapels, make no claim to Darwen Chapel, and it may be concluded that there was neither church nor chapel in Darwen prior to the Reformation. No record of any chapel in Darwen has been found taking us further back than the year 1577. In that year the quaint but careful Elizabethan writer, Harrison, the venerable chaplain of Lord Cobham, described the course of the various rivers of Lancashire, as observed in his itineraries. Referring to the Ribble, he says :—" And then taketh in the Darwent, before it goeth by Pontworth or Pentworth into the sea. The Darwent divideth Leland-shire from Andernesse [Blackburnshire, not Amounderness], and it ryseth by east above *Darwent Chappell*, and soon after vniting it selfe with the Blackeburne and Rodlesworthe water, it goeth thorowe Howghton Parke, by Howghton Tower, to Walton Hall, and so into the Ribell." In the Harleian MSS. there is given a drawing or map of Lancashire as it appeared in the year 1598, and " Darcom Chap." appears on it near the River Darwen. Lancashire at that time was recorded to contain "XV. market townes and 36 parish churches, besides chapels in great nomber." A copy of the drawing made for Gregson in 1821 is reproduced in the new edition of Baines's *History of Lancashire*, vol. 1., p. 253.

We next hear of Darwen Chapel as a chapel of ease belonging to the Parish Church of Blackburn. A survey of the Blackburn Rectory was taken on September 20th, 1616, and from the record kept in the Remembrancer's Office of the Royal Exchequer the following extract is taken :—" A.D. 1616. The Parish [of Blackburn] contained the Mother Church, and Low Church [Walton-le-Dale], Samlesbury, Harwood Church, Lango Chappell, *Darwen Chappell*, Tockholes Chappell, and Balderstone Chappell." There was a "lecturer" at Darwen in 1622, recognised by the Bishop, and probably acting as a sort of curate under the Vicar of Blackburn. The most remarkable thing about this lecturer is his name—" Welch,"—which would lead us to identify him with the Rev. Edward Welshe, Vicar of Blackburn from 1580 to 1606, who, after serving the Church for quarter of a century, was deprived of his benefice for declining to conform to the three articles in the 36th Canon of 1603. He retired to the homestead of his family, Walsh Fold, Darwen, and resided there until his death in 1628. Not only the name of this Darwen lecturer, but his apparent affluence, tends to identify him with the retired Vicar at Walsh Fold, for he was one of the very few clergy-men in the deanery of Blackburn who could afford to contribute towards the King's numerous levies of ship money about that period. The record of his donation is given in the private ledger of John Bridgeman, D.D., Bishop of Chester, now in the possession of his descendant, the Earl of Bradford, where it is recorded as follows :—" Lectur. de Darwin, Mr. Welch, 13s. 4d."[1] The Vicars of Blackburn and Whalley, at that time, gave nothing, the latter, in 1634, excusing himself on the ground that he was poor, and all the rest of the clergy in the Blackburn Deanery were said to be "poor curates." Subsequently, when Adam Bolton was Vicar of Blackburn, he contributed £1, and on another occasion Blackburn's contribution (probably out of the pocket of Mr. Bolton) was 8s. Loans, contributions, subsidies, and ship money were levied on the clergy of the Blackburn Deanery seven times between 1620 and 1639, but these are the only contributions given from this neighbourhood.

In the course of the Commonwealth Church Survey an inquisition was taken at Blackburn, on June 25th, 1650, when the following information regarding the Darwen Chapel was gleaned :[2]—" Over Darwen a chappell distant from their P'ishe Church ffour myles, consistinge of aboue ffour hundred ffamilies being w'thin the sd. Town of Ovr. Darwen and p'te of the fforest of Rossendall, Mr. Josiah Barnards, an(d) able & godly Divine, hath for his Sallery ffourtie pounds p. ann. allowed by the Committee of this Countye : the Inhiats desire it may be made a p'ishe, and competent mainteinance allowed for their minister." The same survey also enumerates the tythes held by the impropriator of the Rectory of Blackburn, Mistresse Marianne ffleetwood, including the following :—In Nether Darwen twentyeseaven pounds per ann. ;" "in Mellor-cum-Eclesill thirty pounds per ann. ;" "besyde Yatebanke and Piccopbanke, part of the forrest of Rossendall, but parcell of the rectorye of Blackburne, theare tythes worth to the above said farmer five pounds per ann."

At this time three separate sums of £10 each had been given by inhabitants of Darwen and neighbourhood to form the nucleus of an endowment of the Darwen Chapel, for the maintenance of a resident minister. Josiah Barnards (or Joshua Bernard), a Presbyterian, is then recorded to be the resident minister, and the people express their desire that a separate parish may be formed. A dispute as to the possession of the old chapel arose in 1687 between the Vicar of Blackburn (Francis Price) and the Nonconformist inhabitants of Darwen, and in 1692 Vicar Price caused the following document respecting its endowments to be prepared :—

[1] Record Society's Publications, vol. xii., p. 68.   [2] Ibid, vol. i., p. 161.

A true account of the money that hath been given to Darwen Chappell to be and remaine as stocke there, and the names of they persones that hath given it, and when they gave it, and in what words, and also by what meanes this stocke hath been invested, and now in whose hands this chappell stocke doth remaine for the present, as followeth :—

Impr. January the 20th, 1638. I, William Haydock, of Audlock Shaw, in Levesay, give and bequeath unto Thomas Fish, of Eccleshill, and John Ellison, of Over Darwen, and theire heires a sume of ten pounds, to be and remain as a stock at Over Darwen Chappell, and the intreas thereof to be and remaine to such a minister as shall be theire resident from time to time.

2ly. March the 28th, and in the 17th year of Charles the First, John Crosse, of Over Darwen, gent., gave ten pounds in these words:—Item. I give and bequeath to Thomas Fish, of Eccleshill, and John Ellison, of Over Darwen, their heires and assignes, a sume of ten pounds of lawfull English money, to be and remaine as a stock at Over Darwen Chappell, and my will is that the intreas and intrest that shall be raised or received for the same shall be paid to such a minister as shall be their resident from time to time.

3ly. November 15th, 1641. I, Thomas Lomas, of Over Darwen, in the Parish of Blackburne, husband man, doe give and bequeath unto Thomas Fish, of Eccleshill, and John Lomas, of Over Darwen, their heirs and assignes, the some of ten pounds, to remaine and continue as a stock at Over Darwen Chappell for ever, and my will is that the intreas that shall be raised or received for the same shall be used and disposed of for the mantayning of God's word and His servis at the said Chappell from time to time.

4ly. At varant times when there was no minister resident at the Chappell, Thomas Fish and John Ellison and John Lomas did keep the intrest of the above said 30 pounds until it was ten pounds, and then it was added to the stock, and at this time it was mayd 40 pounds.

5ly. May the 30th, 1673. I, Thomas Longworth, of Over Darwen, in the County of Lancaster, husbandman, do give and bequeath ten pounds, to be added to the stock or gift formerly given to the chappell at Darwen, to be set or let out upon intrest by my exectrs. and his heirs here after named, and the profet ther of to be paid to such a Gospell minister as shall teach theire.

6ly. July 2th, 1674. Richard Fish, of Heath Charnock, in the County of Lancaster, yoman, in his last will, did give and bequeath four pounds towards a minister at Darwen Chappell.

7ly. Thurston Maudsley, of Ousbooth, in the County of Lancaster, gent., on the 27th November, in the 36 year[1] of the raigne of Charles the 2 gave 5 pound in theese words:—Itam. I give and bequeath 5 pound to wards the maintenance of an orthodox minister at the Chappell at Over Darwen, which shall be conformeable to the Church of England, to be put into the same common stock theire to wards the maintenance of the same.

8ly. There was seventeen shilling interest aded unto the chappell stock by William Bury, and at this time it was mayd six pounds.

January 26th, 1692. This abstract was taken and presented to Fr. Price, Vicar of Blackburn, by me,

THOMAS ELLISON, of Over Darwen.

---

1 This would be the year 1684, three years before the great dispute for the possession of the chapell. Note the phrase, "An orthodox minister" . . . "conformeable to the Church of England."

It appears to have been customary for a curate of the Mother Church in Blackburn to preach occasionally in the Darwen Chapel, and to have been the wish of the people that a resident curate should be appointed. From the wording of the bequests quoted above, there can be no doubt that the endowments of the chapel, from 1638 onward, were all intended to be added together, and used for the same purpose. At first this purpose was the maintenance of a resident minister, and it was not until 1684 that a stipulation was made that the resident minister deriving his income from the endowment should be "conformeable to the Church of England." The first resident curate appointed was a Presbyterian, and for his history we have to turn to the minutes of the Blackburn Presbyterian Classis, from which the following extracts are made:—"Joshua Bernard, Minr. at Over Darwin Chap. By an order of the Com. at Manchester, of the — of Jan., 1648, there is 40*l*. per an. allowed to Mr. Bernard, Minr. at Over Darwin, together with the arrears due unto him. By a certificate of the Inhabitants of the Chappelrie of Over Darwin, it appears that Mr. Bernard was in arreare for two yeares and a qr. ending the 3rd of Decr., 1649. Mr. Bernard was ordained the 4th of Decr., 1649, at the chappel of Over Darwin, by the Classis of Blackborne Hundred."[1]

In the following year Mr. Bernard was still minister at Darwen, as already shown, but after this we lose sight of him. One local ecclesiastical writer (the Rev. R. Nicholls) says:—"Mr. Barnard continued his ministrations at Darwen until the restoration of Charles II. (1660), when, it is conjectured, he, fearing the storm that was about to burst upon the land, emigrated to America." The fact is that we lose sight entirely of Mr. Barnards, or Bernard, and a local antiquary surmises that he may be the same person as the Joshua Barnet who was ordained by the Presbytery minister at Tockholes. The history of Barnet, as given by Calamy[2] is summarised by Dr. Halley as follows:—"During the establishment of Presbyterianism in Lancashire, Mr. Joshua Barnet was ordained by the Classis minister of Tockholes Chapel. As he could not conscientiously subscribe 'the solemn League and Covenant,' he was compelled to resign his situation. He removed to Hodnet, in Shropshire, where he had to submit to a second ejectment for refusing to sign the 'Engagement' under the Republican Government. Not complying with the requirements of the Act of Uniformity, he suffered a third ejectment, which was from Rockwardine, in Shropshire."

[1] *History of Whalley*, i. 222. [2] *Nonconformist's Memorial*, vol. iii., p. 19.

Notwithstanding the rise of Nonconformity the Vicar of Blackburn, who afterwards became so jealous for the cause of the Church, was very lax in his attention to the chapel at Darwen, and evidently took no notice of it, for it fell into a ruinous condition, and the people themselves, as shown in a document hereafter quoted, were allowed to develop their Congregational tendencies by conducting services in their own way. This was probably about 1672-3, and the authority by which the people acted was a license granted under the Indulgence of Charles II. for "The house of William and Henry Berry, in Upper Darwen, to be a Pr. meeting place." Tradition points to a house still standing in Bury Court, as the Presbyterian meeting place thus sanctioned,[1] but the inhabitants declared in 1687 that under that license they had been allowed to use the old Darwen Chapel. In 1683, when the Nonconformists were being vigorously prosecuted, monthly services were conducted in the chapel by a curate sent by the Vicar of Blackburn, who in that year reported to the Archbishop of Canterbury as follows : "Darwen Chapell, four miles from Blackburn Church, four miles from any other chapell. N. N. officiates there once a month. Adjacent, Upper Darwen, Eccleshall, Yate Bank, and Piccop Bank. Endowment: Interest of several small sums of money given by well-disposed persons, £4 ; Mrs. ffleetwood promiseth £2 ; inhabitants will give at least £10, if Mrs. ffleetwood raiseth not her 40s. from the Tith Hay."

A battle royal for the possession of the chapel took place in 1687. James II., having succeeded his brother, stopped the persecution of the Nonconformists, and promulgated his "Declaration" of religious liberty. To him the Nonconformists of Darwen, now not Presbyterian but distinctly Congregational, applied for a new license, and obtained from the King a warrant dated July 25th, 1687, and worded as follows :—" We have allowed and do hereby allow of a Meeting-place erected in Upper Darwen, in the Parish of Blackburn, in our County of Lancaster, to be a place for the use of such as do not conforme to the Church of England, who are of the persuasion commonly called Congregationall, to meet and assemble in, in order to their publick Worship and Devotion." At that time the chapel was in possession of the Vicar of Blackburn, who held the keys, and the services here were conducted (probably once a month) by his curate, William Colton, who was called the "curate of Darwen." The Congregationalists produced their license and applied for the keys, the application being made on the 8th of August, 1687, by William Crosse. The Vicar denied that the license

[1] But the Rev. R. Nicholls, conjectures that "the house" was Bury Fold, a fine Elizabethan homestead at the opposite end of Darwen.

referred to the old Chapel, and refused to give up the keys. He contended that the King meant, in his license, the house of William and Henry Berry, which had previously been licensed and used as a Dissenting Meeting-house, but the King probably knew nothing about the local circumstances, and the Nonconformists themselves undoubtedly meant the old Chapel when they sought and obtained the license. Being certain of their own intentions, and armed with the authority of the King, the Nonconformists forcibly took possession of the Chapel by breaking open the doors, and established in it the Congregational mode of worship which has become so popular among the people of Darwen. The Vicar immediately wrote to his diocesan, Dr. Cartwright, Bishop of Chester, relating the circumstances of the case, and entreating him to intercede with the King for the restoration of the Chapel to his possession. His letter is as follows :—

To the Right Rev. Father in God, Thomas, Lord Bishop of Chester, my honoured diocesan.—May it please your Lordship.—The regard your Lordship has for your clergies' concern, and the justice you administer upon all occasions with so much integrity, have brought me to prostrate myself at your feete, to represent to your clemency, in few words, an affair which ought to be treated at large. Upon the eighth day of this instant, August, 1687, one Mr. William Crosse, of Upper Darwen, in the parish of Blackburne, in the County of Lancaster, demanded of me (the present Vicar of Blackburne), the keys of the chappel of Darwen, to which, as Vicar of Blackburne, I hold an indubitable right and title, pretending that our Sovereign Lord the King had assigned that ancient and sacred fabrick for such of the inhabitants as did not conform to the Church of England, But because, in the license which he showed me, I did not find the word "chappell" once mentioned, nor anything sounding like it, except one expression contained in this sentence :—" We have allowed, and do hereby allow of a meeting-place, erected in Darwen, in the parish of Blackburn,"—I could not consent to the delivery of the said keys till I was fully satisfyed that, by those words, his Majesty did meane the chappel at Darwen ; yet freely did I offer to deliver up the said keys in case that three of the Justices of the Peace did apprehend that those words in the license were to be interpreted, viz., of the chappel of Darwen, and not of another edifice in Darwen, which some of the Dissenters had before signifyed and made known to the Justices of the Peace, they had set apart to assemble in. This reasonable motion was rejected, and since then the doors of the said chappel have been broken open, and the curate of that chappel not permitted to perform his ministerial offices, which, with agitation of grief and sorrow, I most humbly desire your Lordship to make knowne unto the King's most excellent Majesty, and to beseech his Majesty to certify your Lordship whether or no his Majesty did meane the chappel of Darwen, in those words :—" We have allowed and do hereby allow a meeting-place, erected in Darwen." If your Lordship do finde that by those words his Majesty did not mean the chappel of Darwen, I humbly beg that your Lordship would issue out an order to be affixed to the doore of Darwen chappel, that no Minister whatsoever presume to preach in that chappel but such as are duly licensed by your Lordship. But if, on the other side, your Lordship do finde that by the aforesaid words is meant the chappel of Darwen, and that his Majesty thinks fit, from causes best known to himself, to waive my title and to determine against my curate's re-admission, we shall not immediately refuse nor uncharitably censure, much less undutifully disobey, but in all becoming silence sit downe in submission to his Majesty's good will and pleasure; in which desire I will here rest, humbly beseeching the Almighty God to multiply his blessings upon the King's most excellent Majesty; and your Lordship to pardon my great boldness, who am, your Lordship's in all duty, FRANCIS PRICE, Vicar of Blackburne, in Lancashire.

When Bishop Cartwright submitted the dispute to the decision of King James, that monarch did not decide whether he meant the old chapel or not in his license to the Nonconformists, but adopted the simpler expedient of revoking his former order by a second warrant, dated October 20th, 1687, and worded thus :—

James the Second, by the grace of God King of England, Scotland, France, and Ireland, Defender of the Faith, &c — To all to whom these presents shall come, greeting. Whereas, by our warrant under the signett and signe manual, bearing date the 25th day of July last past, we allowed of an erected meeting place in Upper Darwen, in the parish of Blackburn, in our county of Lancaster, to be a place for the use of those who do not conforme to the Church of England, who are of the persuasion commonly called Congregationall, to meet and assemble in, in order to their publick worship and devotion. And whereas it has been since humbly represented unto us that the place claymed by virtue of our said warrant is a chappell belonging by an unquestionable title to the Vicar of Blackborne aforesaid, and that the Vicar thereof for the time being hath constantly, time out of mind, nominated, and the Bishop of Chester licensed, curats to officiate in the said chappel. We have, therefore, thought fit to revoke and annull our said warrant, and we do accordingly by these presents revoke and annull the same, and all and singular the clauses therein contained. And our will and pleasure is, that the Vicar of Blackborne aforesaid now and for the time being, or his curate duly constituted and licensed, have and enjoy the quiet and full possession of the said chappel, there to perform divine service, in such manner as heretofore hath been accustomed without any hindrance or molestation, anything in our said Warrant to the contrary thereof notwithstanding. Whereof all and singular, our officers and ministers, ecclesiastical, civill, and military, and other persons whom it may concerne, are to take notice, and to yield due obedience to our pleasure herein declared. Given at our Court at Whitehall, the 20th day of October, 1687, in the third yeare of our reigne. By his Majesty's command, SUNDERLAND, LD.

By virtue of the King's warrant the Vicar obtained a magisterial order on November 23rd, 1687, restoring the chapel to his possession, as certified in the following document :—

We whose names are subscribed, being churchwardens or the Parish Church of Blackburne, do hereby testify that Thomas Braddyll, Esq., Edward Osbaldeston, Esq., and Ralph Livesey, Esq., three of his Majestie's Justices of the Peace for the County of Lancaster, did give restitution of possession of the Chappell of Darwen, in the County of Lancaster, unto Francis Price, Vicar of Blackburne aforesaid, and William Colton, curate of Darwen aforesaid, upon the 23rd day of November, 1687. In witness whereof we have subscribed our names this 5th day of December, 1687.—(Signed) GYLES WALMSLEY, WILLIAM CHATBURNE, RICHARD COOPER (his mark), churchwardens.

The Nonconformists did not yield their claims without an effort. In the face of the King's warrant produced before the magistrates, and executed in the legal way, they could not retain their hold of the chapel, but they determined to appeal to the King. The Darwen Chapel had probably been built by the inhabitants themselves, and not by any ecclesiastical authority, and it had never been consecrated by any Bishop. When no sect was tolerated, and the only Church of the land was the Established Church of England, the chapel, as a matter of course, came to be regarded and reckoned as the property of the Vicar of Blackburn, in whose parish it was situated, but when the sects which had existed within the Church of England were allowed by law to propagate their various creeds openly, the Low Church section of the inhabitants of Darwen, who must have been very numerous, considered that they had at least as much right to the Darwen Chapel as any other section. In those days of religious fervour, the fact that the Vicar of Blackburn allowed the chapel to fall into a ruinous state, and the equally significant fact that he only sent his curate once a month, led the Dissenting section of his congregation to the belief that they had only to ask in order to obtain possession of the chapel, to form a church after their own model, and worship God in their own way. For three months they used the old chapel, and when they were deprived of it by the magistrates they forwarded this petition to the King :—

> The humble petition of your Majestie's subjects in and about Darwen humbly sheweth—That whereas we formerly have had an erected meeting house in Upper Darwen aforesaid, to worship God in after our own way, which your Majestie's subjects enjoy'd with a great deal of freedome, in pursuance of a license formerly granted to us of the said place by your Lordship's late brother of ever blessed memory, and untill such time as the same was cancelled, and wee, your Majestie's subjects, put under new difficulties, though we behaved ourselves peaceably and loyally towards the Government ; and further, that the said place was never visited by any Bishopp, as fair as your Majestie's subjects can heare or understand, and since your Majestie's gratious declaration, the keys of the said house were taken away by the Vicar of the Parish or his order, on purpose to exclude your Majestie's subjects from the same. Wherefore your Petitioners doe humbly pray your Majestie that you would be gratiously pleased to restore your Majestie's subjects the use of the same house, it being out of repaire, and ready to drop downe ; and we are willing to repaire the same, and your Petitioners, as in duty bound, will ever pray for your Majestie's health and happiness, &c.

No reply appears to have been vouchsafed to this petition, and since that time the Church of England has had undisputed possession of the old Darwen Chapel and the fabric that has succeeded it.

In the following year (1688), while the Nonconformists provided themselves a place of worship in a barn, the adherents of the Church, stimulated, assisted, and encouraged by Vicar Price, began to consider the task of repairing the chapel and providing a stipend for a resident curate. They undertook, in a document dated September 20th, 1688, to repair the chapel within the next two months, but either from lack of zeal, or from a feeling of sympathy with their neighbours the Nonconformists, they neglected the work, and, four years later Vicar Price found it necessary to enforce a compulsory church rate to pay for the repairs. I transcribe hereunder three documents belonging to this period. The first, without date or signature, shows that a house-to-house canvass was made by the leading Churchmen to see how far the inhabitants were disposed to support the Vicar; the second is an agreement made by the Vicar with one William Stones, of Blackrod, whom he appointed to the joint curacy of Darwen and Tockholes; and the third is an undertaking given to the Vicar by the inhabitants showing what they were prepared to do.

OVER DARWEN CHAPPELL.

The Inhabitants w'thin the chappellrie of Darwen to a late mocon and offer of kindnes by his Grace the Arch Bpp of Canterbury and others to us made doe returne o'r answer as foll'e. That ye ffeoffees (who are appoynted for the dispose of some affaires w'thin o'r Chappellrie) w'th some others have made it their busines to goe from house to house to see how p'sons stood affected towards soe good a worke and finding that ye Generallity alledg'd they were either ffarmers or held lands by Lease und'r such as lives remote from us w'th though they are very desireous that such a Ministry should bee embraced as is by Law tollerated, wee are all Constrained unanimously to say that wee shall show o'rselves forward to hyre one (our selves) to officiate att our Chappell. And if his Grace the Lord Arch Bpp is pleas'd to doe any thing for us towards ye mantainance of a Lawfull Minister by way of Augmentaion wee shall all be ready to Denote o'r thankfullnes in a Cheerful laying out our selves (to the full) in what may be reasonably expected from us.

Articles of Agreement had, made, concluded, consented unto and fully agreed upon by and between Francis Price, Vicar of Blackburn, in the County of Lancaster, of the one part, and William Stones, curate of Black Rood, in the said County of Lancaster of the other part, this [blank] day of [blank] anno regni domini nostri jacobi secundi dei gratiâ Angliæ, Scotiæ, Franciæ et Hiberniæ regis, fidei defensoris, &c., quarto anno domini 1688. *Imprimis.* The said Francis Price doth covenant, promise and agree to and with the said William Stones that in consideration of the covenants and conclusions hereafter in these presents mentioned, which, on the part and behalf of the said William Stones are to be observed and done, the said Francis Price will upon the [blank] day of this instant, 1688, admit the said William Stones into the curateship of Tockholes and Darwen, in the Parish of Blackburn, in the County of Lancaster, together with all the profits, dues, members, and appurtenances whatsoever thereunto belonging or appertaining, excepting what hereafter in these presents is excepted. *Item.* The said William Stones, in consideration of the premises doth covenant, promise and agree to and with the said Francis Price by these presents that the said William Stones will at or before the first day of January next ensuing the date hereof resign all his right and title to the curateship of Blackrood in the Parish of Bolton in the said County of Lancaster. *Item.* It is further covenanted and agreed by the said parties that the said William Stones shall constantly reside within one of the said chapelries of Tockholes or Darwen, and diligently attend the cure of souls in the said chapelries of Tockholes and Darwen; and shall publicly and solemnly preach and read prayers appointed to be read by and according to the Book of Common Prayer at such times and places as are by these presents specified, that is to say, shall read prayers and preach both morning and evening every other Lord's Day from the first day of March to the 11th day of November following at the Chapel of Tockholes, and shall read prayers and preach every other Lord's Day during the said term (and as often) at Darwen Chapel and likewise shall read prayers and preach at least once every Lord's Day from the 11th day of November, to the first day of February at one of the foresaid chapels. *Item.* It is further covenanted and agreed by the said parties that forasmuch as the surplice fees within the said chapelries of Tockholes and Darwen have all along, since the alienation of them from the appropriator belonged to the Vicar of Blackburn for the time being, the foresaid Francis Price, together with the free consent of the said William Stones, doth make these following determinations and allotments concerning the said surplice fees, viz., that the said William Stones shall receive churching dues of all such women as shall be churched at Darwen Chapel or Tockholes, supposing they dwell within the chapelries of Darwen or Tockholes, and likewise burying dues for such persons as shall be buried at the said chapels; the said William Stones shall also receive full marriage dues, viz., 2/6 upon a publication of banns and 5/- upon a license of all couples as dwell within the said chapelries of Darwen or Tockholes and are married at the said chapels by the said William Stones; and if it so happen that any person inhabiting within the chapelries of Darwen or Tockholes be married at either of the said chapels to any person inhabiting out of the said chapelries within the proper precincts of the mother church of Blackburn, then the said William Stones shall pay to the Vicar of the said mother church for the time being one one-half of the fees that shall be due for every such marriage, but the said Vicar of the said mother church of Blackburn shall not be accountable to the said William Stones for any surplice fees received by the said Vicar of the inhabitants of the foresaid chapelries of Tockholes or Darwen for any holy offices performed at the said mother church of Blackburn. *Item.* It is further covenanted and agreed by the said parties that the said William Stones shall read prayers as often as he can conveniently at one of the chapels of Tockholes or Darwen upon holy days; and not only read prayers but also preach at one of the said chapels upon solemn days appointed by authority; and shall perform, or cause to be performed, all other holy offices of what kind soever they be that are incumbent upon a curate, and, in fine, shall so lead his life as becomes a minister of the Church of England and as one that appears worthy of the respect and favour which is showed him by the said Francis Price. *And*, lastly, the said William Stones does promise to signify his subjection to the mother church of Blackburn by preaching at it once every year if he be required; and to assist the said Francis Price in getting the Lord Archbishop of Canterbury's lands at Thornley and collecting of the rents thereof, and does firmly oblige himself to the said Francis Price by these presents in the sum of £20 of lawful money of England to perform and accomplish the agreement and covenants expressed in manner and form aforesaid.

We, whose names are submitted, inhabitants within the chappelry of Darwen and parish of Blackburn, do promise in behalf of ourselves and our neighbours to put the chappel of Darwen into some fitting repairation before the 11th day of November next ensuing the date hereof, and we do also promise on behalf of ourselves and neighbours to give to the curate of Darwen by way of benevolence, yearly, the sum of 5 Pounds at least upon condition yt. the said curate will preach and read prayers at the said chappell twice every other Lord's Day from Candlemas to Martinmas, and at least once every other Lord's Day from Martinmas to Candlemas : upon condition likewise that the Lord Archbishop of Canterbury will give to the said curate the sum of 5 Pounds a year, and will allow the said curate 40 shillings a year out of the 14 Pounds a year which the Farmeresse of the Rectory of Blackburn is obliged by covenant in her last lease to pay to the chappels of the foresaid parish, according to the direction of the said Lord Archbishop of Canterbury. In testimony whereof we have subscribed our names this 25th day of September, 688. [No signatures appear on this document.]

The grant of the Archbishop of Canterbury referred to above is probably explained by a document in the records of the Parish Church of Blackburn, dated May 28th, 1688, and headed :—" The Vicar of Blackburn desires to be resolved in these following particulars." Clause 1 is a question concerning the disposal of the sum of £55 5s. 7d. "which is due from him [the vicar] to the Lord Archbishop of Canterbury." Clause 3 reads as follows :—" (3) Whether the remainder of the said sum of £55 5s. 7d. may not be distributed among the curates of Blackburn Parish, viz. : Mr. Abbott, curate of Low and Samlesbury Church; Mr. Colton, curate of Harwood and Darwen ; and Mr. Stones, curate of Tockholes ; in this manner, viz. : 8/- in every pound to Mr. Abbott, 8/- in every pound to Mr. Colton, and 4/- in every pound to Mr. Stones, which in the whole will be very considerable and very thankfully received." The reply to this question is written in the margin—" It may, and must."

Mr. Stones duly became the curate of Darwen and Tockholes,[1] but the inhabitants neglected their undertaking "to put the chappel of Darwen into some fitting repairation," and also objected to the arrangement whereby they only received one-half of the curate's attention. This is shown by the two following extracts from the Vicarage records, the first being dated 1689, and the second, which immediately follows it in the records, being without date :—

Darwen and Tockholes, 2 chappells supplyed by Mr. Stones a conformable minister. Tockholes hath boon given annually by pious persons, a stock of money, the interest whereof is betwixt £7 and £8, which sum of £7 or £8 is given in most or in great part to Nonconformists or at lest not to ye conformable ministr incumbent there. My Ld. Archbp. of Canterbury gives to ye sd. 2 chappells of Darwen and

---

[1] The Tockholes Coucher Book records that William Stones was appointed curate of Tockholes and Darwen, by Francis Price, in January, 1689, and that he died in 1720.

Tockholes £5 p. annum apiece expecting on his voluntary kindness yt. ye interest of ye sd. stock be paid to a conformable minister there. The inhabitants of Darwen did promise (upon ye bounty of my Ld. of Canterbury) to make an addition to my Ld.'s gift of £9 p. ann., but have p'formed nothing of all they promise.

An answer to my lord's instructions concerning the chapelries in Blackburn. [Extract.] Darwen Chapel. The inhabitants desire a fortnight's time to consider what they shall do. The inhabitants of each chapelry are not willing to unite to any other, though they may better consider of it hereafter.

The following account of Darwen Chapel is given in the *Notitia Cestriensis*[1] of Bishop Gastrell written about the beginning of the 18th century :—

DARWEN.— Upper Darwen, Certif.[ied] £9 16s. 8d., *viz.*, out of [the] A'bp. of Cant'y's Lands at Thornley £5 ; Rect'y of Blackburn £2 6s. 8d. ; Int.[erest] of £50, £2 10s. £9 4s. 9d. *Vic's Account*, an [no] 1704. *Pap. Reg.* [The] same curate serves Darwen and Tockholes. Circumf.[erence] about 12 m.[iles.] Upper Darwen, Yate-Bank, Piccop Bank, Eccleshill, and part of Lower Darwen, resort to it. All Div.[ine] Offices [are] performed every other Sunday. [No warden.] White-Hall. Augm.[ented] an.[no.] 1719 with £220, by Mr. Eccles and others. 3 m.[iles] from [the] Par.[ish] Ch.[urch ; and] 2 [miles] from any other Ch[urch.] No school. No charities.

In 1692, by which time the Nonconformists had become thoroughly established, while the promises of the Churchmen had been broken, the Vicar deemed it necessary to take strong measures, and so announced that he would levy a compulsory rate upon the inhabitants of the chapelry to pay for the repair of the ruined chapel. The notice runs as follows :—

Dearly Beloved,—You perceive by this order of the Lord Bishop of Chester how zealously he is concerned for the repairing of the Chappel of Darwen, and to that end, how earnestly in the first place he recommends the carrying on of that pious worke to the care of the inhabitants of that chappelry ; and upon their neglect, how he enjoynes the Churchwardens of Blackburne (after publick notice given) to proceed to make such assessment or lay within the said chappelry, as shall be proportionable and sufficient to the said Chappel of Darwen. Now, in pursuance of that order, I do in the name, and by the directions of the said churchwardens, give publick notice that in regard the time allowed for the repairing of the said chappel is almost expired, and the work still undone, the said churchwardens (God willing) do intend to meet at the said chappel of Darwen upon Thursday next, at one o'clock in the afternoon, to make an assessment or lay for the foresaid purpose. Desiring and hoping that the said inhabitants will vouchsafe them their company, concurrence, and assistance at the time and place aforesaid ; or at least (in respect to religion and their own good) they will not show any dislike to so publick, so useful, and so unavoidable an undertaking ; and in so doing they will oblige the churchwardens, who remain their and the Parish most humble servants.

Published at Blackburne and Darwen, September 12th, 1692. Baulderston people will have notice some other Lord's Day, when their business shall fall under consideration.

[1] Vol. 2, part 2, Chet. Socy's series. vol. 21, pp. 283-4.

Thirty years later, the old Darwen Chapel, which had been the object of such dispute, was pulled down and succeeded by the present Church of St. James, which was built about 1722-3.[1] This church stands almost on the identical site of the old Elizabethan chapel, its foundations having been laid three or four feet to the north of the old ones. The plan of the old chapel, like that of the present church, was a simple parallelogram, and it is said that the present St. James's Church is exactly the same size as the old Darwen Chapel observed by Harrison in 1577. For a long time interments were allowed to take place inside the old chapel, and at the present time the church is completely undermined with vaults, long since closed for burial purposes. It was in order to dig the foundations without disturbing these vaults that the new St. James's Church of 1723 was built a few feet to the north of the old foundations. Tradition says that the Churchmen rebuilt it in emulation of the Nonconformists who erected the old Lower Chapel in 1719, and it is certain that Lower Chapel is the more ancient of the two existing buildings, for the date stone on Lower Chapel is "1719," and a document in the Vicarage records, dated September 16th, 1719, shows that the Higher Chapel was not then re-built. This document relates to an inquiry respecting a trespass. It contains the depositions of Thomas Taylor, John Whewell, aged 78, William Lightbound, aged 30, and James Halliwell, aged 50; it is signed by Thomas Whittaker and William Sudell, and witnessed by John Taylor. The following is an extract :—

September 16th, 1719. Witnesses examined at a difference betweene Henry Maudsley and John ffishe[2] and Wm. Yate abt. a trespass near Darwen Chappel. Tho. Taylor says yt. upon a report yt. he had hindered Mr. ffish and Mr. Yates from having stones for their new building designed for a chappel abt. ye beginning of May he went to his son-in-law, Hen. Mawdesley, and asked him yt. he wod give leave for 'em to get stones, and he replied yt. if they wod send for him, keep himself quiet, and not let his ffather know, he wod treat with 'em abt. stones. That, in Whitsun weeke, Tho. Taylor was call'd in at Wm. Holden's by Tho. Kirkham, and yt. he was publickly; thanked for asking his son leave, and yt. he then told ym yt. they might have stones. Mr. ffish says yt. how hardly soever he is used in this refference *he will give liberty of his delf for Darwen Chappell when it is rebuilt, and likewise to build a house for a curate upon his land and stones for ye same.*

The church was built by the inhabitants after the primitive manner of those times, some giving material and some giving money. The following list of eighty-six persons who promised to subscribe among them nearly £100 towards the cost of the church is of interest as

---

1 A brief was obtained and 1/6 collected at Milnrow for Upper Darwen Chapel, in the County of Lancaster, September 22nd, 1722.—*Milnrow Register.*

2 Dr. Halley jocularly observes :—" It may amuse the people who affect to spell their names with a double f that not only were the ffaringtons and the ffrenches so spelt, but also the ffools and every ffriday in the year. It was the old way of writing a capital F."—*Lanc. Nonconformity,* i. 27.

showing who were the leading Churchmen of Darwen at that period :—
1719.

We whose names are under-written do hereby promise to pay to the trustees of Darwen Chapel the several sums by us subscribed for and towards the re-building of Darwen Chapel aforesaid :—

	£	s.	d.		£	s.	d.
Edmund Eccles	5	0	0	Jno. Livsay	0	5	0
Roger Welsh	5	0	0	Tho. Bayley	0	5	0
James Horridge	5	0	0	James Morris	0	5	0
Mrs. Haworth	5	0	0	Henry Clark	0	10	0
James Marsden	6	0	0	Jno. Clark, senior	0	5	0
John Cooper	5	0	0	Jno. Clark, junior	0	5	0
Tho. Taylor	3	0	0	Widdow Townend	0	5	0
Henry Marsden	2	2	0	Tho. Yeates	0	10	0
Wm. Cross	1	1	0	Tho. Knowles and his 3 sons	1	0	0
Tho. Kerkam	1	0	0	James Yeates	2	2	0
Tho. Yeates	0	15	0	Mr. Folds	2	2	0
Wido. Cross	0	10	0	Tho. Heys	0	5	0
Alce Rideing	0	2	6	Richd. Ellison	0	11	0
Larwence Welsh	0	10	0	Jno. Wadinton	0	5	0
Wm. Holden	1	0	0	Micheall Harwood	0	2	0
Henry Livesay	3	0	0	Thurston Cooper	1	0	0
Larwence Welsh	0	5	0	Richd. Wilkinson	0	5	0
Wm. Fishwick	0	5	0	Roger Taylor	0	5	0
Jno. Elison	1	0	0	Richd. Tompson	0	5	0
James Cunlife	0	10	0	James Tompson	0	5	0
Richd. Leach	1	0	0	Tho. Yeates, senior	0	2	6
Jerimy Leach	0	10	0	Christopher Hargreaves, senr.	0	2	6
Wm. Duxbury	1	0	0	Christopher Hargreaves, junr.	0	2	6
Henry Duckworth	1	0	0	Law. Yeates, Yatebank	0	5	0
Jno. Leach	0	5	0	Henry Ashworth	0	10	0
Edwd. Bradgeshaw	0	10	0	Henry Lighpound	0	5	0
James Almond	0	10	6	Simeon Townend	0	5	0
Nicholes Tomlinson	0	8	0	Christopher Duckworth, senr.	0	10	0
Jno. Wamsley	0	5	0	Christopher Duckworth, junr.	0	5	0
Ralph Fish	0	10	6	Henry Rosthern	0	1	0
Tho. Thomason	1	1	0	Jno. Cokshoot	0	2	6
Jno. Welsh	1	1	0	James Holden	0	10	6
James Hunt	1	0	0	Jno. Ashworth	0	10	6
Richd. Cronkshaw	0	10	0	Jno. Houghton, Inkeeper	0	5	0
Jno. Isherwood	2	16	0	Ann Croston	0	5	0
Geo. Fishwick	0	15	0	Tho. Leaver	0	5	0
Elizabeth Eccles	0	2	6	James Duckworth	1	1	0
Alce. and Margt. Yeates	0	10	0	James Heape	0	2	6
Peter Kay	0	5	0	Richd. Widerington	0	2	6
James Shaw	0	10	0	Hugh Hayhurst	0	2	6
Robt. Yeates, Watterside	4	9	0	Wm. Yates	4	10	0
James Garstang	0	10	0	Mr. Dewhurst	3	5	0
Tho. Pickup	4	10	0				
Robert Peel	1	1	0	¹£94	18	0	

After standing unaltered for nearly 130 years, St. James's Church was found to be in a dilapidated condition, and, in the opinion of the best authorities, unsafe. Several examinations were made, and the reports were conflicting. It was discovered that the coal beneath the church, presumably belonging to the Ecclesiastical Commissioners, had been taken away by the Messrs. Brandwood, proprietors of some

¹ The figures add up to £95 7s.

neighbouring mines, who had tunnelled their way under the edifice, and that the foundations of the church had sunk in consequence. Mr. William Stott, of Kearsley Mount, Bolton, at the request of the Vicar of Blackburn, and with the consent of the Messrs. Brandwood, examined the colliery workings at the end of 1850 to ascertain the cause of the damage done to the church during the past eighteen months, and in his report, dated January 27th, 1851, he expressed the opinion that the chapel was in great danger of falling within a year, not only through having been undermined (unintentionally) by the colliers of Messrs. Brandwood, but because of the existence of an old stone quarry beneath it. He recommended the immediate cessation of work in certain parts of the collieries, and advised that the workings should be securely propped forthwith. In the following September the church was closed, and a survey of its condition was made by Mr. H. P. Horner, architect, of Liverpool, who reported to the Vicar of Blackburn on December 16th, 1851, that the walls of the chapel yard on the north and south sides were separated into distinct portions by cracks, that the graveyard itself exhibited similar appearances, and that none of the walls of the chapel were perpendicular throughout their entire length, the north wall, for instance, bulging out to the extent of $3\frac{1}{4}$ inches. After pointing out in detail the various external cracks, and the size of them, he added that the arches of the interior were all more or less crippled, and sinking beneath the weight of the bulging roof, and being about 12 feet span, and badly formed, it was evident that they were ill calculated to bear any severe stress. Both arcades were thrown outward from the perpendicular, the opening between them under the roof being $9\frac{1}{2}$ inches more than it was originally. A general sinking of the surface was visible in the change of form of the flooring and the pews, and the walls were cracked inside as well as out. During the next two years, while service was conducted in the Holden Fold school, the church fabric was substantially restored, the workings beneath it being carefully propped to prevent further mischief. The unevenness of the stone courses of the church walls at the present day testify to the disturbance of the foundations. The walls of the church were made sound, a new roof was put on, the north and south galleries were added; the organ in the old west gallery was enlarged; the interior was repewed; and the pulpit and reading-desk were altered.

St. James's Church,[1] commonly called by old inhabitants "The Higher Chapel," stands near the summit of the hill on the eastern side

[1] The term St. James's Church or St. James's Chapel has been commonly used in official documents since 1830. I have not met with any account of its origin. Prior to 1830 it was officially called Darwen Chapel, or by some similar name, and in a circular issued in 1843 by the resident curate, the Rev Henry Dunderdale, it is described as "the Chapel of Over Darwen." A separate ecclesiastical district was assigned to St. James's Church by an Order in Council dated Aug. 11, 1842.

DARWEN CHAPEL (St. James's Church). Existed 1577; Re-built 1723.

of the Darwen valley, and very near the borough boundary where it runs through the township of Eccleshill. Its plan is a parallelogram measuring 58 feet by 40 feet, and there is a semi-circular apse of 9 feet radius at the east end. It is built of stone and oak in the familiar mongrel classic style of the last century. There is no tower or spire, but a small cupola or bell turret surmounts the gable at the west end. The arched doorway in the western wall was made about twelve years ago; the old doorway on the south side, where the vestry now stands, was square-headed with a massive lintel. There are four circular-headed windows with projecting keystones on each side, each consisting of three lights, with tracery of late gothic design, and the apse has two windows of the same kind. The side walls are supported by flat pillasters supporting an entablature, and at the west end there are semi-circular doric pillasters with the entablature above. This gable formerly contained three small mullioned windows, but they are now blocked. The principal features of the interior are two arcades dividing the nave from the aisles; the well-lighted apse; and the pulpit; which latter, with its reading desk in front, is of the style sometimes described as an "ancient two-decker."

Mr. Horner's description of the fabric as it stood in 1851 was as follows:—
"The chapel is a parallelogram of about 58 feet by 40 feet externally, with a semi-circular projection of about 9 feet radius at the east end forming the chancel, the walls being about 1 feet 9 inches in thickness, and pierced on each side with three windows and a door. The interior of the chapel is divided into a nave and aisles by two series of four arches, supported on columns and pillasters about 9 feet from the side walls. A gallery at the west end extends beyond the first pair of columns in the centre, and a little past the second pair on either side. The roof is of rather high pitch, constructed of oak on the collar beam principle, and covered with the heavy flag-slates of the country."

There are 450 sittings; and 76 seats are free. The churchwardens take the rents of all the pews in the galleries and apply them to the payment of their expenses. This custom is said to be unique.[1] They have also the income from a pew in the nave which formerly belonged to the late Dr. Samuel Barton, J.P., of Manchester, grandfather of the Rev. E. H. Barton, B.A., lately curate of this church. As Mr. Barton lived in Manchester, and the pew was not used by him, the Rev. Charles Greenway wrote about 1853 and asked him to sell it to the church-wardens. Mr. Barton replied that he would not make merchandise of anything in the House of God, but would give the pew as a permanent endowment, the rent to go towards defraying the wardens' expenses, and his offer was accepted.

[1] In 1825 a rate was levied on the pews on the ground floor of the chapel for repairs, &c., and on the galleries for the organ. The accommodation of the building at that time was stated to be sufficient for 600 or 620 persons.

A faculty was obtained during the progress of the restoration of 1851-3 for the construction of a cellar to contain the new heating apparatus. Many coffins had to be removed, and they were found to be in an excellent state of preservation, owing to the strong clay, but much difficulty was experienced in removing them, and they had to be forced out and broken with pickaxes. In one corner of the churchyard there existed a charnel house, and here the bones from this cellar were deposited. The number of interments in the churchyard was so great that for many years old graves were constantly being disturbed in digging new ones, and the bones thus dug up were invariably removed to the charnel house. At length an Order in Council was obtained for the enlargement of the burial ground, and the charnel house was abolished, together with a similar one connected with the Lower Chapel.[1]

The following clause is contained in an Order of the Queen in Council for the closing of burial grounds, dated 16th November, 1857:—"Over Darwen, in the parish of Blackburn. Forthwith, in the old part of St. James's churchyard, Over Darwen, in the parish of Blackburn, and in such parts of the Independent Wesleyan Association and Primitive Wesleyan chapel yards as are within three yards of any building, and in Trinity churchyard and in the Lower Independent chapel yard on the first day of January, 1859, except in family graves which are free from water and remains. No coffin to be buried within a foot of any other coffin, or less than four feet beneath the surface. Also that in the new part of St. James's churchyard, Over Darwen, the regulations for new burial-grounds are to be observed."

The oldest and most interesting gravestone in St. James's churchyard lies on the south side, and is inscribed as follows:—"Here lyeth the body of Thomas Watson, of this town, chapman, son of Edmund Watson, of Hague Hall, in the County of York, gentleman, who departed this life, the nineteenth day of December, 1732. And gave for the congregation of this Chappel the summ of three hundred eighty-five pounds. DEUS AMAT LÆTUM DATOREM." A curious gravestone in this churchyard has carved at the head an anvil, a stock and die, pincers, and a hammer, followed by this inscription:—

In memory of James, the son of William and Rebecca Gibson, of Over Darwen, died April 26th, 1814, in the 16th year of his age.

My anvil and my hammer are declined,
My bellows, too, have lost their wind;
My fire extinct, my forge decayed,
And in the dust my vice is laid;
My coal is spent, my iron gone,
My last nail driven, and my work is done.

The endowment of St. James's originated in the desire of the inhabitants to have a resident minister, and from 1638 to 1692 the

[1] The number of funerals at St. James's from 1813 to the end of 1887 was 2,206.

various gifts and accumulated interest amounted to £60, as shown in a document already quoted.[1] On Christmas Day, 1718, in anticipation of the building of the new church, " Mr. Edmund Eccles and others " made a benefaction of £220, and next year the governors of Queen Anne's Bounty met this with a grant of £200, making a total of £420. This sum, augmented by other donations to £450, was apparently laid out in the purchase of an estate at Yate Bank, which was conveyed to the trustees of St. James's on November 10th, 1719, by Henry Eatough, of Yate Bank, and Christopher Brandwood, of Inglewhite, the consideration money being £450. In 1733, a sum of £800 was raised in a similar manner. The Rev. John Holme, vicar of Blackburn, and the Rev. John Folds, curate of Darwen, jointly gave £200 which the governors of the Bounty doubled, and ten days later (September 20th, 1733) a donation of £200 by Henry Feilden, Thomas Whalley and J. Cooper, gents., enabled the trustees to obtain a second grant of £200, making a total addition to the endowment at this time of £800. Land and houses in the neighbourhood were purchased with this, and these two estates form one of the chief endowments of St. James's to-day. The tithes of the chapelry of Over Darwen were claimed by Henry Feilden, Esq., of Witton, in the year 1818, in right of purchase from the Archbishop of Canterbury under a special Act of Parliament—not only rectorial tithes of corn and hay, but tithes of vegetables, eggs, calves, &c., usually considered to be vicarial tithes. All these tithes were "purchased out and out " in 1819 by the proprietors of the lands and houses in the chapelry. A return made in 1823 showed the total acreage of the above-mentioned estates to be 54a. 13p. From six tenants in Yate Bank the Vicar received £131 5s., and from four in Over Darwen £69 10s. In addition to this there was £10 5s. from lands in Thornley given as an endowment by Archbishop Sancroft, and £3 from surplice fees, making the total income of the benefice £214. In a more recent return of landowners, St. James's Church is said to possess 49 acres of land yielding a rental of £53. By deed dated December 6th, 1858, the incumbents of St. James's, Over Darwen, Holy Trinity, Over Darwen, and St. James's, Lower Darwen, along with others in the parish of Blackburn, had the surplice fees of their respective churches assigned to them and their successors for ever by the Vicar of Blackburn. The total value of the living of St. James's, which is in the gift of the Vicar of Blackburn, is returned in the Diocesan Calendar for 1889 at £450, but in "Crockford " at £475. The amount of income from the glebe is £335 19s. 5d.

[1] See *ante*, page 74.

Mr. Welch was lecturer of Darwen in 1622; Joshua Barnard, ordained by the Blackburn Presbyterian Classis, was resident curate from 1647 to 1650; William Colton, curate of Blackburn, preached at Darwen occasionally about 1687; William Stones was resident curate of Darwen and Tockholes from 1688 until his death in 1720; John Folds, through whose exertions the new church was built and endowed held the benefice as resident curate of Darwen for 52 years. He was appointed in 1720 and died in 1772. A mural tablet in the church perpetuates his memory. It is inscribed :—" John Folds, clerk, A.B., curate of this chapel upwards of 52 years, interred 15th February, 1772, aged 75 years; Ann, his wife, interred 31st August, 1781, aged 81 years."

The Rev. John Folds married, in November, 1725, Ann, daughter of John Cooper, yeoman, of Brick House, Darwen, and had issue three sons and one daughter. One of the sons, James, became, like his father, a clergyman, and was a most eccentric character. He was curate of Walmsley Old Chapel, near Bolton, lecturer of Bolton Parish Church from 1755 to 1820, and Vicar of West Hythe, Kent. He died on the 13th of August, 1820, in the 93rd year of his age, and was interred in the Bolton Parish Churchyard. The "sayings and doings" of "Parson Folds," as he was usually called, have been collected by the late Mr. Greenhalgh, of Bolton, from whose book the following curious stories are culled :—In going to and from the chapel at Walmsley, Parson Folds was accustomed to bait his horse and have a pipe and a glass at the house of a farmer named Hamer, about half a mile from the chapel. Curious to know how much the Walmsley curacy made, Hamer once said to his guest, " Why, Mester Folds, I reckon you'll not be getting aboon £30 a year fur Walmsley?" " Canst ta keep a saycret?" asked the parson. " Aye," replied the farmer. " An' so can I" was the happy rejoinder. On a certain Sabbath, when Parson Folds had reached the uppermost step of his pulpit he beheld in his sacred rostrum a goose which by some means had hobbled in before him. " Come thee out," said the preacher; "*one's* plenty !" On a child being presented at the font for baptism the parson asked what its name was to be. " Malley," replied the parent. " Take it away, take it away," said he, angrily ; " we'll have no Malleys here." Some of these stories are probably apocryphal, the following, for instance, depending for its force upon an expression too coarse for the tongue of a clergyman :—He was asked by the officials of a certain village club what he would preach them a sermon for on their annual club day. " A guinea," said he ; upon which they began to haggle for a reduction. Parson Folds, not relishing this, sharply told them that he " could do it for half-a-guinea, but it would not be worth a ——."

Henry White had charge of the chapel from 1772 to 1783, and the Rev. William Parker was engaged there as his curate; Jeremiah Gilpin was there from 1783 to 1792; and Thomas Exton from 1792 to 1815. Exton held the curacies both of Darwen and Balderstone, and was also Usher of Blackburn Grammar School. He was drowned in the river, at Lower Darwen, in 1815, while returning home from Blackburn, where he had been conducting a funeral service. Three manuscript sermons were found in his pocket, and they are now in the possession of an old woman at Holden Fold, daughter of a former sexton of St. James's. Two of them are sermons advocating temperance. The next clergyman to hold the living was the Rev. Matthew Yatman Starkie, LL.B., who also held a benefice at Rushbury, Salop, and resided there. He received the appointment at Darwen in December, 1815, and held it, without residence, until his death, at Rushbury, on the 11th of September, 1851. Nearly the whole of this long period his curate, the Rev. Henry Dunderdale, officiated as his substitute at Darwen Chapel. Mr. Dunderdale was a graduate of Trinity College, Cambridge, but only held deacon's orders. On the appointment of the Rev. Charles Greenway, of Darwen Bank, to succeed Mr. Starkie, there was no further necessity for Mr. Dunderdale's services, and he left the town. The correspondence preserved at the Vicarage shows that Dr. J. W. Whittaker did not overlook without strong reasons the claims which this curate's long service gave him to the living. Mr. Dunderdale considered himself discharged, for in his own handwriting in the register at St. James's Church there appears this note:—"Superseded after 33 years and 11 months' service." A fund was got up for the relief of himself and his family, Archdeacon Rushton, of Manchester (afterwards Vicar of Blackburn) being the treasurer. Mr. Greenway's appointment dates from October 20th, 1851. He became "incumbent" in 1858, and he resigned in 1868. He resides at the present time at Darwen Bank, which he inherited from his uncle, James Greenway, Esq., and holds a high position in the town as a county magistrate and a politician (Conservative). The present vicar, the Rev. W. H. Blamire, was instituted on the 17th of December, 1868. He had as his curate in 1887-8 the Rev. E. H. Barton, B.A.

The Rev. W. H. Blamire is singular in the possession of a name which is owned by no other clergyman of the Church of England, for that well-known clerical directory, "Crockford," mentions no Blamire, except the Vicar of St. James's, Over Darwen. It was owing to this curious fact that a still more curious circumstance came to light some ten or a dozen years ago. Mr. Blamire was standing in the shop of Mr. Rowarth, bookseller, St. Ann's Square, Manchester, when a strange clergyman, hearing his name mentioned, asked, "Are you Mr. Blamire, of St. James's, Darwen?" Being answered in the affirmative, he imparted to Mr. Blamire the incredible intelligence that he (the stranger) had possession of some of the old registers of St. James's Church. Mr. Blamire declared that, to his knowledge, none of the old registers were missing, and on an investigation being made, it appeared that the stranger had not the actual registers, but perfect copies of the originals. They had evidently been copied by different persons, as the writing varied, and the copies came into the hands of their present owner through a dealer in old books, he having bought them under the impression that they were originals, and consequently of great value.

The parsonage of St. James's is a modern house, standing in a large garden not far from Lower Chapel, but there was anciently a parsonage in which "Parson Folds" died, called the Bull House, because of its conversion into an inn with the sign of the Bull. This house is believed to have become the property of Lawrence Yates, of Pickup Bank, through the foreclosing of a mortgage, and "Parson Smalley," the Nonconformist Minister, who married Lawrence Yates's daughter, went to live there after Parson Folds's death in 1772. It was built by a man named Fish, and bears the inscription, "I.E.F., 1725."

There were both day and Sunday schools at Chapels in connection with St. James's fifty years ago, for there is a return in existence for the year 1830-31 stating that there were then 198 children on the books of St. James's Sunday School, half of them being boys and half girls. The maximum attendance was 111 (62 boys and 49 girls); and the average attendance 105 (59 boys and 46 girls). St. James's National Day School for the same period had 32 children on its books (26 boys and six girls), and an average attendance of 28 (24 boys and four girls). New schools were built in 1843 (opened on July 24) at a cost of over £280. There were at that time from 250 to 300 scholars and teachers, and the maximum attendance was 215. The day school of St. James's was suspended in 1843-4-5, but one was started in Pickup Bank with 70 scholars, and an average attendance of 59 (35 boys and 24 girls). The Pickup Bank branch school had 245 Sabbath scholars in 1843, with an average attendance of 183. In 1853-4 the number of scholars on the books of St. James's Sunday School was 246, and at Pickup Bank there were 175. The inhabitants of Yate and Pickup Bank complained to the Vicar on November 14th, 1853, that there had been no afternoon school there for ten weeks, that the schoolmaster had been compelled to leave, and that they had only had four services in 14 months. A new school was built at Hoddlesden about this period.[1] A fine new school was built in St. James's parish in 1881, on a site in Olive Lane, much nearer the centre of population than the old school. The foundation stone was laid on May 21st, 1881, by Mrs. Philip Graham, who gave £100 to the building fund, and the school was formally opened on December 31st, the same year, having been erected at a cos of £1,784 18s. 1d.

MODERN CHURCHES OF THE ESTABLISHMENT.

HOLY TRINITY, OVER DARWEN.—A fine new church, dedicated the Holy Trinity, was built in 1827-8-9 on a commanding site near the centre of modern Darwen. This and the church of St. James in Lowe

[1] The Church Sunday School at Pickup Bank dates from 1790, and it was rebuilt in 1832.

Darwen were both established about the same time by men who had formerly been attached to the Darwen Chapel. Applications for aid were made to Parliament in 1823, and Holy Trinity Church was founded in 1827, a Parliamentary grant of £6,799 having been obtained. The consecration took place on September 13th, 1829. Holy Trinity Church is built of reddish stone in a florid Gothic style of architecture, with a massive square tower at the west end surmounted by eight crocketted pinnacles. The tower contains a peal of eight bells, and a clock purchased by public subscription, in 1878, at a cost of £210. The entrance to the church is by a porch on the south side, and the plan includes nave, side aisles, and a pentagonal chancel. There are galleries over the aisles and at the west end. An organ was placed in the latter in 1843. A separate parish was assigned to this church in 1833-4, and schools were built in 1836-46. Marriages have been celebrated here since 1837. The interior was beautified and improved in 1880, at a cost of £500, and the edifice was thoroughly renovated in 1887, when a new vestry was added, and a new organ, presented by Mrs. L. Gregson, was built. The re-opening took place on the 29th of September, 1887. There are 1,812 sittings, of which 1,026 are free. The living is in the gift of the Vicar of Blackburn, and is worth £380. The first vicar was the Rev. G. Park, who was succeeded by the Rev. E. C. Montriou, M.A., and the Rev. R. M. Lamb. The present vicar, the Rev. R. Mayall, was admitted in 1868.—*The Lee School Church*: A new school-church was built on the Lee in 1882, the foundation stone being laid by the Hon. Mrs. Duckworth, on April 29th. This building cost £1,480 0s. 9d., and it provides accommodation for 409 children and 300 worshippers. It was opened on the 11th of November, 1882.— Trinity School-Church, licensed for worship, contains 450 sittings.— Branch day and Sunday schools were opened in Vernon-street in 1877.

ST. JAMES'S, BLACK-A-MOOR, LOWER DARWEN.—An application for aid to build a new church at Black-a-Moor, within the township of Lower Darwen, was made to Parliament in 1823, a site was purchased and the foundation stone was laid in 1827, and the new church was opened by license in 1829. It was licensed for marriages, like Holy Trinity Church, Over Darwen, in 1837. The cost of the building was defrayed by a Parliamentary grant of £5,491 2s. 6d. The church, which is dedicated to St. James, stands on an elevated site, a considerable distance to the east of the village of Lower Darwen, and its embattled hexagonal tower forms a noticeable feature in the landscape. It is built in the decorated gothic style, with nave, aisles, and pentagonal apse. The prinipal windows have each two lights, with traceried heads. There are 654 sittings, of which 410 are free. The living is in the gift of the Vicar of Blackburn, and is worth £300. The Rev. J. K. Glazebrooke, M.A., was appointed Vicar in 1841, but after holding the living for upwards of forty years, he retired into private life, and his curate, the Rev. George Sumner (present Vicar), was preferred to the appointment on the 19th of April, 1884. The Black-a-Moor School was erected in 1837, and enlarged in 1873 at a cost of £850. *Guide School*, in connection with this church, erected in 1855, is licensed for divine service. It was rebuilt and enlarged in 1888 at a cost of £850; sittings, 350.

ST. PAUL'S CHURCH, HODDLESDEN.—St. Paul's Church, Hoddlesden, stands within the township and borough of Over Darwen, but near the extreme eastern border, and separated from the Darwen Valley, in which the town proper lies, by the Blacksnape ridge. It was consecrated on June 24th, 1863. Towards the original cost, £5,050, Mr. W. B. Ranken, owner of the Hoddlesden estate, contributed £3,000. The style of building is decorated gothic. In 1878 a tower was erected at the north end of the edifice, and a peal of bells was placed in it by public subscription. Of the 579 sittings, 209 are free. The value of the living is £140; patron, the Bishop of Manchester. Vicars :—The Rev. G. W. Reynolds, 1863-7; Rev. W. B. Berry, 1867-81 (now Vicar of Smallbridge); Rev. Stanford Harris, M.A., 1881 (present vicar). The church in this valley originated with the Pickup Bank School, connected with St. James's. This was succeeded by the Hoddlesden National School, the foundation stone of which was laid by Mrs. Hargreave on May 19th, 1852, on a plot of land given by Oliver Hargreave, the principal landowner in the locality at that time, who also contributed £400 towards the total cost of £900. Accommodation was provided in the first instance for 75 boys and as many girls, but the school was enlarged in 1883.

ST. JOHN'S, TURNCROFT.—The Church of St. John the Evangelist was built and endowed at a cost of £11,500 by the late Mrs. Graham (daughter of John Brandwood, Esq.), and her husband, the Rev. Philip Graham, became its first Vicar. It is a beautiful example of gothic architecture, and comprises nave, clerestory, side aisles, chancel, north and south transepts, tower, and spire. There are no galleries. Of the 740 sittings 240 are free. The consecration took place on July 7th, 1864. An organ by Willis was built in the church in 1867. The gross value of the living is £300, and the patronage was vested by the donor in the Bishop of Manchester. The Rev. Philip Graham was the son of a Cumberland yeoman, whose occupation was that of head woodman (or wood steward) under a gentleman of the same name as himself. He was born in the year 1823, educated at a village school, and, as he showed a preference for books, he was sent at the age of 19 or 20 to fill the place of usher at a small private school in Liverpool. He saved as much as he could out of his salary, and eventually went to St. Bees College, Cumberland, to be educated for the ministry. He was ordained deacon on St. Thomas's Day, 1850, by Dr. Prince Lee, Bishop of Manchester, and two years later he took priests' orders. At that time he held the position of curate at Holy Trinity Church. But he left Darwen in 1854 to become curate of St. Mark's, Cheetham Hill, Manchester. Soon afterwards he married the widow of Eccles Shorrock, Esq. (formerly Miss Jane Brandwood) and came to reside at Turncroft. Mrs. Graham having built and endowed St. John's Church and Vicarage, her husband, with the consent of the Bishop, was appointed its first incumbent. On April 17th, 1867, Mrs. Graham died, leaving her property to her husband, who married again, retiring from his living and betaking himself to politics, in which he played a very active part, being for some years Chairman of the Conservative Executive for North East Lancashire, and personally responsible in a large measure for the introduction of Lord Cranborne to the Darwen Division. His curate, the Rev. H. H. Moore, M.A., succeeded to the living on July 6th, 1869, and holds it at the present day. When Mr. Graham's will was proved, his personalty was sworn to be under £35,000. His widow gave a hundred pounds to each of the four churches of Darwen after his death, which occurred on May 10th, 1887. A faculty was obtained on November 2nd, 1888, for erecting a monument to the memory of the late Rev. Philip Graham in the chapel on the north side of the chancel of St. John's Church. St. John's Schools in Barton Brow, opened in August, 1866, were erected by Mr Graham at his own cost. Branch schools of St. John's exist at Grimehills and in the Culvert district.—*St. Barnabas's Mission Church* : In connection with the Culvert School a Mission Church dedicated to St. Barnabas was built in 1884 providing accommodation for 300 worshippers at a total cost of £1,480. It was opened on August 7. The curates of St. John's parish have had charge of the mission in Culvert district since 1865. The present curate, the Rev. Evan T. Powell, was appointed in 1889, in succession to the Rev. I. Rangeley, deceased.—*Grimehills School* is used as a mission room, and it contains 120 sittings.

St. Cuthbert's, Hollins Grove.—The Church of England schools at Earcroft, Lower Darwen, in connection with St. Stephen's Church, Tockholes, were built in 1864-5. Here began a mission which resulted in the formation of the new parish of St. Cuthbert, carved out of the four parishes of St. Stephen, Tockholes, St. James, Lower Darwen, St. James, Over Darwen, and Holy Trinity, Over Darwen. The Rev. F. E. Broderick, M.A., was appointed curate-in-charge of the Earcroft Mission in 1867. In 1871 a new school was opened at Hollins Grove, and in the following year the Rev. W. G. Procter, B.A. (present vicar), succeeded Mr. Broderick as curate-in-charge. A parish was mapped out and allotted to the proposed new church on January 26th, 1874, and a site for the edifice in Blackburn-road, Hollins Grove, was given by the Rev. Charles Greenway, M.A., together with a donation of £500. Miss C. Greenway laid the foundation stone on August 14th, 1875. The cost of the church, £6,000, was readily raised by subscriptions. On January 31st, 1878, the building was opened and consecrated by Bishop Fraser. The bright red colour of the stone of which the church is built and of the tiles with which it is roofed, make it a prominent roadside object at the northern entrance to the town. Its style is gothic, of the early decorated period, and its design includes a tower with massive square base working off into an octagon with angle weatherings. There are 500 sittings. The beautiful window at the east end of the south aisle was given in August, 1880, by Mrs. Gillibrand, of Hollins Grove House, in memory of her late husband. An organ, which cost £700, was placed in the church in 1880, and opened on April 29th. A new reredos of sculptured alabaster was presented by the Rev. Charles Greenway, M.A., J.P., in 1887, and two 21-light brass gas standards were placed in the chancel at the same time by Mrs. Philip Graham in memory of her late husband. The church contains 462 sittings, all free. The living is worth £300 a year, and is in the gift of the Bishop of Manchester. Mr. Gladstone originally nominated the Rev. C. W. Firmstone to it, but the parishioners desired to retain their curate-in-charge, the Rev. C. W. Procter, B.A., present vicar, and Mr. Firmstone voluntarily withdrew in his favour. Mr. Procter has been for years in delicate health. In December, 1879, while he was residing near Clitheroe, his congregation presented him with an address of sympathy and a purse containing £115 in gold. Since then he has travelled abroad, and spent some months at the Azores.—*Earcroft School*, licensed by the Bishop, contains 300 sittings.

ORIGIN OF CONGREGATIONALISM. —THE LOWER CHAPEL.

Nonconformity in Darwen, according to the modern interpretation of the term, dates from the Act of Uniformity, passed in 1662. Prior to that, Darwen Chapel apparently belonged to the Church of England, which embraced all sects of Protestants from the High Churchman (whose creed was very much akin to that of the Catholics, except that the King of England instead of the Pope of Rome was the recognised head of the Church) to the rigid Puritan (who was a strict Sabbatarian and a stern opponent of all ceremonies and artificial aids to worship that reminded him of the Church of Rome). The Darwen Chapel, as already mentioned, was in existence so far back as 1577, and until 1672 it was the only place of worship in Darwen. In this church the Royalists, or High Church Party, and the Puritans grew up together, and there is no evidence to confute the traditions of the Darwen Nonconformists that Puritanism preponderated and that the original Darwen Chapel was a Presbyterian or Congregational meeting house, where services were conducted in the simple manner that suited the inhabitants, without any interference on the part of bishops or priests.

When, on the 23rd of August, 1662, two thousand rectors and vicars—a fifth of the English clergy—were ejected from their parishes for not conforming to the provisions of the Act of Uniformity, there was no minister at Darwen to eject, as its Presbyterian minister, the Rev. Joshua Barnard, appointed in 1647, had left; but the chapel at Darwen was supplied by a curate from Blackburn Parish Church once a month, and the Nonconformists, owing to the stringency of the law, had to worship in secluded places on the moors.

Being driven from the Church by the rigorous measures of Charles II., the Nonconformists of Darwen worshipped in secret for ten years, having Charles Sagar, of Blackburn, for one of their preachers; but in 1672, under an "Indulgence" from the King, licences were issued to Presbyterian preachers, and "the house of William and Henry Berry, in Upper Darwen," was licensed "to be a Pr. meeting place." This indulgence lasted only for ten months, and then persecution was renewed with increased vigour. During the brief period of indulgence the Nonconformists, though they had now a licensed meeting-place of their own, were allowed, it is stated,[1] to conduct their service in the old chapel, and this practice of Nonconformist worship in the chapel was suspended in 1673, on the withdrawal of the Presbyterian licenses. Mr. John Parr, who "preached sometimes at Preston and sometimes at Walton, about a mile off," appears to have been the minister at the house of William and Henry Berry at the time Presbyterian licenses were granted. I have found no clear record of this, but in 1672 Mr. Jollie made an entry in his Church Book relating a curious circumstance about a certain man being prevented by a dream from going "to hear Mr.

[1] See *ante*, p. 79.

Parr, of Darwen." Calamy says of Parr :—" His conversation was strictly pious and regular; his temper meek and peaceable; and his preaching affectionate, searching, and useful. He met with many hardships and sufferings," and died about 1714.

Lower Chapel, the first recognised Nonconformist place of worship in Darwen, except the house of Wm. and Henry Berry, was founded in 1688, by the purchase of a thatched barn at Bottoms, and the licensing of this as a Congregational Chapel. It was called Lower Chapel to distinguish it from the old chapel, which stood higher up the hill. But, by the celebration of their bi-centenary in 1887, the congregation of Lower Chapel date back their church to the 25th July, 1687. On that day King James II., having promulgated a "Declaration" of religious liberty, granted a license to the Nonconformists of Darwen, worded as follows :—" We have allowed, and do hereby allow of a meeting-place, erected in Upper Darwen, in the Parish of Blackburn, in our County of Lancaster, to be a place for the use of such as do not conforme to the Church of England, who are of the persuasion commonly called Congregationall, to meet and assemble in, in order to their publick Worship and Devotion." Upon this authority the Nonconformists forcibly took possession of the old chapel, and held it until the following November, when the "warrant" was revoked, and they were ejected. In the following year, 1688, they obtained a license for public worship in the barn at Bottoms, which was the original Lower Chapel. The spot where this old meeting-house stood is at the junction of two lanes, between the present Lower Chapel School and the minister's house.

Dr. Halley says, "The tradition of the Darwen people the truth of which nobody doubts, is that our fathers worshipped in this mountain," and, from the stories which he had heard of the old Nonconformists worshipping in unfrequented parts of the hills and moors, he seems to have mistaken or exaggerated the position of Lower Chapel, which he speaks of as being on a "bleak mountain exposed to many a storm." He also says, "The Lower Chapel, often supposed by strangers to be situated in the valley, is inconveniently high on the mountain. It was called the Lower Chapel because another chapel stood a few yards higher on the ascent." Now, the ridge on the eastern side of the Darwen valley, on the breast of which stand the Higher and the Lower Chapels, cannot by any stretch of the imagination be called a "mountain," especially with the rugged heights of Darwen Moor towering on the opposite side of the valley, and tending to dwarf the lesser hill by comparison; but Dr. Halley is right about the tradition,

RUINS OF JOLLIE'S CHAPEL ON PENDLE HILL. 1668-1888.

for the Nonconformists of Darwen, Tockholes, and Haslingden, worshipped among the hills and moors of the neighbourhood during the troublous times of Charles II., and even went as far as Pendle Hill to Thomas Jollie's chapel at Wymondhouses. On page 23 of the second portion of this History, in " Jeremy Hunt's Recollections of Old Darwen Families," there is a tradition touching this point. It was first told to me by Jeremy Hunt, about the year 1882, and he had it direct from his own father, to whom it was told by " Owd Timothy o' th' Looms," 120 years ago. The old chapel is still standing, roofless, and in ruins, near the top of "Little Pendle," and not far from that miniature mountain pass, the " Nick o' Pendle," through which runs a cart road leading from Clitheroe to Sabden. It was used on Easter Sundays up to a quarter of a century ago. There was originally a stone over the doorway inscribed:—

T. I.
Luke VII. v.
1688.

This grandfather of Timothy Holden (otherwise " Owd Timothy o' th' Looms ") lived at Scotland Farm, Hoddlesden, and belonged to a branch of the Holden family, of Holden Hall, Haslingden, who migrated to Darwen between 300 and 400 years ago. The Rev. J. Horatio Johnes, pastor of the Congregational Church, Haslingden, and author of an historical pamphlet on the Nonconformity of Haslingden, furnishes me with the following story of a family tramping every Sunday from Haslingden to Darwen Chapels. They would come into Darwen over the Pickup Bank Brook along an old Saxon road forming part of the Limersgate. The story is told by Mr. J. Stott, of Springfield Lodge, Haslingden.

Henry Haworth, whose ancestry can be traced in a direct line from one Ottiwell Haworth, in the year 1625, and who was originally a " Presbyterian," resided at Sykeside (the farm now occupied by Mr. Eaton), and the house in which he lived is believed to be the first house in this locality licensed for Nonconformist worship. A stone mantelpiece in one of the rooms bears the initial letters, "T. H. A." (*i.e.*, Thomas and Alice Haworth, parents of Henry), and also the date, "1748." In Henry Haworth's early days the male portion of his household went regularly every Sabbath morning, with others like-minded, to Darwen to worship. Their route was over the fields to Flaxmoss, then along very rough and primitive roads, over Hutch Bank, through the Grane and Halley Cross. In fine weather the female portion of their household walked with them. But wet or fine, summer and winter, the men went constantly; and such was their regularity that many years later Mr. Henry Wood, a London merchant, who in his boyhood had lived at Flaxmoss, bore testimony that he could tell the time to within five minutes on a Sunday morning when he saw Henry Haworth and his company coming across the fields on their way to Darwen. My father, who resided with Henry Haworth for five or six years before his death, always spoke of him with the most profound respect as the most upright, consistent, godly man he ever knew. Every morning he assembled his household, consisting of his wife, a domestic servant, and a farm labourer or two, for family worship; and the impression made on my father's mind by observing the principles and daily conduct of his great-uncle remained with him as a powerful influence for good to the end of his days. Often have I heard my father speak, also, of the solemn scene when he was called to the bedside of the good man a day or two before his death—how he placed his hands on my father's head, gave him his blessing, and charged him so to live that he would always have God for his friend, and when he succeeded to the property to be kind to the poor. Henry Haworth died May 31, 1814, aged 67 years. He was interred inside the Parish Church, and a tile in the centre aisle bears the record, as well as a gravestone at the south-west corner of the church.

Among the two thousand divines ejected from the pulpits of the Church of England and the public schools by the Act of Uniformity in 1662, were Thomas Jollie, the founder of Wymondhouses, on Pendle Hill, and Charles Sagar (or Seagar), an early minister of Lower Chapel. Charles Sagar was the son of John Sagar, of Burnley, who at one time held the office of churchwarden at Burnley Parish Church, and the church registers there show that he was baptised in October, 1636. After being trained at Burnley Grammar School, he completed his education at St. John's College, Cambridge, where "the most religious students were his companions," and in January, 1656, received the appointment of "Schole Master" of the Blackburn Grammar School. Nonconformists were prohibited by the enactment of 1662, from holding appointments in public schools, and Sagar, though in favour with the governors, declared his Nonconformity, and voluntarily resigned his position. He received "his wage" "in full" up to the 28th of May, 1666, which was the date of his leaving, and he appears to have been temporarily engaged by the governors at subsequent dates, before his successor was appointed. Calamy says the governors "connived" with him in evading the law. For twenty years he conducted a private school for the gentry of Blackburn with marked success, and at the same time preached in secret to congregations of Nonconformists, "and especially to a congregation accustomed to meet on the hills of Darwen." A preaching license was granted to "Chas. Sagar, Pr. Teacher of Blackborne," in 1672. Sagar's "great enemy," Major Nowell, of Read, a magistrate who persecuted the Nonconformists without mercy, had him arrested in 1683, and sentenced him to six months' imprisonment in Lancaster Castle for unlawful preaching. But "during his confinement he was useful among the prisoners, and several persons also of the town, by setting up a conference on the Lord's Day. His prison comforts and improvements were very great."

On his release he resided in Blackburn, and resumed his preaching among the neighbouring moors. His first regular pastorate was not at Darwen, but at Walmsley, for in Jollie's Church Book, under the date 1687, I find the entries:—" Sagar ordained," and " Mr. and Mrs. Sagar dismissed to Walmsley." He, however, became the first pastor of the now recognised Congregational Church at Darwen under the license of King James II. (1687), and laboured with much acceptance in the old chapel at Bottoms, provided in 1688. He continued to reside in Blackburn until 1691, but the Nonconformity which had sprung up amid the seclusion of the moors of Darwen and Tockholes did not take root in Blackburn until nearly a hundred years after it had been firmly established in Darwen. Nonconformity was so strong in Bolton that that town received the appellation "The Geneva of Lancashire," but it obtained no hold in Blackburn in those early days, although Mr. Sagar, the minister of the Darwen Nonconformists, lived in the town, and was much respected. Calamy describes him as "a good scholar, very affable, blameless in conversation, and generally beloved." The Rev. Henry Newcome, of Manchester, one of the ejected ministers, writes thus in his diary, under date October 20, 1691 :—

> From Bolton lecture I went to Blackburn. Strangers, and in the night, the way was perilous, but the Lord brought us in safety. Mr. Green came in late at night. In the interim I had the company of *my old hearty friend, Mr. Sagar*. The next day we went to Ribchester, when we visited and attempted to order the Charity School there, and despatched so as I came to Hoghton Tower in good time. Mr. Sagar came to me, and there I stayed the next day in much content and freedom and hearty welcome with our old friend Sir Charles Hoghton.

Mr. Sagar married in 1663 Isabell, daughter of Henry Astley, of Blackburn, and had a son, Joshua, born on the 29th of April, 1666. This Joshua was educated for the ministry, and ordained as a Congregational minister at Wymondhouses on September 20th, 1693, by Mr. Thomas Jollie, Mr. Waddington, Mr. John Walker, and his own father. He then became pastor of the Independent Church at Alverthorpe, near Wakefield, and died there in 1710. The elder Sagar, after preaching about the moors of Darwen for twenty years, and openly as the recognised pastor of the Darwen Nonconformists for ten more, died of paralysis on February 13th, 1697, aged 61, and was buried at Blackburn Parish Church. He maintained his intimacy with Jollie to the last, for in Jollie's Church Book I find this entry:—"1696. Sept. 29, Mr. Sagar badly." A few years before his death he was a prominent member of the United Brethren—a body of Lancashire Nonconformist ministers—and held the office of scribe or secretary.

The Rev. Griffith Griffith, who, according to Jollie's Church Book, was ordained on June 24th, 1699, succeeded Mr. Sagar. He was "an earnest, affectionate, soul-stirring Welshman," whose popular preaching attracted greater numbers to the meeting-house than it could accommodate—"a man of patriarchal simplicity and general influence of character." In the year 1714, when Mr. Griffith was in the height of his popularity and power, there were only fortnightly services in the Higher Chapel, and it was reported to the Bishop of Chester that "a great many of the inhabitants frequent a Presbyterian Meeting-house there is within the chapelry those Sundays they have no service in their own chapel." Lower Chapel was reported by Dr. Evans, between 1717 and 1729, to have a congregation of 648 persons, of whom 25 were county voters. The significance of these figures is best understood by calling to mind the fact that at that time the township of Over Darwen only contained about 500 people, and that there was a newly-erected Independent Meeting-house so near as Tockholes. Mr. Griffith's congregation must have been drawn not merely from Over Darwen, Lower Darwen, and Eccleshill, but from Blackburn and Haslingden as well, to muster such a roll.

It was during the ministry of Mr. Griffith that the old Lower Chapel of 1719 was built, to succeed the barn at Bottoms. There are about twenty deeds in existence relating to the property of the church worshipping at Lower Chapel, and they are preserved in the Lancashire Independent College, to which place they were sent shortly after the formation of the Duckworth Street Church. The most important are a lease and release dated 1 and 2 January, 1718, conveying to trustees the land upon which Lower Chapel was built in the year 1719. The provisions of these were summarised in the statement of a case for the opinion of counsel in 1736, when a dispute arose, and it will be sufficient to quote the summary here.

Several Protestant Dissenters, Presbiterians, inhabiting or near the townships of Over Darwen, Lower Darwen, Eccleshill, Blackburn and Yatebank, in the County of Lancaster, did by contributions amongst themselves purchase a plot or parcel of ground in Over Darwen aforesaid, and thereupon erected a meeting house, or place for worship, which was licensed pursuant to the Act of Tolleration. This plot of ground was purchased by one John ffish, and the conveyance thereof, as also the deed declaring for what purposes the said plot of ground was purchased and the said meeting house erected, are to the following effect :—

1 and 2 January, 1718. The said John ffish by indentures of lease and release, in consideration of £5, conveys unto William Yates, Richard Saunderson, and fourteen other persons therein named, and their heirs, a plot of ground in Over Darwen aforesaid, part of the close called Clark's Field.

2 January, 1718. The said John ffish, William Yates, Richard Saunderson, and the other grantees in the said indentures of lease and release, make and execute a deed poll, whereby, after reciting the said indentures of lease and release, that the congregation of Dissenting Protestants in and about Over Darwen, Lower Darwen, Eccleshill, Blackburn, and Yatebank aforesaid, had concluded and agreed to erect an edifice, oratory, or meeting house, upon the said plot or piece of ground, for the uses therein mentioned, and had subscribed considerable sums for doing thereof, they, the said John ffish, William Yates, Richard Saunderson, &c., did thereby declare that the said plot of land was so conveyed to them, the said William Yates, Richard Saunderson, &c., their heirs and assigns, in trust, to permit the said edifice, oratory, or meeting place to be erected thereon, and, after the erecting thereof, upon trust to let, manage, and improve the same to the best yearly proffit and advantage that might be, and as they, the said trustees, and the survivors or survivor of them, should in their discretion think fit, and employ the clear yearly rents and proffits thereof, either for binding poor children apprentices, born and resident within Over Darwen, Lower Darwen, Eccleshill and Yatebank aforesaid, or some of them, to callings or trades, or for purchasing woollen or linnen cloath for such poor children, as they the said John ffish, William Yates, Richard Saunderson, &c., and the survivors or survivor of them, their and his heirs and assigns, should in their discretion think fit. And it is thereby provided, and the said deed poll is upon this further trust, that when, and so often, and so long as the laws of this realm should allow and suffer any preaching and teaching minister (such as are usually called a Protestant Dissenting minister or Presbyterian minister) to preach and teach God's word in any chapel or place within England, they, the said John ffish, William Yates, Richard Saunderson, &c., and their survivors or survivor, their and his heirs and assigns, should and would permit and suffer Mr. Griffith, then minister there, and such other said Dissenting minister as should from time to time be nominated, elected, and chosen by the trustees for the time being, or the major portion of them, and the communicants (or such as do usually partake of the sacrament of the Lord's Supper at the said meeting place) and the constant contributors to the maintenance of the ministry there, or the major part of them, for the time being, to preach and teach God's Word in the said edifice or or meeting place, and to administer the sacrament of the Lord's Supper, and exercise all other offices belonging to that sacred function therein, it being the true intent of the said deed poll and the parties thereto, and according thereby declared that when, and so often, and so long as the laws of this realm would permit and allow of such minister aforesaid, and such ministry, preaching, and teaching aforesaid, to be exercised within the the said edifice or meeting place, or within Over Darwen, Lower Darwen, Eccleshill, or Yatebank aforesaid, or any of them, that then, and so often, the trust before declared, and during the allowance and permission of such ministry, teaching, and preaching aforesaid, give place thereto and be suspended, and that when, and so often as, such ministry should not be permitted, then the other trusts should be revived and take effect, and so that order and course to be, from time to time, for ever thereafter observed. And then directs two anniversary sermons on Whitson Tuesday and the fifth day of November, and that the trustees should meet on these days for the better management of the said trust. And it is thereby further covenanted, agreed, and declared that when and so often as any of the trustees should die, that then and so often such and so many of them as should survive and be living should, with all convenient speed, elect and choose one or more able, substantial, and religious person or persons, most likely

to favour and promote the uses or trusts aforesaid, as would accept thereof, to make up the number at the least ; to the end that the charities and trusts aforesaid might be continued by the choice of new trustees, and that whensoever all the trustees but five are dead, in whom the estate in law of the said edifice or meeting place, plot of ground, and premises, should be, that then, if not sooner, the surviving trustees should with all convenient speed, convey the same to the new trustees and their heirs, to the use of the old ones and also of the new ones, and their heirs, upon the trusts aforesaid, the expense thereof to be defrayed out of the rents and proffits of the said premises. And it is thereby lastly declared and agreed that if any of the trustees for the time being should decline or withdraw him or themselves from being constant hearers at the said edifice or meeting place, and constant contributors to the said ministry there, or should or did fall into any error or vicious, sinfull practices, and should by the other trustees for the time being, or the major part of them, be publickly voted and adjudged so to be, and shall not, in due and convenient time after, join himself to the said congregation and contribute, or shall not retract his error and live his life to the satisfaction of the minister there for the time being and the said other trustees, or the major part of them, that then, in any of the cases aforesaid, the said person or persons so withdrawing, neglecting or offending should be, and is, thereby excluded and debarred from voting or acting in any of the trusts aforesaid, and should forfeit to the said other trustees all his or their right or benefit and advantages of and in the said premises and the uses and trusts thereof.

NOTE.—On the attestation of this deed poll before the witnesses subscribed their hands, it is mentioned to be agreed that Robert Yates and four other persons should be esteemed trustees, along with the trustees within-named, for the uses and trusts aforesaid, to all intents and purposes as if their names had been inscribed in the within-written deed and conveyance, and the within-mentioned premises.

Mr. Griffith married, at Manchester, in 1711, Elizabeth Coulburne, of Leyland, and had a son, Nathaniel, born in 1714. He died at Darwen in 1723, and was buried at the foot of the pulpit stairs on April 19th.

Dr. Raffles has preserved a curious anecdote of this good Welshman, which, if not true, deserves to be. It is given on the authority of one of his successors. During the time of his ministry, the black cap of the Puritan minister was going out of fashion in genteel congregations. Some of the young people of Darwen had been to Liverpool, and had seen the graceful wigs which polite ministers wore in that town. Esteeming their minister worthy of so honourable a decoration, they generously purchased one for him. The old gentleman, pleased with this mark of respect from his young friends, somewhat incautiously, without consulting the elders, appeared the next Sunday doing duty in his fashionable wig. It was a sad scandal to the elders. Was their minister conforming to the fashions of the world? Or was it a new sort of conformity with the Church? Had he appeared in a surplice they could not have been more offended. They left the place, and in the afternoon their seats were vacant. The good minister was sorely distressed. He wished to conciliate both old and young, and succeeded by appearing the next Sunday with his black cap over his wig, the graceful curls of which hung beneath it. Endeavouring to "please all men in all things," he seems to have succeeded.[1]

[1] *Lancashire Nonconformity*, vol. ii., p. 424.

After Mr. Griffith came the Rev. James Burgess, who was born near Oldham towards the end of the previous century, and educated for the Congregational ministry. He ministered for ten years at a Yorkshire village called Long Row. He married Miss Rebecca Livesey, of Clayton-le-Moors, whose mother, for her second husband, had the Rev. John Jollie, of Wymondhouses. On the appointment of Mr. Burgess, shortly after the death of Mr. Griffith, an influential section of the congregation seceded from Lower Chapel, and built a place called Yates's Chapel, for a young minister named Robert Yates, belonging to a local family. The following anecdote is given in " Peter Walkden's Diary " :—

May 18 [1725.] Went to Tockholes Chapel ; after service some of the ministers were in a parl[ey]. We understood they were consulting about the time appointed for Mr. Hesketh's ordination, and Mr Gillibrand said if they could but get Mr. Jolly into the same meaning they might undoubtedly carry it. Mr. Burgess asked Mr. Gillibrand what that was he said of Mr. Jolly. He answered Mr. Burgess to the effect above said, and much in the said words. *Mr. Burgess assured him that Mr. Jolly would not consent to these matters, to have Mr. Yates joined in,* Mr. Jolly having several objections to offer against it, at which Mr. Burgess went his way in some displeasure, and I followed, being in a mind as far from complying as Mr. Burgess ; and we came directly to Andrew Berry's, where we called, and smoked each our pipe. Then called at another of Mr. Burgess's hearers, where were several young persons who did sing psalms very well. We stayed an hour full, hearing them sing ; then came to Mr. Burgess's, where was my son's master waiting on me, with whom I went home and supped.[1]

Mr. Burgess left Darwen in 1733, and became pastor at Greenacres. He was "an evangelical and faithful preacher, who possessed some knowledge of medicine, which he made useful to his neighbours." He died at Oldham about 70 years of age. His eldest son, James, born in 1721, spent his boyhood in Darwen, was educated by Mr. Kirkpatrick, at Bedworth, and settled at Whitworth, as a Congregational minister, in 1752. This James Burgess the younger was "an extraordinary man," and a somewhat noted author of theological tracts.

The Rev. Benjamin Mather succeeded the elder Mr. Burgess as pastor of Lower Chapel, about 1736. He had been trained by the Rev. James Coningham, of Manchester, and was a man of considerable learning After ministering at Darwen for twelve years he died there, and his tombstone in the graveyard, on the south side of Lower Chapel, is inscribed as follows :—" In hoc tumulo mortalitatis suæ Exuviæ spe lactæ Resurrectionis deposuit Benjaminus Matheriis, S.T.P., hujus Ecclesiæ per annos duodecim fidelis Pastor et inter omnes Pietatis et

[1] *Peter Walkden's Diary*, p. 17.

Amicitiæ assiduos cultor. Eadem qui vixit æquanimitate sine ulto nisi cordis ad Christum suspirio animum expiravit 23 Januarii anno 1748-9, ætatis 60. Amantissimi conjugis, optimi Patris, Theologi vere Xtiani clarum reliquit posterio exemplum. Exuviæ Edwardi Matheriis hujus Ecclesiæ Pastoris Filii, nati Decembris 31, 1727, denati 19, Decembris 13, 1746."

For forty years, commencing in 1751, the pulpit at Lower Chapel was occupied by the Rev. Robt. Smalley, "the prince of the pastors of this church." He was a native of Darwen, and brother of a local chapman who was a somewhat noted musician. It was Mr. Smalley's marriage with Miss Ann Yates that brought about the reunion of the two Nonconformist congregations at Darwen Chapels, and gave rise to the enlargement and re-edification of the Lower Chapel, which was not capable of accommodating the joint congregations. The gallery was added at this period (1753). Robert Smalley was born in 1729, and educated by those illustrious Nonconformists, Dr. Doddridge and Dr. Jennings. At the age of 20, and before he had completed his college course, he received a call to Lower Chapel, where he was ordained on the 14th of August, 1751, Dr. Jennings preaching the ordination sermon. He was a man of culture, learned both in literature and science, and accustomed to associate with some of the leading men of his day, but, according to Jeremy Hunt, he was also a believer in astrology, and his belief received remarkable confirmation by the drowning of his child on the day on which he had predicted it should be drowned.[1] Fully half the population of the neighbourhood must have been attached to Lower Chapel in Mr. Smalley's days, for Dr. Percival, on Mr. Smalley's authority, wrote, in 1775—"The Rev. Mr. Smalley's congregation at Darwent consists of 1,850 individuals, viz., 900 males, 950 females, 640 married persons, 30 widowers, 48 widows, 737 persons under the age of 15, and 218 above 50. During the last seven years the births have amounted to 508, the deaths to 233." The Rev. Robert Smalley died, aged 62, on January 26th, 1791.[2] He commenced the Registers at Lower Chapel, which date from August 20, 1751. The oldest of these registers is now preserved in the archives of the Lancashire Congregational

---

[1] *Jeremy Hunt's Recollections of Old Darwen Families*, page 34.

[2] "Twenty respectable families," belonging to the town of Blackburn, had regularly attended Lower Chapel during Mr. Smalley's ministry, but, with the approval of the "mother church," they separated themselves from the flock in 1777, and built Chapel Street Church, the first Congregational place of worship in Blackburn, engaging for their pastor the Rev James Mc.Quhae, of Tockholes. Thus, the seed sown by Chas. Sagar a hundred years before, at length sprang up in the town where he had lived and laboured.

Union at Manchester.   I here transcribe the first batch of baptisms :—

Names of Parents.	Names of Children.	Place of Abode.	When Baptised.
John and Martha Ormerod	James	Darwen Chapels	August 20, 1751.
James and Ann Harwood	Genet	Darwen Chapels	August 20, 1751.
Thomas and Ann Watson	Mally	Lower Eccleshill	August 20, 1751.
Michael and Betty Briggs	Alice	Highlumole, Darwen	August 20, 1751.
James and Mary Holden	Ellen	Darwen Chapels	August 20, 1751.

There were 24 baptisms before the end of 1751; 54 in the year 1752; and 63 in the year 1800. The last entry in the old register is dated May 13th, 1829. The Rev. Thomas Davies says :[1]—"I find upon referring to the register of baptisms for 1778--that is just 100 years ago—that no fewer than 138 children were baptised in the year 1778. That represents a population of 4,000 persons, and it indicates that there were 4,000 people in this neighbourhood who regarded Lower Chapel as their spiritual or ecclesiastical home."

Richard Smalley, eldest son of the Rev. Robert Smalley, had been educated for the ministry,[2] and accustomed to take duty occasionally for his father. But his habits led the people to think that he was not suited for the ministerial calling, and a considerable section seceded and built Pole Lane Chapel when he was chosen to succeed his father in 1791. He, however, only held the post 12 months, for in 1792 the Rev. Joseph Barratt (of Manchester New College), who afterwards became well known as minister of Carter Lane Chapel, Doctors' Commons, London, was called to the place. In the year 1795, about the time Mr. Barratt resigned, the present minister's house was built. The Rev. Richard Bowden, an earnest preacher of the Gospel, succeeded Mr. Barratt in 1796, and laboured worthily at Lower Chapel until 1813. He was the son of the Rev. James Bowden, of Tooting, Surrey, and edited a volume of his father's MSS., published in 1814. On page 257 is to be found "A charge delivered [by the Rev. James Bowden] at the ordination of the Rev. Richard Bowden, August 15, 1799, from 2 Timothy ii., 15." It is from the younger Bowden's MSS., preserved in Dr. Raffles's "Collections," that Dr. Halley has drawn—overdrawn, I should say—the following picture of the of the irreligious state of Darwen :—

> During the time of doctrinal transition among the Dissenters, the pulpit was occupied by preachers who gave little prominence to their doctrine, whatever it may have been, or stayed too short a time to leave any definite impression upon the people. or, like the good man in both cap and wig, were careful to give no offence to any party. There was, however, one exception. A student from Daventry preached Unitarianism, and afterwards denied that he had preached anything of the kind. His conduct, however, became so irregular and immoral as to render his ministrations in-

1 History of Independency in Darwen, p. 12.

2 In the records of the Manchester New College there appears the following entry :—"Richard Smalley, admitted Oct. 19, 1790; left in June, 1792."

tolerable. Whether he was or was not a Unitarian, the people believed he was one, and imputed to his doctrine the scandal of his life. Amidst these changes the congregation sank into a low state of irreligion and even of immorality. While they retained some sort of connection with the old sanctuary, many of them seldom attended its religious services, and of many others it was not easy to explain the more regular attendance. They had a sort of proprietary interest in the Lower Chapel, for there were their family pews, there they were baptised, and there they claimed their burial-places, inside or outside the building. It was commonly said that if all the Lower Chapel people had gone on the same Sunday to their sanctuary they could not have found room within its walls. There was, however, little fear of such a crowd. The Rev. Richard Bowden, who was invited to be their minister in 1797, says of them :—
"Among the people were professed infidels, while the greater part were working all iniquity with greediness. Many, however, were sufficiently religious to express their approbation of earnest and faithful address when delivered from the pulpit."[1]

It is said that the Lower Chapel people, "after sitting under preachers of different sentiments," had now received in Mr. Bowden one who "in his confession of faith bore unequivocal testimony to the truth as it is in Jesus." He married Miss Nancy Catlow, of Darwen, whose untimely end is here recorded. Mr. Bowden afterwards became pastor of Holloway Chapel, London, and died there. During his residence at Darwen he laboured unceasingly amongst the neighbouring hamlets, and "exposed himself to the chilling blasts of the Lancashire moors, and not unfrequently waded through the swollen brooks with which that district is so much intersected." This laid the foundation of an illness to which he succumbed on January 20, 1829, aged 55 years. The account of Mrs. Bowden's death reads as follows :—

On the afternoon of the 21st of November, 1804, Mr. and Mrs. B., with a select company, had been on a friendly visit about two miles from home. A very heavy fall of rain, commencing soon after their arrival, constrained their stay much beyond the intended hour. They had to re-pass a brook, which during this interval the waters from the adjacent hills had unusually swollen. Mrs. B., with two ladies, her sisters, was on horseback, and, not without impressions of fears, was inclined, with cautious steps, to try the passage. The attempt, hazardous beyond her apprehension, proved fatal. The horse was unable to sustain the impetuosity of the stream. In a moment the distracted husband, now standing on the bridge for foot passengers, had the desire of his eyes, youthful, lovely, and pious, snatched from his sight, and with such distance precipitated down the flood that instantly she was no more! Not one cry of distress was heard. It was a night of agony and gloomy horror, especially as the most anxious search for the body was ineffectual till the morning, but

"God moves in a mysterious way
His wonders to perform."

Though He cause grief, yet will He have compassion, according to the multitude of His mercies.

A religious revival was the direct result of this accident. Mr. Bowden wrote in 1806 a sixpenny pamphlet published in London

[1] *Lancashire Nonconformity*, vol. ii., pp. 424-5.

entitled "A Memorial of the Power and Grace of God in the Conversion of Many Persons in the Village of Darwen, Lancashire." Referring to this pamphlet, the *Evangelical Magazine* describes it as a "more substantial and impressive" account than the one published in the previous year and quoted above, and adds :—" It seems that out of about 200 who attend a prayer meeting nearly 50 are able to exercise their gifts in prayer. . . . . There is such a vein of good sense, modesty, and seriousness in this pamphlet that our critical powers are suspended." Mr. Bowden is referred to as " the amiable writer."

The Rev. Robert Blake, who succeeded Mr. Bowden, and settled in Darwen on February 21st, 1814, had entered the ministry in 1793 at Pocklington, in Yorkshire, and afterwards served for a short period at Pickering and Shelley, in the same county, and at Ossett for six years. He was "clear-minded and evangelical," "zealous and laborious in the discharge of his ministerial duties," and "blessed with a lively soul and a healthful body." He "manifested cheerfulness and kindness towards the people, yet was always firm and fearless." He retired from the ministry in August, 1819, and in 1822, for family reasons, emigrated to America, where he became pastor of a congregation at Piermont, Grafton county, New Hampshire, in July, 1823. After 16 years' labour there, he removed to Woodburn, co. Macouri, Illinois, and in the course of three years increased the church membership there from 13 to 80. In one of his letters home he wrote :—" Often I look across the ocean and wish for a plausible errand to Darwen," but the opportunity never arose, and he died at Woodburn on the 21st of March, 1842, aged 71 years.

A scholar of no mean repute—the Rev. Robert Littler—became the next pastor of Lower Chapel. He was trained at Hoxton Academy, and displayed such ability and erudition that on the completion of his college course he was offered a professor's chair. Preferring to enter the ministry, he was ordained at Darwen, in July, 1823, but only remained there five or six years. He afterwards ministered at London, Matlock, Buxton, and Hanley.

Mr. Littler was succeeded, in November, 1829, by the Rev. Samuel Nichols, who was born at Bath on July 24th, 1797, and educated at Wymondley College under the Rev. William Parry, who ordained him at Chatford, near Stroud, on the completion of his college course. In 1823 he went to Camomile Chapel, London, but retired on account of failing health at the end of two years. He afterwards became pastor of the church at Bawtry, in Yorkshire, whence he removed to Darwen. After

19 years' labour in "that important district"—Darwen—he was stricken with paralysis, which utterly disabled him, but in a few years he recovered sufficiently to be able to preach occasionally. He retired in 1860, and spent the last 12 years of his life at Greenwich, where he died on June 15th, 1873. He was a man who "needed being known only to be loved." "His affliction was sometimes severe, but he never murmured." Mr. Nichols originated the first "Church Book" at Lower Chapel, and published an historical account of the place, compiled from the valuable manuscript collections of Dr. Raffles. I have extracted the following interesting passages :—

> The ancient Dissenting interest now connected with Lower Chapel had its origin in persecution for conscience sake. It seems that, before the year of our Lord 1688, many Protestant families from surrounding towns and villages, prevented from meeting together for the worship of God in the usual way, were accustomed to assemble in an adjoining wood, there to enjoy the means of grace in peace and quietness; but when the glorious era of the Revolution dawned, and secrecy was no longer necessary, because publicity was no longer dangerous, these good people left their retreat and jointly purchased a barn, which is still in existence as a dwelling-house. Having fitted up this humble sanctuary in as decent a manner as circumstances would allow, they invited the Rev. Charles Sager to become their pastor. . . . . Referring to the erection of Lower Chapel in 1719, Mr. Nichols says :—It is recorded that without calling in the aid of any extra labourer, they all set themselves to work, minister and people, men, women, and children, some using the barrow, some the spade, some the trowel, some the spade, some the trowel, some the hammer, till in a very short time the building was erected, free from debt. . . . .In the year 1777, a friendly separation of 20 respectable families residing in Blackburn took place, and thus commenced the present Independent interest in that town.

On March 6th, 1849, the Rev. R. P. Clarke, of Western College, was ordained pastor of Lower Chapel; the Rev. R. Fletcher, of Manchester (formerly of Ebenezer Chapel, Darwen), delivering the introductory discourse to a crowded congregation. During his ministry a division took place, the minister and major portion of the congregation removing to Duckworth Street, where they built a new chapel in 1853. The small section which remained on the hill-side had the chapel partially taken down, the foundations made firm, and the fabric rebuilt of the old materials. It was a hundred years since much attention had been paid to the fabric, and this extensive renovation was what it really needed. The mullioned windows were enlarged and increased in number, a new east frontage was put in, and the building, thoroughly restored, was re-opened on the 10th of July, 1853—nearly three weeks after the formal opening of the new Duckworth Street Chapel.

Mr. Clarke having gone to Duckworth Street, the Rev. George Berry was engaged to succeed him at Lower Chapel. George Berry

LOWER CHAPEL DARWEN, A.D. 1719.

was born at Ingleton, on January 23rd, 1811. He was the son of a yeoman who trained his children in the principles of the Church of England, and George became a candidate for confirmation. It is recorded that "whilst the Bishop was pronouncing the usual formula, some doubts arose in George's mind as to the scripturalness of the rite in which he was taking so solemn a part," and immediately afterwards "he became from conviction a Dissenter from the Established Church, and joined the Independent Church meeting in High Street, Lancaster." In order to attend the services at this chapel, he had to walk a distance of 14 miles every Sunday. In June, 1839, he became the minister of the Congregational Church, Inglewhite, and in 1844 he removed to Mount Zion Chapel, Gisburne, where he was ordained on the 26th of June. He remained there ten years, preached three times every Sunday, and regularly visited the surrounding villages and hamlets, some of which were ten miles distant from his house. In March, 1854, he received a call to the pastorate of Lower Chapel, where he laboured 23 years, preaching his final sermon on August 23rd, 1877. He continued to reside at Chapels—"a place, which to him, was undoubtedly the most precious spot on earth"—and accepted occasional preaching engagements until his death, on the 18th of November, 1885. He was interred at the Darwen Cemetery.

The Rev. W. C. Talbot, an Airedale student, came to Lower Chapel in 1878, but is now at Wimbledon. He was succeeded at Darwen on March 31st, 1881, by the Rev. Richard Nicholls, the present pastor, who was trained at Richmond, and has held pastorates at Horwich and Bacup.

The oldest portion of the present Lower Chapel was built on a cornfield that was tilled by "Owd Timothy o' th' Looms.[1] Having purchased the land, the Nonconformists, led by their minister, the Rev. Griffith Griffith, built a new sanctuary with their own hands. Minister and people, men, women and children all lent a helping hand. Old Timothy, who was a corn-grower, a handloom weaver, and a schoolmaster all rolled into one, lent his cart to cart stones on the land which had hitherto been his cornfield; other residents lent their barrows and their spades, carpenters brought their own tools and worked with them, without expecting or receiving pay, and the chapel was built so substantially by the amateur builders of the congregation that it has stood to the present day, although three times restored and enlarged. Labour and material having been given, and tools and implements lent, the actual cost of the chapel in cash was not very great, and it was opened

[1] *Jeremy Hunt's Recollections*, pp. 25-6.

in 1719 free from debt. It stands with a frontage to a street called
"Chapels," bearing four date stones, namely, "1719," "1753," "1853,"
and "1883." The back portion, surmounted by its peculiar belfry, is
the oldest portion of the structure. This part of the chapel is built of
thick walls, consisting of small stones laid in irregular courses. The east
end, with its porch, is modern, as is plain to be seen. The chapel, an
adaptation to ecclesiastical uses of 16th century domestic architecture,
is lighted by ordinary mullioned windows, and the principal feature of
its exterior is the stone belfry crowning the west gable, formed
of short pillars, and surmounted with stone balls. The windows were
enlarged in 1853, and their number was increased. The chapel stands in a
well-filled graveyard, with the houses of "Chapels" adjoining it on the
north and south, and a low iron railing close to the porch, dividing
it from the street on the east. The land on the west end of the chapel,
which is lying in waste, slopes rapidly down to the valley of the river
Darwen, which is 200ft. or 300ft. below. The interior of the chapel is
furnished with modern wooden benches, introduced in 1875 to
replace the old high-packed pews, but there is one old square pew
preserved, bearing the initials "L.W.I." and the date "1704." This
was brought from the old chapel at Bottoms in 1719. The pulpit is on
the northern side of the edifice, with the organ in an apse on its right.
There are several inscribed gravestones in the floor near the pulpit and
communion, there having been a custom in olden times to bury the
ministers and prominent members of the church within the sanctuary.
This custom originated, so far as the Lower Chapel is concerned, with
the Rev. Griffith Griffith. The chapel contains 1,000 sittings.

In 1829, the Lower Chapel had 51 members; in December, 1848,
106; in December, 1851, 137. In December, 1852, the church, now
transferred temporarily to Belgrave Schools, had 136 members; and in
June, 1854, the membership of the church at Duckworth Street was 131.
A new society was formed at Lower Chapel upon the removal of the
church to Duckworth Street in 1852, and this was received into the
Lancashire Congregational Union in 1856.

There was a school connected with Lower Chapel in the Rev.
Robert Smalley's days. A new school, to accommodate 300 children,
was erected in 1883 at a cost of £1,055, and opened by the pastor on
December 8th.

YATES'S CHAPEL.

In the history of Lower Chapel reference has been made to the
building of Yates's Chapel on an adjacent plot of land about the year
1723. An influential party seceded from Lower Chapel on the

appointment of Mr. Burgess to succeed Mr. Griffith, having been unsuccessful in their attempt to appoint to the vacant post Mr. Robert Yates, of Pickup Bank, who had been educated for the ministry at Glasgow. "Yates's Chapel," which these seceders built, somewhat resembled in external appearance the old Lower Chapel. It is now converted into four dwelling-houses. Viewed from the croft in the rear, that is at the west end, it still exhibits one or two architectural features, such as the balls of stone on the roof, similar to those of Lower Chapel. In this building Mr. Yates laboured until his death. On the removal of Mr. Mather in 1733 the congregation at Yates's Chapel desired to return to the Lower Chapel and instal Mr. Yates as their pastor, but, though now very numerous and powerful, they had given up all their rights in the management of the affairs of Lower Chapel, and were unable to do anything. Accordingly, after a three years' vacancy, the Rev. Benjamin Mather was chosen to occupy the pulpit, and Yates's Chapel was continued as a separate church. A legal document, dated Nov. 22, 1736, gives some interesting facts concerning the position of the contending parties. After reciting the conditions of the trust, already quoted, it proceeds :—

Mr. Griffith continued minister of this [Lower] Chapell or meeting house from the erection thereof untill about thirteen years ago, when he died, and thereupon a dispute arose amongst the trustees about the election of a succeeding minister. One Mr. Burgess was a candidate, and ten of the trustees were for him and also the majority of the communicants and contributors, but the other eleven trustees (there being then only twenty-one in number) were against him, and did not appear for him, so that he had not a majority of the trustees. However, Mr. Burgess got into possession of the meeting house, and has officiated there ever since. This raised uneasiness, and the trustees that opposed Mr. Burgess's election built another meeting house in the same close of land with the former, and withdrew themselves and their contributions from the old one, and very seldom, or never, went thither to hear divine service, but on very extraordinary occasions. However, the other trustees have not had any public meeting, passed any vote or resolution, whereby to exclude them from being trustees pursuant to the last clause in the deed poll. There are now living eight of the trustees that opposed Mr. Burgess's election, to wit five that were named in the conveyances from John ffish, and three that are only named in the attestation or endorsement upon the deed poll, and there are only now four living that favoured Mr. Burgess's election. There is another trustee that is become insolvent and gone beyond seas, and also another that is disordered in his senses and not capable of transacting any business. The trustees that favoured Mr Burgess's election have since that time had the direction of the first meeting house, but have now quarrelled with Mr. Burgess, and have obliged him to quit or resign his place of minister there, so that there is a vacancy, and a new minister is to be elected. But those trustees who are only four in number now insist that the other trustees that withdrew themselves and built the new meeting house (though now the major part) have by withdrawing themselves and their contributions forfeited their right of being trustees, and have no votes in the election of a new minister to fill up the present vacancy. The eight surviving trustees that opposed Mr. Burgess's election have chosen Mr. Robert Yates to be minister to supply the present vacancy, and the other four trustees have chosen Mr. Mather.

Here follows six queries put by the solicitor acting for the eight trustees and answered by counsel. The eight trustees, now attached to Yates's Chapel, wanted to know "how to proceed." "so as to regain possession of the said old meeting house," &c., and sought counsel's opinion on the various questions arising out of the case stated. Counsel's opinion is given on the six queries, and in reply to the crucial question, how to regain possession of the Lower Chapel, he says :—"Their proper method of relief would be by a bill in the Court of Chancery, but this seems to be a matter much fitter to be accommodated in an amicable way than brought into a court of justice."

The two chapels were continued side by side for eight years longer, no agreement having been arrived at for coalition, but on the death of Mr. Yates, in 1748, a happy event re-united the two congregations and caused Yates's Chapel to be converted to secular uses. This auspicious occurrence was the marriage of the Rev. Robert Smalley, who succeeded Mr. Mather at Lower Chapel, to Miss Ann Yates, a sister, or, at any rate, a near kinswoman of the Rev. Robert Yates.

POLE LANE, EBENEZER, AND BELGRAVE CHAPELS.

Belgrave Chapel, which stands in the centre of Darwen, represents the oldest living branch of the Lower Chapel. Though Mr. and Mrs. Smalley, who were noted for their virtues, succeeded in healing up the first real breach in the Congregational Church of Darwen, their son Richard, "a rollicking young gentleman," was the cause of a second secession, which occurred in 1792. An appeal for support which the seceders issued was "commended" to Nonconformists generally by four neighbouring ministers—the Revs. John Hughes, of Bury; George Watson, of Horwich; Thomas Whiteley, of Tockholes : and James Mc.Quhae, of Blackburn. It was set forth that 70 or 80 families had been compelled by the "most important motives" to withdraw from joining in public worship with their former brethren at the usual place, that they had resolved to erect a new place of worship and had subscribed £160 for that purpose, but that £200 more would be required. The appellants further say—"We are not prompted by malevolence, or a spirit of faction," but "we desire a faithful and evangelical preacher who may deliver, *in substance*, the same important doctrines to which we have been accustomed." Jeremy Hunt's father was one of the seceders of this period. They built Pole Lane Chapel, the graveyard of which still remains, although the little chapel, having been succeeded by larger and more convenient structures has not one stone left upon another. Some of the graves were dug up when the church removed to the centre of Darwen, and the bodies were carried thither, and only half a dozen tombstones now remain in the deserted and dismantled burial ground, Some account of these has been given in a previous chapter.[1] Pole Lane Chapel was opened on the 6th of May, 1793, with the Rev. Henry Townsend, of Cockermouth, as its pastor. In 1806 Mr. Townsend resigned, and with the assistance of his followers built a new chapel at the bottom of Bolton Road, called "Townsend's Chapel," or "The Refuge." This was a plain, small, rectangular edifice, without galleries. and was opened in 1808. Mr. Townsend did not long remain in the chapel which his adherents had built for him, but retired from the ministry. Both chapels, however, continued to be used until 1822, when the two congregations, being without minister, amalgamated, and decided to build a new and commodious church. Mr. Townsend's chapel was selected as the having the most suitable site, and after it had been enlarged and improved, it was re-named Ebenezer Chapel. It was opened in 1822, during the ministry of the Rev. Richard Fletcher, and the Pole Lane Chapel was abandoned. It occupied the site where the the Belgrave Schools now stand. Owing to the rapid increase of the congregation, it was decided to build a new chapel on an adjacent plot of land, at a cost of £8,000. This edifice, called the Belgrave Meeting House, was opened by Dr. Raffles in 1847, and it has ever since been one of the most important places of worship in the town. Its architecture is early English in style, and of a good type for modern work. The main feature of its exterior is the pinnacled, gabled, and arcaded "screen" which stands above the roof between the principal porch and the nave. In the interior it is surrounded with galleries, and contains 1120 sittings. The plan comprises nave, side aisles, east transept, and chancel apse. An organ, built by Messrs. W. Hill and Son, was placed in the chapel in 1880, at a cost of £1200. In 1886, Mr. Jeremy Hunt, a life-long official of the Pole Lane, Ebenezer, and Belgrave Chapels, presented to the church at Belgrave a list of ministers of the successive chapels, sampler-worked by his own hand, and completed on his 80th birthday. He furnished all the names and dates from memory,

[1] See *ante*, pp. 28-9.

having known everyone of the ministers personally. The "record" is as follows:—

A RECORD of the MINISTERS

OF

Pole Lane, Ebenezer, and Belgrave Chapels,

DARWEN.

POLE LANE CHAPEL, OPENED MAY 6, 1793.

First Minister:

Rev. Henry Townsend,
FROM SEPTEMBER, 1793, TO AUGUST, 1806.

Rev. William Hacking,
FROM SEPTEMBER, 1807, TO DECEMBER, 1821.

EBENEZER CHAPEL, OPENED SEPTEMBER 24, 1822.

Rev. Richard Fletcher,
FROM AUGUST, 1823, TO APRIL, 1831.

Rev. Joseph Hague,
FROM OCTOBER, 1831, TO AUGUST, 1835.

Rev. S. T. Porter,
FROM AUGUST, 1836, TO AUGUST, 1848.

BELGRAVE CHAPEL, OPENED OCTOBER 21, 1847.

Rev. G. B. Johnson,
FROM MAY, 1849, TO OCTOBER 1857.

Rev. David Herbert, M.A.,
FROM OCTOBER 1858, TO SEPTEMBER, 1865.

Rev. James Mc.Dougall,
FROM AUGUST, 1866, TO MAY, 1880.

Rev. Henry Irving,
FROM OCTOBER, 1881, TO THE PRESENT TIME.

THE WORK OF JEREMY HUNT, AGED 80 YEARS, FEBRUARY 27, 1886.

The Rev. James Mc.Dougall, who preached his farewell sermon in Darwen (at Bolton-road School) on September 29th, 1880, was recognised, on the 26th of the following month, as pastor of the Broughton Congregational Church, Manchester, where he still labours. The splendid schools attached to the Belgrave Chapel contain a Great Hall and a Lecture Room, the former being furnished with an organ.

They were opened on November 8th, 1879, with an Art Treasures Exhibition, attended by upwards of 40,000 persons. The smaller schools which preceded them were founded in 1867. A mission school is attached to this church at Blacksnape, having been built in 1823, chiefly through the exertions of John Harwood.

BOLTON ROAD CONGREGATIONAL CHURCH.—Spacious branch schools were built by the Belgrave Church at the upper end of Bolton Road near the southern extremity of the town, in 1867, at a cost of £2,000. A meeting was held here on June 6th, 1883, to form a separate and independent Congregational Church. The Revs. Henry Irving, and W. C. Russell, M.A., of Darwen; the Rev. A. Foster, M.A., secretary of the Blackburn District of the Lancashire Congregational Union; and Mr. R. S. Ashton, B.A., J.P., took part in the proceedings. The Rev. W. Lloyd Robinson, formerly of Chudleigh, South Devon, became the first pastor, and was publicly recognised on March 12th, 1884. The place contains accommodation for 500 worshippers.

DUCKWORTH STREET CONGREGATIONAL CHURCH.

The church worshipping in Duckworth Street can establish its position as the oldest Congregational Church in Darwen, and the direct representative of the body which founded Lower Chapel in 1719. In 1851 the church and congregation of Lower Chapel were engaged in preparing for an extension of their work, with the view of supplying the needs of the people in the valley where the population was growing rapidly. Sums of money had been collected in the chapel and the Sunday school towards this object, and the preparations were proceeding rapidly when, one Sunday morning, it was found that, owing to a subsidence of the foundation of Lower Chapel, the fabric was seriously injured. The doors were awry, large portions of plaster had fallen down, and the walls were cracked. Nine-tenths of the people believed that the subsidence was due to the existence of coal mines underneath, but it has since been disputed that any coal was ever taken from beneath Lower Chapel. There was general consternation at this accident, and at a church meeting held on Sunday, February 22nd, 1852, it was resolved—"That the pastor seek to obtain the Belgrave Lecture-room or Assembly-room for worship, for three or four Sabbaths, on account of the dangerous condition of our chapel." This room having been obtained it was used for service, not merely for "three or four Sabbaths," but for sixteen months, for the scheme of church extension so long talked about was suddenly developed into a resolution to build a new chapel nearer the centre of the population. Only five days after the alarming subsidence of the ground beneath the old chapel a church meeting was held in the Lower William Street School (Feb. 27th, 1852), when it was resolved—(1.) "That the pew-holders and church and new chapel subscribers meet on Monday evening, and that the church determines, by God's help, in union with the congregation, to erect a new chapel." (2.) "That the thanks of the church be presented to the church meeting in Belgrave Chapel for the kind accommodation offered to them." At this early stage some disagreement arose. Most of the church members and congregation were sincerely attached to the temple of their forefathers, and while, as a body, they resolved to build their new chapel in the centre of the town, a fear arose among some of them that the old chapel would be deserted altogether. To dispel this a church meeting was held in Belgrave Lecture-room on Sunday, March 14th, 1852, at which the following resolution was passed unanimously:—"That this church hereby expresses its intention by no means to neglect the spiritual interests of Darwen Chapels, and resolves, as soon as practicable, to commence a district Sabbath school, and to employ other means for the good of the inhabitants; also, with the concurrence of the congregation, that the interest of the old chapel and the new one, when erected, shall be one, and that the graveyard shall be the graveyard of the congregation of the new place; and, also, that the trustees be requested to appropriate any moneys that may arise from the sale of anything on or about the place to the purchase of more graveyard and to the repair of the graveyard walls, &c."

About this time there gathered, chiefly around the grave-digger, who was also a trustee and chapel keeper (named Shorrock), a number of dissentients, who resisted by every means in their power the general purpose of the church and congregation of leaving the old chapel and building a new one. Only from seven to twelve of the church members joined this dissentient party, and at that time the membership numbered 137. The minister, all the office bearers, and the great majority of the church members, had decided to build a new church in Duckworth Street, to succeed the old fabric, which they considered to be unfit for further use. Numerous scandals arose out of the division in the church, chiefly in relation to burials. Finding the old sexton quite unmanageable, the church exercised its assumed right to dismiss him and appointed a new sexton in his place, but Mr. Shorrock would not be dismissed, and he was supported generally by the residents in Chapels, including the congregation of St. James's Church. A grave was dug in the old graveyard of Lower Chapel for the first funeral, but on the arrival of the funeral, it was found to have been filled up. A scene was then witnessed which caused a great scandal. As fast as one sexton shovelled earth out of the grave the other sexton shovelled it in. This was continued until nightfall, when it was arranged that the body should be taken into the chapel and left there. For sixteen nights the corpse remained in the chapel, guarded by a body of Churchmen attached to St. James's, who were supplied with bread and cheese and beer, and engaged to watch the coffin in order that it might not be buried secretly. One night the hamlet was aroused by the ringing of St. James's Church bell, and the inhabitants flocked to the scene from every corner of the town. A pitched battle ensued. A woman named Margaret Hutchinson, who is still living (1887), caught hold of a notorious prize-fighter of that day and demanded to know his business. He said they had made up their minds to bury the child, to which she replied by throwing him against a tombstone with such force that he was compelled to retire. Worn out by watching, the "garrison" succumbed to fatigue on the evening of the seventeenth day, and the child was buried in the dead of the night without any service whatever. Before daylight, however, the coffin had been disinterred and the grave refilled with earth. The coffin was propped on end on the graveyard wall and left there. It was eventually taken away and buried in the Primitive Methodist burial ground, Redearth Road. The Chapels section after this got their own way so far as to retain possession of the Lower Chapel, which they put in a good state of repair and used for worship under a new pastor, the Rev. George Berry. But the church at Duckworth Street was recognised as the continuation of the Lower Chapel church, and it was not until 1856 that the section remaining at Lower Chapel was received into the Lancashire Congregational Union as a new church. In the Lancashire Congregational Calendar both Lower Chapel and Duckworth Street Chapel give 1687 as the date when their "church" was formed. At a church meeting, held in Duckworth Street School, on Sunday, February 17th, 1856, the pastor stated that the church at Lower Chapel stood proposed to come into the county Union at the next annual meeting, and the Duckworth Street Church, "deeming it advisable that certain matters connected with the foundation of that church, and with the conduct of some of its members, should be inquired into," resolved unanimously "that Messrs. Thomas Eccles, of Lower Darwen, and William Hoole, of Blackburn, be requested to represent this church in the Committee of Investigation, with the view of healing existing differences, and that Messrs. John Pickup, Andrew Eccles, James Eccles, and the pastor, be deputed to express the feelings of this church in the matter referred to above." Both churches being now amicably disposed to each other, the points in dispute between them were settled, and the two churches became united in Christian brotherhood. The Committee of Investigation referred to in the above resolution consisted of the Rev. A. Fraser, M.A., of Blackburn; Mr. G. B. Johnson, of Darwen; Mr. Thomas Eccles, of Lower Darwen; and Mr. William Hoole, of Blackburn, and they eventually adopted unanimously a resolution in these terms:—" That from the statements laid before us this evening it is manifest that some irregularities have been connected with the formation and growth of the church at Lower Chapel, but from the feeling that has been shown on each side we confidently hope that fraternal services of some kind may be held in Lower Chapel in recognition of the church existing there, and we heartily join in recommending that such services should be held as soon as practicable."

On Monday, July 28th, 1852, the foundation-stone of the new chapel, in Duckworth-street, was laid by Charles Potter, Esq. The prayer was offered by the pastor, and the address was given by the Rev. Samuel Martin, of Westminister Chapel, London. Meetings were held in the evening in the Belgrave Schools. In the words of the Rev. R. P. Clarke, "the services were most delightful and refreshing." The new chapel, which cost £4,000, was opened on Thursday, June 23rd, 1853. The Rev. T. Raffles, D.D., LL.D., from Liverpool, preached in the morning, and the Rev. Newman Hall, B.A., of Hull, in the evening. On the following Sunday, the Rev. James Baldwin-Brown, B.A., of London, preached in the morning, and in the evening the Rev. John Lyeth-Feaston, of Wotton-under-Edge. The congregations were large, and the collections amounted to £358 14s. Again the Church Book records—" The services were delightful; to the pastor of the church they were times of refreshing." At first the Sunday school connected with the Duckworth Street Church was in the gallery of the chapel, but at Christmas, 1853, the teachers and scholars requested the church to erect a new school, and in the following February the church decided to build a school at once, This cost £2,000, and a manse was provided at a cost of £1,200. In 1868 the church had to be restored, as it was built of stone which did not stand the atmosphere. Longridge stone was used in the exterior restoration, a new roof was put on the building, vestries were added, and an organ was erected in the chancel. The church is of a decorated design, in the 14th century style of gothic architecture, with a handsome arcaded porch in the west front, facing Duckworth Street. There is no tower, but a lofty pinnacle on the high-pitched gable of the nave. The nave, aisles, and three galleries contain seats for 1110 worshippers. The chapel was renovated in 1877. Splendid new schools were built in 1883-4, the foundation-stone being laid on May 26th, 1883, by James Hunt Eccles, a gentleman nearly 90 years of age. The schools are in the gothic style of architecture, well-arranged and lighted, and they provide accommodation for over 1,000 scholars. The cost was £4,800, towards which Mr. Joseph Eccles, J.P., contributed £400. Mr. Joseph Eccles opened the building on the 11th April, 1884.

The Rev. R. P. Clarke, first minister of the church in Duckworth Street, left Darwen for Uxbridge in 1859, and next year the Rev. Thomas Davies was called to the pastorate. He retired in August, 1880, after 46 years' service in the Congregational ministry, including upwards of 20 years at this church; and the present pastor, the Rev. W. C. Russell, M.A., succeeded him in November, 1881. Mr. Russell is a graduate of Aberdeen (1866), and a student in theology of the Lancashire Independent College, Manchester, where he spent five years as a tutor.

HOLLINS GROVE CONGREGATIONAL CHURCH.—A branch of Duckworth Street was established at Hollins Grove, the northern extremity of Over Darwen, about the year 1876. The Rev. M. Braithwaite, of Barrow-in-Furness, became the first pastor of the church formed here, and entered on his ministry on March 13th, 1881. In the following month contracts were let for the erection of a new chapel and school, the foundation-stone of which was laid on May 7th, the same year. The building, which contains 460 sittings, cost £3,300, and was opened on April 7th, 1882. It has a fine frontage to Blackburn-road. In the following November Mr. Braithwaite died suddenly from apoplexy, a few hours after having delivered a lecture in the Co-operative Hall. In November, 1883, the independence of the Hollins Grove Church was recognised. It had hitherto been a branch of the Duckworth Street Church, but was now considered able to take care of itself. The Rev. J. Ernest James, a student of the Lancashire Independent College, was ordained minister here on the 5th of the following month. Present pastor, the Rev. Jenkin Jones.

CONGREGATIONALISM AT PICKUP BANK, BELTHORN, AND LOWER DARWEN.

The Independent School at Pickup Bank was erected in 1835 chiefly through the exertions of Mr. Jeremy Hunt.[1] An Independent Church was founded there in 1860. The Rev. Joseph Clyde was

1 *Jeremy Hunt's Recollections*, pp. 9-10.

resident minister for twenty years, until his death in 1886. Sittings, 300. Present pastor, the Rev. Henry Ogle, formerly minister of the Baptist Church, Darwen.

Belthorn Independent Church (in the township of Yate Bank), was formed in 1858, and a school chapel was built in 1878 at a cost of £1,140. This was succeeded by a new edifice, erected in 1885 at a cost of £2,000. There is a manse connected with the place which cost £800. Pastor, the Rev. E. Apperley. Sittings, 500.

Messrs. R. and T. Eccles, cotton manufacturers, Lower Darwen, built a "village school" near their mill in the centre of Lower Darwen, Darwen, and in 1872 a Congregational Church was formed in connection with it. A new gothic chapel between Lower Darwen and Golden Cup was built in 1885, providing accommodation for 280 worshippers, at a cost of £1,800. Pastor, the Rev. A. A. Dauncey.

METHODISM IN DARWEN.

A private house at Top o' th' Coal Pits, Lower Darwen, where a class was formed in 1758, was the place where the "first approach towards any Methodistical organisation in this part of Lancashire" was made. It arose from the preaching of John Nelson, the Yorkshire stonemason, whose first converts at Lower Darwen were a farmer named John Haworth and three of his brothers. James Oddie, another of the first Methodist preachers, who followed Nelson on this ground, formed the scattered converts into a class. The first leader was James Clegg, but subsequently Mr. Haworth was the class-leader until his death in 1811. Mr. Haworth's son, William, entered the ministry and laboured for nearly 50 years. John Wesley passed through Darwen twice on his travels between Bolton and Lancaster. He preached at Lower Darwen in May, 1759, as recorded in his diary. "Wednesday, 9. In the evening I preached at Bolton, and on Friday, 11, about nine, at Lower-Darwent, a small village near Blackburn."[1] Two years later he paid a second visit to this "small village," for on April 16th, 1761, he recorded in his diary, "After preaching at noon I rode to Lower Darwen, near Blackburn, where a large congregation behaved with deep seriousness." Harwood Barn, bearing the date 1691, and the initials W. H. M., is said to have been the place where Wesley preached.

Mr. William Banning, of Blackburn, preached regularly on Darwen Green (Over Darwen) between 1785 and 1788; and a preaching place was afterwards engaged over a blacksmith's shop in Wellington Fold, occupied by Thomas Ainsworth. In 1788 a room at

[1] *Wesley's Journal*, vol. ii., p. 455.

the bottom of Water Street was rented and furnished as a place of worship and Sunday School. The Sunday School was opened in 1789 with 100 scholars, and the attendance increased so rapidly that in 1790 the room was found to be too small for them, and the society purchased from Mr. James Greenway a plot of land in Back Lane, upon which they erected their first chapel in 1790 at a cost of £1,000. Mr. Wesley visited this chapel in the 86th year of his age, and probably preached there.[1] Mr. Greenway gave a subscription to the building fund, but it is said that "the opposition to Methodism was so strong that no masons in the town would touch the chapel, and that workmen had to be obtained from Preston to build it." An enlargement of this edifice was made in 1839 at a cost of £2,500, with a frontage to Belgrave Square. This "Centenary Chapel," as it was called, was reconstructed at a cost of £1,000, and given up to day and Sunday School purposes in 1866, when the noble classic structure in Railway Road, called the "Wesley Chapel," was opened. This handsome sanctuary cost £7,750, and it contains 1,250 sittings. The principal features of its exterior are the massive corinthian columns supporting a bold entablature, surmounted by a sculptured pediment.

A small Methodist Society was formed in Over Darwen about 1785, and the members were pelted with stones and rotten eggs by their persecutors on their way to the meetings at Blackburn. Mr. Ralph Entwistle, of Sough, had entertained John Wesley on his journeys through Darwen from Bolton to Blackburn, and he joined the Methodist Society formed by William Greenwood, tailor, William Crook, tailor, and Richard Cross, shoemaker. Burgoin Fish was one of their earliest and most noteworthy converts. He joined the Society in 1788. A pamphlet was published in Halifax in 1848, entitled "The Power of Divine Grace, as illustrated in the Conversion, Consistent Life, and Peaceful Death of Burgoin Fish, of Waterside [Glossop], late of Darwen. (By his Class-Leader.)" It relates that Burgoin was born at Darwen Chapels, in May, 1766, and that he grew up a strong athletic young fellow and a notorious prize-fighter. At the age of 22 he was going to fight the champion of Turton, at Turton Fair, when "the Lord arrested him by the way as he did Saul of Tarsus. . . . . as sudden as the lightning's flash." At that time (1788) the Methodists were few in Darwen and much persecuted, Burgoin being one of their persecutors, but immediately after his conversion he went to the Methodist meeting in Water Street and joined the class. The "rage of persecution" in

[1] Ward's *Methodism in Blackburn*, pp. 27-8.

Darwen was stopped, Burgoin being now a stout defender of the new sect.[1] He removed to Waterside in the Glossop circuit in 1837, and died there in the 81st year of his age, having been for 59 years an earnest and consistent member of the Wesleyan Society. In 1809 Giles Haworth was the class leader at Lower Darwen, and the names of four other members are on record. There were at that time 70 members of the Society in Over Darwen, the leaders being William Greenwood, Joseph Whittaker, John Entwistle, James Smith, and Burgoyne Fish.

The Blackburn Circuit was separated from Colne in 1787, and in the record of the Quarterly Meeting held at Haslingden on January 8th, 1788, there is an entry of 3s. received from Pickabank [Pickup Bank], where a Methodist society evidently existed. Meetings were held in a house at Oakenhurst, Lower Darwen, about this time. Black Snape is found in the Circuit Book under the date July, 1789; Darwen in 1790; Grimshaw Bridge in 1804; New Row in 1815; Lower Darwen in 1819; New Field and Waterside in 1827; Bellthorn in 1830; and Hoddleston in 1859. Each of these entries indicates that Methodism had an "agency" at the place named.[2] In 1830 Bellthorn was received on the plan; in 1831 Newfield. Guide was taken on in 1837; Lower Darwen discontinued in 1851. Huddleston was taken on in 1859. June, 1862, "Out-door service to be held at Lower Darwen;" December, 1863, "Evening service discontinued at Lower Darwen;" September, 1869, "Darwen branch school taken on;" June, 1873, "Astley Street, Darwen Ragged School, taken on;" December, 1873, "Hoddlesden to be taken on if a suitable place be found." These extracts from the Local Preachers' Minute Book indicate the nature and extent of Methodist enterprise in the neighbourhood of Darwen.

The modern Blackburn-Darwen circuit (formed out of the Blackburn circuit in 1878) comprises chapels in Railway Road, Bolton Road, and Hoddlesden (all in Over Darwen), at New Row (in Lower Darwen), and at Witton (Blackburn). *New Row:* The New Row chapel, which stands on the borders of Lower Darwen and Livesey, was built in 1828, and it has superseded the original meeting-houses of Top o' th' Coal Pits and Lower Darwen village. Galleries were added about 1860, and there is sitting accommodation for about 400 people. New Row was formerly joined with Tockholes, and the society there existed in 1805. In 1816 the New Row society was distinct from that at Tockholes. The building of the new chapel arose out of a religious evival in 1828, and it is said that the edifice was used for Sunday school purposes forty-two days after the laying of the foundation-stone. The land

---

[1] *Jeremy Hunt's Recollections* p. 127.   [2] *Clayton Street Centenary Volume*, p. 54.

and stone were given by Mr. William Turner.—*Bolton Road:* Bolton Road school-chapel was built by the Over Darwen society in 1880-1 at a cost of £1,000, and opened on April 15th of the latter year. It contains 400 sittings. This place succeeded the Astley Street school, taken by the Wesleyans from the Congregationalists about 1869. —*Hoddlesden:* At Hoddlesden the Wesleyans have a school-chapel that was built by the Primitive Methodists in 1879. Cost, £450; sittings, 250. They for some years temporarily occupied the Old Workhouse as a mission room, and at the present time they contemplate building a new chapel at Hollins Grove.

PRIMITIVE METHODIST CHAPELS.—The Primitive Methodist Connexion has four chapels in Darwen. A society of Primitive Methodists was formed at a temporary meeting-place in Winter Street, Over Darwen, in 1825, and in 1832 this community built a chapel in Redearth Road. A burial ground, adjacent, was used for interments until the year 1859. The original chapel was enlarged and had schools added, but in 1875 the premises were found to be inadequate for the accommodation of the increasing congregation, and it was resolved to erect a new building on an adjoining plot of ground. The new chapel and schools in Redearth Road, which had been three years in building, were opened on Good Friday, 1878. The structure is of stone, in the gothic style of architecture, and the chapel provides accommodation for 720 worshippers. Towards the total cost of £4,000, £1,300 had been contributed prior to the opening ceremony.—*Sandhills:* A branch school-chapel was built by the Primitive Methodists at Sandhills in 1869 at a cost of £300, its sitting accommodation being for 200 persons.—*Sough:* A similar school-chapel was built in the hamlet of Sough in 1874, and opened on September 5th. Cost, £350; sittings, 200. Mr. John Muncaster, who died in 1881, left a legacy of £200 to this place, and a new chapel was built shortly afterwards, opened on January 20th, 1884. Its cost was £670, and it provided seats for 200 people.—*Lower Darwen:* At Lower Darwen the Primitive Methodists have had a chapel containing 300 sittings since 1873. This building was originally erected by the Wesleyan Association, and afterwards used by the United Methodist Free Church.—*Hoddlesden:* A Primitive Methodist mission was commenced in Hoddlesden in 1874, and in 1879 a new school-chapel was built and opened. This chapel has since been conveyed to the Wesleyan Methodists.

On August 7th, 1873, the Rev. James Crompton, Primitive Methodist minister, residing in Over Darwen, and Mr. John Haworth, local preacher, of Blackburn, were summoned for obstructing the footpath and highway, at the bottom of Railway Road and Bridge Street, and the highway from Railway Road to the Big Lamp on the Cross. It was customary to hold a camp meeting here on Sundays and to go through the streets six deep singing hymns. One of the witnesses, Mr. John Muncaster, said he had lived in Darwen nearly 38 years, and the Primitive Methodists had held annual services similar to this one during the whole of that time. The Bench imposed a fine of one shilling and costs. Mr. Crompton refused to pay this, preferring to go to prison, and he was consequently locked up. Being a widower, with three children, the position in which this determination placed him excited much sympathy among his friends and the general public, and next day 3,000 people assembled to see him taken off to Preston Gaol. He was conveyed to the railway station as a prisoner in a carriage belonging to Mrs. Preston, but on reaching the station he was set at liberty, Mr. Whiteman, without consulting Mr. Crompton, having undertaken to pay the fine and costs. The incident resulted in what was called a "demonstration in favour of religious liberty," held in the Co-operative Hall on the 23rd of the same month. Between 5,000 and 6,000 persons attended, and after the meeting a procession, led by the Temperance Band, marched through the principal streets, the banner of the Primitive Methodist School being carried at the head of the procession. Several ministers and one or two prominent laymen were present and made stirring speeches.

UNITED METHODIST FREE CHURCH.—The original chapel of the United Methodist Free Church, in Duckworth Street, Darwen, was built by the Wesleyan Association in 1839, at a cost of £2,200, and enlarged in 1861 at a cost of £2,400. It was galleried, and contained an organ. The sitting accommodation was for 700 persons. A new chapel was built on the same site in 1887-8, projecting forward, towards Duckworth street, 14 feet more than the old one. It is in the Italian style of architecture. The interior is arranged in the amphitheatre style, and contains 750 seats, and the principal school-room, in the basement, will seat 700 people. Its total cost was £5,000. The handsome pulpit is the gift of Mrs. Lightbown, of Falcon House.—*Lower Darwen:* The United Methodist Free Church, Lower Darwen, was opened on the 19th of June, 1873. It provides accommodation for 550 people, and cost £2,000, towards which one half was raised at or before the opening services. It is a handsome gothic edifice, with traceried windows and pinnacled buttresses. The interior is galleried.— *Hollins Grove:* In 1870 the United Methodists of Over Darwen built a school chapel at Hollins Grove, at a cost of £300; sittings 300. This was afterwards used by the Congregationalists, but its site is now covered with cottages.

OTHER NONCONFORMIST CHAPELS.

BAPTIST CHAPEL.—A Baptist church was formed in Over Darwen in April, 1858, and its members built the Baptist Chapel and School in Bolton Road in 1862. It is a classic structure, galleried in the interior, with school accommodation in the basement. Cost, £3,000; sittings, 550. Present pastor, the Rev. B. Davies.

UNITARIAN FREE CHURCH.—A neat iron chapel, capable of accommodating 250 persons, was opened on September 28th, 1878. It was erected at a cost of about £500 on a plot of land in Bolton Road purchased by the East Lancashire Unitarian Union. Pastor, the Rev. Herbert Clarke.

The Salvation Army have a "barrack" in Bridge Street, and the Spiritualists a meeting room in Church Bank Street.

THE ROMAN CATHOLIC CHURCH.

ST. JOSEPH'S.—The Roman Catholics built a mission room in Radford Street, used for both school and church purposes, in 1856, and subsequently enlarged it, so as to have distinct portions for these separate uses. The total cost was £1,500: sittings, 250. This church, dedicated to St. William, was succeeded, in 1884, by a new building dedicated to St. Joseph and built on a plot of land in Bolton Road. The foundation stone of St. Joseph's was laid by Bishop Vaughan on May 3rd, 1884, and the church was opened on October 15th, 1885. Messrs. Pugin and Pugin, of Westminster, were the architects. The church is in the early decorated style of architecture, and consists of nave, chancel, and sacristy, with two porches in Bolton Road, at the west end, surmounted by a turret. Cost over £3,000; sittings, 700. Two priests of St. William's sacrificed their lives to their duty by visiting the sick. The first, Father W. J. Hampson, assistant priest, died on September 14th, 1877, from scarlet fever, after labouring here only a few weeks, and on the 23rd of March in the following year, Father Peter Kopp died of a fever. Like Father Hampson he had only been in the town a few weeks. Each clergyman was in his 25th year, and each contracted his disease by visiting the sick. The priest at present in charge of St. Joseph's is the Rev. David Vandenweghe.

CHURCH OF THE SACRED HEART.—A school at the northerly end of the town, in the township of Lower Darwen, built in 1872, was converted into a mission room on January 20th, 1878. This school-church was dedicated to St. Edward, but a new edifice was erected in 1882-3, on an adjacent plot of land, and named the Church of the Sacred Heart. It seats 400 people, and its cost was £2,000. The consecration ceremony was performed by Bishop Vaughan, on April 11th, 1883. A statue, carved in wood, representing our Lord showing his heart to the people, was unveiled on June 22nd, 1884. It was the gift of Mr. Richard Holden, of Blackburn. Priest in charge, the Rev. Rudolph Classé.

CENSUS OF CHURCHES AND CHAPELS.

Returns published by the *Nonconformist* show that in 1851 there were seven places of worship in Over Darwen with 5,794 sittings, and, in 1872, 22 places of worship with 14,131 sittings. Mr. J. J. Riley, proprietor of the *Darwen News*, and author of a chronological History of Darwen, published annually from 1878 to 1884, caused a "religious census" of Over Darwen to be taken on February 19th, 1882, and the following is his summary of the returns, the estimated population being 33,557, and the number of places of worship 20, eleven belonging to the Church of England :—

	Sittings.	Morn.	Aftern.	Eveng.	Total.
CHURCH OF ENGLAND,—Holy Trinity	1350	710	—	537	1247
St. John's	1660	598	56	449	1103
St. James's	530	242	250	—	492
St. Paul's	579	166	238	—	404
St. Cuthbert's	462	343	—	252	595
Church of England Total	4581	2059	544	1238	3841
CONGREGATIONALISTS…Duckworth Street	1310	855	—	603	1458
Belgrave	1768	591	—	835	1426
Lower Chapel	700	311	452	—	763
Congregationalist Total	3778	1757	452	1438	3647
METHODISTS…Wesleyan	1636	663	—	492	1155
Primitive	1325	207	70	294	571
United Methodists	608	236	—	220	456
	3569	1106	70	1006	2182
MISCELLANEOUS…Baptists	480	174	—	91	265
Unitarians	200	55	—	69	124
Salvation Army	250	78	158	430	666
		(Early Mass)	(Mass)	(Vespers)	
ROMAN CATHOLICS…St. William's	500	372	329	192	893
St. Edward's	140	141	137	105	383
Roman Catholic Total	640	513	466	297	1276
	Sittings.	Morn.	Aftern.	Eveng.	Total.
Church of England	4581	2059	544	1238	3841
Congregationalists	3778	1757	452	1438	3647
Methodists	3569	1106	70	1006	2182
Baptists	480	174	—	91	265
Unitarians	200	55	—	69	124
Salvation Army	250	78	158	430	666
Roman Catholics	640	513	466	297	1276
	13498	5742	1690	4569	12001
Church of England	4581	2059	544	1238	3841
All Other Bodies	8917	3683	1146	3331	8160
	13498	5742	1690	4569	12001

DARWEN AND ITS PEOPLE.

	Sittings Provided for.				Per Centage of Sittings Occupied.
Church of England	13·65	per cent. of the population	...	52·69
Congregationalists	11·25	,,	,,	,,	... 64.34
Methodists	10·63	,,	,,	,,	... 40·79
Baptists	1·43	,,	,,	,,	... 45·62
Roman Catholics	1·90	,,	,,	,,	... 132 03
Unitarians	0·59	,,	,,	,,	... 39·00
Salvation Army	0·74	,,	,,	,,	... 120·00

REVENUES OF THE NON-ESTABLISHED CHURCHES.

The following statement of the revenues of all the non-established churches in the town of Darwen, from exclusively private sources, during the year ended June 30th 1873, was published at the time by the Rev. James Mc.Dougall.

Church.	Income for the year.
	£ s. d.
Wesley Chapel, Railway Road	900 0 0
Baptist Chapel, Bolton Road	333 15 11
Duckworth Street Congregational Church	1030 0 0
Belgrave Congregational Church	1063 15 5
Lower Chapel Congregational Church	580 3 9
Primitive Methodists (two chapels)	287 0 0
United Methodist Free Church (two chapels)	300 0 0
Roman Catholic Church, Radford Street	200 0 0
Total	£4694 15 1

Mr. J. J. Riley notes in July, 1881, that "the total amount collected at the Sunday School sermons held in Darwen alone amounts to the handsome sum of £1,268 8s. 11½d." On June 14th, 1885, the Sunday School collections at Belgrave Congregational Church amounted to £1,663.

STATISTICS OF DAY AND SUNDAY SCHOOLS.

Baines, the historian of Lancashire, recorded in 1825 that there were then about 1,500 children receiving instruction at the Sunday Schools attached to the various places of worship in the township of Over Darwen. An anonymous document sent by post to the Vicar of Blackburn on December 20th, 1828, and preserved in the Vicarage Records, gives the following statistics of Sunday Schools.

OVER DARWEN SUNDAY SCHOOLS.

The Church (boys and girls)	168
Lower Independent Chapel	370
Ebenezer	250
Blacksnape	170
Methodists	550
Ranters	100
New Jerusalem	100
Total	1708

On February 26th, 1882, Mr. J. J. Riley caused a census of the Darwen Sunday Schools to be taken, and the result showed that 3,138 teachers and scholars attended in the morning; and 6,191 in the afternoon; total for the day, 9,329. The detailed return is as follows:—

		Morn.	Aftern.	Total
CHURCH OF ENGLAND.—Holy Trinity Central School...	242	564	806
	Vernon Street...	136	185	321
	Wood Street ...	45	88	133
		——423	——837	——1260
	St. John's Central School	158	386	544
	Culvert	145	283	428
	Grimehills	17	34	51
		——320	——703	——1023
	St. James's School	188	251	439
	St. Paul's School..................	63	103	166
	St. Cuthbert's Central School .	171	304	475
	Earcroft	44	96	140
		——215	——400	——615
CONGREGATIONAL............Duckworth St. Central Schools	252	502	754
	Hollins Grove .	120	230	350
		——372	——732	——1104
	Belgrave Central Schools	209	481	690
	Bolton Road	146	320	466
	Mission Schools	73	113	186
	Blacksnape	—	58	58
		——428	——972	——1400
	Lower Chapel School	230	321	551
METHODIST......................Wesleyan Meth. Central School	262	491	753
	Bolton Road .	70	161	231
		——332	——652	——984
	Primitive Meth. Central Schools	109	251	360
	Hoddlesden ...	32	41	73
	Sough	46	60	106
	Sandhills	60	126	186
		——247	——478	——725
	U.M.F.C. School..................	120	286	406
MISCELLANEOUS. ....Baptist School.....................	137	205	342
	Unitarian School.................	63	83	146
ROMAN CATHOLIC...... ...St. William's	—	143	143
	St. Edward's	—	25	25

Whittle says:—" In 1851 the population of Darwen may be computed, in round numbers, at 12,000; 2,400 children in all, 547 receiving education on the voluntary system, 380 under the Factory Act, and 1,473 attending no school at all. Two day schools exist: the British and Foreign School, in connection with the Independents, Belgrave Square, with 140 boys and 112 girls, and the schools in connection with Holy Trinity Church, attended by 135 boys and 80 girls.[1]"

[1] *Blackburn as It Is*, p. 302.

There are 18 day schools under Government inspection within the borough of Darwen, and five more in the district covered by this History. The statistics in the first, third, and last columns of the following tables are compiled from the Parliamentary Blue Book issued in 1888, and those in the second and fourth columns from the Diocesan Calendar for 1889. The 19 day schools of the borough provide accommodation for 9,239 children, the average attendance is 4,517, and the annual grant shown in the latest published return was £4,459 9s. 9d. Mr. Abram notes[1] that in 1874-5 the school accommodation in the same area was 5,000, average attendance 2,131, annual grant £1,591 6s. 9d.

DAY SCHOOLS WITHIN THE BOROUGH.

CHURCH OF ENGLAND:—

	Accommodation. Govt. Retn.	Dioces. Retn.	Average Attendance.	Present at Dioc. Exam.	Government Grant. £ s. d.
St. James's, Chapels	570	572	221	331	202 6 0
Holy Trinity, Central	429	772	359	443	396 16 1 }
			27[2]		19 2 0 }
do. Vernon St	228	220	135	140	101 17 6
do. Lee School	354	365	218	284	176 6 0
St. Paul's, Hoddlesden	327	—	161	—	177 2 10
St. John's, Central	938	669	315	354	312 13 0
do. Culvert	669	669	319	408	339 5 7
St. Cuthbert's, Central	549	536	267	346	285 4 9
do. Earcroft	356	200	115	146	99 17 9
	4420	4003	2137	2452	2110 11 6

CONGREGATIONAL:—

Lower Chapel	552		200		205 12 0
Belgrave	948		326		303 3 0 }
			41		28 12 0 }
Duckworth Street	830		412		431 19 0
Bolton Road	534		323		346 0 8 }
			40		27 12 0 }
Hollins Grove	403		210		234 14 8
	3267		1552		1577 13 4

METHODISTS:—

Wesleyan	610		337		371 15 8
Prim. Meth, Sandhills	263		86		75 3 10
	873		423		446 19 6

ROMAN CATHOLICS:—

St. William's	522		243		223 0 2 }
			30		13 12 0 }
St. Edward's	157		84		54 1 3
	679		357		290 13 5

[1] *History of Blackburn*, p. 528.
[2] The figures bracketted with the line above refer to night schools.

HISTORY AND TRADITIONS OF

	Accommodation. Govt. Retn.	Dioces. Retn.	Average Attendance.	Present at Dioc. Exam.	Government Grant. £ s. d.
BOROUGH EVENING SCHOOL			48		33 12 0

DAY SCHOOLS OUTSIDE THE BOROUGH.

Lower Darwen Factory School	300		135		120 18 10
St. James's, Black-a-Moor	385	200	80	100	65 4 4
Do. Guide	280	160	107	116	91 1 6
Belthorn Independent	274		68		47 17 2 ⎫
			10[1]		3 6 0 ⎭
St. Michael's (Belthorn and Daisy Green)[2]	190		91		93 15 3
	1429	360	491	216	422 3 1

[1] The figures bracketted with the line above refer to night schools.

[2] St. Michael's School, Belthorn, is a branch of St. Paul's, Oswaldtwistle, and is used for divine service.

Chapter 5.

The Progress of Two Centuries.

Modern History—Darwen 200 years ago—Rise of the Staple Trades—A Few Fragments—Pack-Horse Roads of the Eighteenth Century—The New Road—Nineteenth Century Progress—Directory of Darwen for 1824—The Cotton Trade—Handloom Weaving—Introduction of the Spinning Jenny—The Old Mill, Lower Darwen—Th' Top Factory—The Loom Breaking Riots—Mr. Eccles Shorrock—Spread of the Factory System—Cotton Trade Statistics—Calico Printing—The Paper Trade—Crompton's Bleach-Works—Mining and Quarrying—The Railway—Local Government—The Local Board of Health—Incorporation of the Borough of Over Darwen—Name Changed to "Darwen"—Municipal and Sanitary Progress—Public Buildings and Public Works—The Moors and Parks—The Steam Tramway—Political Annals—Extension of the Franchise and Re-Distribution of Seats—Election of Lord Cranborne in 1885 and 1886—Census Returns—Co-operation—Miscellany.

MODERN history in Darwen may be conveniently dated from the year 1688, and summed up in the annals of the social and commercial progress of the last two centuries. In the four preceding chapters, following a general, but not precise, chronological order, I have traced the history of Darwen from pre-historic times through the eras of the Roman occupation and the Saxon settlements, and on through the great mediæval period of feudalism and warfare, stretching from the Norman Conquest in 1066 to the peaceful Revolution of 1688, and so reaching the local climax of the great struggle for religious liberty which ended in the establishment of Congregationalism at Darwen Chapels,—one of the most ancient and interesting of the historic strongholds of Nonconformity. The classification of the subjects under notice has made it desirable to avoid a strictly chronological arrangement, and in dealing with the modern period of 1688-1888 the same course will be followed.

Two hundred years ago, just about the time of the great struggle for the possession of Darwen Chapel, the rectory estate was held by Mrs. Fleetwood, and it was reported that most of the under-tenants were miserably poor and the housing out of order, tenants being loth to build new houses for fear of eviction at the expiration of their lease. A better state of things, however, prevailed on the estates of other landlords in the neighbourhood. A considerable amount of coal-getting took place in Darwen at the beginning of the eighteenth century, but the majority of the inhabitants of Darwen appear to have been weavers or "websters," judging from their description in the parish registers, while the principal yeomen and freeholders were "chapmen" or "putters out" of pieces to the handloom weavers. Even in those early days there were periods of stagnation that were felt by the whole community. We may judge of the state of Darwen from a petition quoted in the Linsey MSS. concerning the neighbouring town. The writer says:—"The state of Blackburn was such in the year 1706 that people were seen walking their desolate streets, hanging down their heads under disappointments, wormed out of all branches of their trade, uncertain what hand to turn to, necessitated to become apprentices to their unkind neighbours, and yet, after all, finding their trade so fortified by companies and secured by prescriptions that they despair of any success therein."[1]

That quaint rural parson, Peter Walkden, Nonconformist minister at Chipping, had frequent dealings with the people of Darwen in the early part of last century, although he lived 15 miles away, and there was no road except for pack-horses. We read that he "wound the yarn for one of his sons who was a weaver, and sold the 'web' (woven cloth) at Darwen,"[2] and it is further recorded that one of his sons "wove at home for the Blackburn and Darwen manufacturers." The homely pastor himself states in his diary for September 17, 1729, that his son John "washed potatoes to send to Over Darwen to be sold there."[3] Again, "October 19. Lord's Day, so we got ready for Darwen Chapel, and betwixt 9 and 10 a clock I and the family set forward and rid to Richard Smalley's, where I put in my mare and went to chapel. . . . At noon I went to Holden's and got some refreshment there; then went to chapel again. . . . [Having dismissed the congregation at the close of the afternoon service] I got my mare and went to Mr. Burgess's and dined there. . . . Went to Fernhurst" [where he was lodging for a few days]. "December 10. Son John being to Eccleshill coal-pits with my mare and horse," &c. "December 13. Son Thomas got home from Fernhurst about 7 a clock." "December 17. Son John went to Eccleshill coalpit for two loads of coals for Henry Richmond's."

Some interesting incidents in the local history of this period will be found in the preceding chapter, the eighteenth century being one of great activity and rapid development ecclesiastically.

1 Whittle's *Blackburn as it Is*, p. 217.
2 *Rural Life* (Transactions of the Lancashire and Cheshire Historical Society, vol. xxxii.), p. 31.
3 *Peter Walkden's Diary*, p. 44.

The following is a curious notice published in the *Manchester Advertiser* by Christopher Hindle, Constable of Over Darwen, on September 6th, 1757. This Constable was probably a member of the Hindle family of Great Harwood, who bought the Highercroft estate and mansion, Lower Darwen, toward the end of last century, for it is a coincidence that another Christopher Hindle, son of Christopher Hindle of Highercroft, became Chief Constable not merely of Over Darwen, but of the whole of the Blackburn Lower Division, and died in 1847, aged 70. The notice runs as follows :—" Wednesday night, August 31, 1757. Run away from Over Darwen, a man called Joseph Holt, born in the parish of Linn, in Cheshire ; about 25 years of age, 5 feet 6 inches high, a little mark't with the small pox ; had on a blue plush coat, white stockings and a short wig, he being convicted by Richard Whitehead, Esq., for stealing a horse, the property of Peter Warburton, in the parish of Linn aforesaid. Whoever will secure the said Joseph Holt shall receive a handsome reward and all reasonable charges, from their humble servant CHRISTOPHER HINDLE, Constable of Over Darwen aforesaid."

A note concerning a malignant fever which occurred in the year 1759 was published in the " Sketches in Local History " in the *Preston Guardian* of September 13th, 1879, the circumstances having been related by Mr. Jeremy Hunt, " whose retentive memory," remarks the editor, " in his old age is a storehouse of local facts connected with the period of his youth." In the year 1759, a malignant fever was raging in the district of Darwen and Eccleshill, and both the sons of Nathaniel Hunt (Jeremy's great-grandfather) were stricken down by it. The son John died in the summer and the son Nathaniel died in the following August. The senior Nathaniel Hunt's lease of Harwood Fold Farm, Eccleshill, was valid so long as his two children and a woman named Margery Morris lived, their names being specified in it, and when his second son was lying dangerously ill Nathaniel the elder went to see him, and said, " Our John's dead, and if thou dies there'll be nobody left but Margery," *i.e.*, in the lease. Margery lived fifty years after this, and so secured to the Hunts a long tenure of the farm. She was the daughter of James Morris, of Eccleshill, a reputed centenarian.

In the *Manchester Mercury* of May 25th, 1779, appears the following advertisement respecting Oakenhurst Fold :—" To be sold by auction, at the sign of the Black Bull (Samuel Rixton), in Over Darwen, near Blackburn, in the County of Lancaster, upon Wednesday, the fourth day of August next, at three o'clock in the afternoon. Lot 1st. The fee simple and inheritance of and in all that messuage and tenement called Oakenhurst Fold, with the several closes or parcels of land and appurtenances thereunto belonging, situate, lying and being in Over Darwen aforesaid, containing by estimation twenty acres of land of the large measure there used, or thereabouts, be the same more or less, late the inheritance of John Bent, and in the possession of Thomas Aspden as tenant thereof. Lot 2nd. Also, of all that other messuage and tenement called the Diveling, and the closes of land and appurtenances thereunto belonging, situate in Over Darwen aforesaid, containing by estimation four acres of land of large measure, late the inheritance of John Bent, and in the possession of Thomas Aspinall as tenant thereof. N.B.—An Act of Parliament has lately been passed for inclosing the commons within Over Darwen aforesaid, from which there will be valuable allotments more in respect of the last-mentioned estates, which will be sold therewith, in such manner as shall be fixed upon at the time of the sale. And for particulars in the meantime apply to Mr. Buckley, of Tunstead, within Saddleworth, in the county of York; or to Messrs. Turner and Kerfoot, Warrington."[1]

In the year 1780, under a local Act of Parliament, Lower Darwen Moor, containing about 600 acres, was parcelled out among the freeholders of the township by Commissioners appointed for that purpose, the chief claimant under the appointment being Catherine, Lady Stourton, lady of the manor. Provision was made for the preservation of common rights, the getting of stone, and the maintenance of highways. The original award specifying the details of the allotment is preserved among the records of the Blackburn Parish Church, and a full abstract may be consulted in the *Preston Guardian* of May 4th, 1878.

In the *Annual Register* for 1787 appear two letters respecting an extraordinary case of a woman who had been delivered of five children at a birth in the previous year. One letter is by Dr. Blaine, physician to St. Thomas's Hospital, introducing the other, which is from Mr. John Hull, "a very sensible and ingenious practitioner of physic at Blackburn, in Lancashire." Dr. Hull, who, together with Dr. Lancaster, of Blackburn, attended the case, says that the mother was Margaret Waddington. aged 21, a poor person residing in the township of Lower Darwen. Her five children were prematurely born, but two of them were born alive. All five were girls. They were born on April 25th, 1786. The mother recovered rapidly. Sixteen days after her confinement she was out of doors, and on the 21st of May she walked to Blackburn, a distance of two miles from her abode. Her husband was,

---

[1] *Vide* Sale of the Manor of Over Darwen, p. 37, *ante*.

at the time, and had been for three years, in an infirm state of health, suffering from confirmed phthisis. The account of the extraordinary case was signed and dated "John Hull, Blackburn, Lancashire, June 9th, 1786."

An eminent Nonconformist divine and author, the Rev. Edward Harwood, D.D., was born at Lower Darwen in 1728, and educated by Mr. Belsborrow, of Darwen. In 1745 he was put under the Rev. Thos. Hunter, of Blackburn, afterwards vicar of Weaverham, Cheshire, "who had the best school of any gentleman in the county." "This most learned and worthy clergyman," says Dr. Harwood, "in the year 1748 wished to place me at Queen's College, Oxford, to which he belonged; but my father, who was a stiff Presbyterian, I believe would have died if he had seen me in a surplice." In the year 1750 Mr. Harwood taught a boarding school at Peckham, and preached occasionally for Dr. Benson at Crutched-Friars. In 1754 he began to teach a Grammar School at Congleton, in Cheshire, and for seven years, while there, preached on alternate Sundays to two small societies at Whitelock and Leek. He took charge of a small church at Bristol in 1765, but upon publishing a second edition of "The Supremacy of the Father," written by one Williams, he was so constantly calumniated in a Bristol paper as an Arian, a Socinian, a Deist and worse than Deist, that his salary diminished year by year although he had a considerable family. In 1772 he obtained a situation among good friends in London, and lived there until his death in 1794. For the last twelve years of his life he suffered from palsy. Greek was as familiar to him as French to any English gentleman, and for twenty years he had no occasion to consult a lexicon. In an autobiographical letter written shortly before his death, and published in Nichols's Literary Anecdotes, he says—"I have written more books than any other person now living except Dr. Priestley; having never spoken evil of dignities, but have lived on the best of terms with the established clergy, who ever respected me as a scholar. After expending a great deal of time in discussing the subject, I am neither an Athanasian, Arian, or a Socinian; but die fully confirmed in the great doctrines of the New Testament, a resurrection, and a future state of eternal blessedness for all sincere penitents and good Christians." He obtained his degree of D.D. from Edinburgh University in 1768. Among his many publications were "An Introduction to the Study of the New Testament," "Translation of the New Testament into Modern English," and "A View of the Various Editions of the Greek and Roman Classicks." His eldest son, Edward, a surgeon in the Royal

Navy, wrote the following epitaph for the grave of his father and mother:—

"H. S. E. Edwardus Harwood, D.D., Vir summo ingenio præditus, qui literas sacras, æque ac humanas, mirâ felicitate coluit, et ornavit. Ob. 14 Jan., anno 1794, ætatis suæ 65. Reliquiæ ejus uxoris, filiæ minoris natu S. Chandler, D.D., juxta hunc tumulum sitæ sunt ; ob. 21 Maii, anno 1791, æt. suæ 58. E. H. Fil. pos."

In connection with the Chapelry of Over Darwen we note a charitable bequest of 30s. annually, made by Mrs. Mary Smalley in 1794, payable to the churchwardens of Over Darwen as a rent of a portion of the tenement called Whitehall, to be spent in linen cloth for distribution among the poor. The bequest was annulled by the Act 9 George II. c. 36, but the charity has been kept up annually by Mrs. Smalley's heirs.

The rise of the staple trades of the town also took place during the eighteenth century, as will be hereafter narrated, and before the dawn of the nineteenth, as shown in Aitken's *Descriptions*, Darwen had become an important and populous manufacturing district. Writing in 1795, Aitken says :—"At Darwen, four miles south of Blackburn, there are plenty of coals. This was formerly a small village, but is now a populous district manufacturing a large quantity of cotton goods. It contains two printing works, and there are a proportionate number of mechanics and shopkeepers. Twenty years since a return was made by Dr. Percival of a Dissenting Congregation here consisting of 1,850 individuals, among whom the annual proportion of births was more than double that of deaths. Darwen is in a bleak and elevated situation, surrounded with moors, and little cultivated."[1]

A small estate in Eccleshill, consisting of two houses and 36 acres of land at Waterside, was in 1796 purchased for £890 by the Governors of the Bolton Grammar School to form part of the endowment of that institution. The conveyance also included a chief rent of 20½d. "and two barbed arrows," payable out of the lands of Sir Richard Clayton, Bart. More recently the Governors have purchased another estate in Darwen.

Mr. Abram prints in the *Blackburn Standard and Weekly Express*[2] a list of 119 patriotic inhabitants of Lower Darwen who in the summer of 1798 raised by subscription the sum of £21 10s. 6d. for the defence of the country in case of invasion by the French or other foreign power. He adds that the National Patriotic Fund was subscribed to by every town and village in Lancashire, but that "in none of the rural townships in Blackburn Parish was the effort more heartily joined in than by the

[1] *Descriptions of the Country Round Manchester*, p. 273.   [2] December 29th, 1888.

inhabitants of Lower Darwen, where the gifts, large and small, were so numerous that the list of names of the givers . . . . must have included nearly every householder and head of a family resident in Lower Darwen." The list is headed by Messrs. Thomas Eccles and Sons with a donation of ten guineas.

On August 17th, 1799, there occurred the heaviest storm remembered by the oldest inhabitant, the river Darwen sweeping away several bridges, inundating land and destroying property.

The Whitehall estate was advertised for sale in 1805, when it was described as freehold, and containing a mansion house (Whitehall) and two farmhouses, 279 statute acres of arable, meadow and pasture land, the whole in the occupation of Messrs. Richard and William Hilton, "who have lately made considerable improvements upon the estate for the convenience of their business of whitsters, and who hold the same for the remainder of a term of 31 years, which commenced at Candlemas and May Day, 1798, under the clear annual rent of £120." A mine of coal about one yard in thickness had just been found on the estate.

PACK-HORSE ROADS OF THE EIGHTEENTH CENTURY.

James Grime, of Bobbin Hall, who died in February, 1857, aged 80, once told Mr. William Thomas Ashton that he remembered the first wheeled vehicle coming into Darwen. When he was a boy the roads were so bad that all merchandise had to be carried on pack-horses, and the river Darwen had to be forded, or crossed by footbridges.

Grime, in his youth, was a friend of Crompton, and the elder Hilton, and was often employed by them in making the wooden rollers used in their respective trades of bleaching and papermaking. His water-wheels on the Kebbs Brook will be remembered by many old inhabitants. For a time he carried on the business of bobbin turner, but, giving this up, he took to the cultivation of the land, enclosing and farming Hall Moss and Lyon's Den, with great industry and a certain amount of success. He laboured long and faithfully as superintendent of Belgrave School.[1]

A petition of the merchants, landowners, cotton manufacturers, and other influential residents of the neighbourhood was presented to Parliament in 1797 stating that the road from Blackburn to Bolton, through the village of Over Darwen, was fifteen miles in length and might easily be shortened to twelve miles; that in many places it was so narrow and bad that carts could not pass without much difficulty; and that it crossed steep hills rising seven inches in the yard, although it was not necessary to have gradients of more than two inches in the yard. After this petition a Bill was passed for the reconstruction of the road, and a great impetus was given to trade by the improved communication then made.

[1] See also *Jeremy Hunt's Recollections*, pp. 107-8.

The old road from Blackburn to Bolton through Darwen was the most important of the local pack-horse roads of the eighteenth century. It entered "the village of Over Darwen" from Blackburn by way of Chapels, running down Robin Bank, across the River Darwen by a ford,[1] where Union Street Bridge now stands, round the back of Smalley's Hotel, down the Green, up Bridge Street and Redearth Road to Sough, along Watery Lane to Culvert School, then away southward over the fields to Cadshaw Bridge. The river was often impassable at the two fords, but narrow footbridges, each with one slight handrail, were used by pedestrians, and horsemen had to wait, in flood times, for the subsidence of the water. These fords and footbridges connected the centre of modern Darwen not only with Blackburn and Bolton, but with the important hamlets of Sough, Blacksnape, Hoddlesden (by way of Princes), and Chapels. Behind Culvert School there is a green cutting through the fields which is a remnant of the old road, now disused. Early in the present century, instead of leading to Cadshaw Bridge along this track, Redearth Road was continued straight on to Cranberry Moss. Over the Moss the track was very faint, but it emerged on the Entwistle side, and continued through Chapeltown to Bolton. The Cadshaw Bridge branch, which was probably the older of the two, led past Walmsley Chapel and through Sharples to Bolton.

On the Blackburn side of Darwen Chapels the road kept to the west of the river, and as far as Lower Darwen there were two tracks, a higher and a lower one. The latter crossed and re-crossed the river at Lower Darwen and Ewood. The former was a continuation of the road running along Blacksnape ridge, and in this section it was identical with the old Roman road. Skirting modern Darwen, but providing a good road for the inhabitants of Chapels, Hoddlesden, and Sough, and the country-side west of the river, this road led from Blackburn to Ramsbottom and Bury.

There was a second road from Blackburn to Bolton prior to 1797, running through Tockholes, Belmont, and Sharples, skirting Darwen on the west. Both Blackburn and Bolton were market towns of considerable importance, and Bolton had a weekly yarn and cloth market that was much frequented by Blackburn manufacturers. Strings of pack horses were employed to carry the piece goods from Blackburn to Bolton, and return with yarn to be distributed to the handloom weavers. The whole of the pack-horse roads were also much used by strings of "lime-gals" travelling with sacks of lime from Clitheroe to Bolton, Bury, and Manchester, and by pack-horses fetching coal from the Darwen

[1] It was at this ford that the wife of the Rev. Richard Bowden was drowned in 1804. See *ante*, p. 108.

mines for use in Blackburn and neighbourhood. The Sharples road, like the one along the Blacksnape ridge, is now almost deserted, and the winding road through Darwen is used merely for local purposes.

THE NEW ROAD.

The construction of the road from Blackburn to Darwen and Bolton in 1797, still called by old inhabitants "The New Road," was really the making of the town of Darwen. Instead of living in scattered hamlets about the hill-sides and valleys, the inhabitants collected by the roadside, and the town gradually assumed its elongated shape, having the new highway as its backbone and the river Darwen as its main artery. From Cadshaw Bridge at the southern extremity of the modern borough to Golden Cup at its junction with Blackburn, the highway runs nearly in a straight line for a distance of three miles and three-quarters, and to-day it is thickly populated on both sides along almost the entire length. The Blackburn and Bolton road is the principal business street, and the only street, except Redearth Road, which is entitled to be called a main thoroughfare. All the streets branching off it are of minor importance, and in no case has the population settled thickly away from the road. The principal populous districts of the borough away from the road-side are the districts of Sough, Hoddlesden and Chapels, —all ancient hamlets that existed before the road was made. On the eastern side of the highway the buildings have spread more than on the western side, because the gradients are easier, and there is therefore a broad band of dwellings extending from Chapels to Sough, but all having their traffic trained into the main thoroughfare or into Redearth Road. The mansions and villas of the local gentry are built, almost without exception, on the western or Darwen Moor side, the older ones being in the southern portion of the town about Whitehall and Thorney Height, and some of the more modern ones towards the northern extremity, in avenues on the Sunnyhurst side. The cottages and other dwellings of the working-classes are spread all over the town. There has been a marked development of the northern portion of the town during the last few years, and there is very little division between the boroughs of Darwen and Blackburn except by an imaginary line indicated near the Golden Cup by an iron signpost having "Blackburn" inscribed on one side and "Darwen" on the other.

NINETEENTH CENTURY PROGRESS.

A century ago the Darwen Valley contained mere scattered collections of houses and detached hamlets, and the only branches of industry in the place were calico-printing, handloom weaving, and the getting of coal. Calico-printing was only introduced in the year 1776; but the low ridge on the eastern side of the valley has been dug for coal for at least 200 years back; and handloom weaving was an important industry during the seventeenth century. At the commencement of the nineteenth Darwen had become quite a populous manufacturing village, and contained two printing works. Since then it has constantly increased in size and importance, concurrently with the introduction and extension of the staple manufactures, and its improved connection with the towns of Blackburn and Bolton. During the eighteenth century the population had increased from about 500 to upwards of 3,000, and by the end of that period the new road had been constructed, calico-printing had been introduced, and two places of worship, in addition to the two at Chapels, had sprung into existence. The rise of the town dates from the beginning of the present century. The hamlets on the Green, at Chapels, and at Sough, began to coalesce and form one town, and the trade has grown rapidly ever since. In 1801 the population, according to the census, was 3,587; during the next 10 years the Dob Meadows Printworks were built, the new public road proved a boon to the colliery proprietors who had supplied Blackburn and other places northward, and the population increased to 4,411. Between 1811 and 1821 the increase of population was much more marked. In 1812 Samuel Crompton, inventor of the spinning mule, came to Darwen, and commenced business as a bleacher. In 1820 the oldest portion of Bowling Green Mill was built, and the factory system, which has since spread so considerably, was introduced into Over Darwen; and the census return in the next year showed the population to have increased to 6,711. Between 1821 and 1831 the only record materially affecting the industry of the people is that of the introduction of power-looms, and of a riot, in 1826, when a number of roughs came from Blackburn and broke 52 of the new machines; and it is noticeable that during that period the population only increased by about 260—a marked contrast to the increase of 2,300 during the preceding decade. In 1831, then, the population was only 6,972. Between 1831 and 1841, however, there was again an improvement. A printshop was built on the Bury Fold Brook; Mr. Eccles Shorrock, who purchased Bowling Green Mill in 1830, built the New Mill in 1835; Hilton's extensive paper works were erected; a Mechanics' Institute was founded; and the Gasworks were established at a cost of £8,000; so that when the census was taken in 1841 the population was found to have increased to 9,348. About the year 1841 Messrs. Potter and Co. established their paper-making and paper-staining business at the Livesey Fold and Belgrave Mills; in 1845 the old Market House was erected at a cost at £3,500; between 1845 and 1848 the railway from Blackburn to Darwen, Bolton, and Manchester, was constructed; and in 1851 the population was found to have increased to 11,702. In 1853 the Peel Baths were erected at a cost of £1,300; in 1854 the Local Board was formed; and in 1855 the *Darwen Examiner*, which was afterwards transferred to Blackburn, and rechristened the *Blackburn Weekly Times*, was issued for the first time, being printed and published in Darwen. The increase of population during this period was very marked, and it has been so until the present day. In 1861 it was 16,492; in 1871, 21,278; in 1881, 33,433. Between 1861 and 1871, the Cemetery was opened; the Co-operative Stores in School Street were built; India Mills were erected; and an Art Treasures Exhibition was held. In 1871 a Free Public Library was established, and since then a number of new places of worship have been built; the town has been converted into a corporate borough; the boundaries have been extended; important and extensive sanitary improvements have been carried out; and Darwen has become the name-town of an electoral division returning one member to Parliament. Having thus glanced summarily at the rapid progress of the nineteenth century, I proceed to deal with some of the more important events in detail.

DARWEN IN 1806 AND 1824.

Gough, the editor of Camden's *Britannia*, writing in 1806, says:—
"At Darwen, four miles south of Blackburn, there are plenty of coals. This was formerly a village, but it is now a populous district, manufacturing a great quantity of cotton goods.[1]

Baines, the historian of Lancashire, wrote of Darwen in 1824:—
" The three townships of Lower Darwen, Over Darwen, and Eccleshill, form the southern townships of the parish [of Blackburn]. The inhabitants, who are chiefly Dissenters, are men of industrious habits, and the whole district exhibits in the print works and bleach works, as well as in other branches of manufacture, the unequivocal symptoms of an active and successful industry. Coal is here very plentiful, and slate is dug up in the adjoining quarries. Within the last 20 years the population has nearly doubled.

DIRECTORY OF DARWEN FOR 1824.

The following list of tradesmen, &c., in Over Darwen, Lower Darwen, Eccleshill, and Yate-and-Pickup Bank, is taken from the "Village Directory of Blackburn Parish," published in the year 1825 in the second volume

[1] Gough's *Camden*, vol. iii, p. 387.

of Baines's *History of Lancashire* (original edition), pages 631 and 643:—

OVER DARWEN.

POSTMASTER, John Green; letters arrive at 7 morning, depart at ½ past 4 afternoon.
Allred, John, nail manufacturer.
Allred, Jno. and Co., iron and brass founders and engineers.
Aspinall, John, attorney.
Banstead, Christopher, bookkeeper.
Beswick, Michael, coal agent, Chapels.
Burns, Jos., druggist, &c.
Carr, Geo., cotton spinner.
Dunderdale, Rev. Hy., Hayfold, Chapels.
Fletcher, Rev. Rd. (Independent).
Greenway, Jas., Esq., Green Bank.
Greenway, Potter, and Co., calico printers
Greenwood, John, glazier, &c.
Harwood, Seth, agent, Whitehall
Holden, James, overseer.
Haworth, Rd., sizer, Turncroft.
Jackson, Jas., coal agent, Whitehall.
Kirkman, Lawrence, plumber and tinman.
Littler, Rev. Rt. (Independent), Chapels.
Maxwell, John, saddler.
Shorrock, Mr. James.
Walsh, Jas., coal agent, Sough.
Whittaker, Geo., blacksmith.
Whittaker, John, bookkeeper.

Inns, &c.
Angel, Ann Walsh.
Black Dog, Chapels, David Nevill.
Board, Chapels, Jas. Booth.
Bowling Green, Gabriel Shaw.
Bull, Chapels, Michael Beswick.
George and Dragon, Jas. Whittaker.
Greenway's Arms, Wm. Hutchinson.
Mason's Arms, John Catlow.
Millstone, Christopher Gibson.
New Inn, Lawrence Yates Smalley.
Punch Bowl, Blacksnape, Jas. Aspden.
Punch Bowl, Wm. Kay.
Red Lion, Blacksnape, Thos. Kay.
Red Lion, Robt. Shorrock.
Rose and Crown, Wm. Low.
Wellington, James Walsh.
White Lion, John Ainsworth.

Academies.
Kenyon, Thos., Hayfold.
Nuttall, Jas., Blacksnape.
Rothwell, James.
Slater, John.
Wells, Ebenezer.

Bleachers.
Grimshaw, G. and Co., Whitehall.
Hilton, Richard.

Coal Proprietors.
Brandwood, J. W. and J., Turncroft.
Briggs, Jas., Blacksnape.
Entwisle, Wm.
Heap and Hindle.

Hilton, Henry.
Hindle, Wm., Newfold.
Miller, J. and Co., Whitehall.
Pickup, James.
Pickup, John, Marsh House.
Smalley, Rd. Kershaw, Sough and Astley Bank.
Sudell, H., Esq., Ellison Fold.

Corn and Flour Dealers.
Hainsworth, W.
Leach, Simon.

Cotton Manufacturers.
*Brandwood, J. W. and J., Turncroft.
Briggs, Jas., Cranberry Fold.
*Briggs, Jas., Blacksnape.
Broadbent, S. and J., Whitehall.
Carr, Wm., Hatton, & Co. (and spinners).
Collins, Jos., waste spinner.
*Cook, John, Blacksnape.
*Duckworth, J.
Eccles, Wm.
Fish, F. Dewhurst.
Garsden and Co., Vale Rock
Grime, Jas.
*Harwood, J., Blacksnape.
*Holden, John, Day Eye.
Kay, Wm.
*Leach, Robt.
*Pickup, J., Chapels.
Shorrock, Jas.
*Walsh, Rd.

Grocers, &c.
(See also Cotton Manufacturers.)
Aspinall, Jas.
Aspinall, Roger.
Bury, Molly.
Livesey, Rd.
Shorrock, John.

Joiners.
Barber, John.
Eccles, John.
Gileson, John.
Hacking, John, (and Constable).
Harewood, J., Hoddlesden (joiner and cabinet maker).
Kay, A., and Co., Cranberry Fold (joiners, cabinet makers, and machine makers).
Nowell, Thos.

Stone Merchants and Builders.
Brandwood, J. W. and J., Turncroft.
Holden, Saml. (mason).
Hilton, Rd.
Hutchinson, T.
Hutchinson, W.
Walsh, Jas.

Surgeons.
Bury, Roger.
Gautler, Wm.

Those marked (*) are also grocers and flour dealers.

LOWER DARWEN.

Croft, Mr. Christopher.
Crompton, Geo., bookkeeper.
Dearden, Joseph, "Bird i' th' Hand."
Eccles, Joseph, cotton spinner.
Hargreaves, Thos., Esq., Top o' th' Coalpits.
Haworth, John, overseer.
Hindle, Christopher, Esq., Highercroft, chief constable for the Lower Division of Blackburn Hundred.
Hindle, Wm., Newfield, land surveyor.
Johnson, Geo., "King's Arms."
Shorrock, Lawrence, "Swan."
Turner, Robt., junr., and Co., calico printers.
Whittaker, Lawrence, Black-a-Moor.
Wood, Abraham, "Golden Cup."
Pomfret, Thomas, carrier to Preston, on Saturdays.

ECCLESHILL.

Bateson, Richard, black earthenware manufacturer.
Hacking, Richard, mason, Grimshaw.
Hargreaves, Richard, farmer, Davyfield.
Holden, John, blacksmith and wheelwright. "Handel's Arms."
Morris, William, accountant.
Sharples, John, "Punch Bowl."
Walmsley, Joseph, cotton spinnner and manufacturer, Grimshaw Bridge.
Walsh, James and Son, coal merchants.
Walsh, Thomas, land agent and overseer.
Hacking, James, carrier to Preston (Saturday), and Blackburn (Wednesday).

YATE AND PICKUP BANKS.

Butterworth, Thomas, "New Inn," Pickup Bank.
Duckworth, George, "Bell i' th' Thorn."
Houghton, Edward, "Dog."
Thompson, William, cotton manufacturer.
Thornber and Bilsborough, calico printers.
Walmesley, Joseph, cotton spinner.

THE COTTON TRADE.

Linen and woollen have been spun and woven in this part of Lancashire since the time of Elizabeth, but the origin of the textile manufactures which now form the staple trade of the county has not been traced further than this. The flax was imported from Ireland; the wool doubtless obtained from the backs of the sheep on the local moors. Cotton was probably introduced about the time of the Commonwealth, and the blue and white "Blackburn checks" woven of linen and cotton became thenceforward a special product of this neighbourhood. "Blackburn greys" were afterwards extensively introduced, and "calicoes" intended for bleaching and printing. In the latter half of last century a great change took place in the method of producing cloth. Originally the weaver's children were employed at a very early age picking clean the cotton-wool with their fingers, and then it had to be carded and spun by his wife and the elder girls. The men and boys worked the hand-loom, and before the invention of the fly-shuttle by James Kay, of Bury, in 1738, they had to throw the shuttle from hand to hand. When the picking-stick came into use a weaver often found that his wife and children could not keep him supplied with weft, and this necessitated the invention of the spinning jenny, a machine which enabled the spinster to spin from 16 to 20 cops at once. James Hargreaves, of Stanhill, invented and made several spinning jennies between 1764 and 1768, and a new spinning mill of Mr. Peel, at

Brookside, Oswaldtwistle, was supplied with them. This early sign of the change from the cottage system to the factory system caused a mob of some hundreds of weavers to assemble in Blackburn in the Spring of 1768, a section of them coming from Darwen. They broke into Hargreaves's cottage at Stanhill, smashed his jenny and his looms, and afterwards demolished Mr. Peel's mill and the machinery contained in it. Hargreaves patented his spinning jenny in July, 1770, and described it as a "wheel or engine" to "spin, draw, and twist sixteen or more threads at one time by a turn or motion of one hand and a draw of the other." Another spinning machine was invented in 1767 by Richard Arkwright, a Preston barber, and in 1779 Samuel Crompton, of Bolton (afterwards of Darwen), invented the spinning mule. A second uprising against the spinning jenny took place in 1779, and the rioters "scoured the country for many miles round Blackburn, destroying all the jennies, carding engines, and every machine driven by water or horses."

A middle-class of manufacturers or merchants commonly called "chapmen," existed in Darwen as early as 1700. They were resident employers of labour, and the most successful of them kept warehouses for the storage of their goods. "The master gave out a warp and raw cotton to the weaver, for the weaving, &c. The weaver, if the spinning was not done by his own family, paid the spinner for the spinning, and the spinner paid the carder and rover." But in 1774 the "Old Mill" was built in Lower Darwen by Thomas Eccles,—"Thomas o' Owd Sapling Bough's,"[1] and furnished with spinning machinery of the new type. It is related that "this spinning and weaving mill has always escaped the wrath of the rioters, probable owing to the amicable relations existing between employers and employed." A village day school called Lower Darwen Factory School has long been conducted in connection with the mill, and it has been an important centre of a philanthropic work in which both Churchmen and Nonconformists have united under the patronage of the Eccles family. The mill has been several times enlarged. Mrs. Ellen Fielding, a native of Lower Darwen, now over 90 years of age, says :—"There were two little straight-up buildings for spinning built at Lower Darwen when I was about five years old. [1804.] They were new buildings and they were used for nothing but spinning. They were built close to Lower Darwen House [Highercroft]." From this it appears that spinning on the factory system was carried on at Lower Darwen without let or hindrance while the district around Blackburn generally was disturbed by rioters ; but the spinning jenny was so un-

[1] *Jeremy Hunt's Recollections*, p. 50.

popular or so expensive that it was not introduced into the cottages of the Darwen weavers until thirty years after the first building of the Old Mill at Lower Darwen. My authority for this statement is the nonagenarian native of Lower Darwen just referred to, Mrs. Ellen Fielding (formerly Ellen Holden), who now resides at Daisyfield, Blackburn. She informs me that she saw the first 20-spindle bobbin-wheel that ever came into Darwen or the district, and wound the first bobbin on it. She was born at Lower Darwen on April 30th, 1799, and in 1801 her parents went to live at Higher Bog Height, Over Darwen, next door to a farmer named Richard Holden. They left Darwen for Oozehead, Blackburn, before she was seven years of age, and it was while they resided at Bog Height that my informant wound the first bobbin on the first 20-spindle spinning jenny known to have come into Darwen.

The following is a statement I have taken down from her own lips :—Our folks brought the first twenty-spindle bobbin-wheel that came into the country, and I turned the first bobbin on it. It was a thing they had heard of, and they had been on the look-out for it, and when my father brought it from somewhere towards Bolton, the whole neighbourhood came in to look at it. It had guiders to guide the wheels, and our folks had to put it in working order with all the neighbours standing round watching. It was the first machine of the kind that had ever come into the neighbourhood or anywhere near, and my father said, "Our Ellen s' turn t' first bobbin on it." I was too little to hold the thread, but I turned the wheel, with all the neighbours standing round watching me. We had not room for the looms at Bog Height, and I was getting old enough to start weaving, so when I was about seven years of age our folks removed to Oozehead, Blackburn, where they had a shop containing five looms.

"In 1779, when calicoes began to be woven in Lancashire, a weaver received £1 16s. for the weaving of a piece, out of which he paid 18s. 6d. to his family, or others, for the carding of cotton and spinning the weft, &c. At that period, oatcake, or jannock (bread made from oatmeal) was the common food of the operatives in the whole line from Blackburn to Bolton; and water-porridge made from meal, boiled in the water and stirred with a thible, was generally taken with milk, treacle, or beer, by the middle classes of society. Oats were 2s. per bushel; wheat was 5s. for 70lbs.; meal was 20s. per load of 240lbs.; jannock, 15lbs. for 1s.; beef, 2d. per lb.; a neck of mutton, 9d.; a goose, 1s. 3d.; cheese, 2¼d. per lb.; and malt, 23s. per load."[1]

The atmospheric conditions of the Darwen valley are very favourable to the manufacture of cotton cloth; and cotton manufacture has therefore become the staple industry of the town. Mr. Abram has noticed from the parish registers in Blackburn that so long ago as 1700-

[1] Whittle's *Blackburn as it Is*, p. 221.

1720 a large proportion of the natives of Darwen were "websters" or weavers, and that half-a-dozen yeomen or freeholders of the township were "chapmen" or handloom cotton manufacturers. Among the chapmen of Darwen prior to 1720 were Ralph Ellison, John Fish, and Richard Smalley, of Upper Darwen; Thomas Watson, of Over Darwen, gentleman, whose gravestone is to be seen to-day in St. James's Churchyard; Richard Sanderson and Edmund Haworth, of Lower Darwen. Some years later the names of Eccles, Barton, Ainsworth, and Shorrock are mentioned among the chapmen or handloom cotton manufacturers. Many prominent gentlemen of the present day were handloom weavers in their youth. Mr. Jeremy Hunt, the joint author of the second portion of this book, was a handloom weaver, like his father before him, and Alderman Henry Green, J.P., the second Mayor of the borough, is another old inhabitant who sometimes relates how he and many other cotton manufacturers of repute used to "pick" the shuttle for a livelihood. The rise of the factory system in the early part of the present century has gradually but certainly stamped out the handloom system. The first factory in Over Darwen was Bowling Green Mill, commonly called "Th' Top Factory," built in 1820. The oldest portion of it was built by Messrs. John and William Eccles, son of Mr. Thomas Eccles, of Princes,[1] and its original purpose was to serve as a warehouse for the handloom weavers of Darwen who came here for their cotton, and came again with their cloth, manufactured in their own houses. Prior to this many weavers of the Darwen and Hoddlesden valleys had had to carry their cotton all the way from Blackburn and back again. Within a few years of the building of this warehouse or mill, power looms were introduced into Darwen, and in April, 1826, there was a great riot among the handloom weavers, when a gang of loom breakers came from Blackburn and smashed 16 power-looms in a factory belonging to Mr. James Grime, and 18 in the "Top Factory," which at this time was being worked by the firm of Carr, Hatton, and Co., cotton spinners and manufacturers.

The following contemporary account of the riot appeared in the *Blackburn Mail*, dated April 26th, 1826:—"On Tuesday, April 25th, 1826, a detachment of the mob, amounting to near 4,000, went from Blackburn to Over Darwen, and being joined by some of the weavers there, attacked and entered the factory of Mr. Carr, where they destroyed all the power-looms (about 18 in number); they then went to the factory of Mr. James Grime (Vale Rock), at which place they destroyed about 16 looms; after which, without doing any further damage to the factories or other property, they departed for Haslingden, where a troop of horse was awaiting them. . . . . Pall Mall Factory, Over Darwen, was reported to be destroyed."

1 *Jeremy Hunt's Recollections*, p. 52.

Mr. Eccles Shorrock, the famous merchant and cotton spinner, came from Blackburn and settled in Over Darwen in 1830, when he purchased Bowling Green Mill and other property of Mr. Carr. He was uncle to the present Eccles Shorrock, and great-uncle of the present Eccles Shorrock, junr., who has succeeded to the property, and was a good specimen of the best class of cotton spinners of the last generation. Born in Over Darwen, the son of a small tradesman, he sprang from a family of yeomen and manufacturers in Lower Darwen who have been engaged in the cotton trade for more than a century. Being fairly educated, very industrious, and reliable, and having a thorough knowledge of his business, he in early manhood became the manager of extensive cotton mills in Hoghton and Chorley, and shortly afterwards was taken into partnership by his cousin, Mr. Bannister Eccles, a large spinner and manufacturer in Blackburn. He retired from this concern about 1831, having then commenced business at Bowling Green Mill, Over Darwen, which he enlarged. In the course of time he took as partners the late Mr. James Shorrock and Mr. Thomas Ashton, and in conjunction with them, built and purchased other mills and estates in the township of Over Darwen, Lower Darwen, Tockholes, &c.[1] New Mill and Darwen Mill were erected by them, the latter on the site of Hilton's Paper Works. Brookside Mill Mr. Eccles Shorrock purchased shortly before his death. In person he was above the middle height, rather handsome, reserved in his manners, and not given to many words. His character was more calculated to inspire respect than to win that abiding affection which keeps a man's memory green. A first-rate horseman, fond of land and the pursuits of a country gentleman, he spent large sums in planting and improving his estates, and some of his happiest hours were passed in slowly riding through the districts he had done so much to adorn. He purchased and enlarged Low Hill House, originally built and occupied by Samuel Compton and afterwards held by Mr. William Eccles, one of the two brothers who built Bowling Green Mill. He was twice married, but died without issue in the year 1853, and was buried in St. Paul's Churchyard, Blackburn, by the side of his first wife. His nephew and heir, Mr. Eccles Shorrock Ashton, who dropped the paternal surname of Ashton on the death of his uncle, married in 1851 the daughter of Timothy Dimmock, or Dymock, of Hanley, Staffordshire, Esquire, a family as old and well-known as the Bagot Oaks.[2] Messrs. Eccles Shorrock, Brother, and

[1] In 1833 there were only ten steam engines in Darwen. Trade was so depressed in 1841 that a body of philanthropists in London called "The Manufacturers' Relief Committee" sent on December 21st for distribution in Over Darwen £300; Lower Darwen, £75; Eccleshill, £25; Yate and Pickup Bank, £75. There was distress again in 1843 and 1847. [2] *The Heart of Lancashire*, ch. ii.

Co. carried on business until the end of 1882, when their failure caused great distress in the town, and threw more than 1,000 people out of work by the stoppage of Darwen Mill, New Mill, Brookside Mill, and Hollinshead Mill. Their liabilities amounted to £130,000, and they paid a composition of 6s. 8d. in the £. On the 21st of February, 1883, Judge Hulton heard an application at the Blackburn County Court, on behalf of Messrs. Cunliffes, Brooks and Co., bankers, to set aside the decision made by Mr. Adamson, trustee in the liquidation proceedings, by which he rejected proof of a claim by Messrs. Cunliffes, Brooks and Co. for £20,270, being the amount of their original debt under a previous composition proceeding, a claim which they had set up in consequence of the instalments not having been paid. The judge decided in the bankers' favour.

India Mill, an extensive stone building with a magnificent campanile chimney, was built in 1867, and opened with an exhibition, the proceeds of which, £1,115, were utilised to build Belgrave Congregational School. The stone on which the foundation of the chimney rests is said to be the largest block quarried since Cleopatra's Needle was dug out of the earth. It was obtained from a plot of land at the southern extremity of Darwen, near Cadshaw Bridge, and a road had to be cut through a meadow from the quarry to the highway for the purpose of transporting it and other materials. This road is still to be seen at the rear of the Half-way House Inn. Thirty-five horses were employed to draw the huge block from the quarry to its destination. It was then buried in the ground, and a chimney which cost £14,000 was built upon it, forming the most conspicuous architectural pile in the town.

The year 1878 is memorable in the history of cotton manufacture. On the 19th of March—six days before the arrival at Over Darwen of the Charter of Incorporation—a meeting of the manufacturers of North-East Lancashire was held in Manchester, at which it was resolved to give a month's notice of 10 per cent. reduction of wages, both in the spinning and weaving trades. On the 20th of April, with very few exceptions, the whole of the mills in Darwen were closed by the general strike; the operatives having decided to resist the reduction. Among the mills which continued working were Cotton Hall, Lower Wood, Dove, Whitehall, Ellenshaw, Hanover Street, and Atlas Mills. It was estimated that this strike threw out of work 5,000 hands in Darwen, from 20,000 to 25,000 in Blackburn, 4,000 in Accrington, and from 10,000 to 15,000 in Burnley, the smaller villages in North East Lancashire being proportionately affected. The strike generally lasted nine weeks; in Darwen ten weeks. At a mass meeting of weavers on the Fair Ground on May 1st, between 2,000 and 3,000 persons being present, it was resolved "that in order to continue the strike, weavers working full-time at the old rate of wages pay a weekly levy of sixpence per loom; those working five days at five per cent. reduction fourpence per loom; and those working four days at full reduction twopence per loom." The operatives in deciding to resist the reduction had contended that a curtailment of production, to be brought about by working short time, was the proper remedy for the depressed state of trade. They had agreed to accept the 10 per cent. reduction, on the condition that the mills were only run four days per week, or to accept a five per cent. reduction at mills working five days per week; but if the masters insisted on running full time then the operatives demanded full wages.

The strike was marked with much rioting and disturbance. At Blackburn the mob burned down the house of Colonel R. Raynsford Jackson, chairman of the Masters' Association, and drew his burning carriage through the streets of the town, besides smashing windows of mills and gentlemen's residences. Several of the rioters were sentenced to long terms of penal servitude The first disturbance in Darwen took place on May 7th, when windows were broken and the effigies of Mr. and Mrs. W. T. Ashton were burnt near Jack's Kay Lodge. Next day a soup kitchen was opened for the free distribution of pea soup and bread to the distressed operatives. The rioting was renewed on the 9th, when the effigy of Richard Sharples, beerseller, was burnt, and the mob broke all the front windows of Mr. Ashton's residence, Ashdale, beside damaging his grounds considerably. Marching down Bolton Road and Market Street, they threw their stones through the windows of the police office, then went down to Lynwood Avenue, stopping opposite the house of Mr. G. B. Snape, where, at a given signal, a volley of stones was fired, breaking all the front windows. The mob rambled about the streets until the small hours of the morning, levying black-mail at the public-houses. On the 10th a large force of additional police arrived. The town was in an excited state until midnight; 150 policemen scoured the streets, dispersing the crowds, under the command of Captain Legge, Chief Constable of the County. Many of the men wore cutlasses and most of them carried their staves in their hands. Several of them were injured, the local Inspector, Mr. Norris, being among the number. By ten o'clock at night they had a dozen prisoners. On this day a meeting of tradesmen convened by Mr. James Huntington, J.P., was held in Berry's Room, Foundry Street, to organize a relief scheme. Mr. John Riley, grocer, afterwards a town councillor, was appointed honorary secretary, and Mr. H. Broadbent, of the Manchester and County Bank, treasurer. The relief committee distributed tickets for loaves, meal, &c., next day. On the morning of the 11th the prisoners were brought before a full bench of magistrates; six were sentenced to a month's imprisonment and others were fined. At five o'clock in the afternoon a meeting was called by the bellman, to be held at the top of High Street, and it was attended by the roughest of the operatives. The Rev. P. Graham, J.P., addressed the crowd from the steps of the police office and strongly urged them not to carry out the threats of destruction which were freely uttered on every hand. The people expressed their willingness to comply with his request, providing the police were withdrawn from the streets. While Mr. Graham and Mr. Charles Costeker, Clerk to the magistrates, were consulting with the officers in charge of the police as to this suggestion, a disturbance arose outside, and stones were thrown. The police rushed out immediately, but, at the request of Mr. Graham, they were recalled. The crowd then marched about the town for an hour, good-humouredly singing ditties, and the riot was considered to be at an end. On the 12th—Sunday—a sitting of the court was held to try three persons taken into custody for rioting on the previous night, and the court, being thrown open to the public, was crowded. In order to allay the popular feeling of indignation against the increased force of police, the Bench dismissed all three cases. On the 14th a meeting of delegates of employers and employed was held in Manchester, but no settlement was arrived at, and on the news being wired to Blackburn, the serious riots in that town, accompanied by the burning of Clayton Grange, broke out. The Riot Act was read and the military were called out, a company of Dragoons galloping over from Preston about midnight. During this week serious riots occurred in nearly all the towns of North-East Lancashire, the Riot Act having to be read, not only at Blackburn, but at Preston, Burnley, and Accrington. A company of the 17th Lancers, numbering 22, and another of the 15th Foot Regiment, numbering 45, visited Darwen on the morning of the 17th, fully equipped, but, after parading for half-an-hour, returned to Blackburn. Sough Tunnel was guarded by a dozen policemen at each end, on the 21st, a rumour being current that the operatives intended upsetting the express from Manchester due at Darwen at 5 20 p.m., and generally known as "the manufacturers' train." On the 22nd, claims were made upon the county rates for damages. The total for the county amounted to £20,000, including £6,000 for Clayton Grange and £6,000 for the furniture which it had contained, The claims from Darwen did not exceed £90, the principal one being Mr. W. T.

Ashton's account for £30. The strike ended on the 21st of June, all mills then resuming work, the operatives having consented to the ten per cent. reduction of their wages. The relief committee issued a balance-sheet, showing subscriptions from all sources, £365 1s. 1d.; expenses, £362 11s. 8d. Mr. James Huntington, originator of the relief fund, died on the 24th, aged 52; and the same day the extra police left Darwen to return home. On this day also 18 Liberal candidates, nominated for the Town Council, were elected unopposed, at the least possible cost and with the least possible excitement.

In 1879, there being again very bad trade, there were strikes in the building trade, among painters, joiners, masons, and plumbers; and on the 1st of April a stormy meeting of cotton operatives was held in the Co-operative Hall to consider a proposed further reduction of five per cent. in weavers' wages, to which, however, they submitted without a strike. On the 8th of January, 1881, this five per cent. was voluntarily returned, Councillor Beads, of Blackburn, cotton manufacturer, having a few weeks before publicly expressed the opinion that the improved state of trade would warrant it.

A further reduction of 10 per cent. in weavers' wages was threatened in October, 1883, and the operatives subscribed a penny per loom towards a fund for resisting it. A compromise of five per cent. was subsequently suggested, and a ballot of the factory operatives of Darwen was taken on the 12th November, when it was decided by a large majority to come out on strike rather than submit to any reduction. Fourteen notices of the reduction in the weaving departments were posted on the 28th and 29th of November at mills containing 15,773 looms; and simultaneously in the mills of other towns and villages in North-East Lancashire. On the 7th of December a public meeting of weavers was held in the Co-operative Hall, when a large majority decided to come out on strike on the expiration of the notice. The strike did not affect the whole town, as the reduction was not enforced at every mill, and the weavers decided at a meeting in the Co-operative Hall, on December 18th, that those working full time should contribute sixpence per loom, and those working short time twopence per loom to the strike fund. Another public meeting was held in the Co-operative Hall on the 14th January, when it was decided to continue the strike. Much excitement was caused, both in Darwen and Blackburn, on the 6th of February, by an announcement that the representatives of the operatives had settled the strike. The basis on which it was settled was that the whole of the operatives should return to work forthwith at the reduction of five per cent., on condition that the question should be reconsidered in the following May with a view to the restoration of the five per cent. if the state of trade should warrant it. A weavers' meeting was held next day on the old Fair Ground, at which 5,000 persons were present, and it was resolved, with great enthusiasm, " that we continue the strike until the masters run four days per week or full time with full wages." A large crowd assembled in the Circus and marched down Blackburn Road, bearing an effigy, of which the police obtained possession near Hollins Lane. A meeting was held in the Co-operative Hall on the 9th to hear an explanation from Mr. David Holmes, a member of the Committee which had settled the strike. There was a crowded attendance, and the proceedings were very orderly, but notwithstanding Mr. Holmes's explanation, it was resolved, almost unanimously, to continue the strike. Another meeting was held on the 19th, by which time the weavers in the rest of North-East Lancashire had resumed work on the terms of the compromise. It was reported that a meeting of weavers' delegates from North-East Lancashire had, on a previous Sunday, decided to send no more pecuniary support to Darwen, and, in these circumstances, the weavers resolved to resume work on the following Thursday; and the strike was thus settled after having been prolonged rather more than the Great Strike of 1878. A public report of the strike showed that £18,500 was distributed by the Weavers' Associations in North-East Lancashire, among those out of work. £4,500 of this came out of the funds of various societies, and the rest was specially contributed by the operatives in work and friends.

On October 21st, 1886, notice of five per cent. reduction was given at six of the largest spinning mills in Darwen, and the spinners at the end of 14 days came out on strike. The spinners, who in Darwen were paid by *weight*, desired to be paid according to the *length* of the yarn spun, as at Oldham, and the strike was settled on these terms on November 11th, the masters agreeing to fix the necessary indicators. A return circulated amongst the master spinners, during this strike, showed that the wages paid in Oldham mills were lower by about £20 per 1,000 spindles per annum than the wages paid for spinning the same counts of yarn in the Darwen mills; or, in other words, that it cost £6,860 more in wages per annum to run 345,000 spindles in Darwen than it would in Oldham. On this basis it was shown that the largest mill in the town, India Mill, was paying £1,720 per annum more than a similar mill would pay in Oldham, and that the next large mill in the town, Mr. James Walsh's, was paying an excess of £1,000 per annum. This return also showed that the wages paid per annum at India

Mill amounted to £14,036; at Mr. James Walsh's to £8,032; at Cotton Hall Mill to £6,152; at Albert Mill to £5,688; and at "No. 1" Mill—Darwen Spinning Co.—to £5,020.

On May 26th, 1883, the *Preston Guardian* recorded the number of spindles in Darwen and the adjacent villages to be 421,442 and the number of looms 21,042. These provided employment for 11,100 people, of whom 800 were out of work at that time by stoppages. It was estimated that the 10,300 workpeople then employed received in weekly wages about £9,000; every man, woman, and child in the town engaged in the cotton trade—one third of the entire population—receiving something like 17s. 6d. per week. The raw cotton imported weekly weighed 176 tons, and the cloth exported about 550 tons. The average wages of weavers for the whole town was about 11s. per pair of looms, but at the best mills the average was 12s. 2d. During the strike of 1884, it was recorded on February 2nd that there were 9,758 looms stopped and 4,747 workpeople thrown out of employment, the number of looms running either full time with full pay, or short time with reduced wages, being 8,712, finding employment for 4,176 workpeople. This was exclusive of the spinning mills pure and simple, and of the mills at Lower Darwen which were affected more by Blackburn than by Over Darwen. Two thousand more looms were under notice to stop during the ensuing week. The cotton trade was again at a very low ebb in September, 1885. At that time there were 62 mills in the town worked by 50 firms. They contained 429,892 spindles and 20,913 looms, finding employment when in full work for no fewer than 11,026 hands. Eight mills at that time were completely stopped, and at nearly every mill in the town that was not stopped there were many looms standing empty and idle. The total number of spindles idle was 46,000, looms 3,085; and 1,510 workpeople were on the streets.

The table below, compiled from the most authentic detailed information obtainable, shows that in the four townships dealt with in this history there are 62 cotton mills, containing roundly 415,000 spindles and 23,600 looms, which find employment for 12,400 men, women, and children—the spinning branch employing 1,350 and the weaving branch 11,050. A number of cotton spinners and manufacturers have very kindly given me exact statistical information from their books, and taking eight or ten mills as the basis, I estimate that the raw cotton consumed annually in Darwen and District is worth £575,000, while the cotton cloth produced on Darwen looms is of the annual value of 3¼ millions. The total wages paid in the Darwen cotton trade amount to £540,787, or an average of 17s. 5d. each working week for every man, woman, and child employed. Wages are slightly higher in the spinning branch, where the average is 18s. 5d. per head as against 17s. 4d. in the manufacturing branch.

COTTON SPINNERS.

	Spindles	Looms	Wkpple.
Albert Cotton Spinning Co., Limited, Albert Mill	36198	...	108
Bolton Road Spinning and Manufacturing Co., Darwen Mill	50000	...	120
Cotton Hall Spinning and Manufacturing Co., Ld., Cotton Hall Mill	43792	...	120
Darwen Spinning Co., No. 1 Mill	36490	...	110
Hindley, Peter, Atlas Mill	20000	...	100
India Mill Co., India Mill	84308	...	270
Shorrock, Christopher and Co., Moss Bridge Mill	39000	...	120
Shorrock, Eccles, junr., New Mill	27200	...	95
Watson, James, Sunnybank Mill	2500	...	30

SPINNERS AND MANUFACTURERS.

Eccles, T. and R., The Old Mill, Lower Darwen	24000	900	600
Haworth, H., Vale Rock Mill, Hoddlesden	2500	80	60
Orchard Mill Co., Limited	30000	800	600
Rawlinson and Boyle, Atlas Mill	19000	400	258
	414988	2180	2591

COTTON MANUFACTURERS.

Ainsworth and Co., Highfield Mill	280	140
Ashton, W. T. and Son, Hope Mill	676	350
Aspden, James, Springfield Mill, Sough	300	150
Barnes, Bros., Belthorn Mill	216	100
Baynes, Taylor and Co., New Mill	830	360
Baynes, Taylor, and Co., Townsfield Mill	370	160
Baynes, Taylor, and Co., Lorne Street Mill	352	160
Bell, H., and Co., Tackfield Mill	224	90
Birtwistle and Thompson, Woodfold Mill	532	230
Brookside Weaving Co., Brookside Mill	325	216
Brookside Weaving Co., Dove Cottage Mill	226	105
Bullough, Adam, Waterside	616	300
Carus, Alexander, Vale Rock Mill, Hoddlesden	576	250
Cooper, Henry, and Sons	226	100
Darwen Manufacturing Company, Limited, Carr's Mill	870	430
Deakin, J. B., Whitehall Mill	480	250
Duckworth and Cooper, Vale Brook Mill	345	180
Eccles Bros., Bottomcroft Mill	492	250
Eccles, Holden, and Co., Speculation Mill	390	190
Eccles, Holden, and Co., Sudellside Mill	259	90
Eccles, N. and J., Two Gates Mill	520	210
Eccles, William and Co., Culvert Mill	120	60
Fish, Graham, and Co., Woodside Mill	943	471
Fish, N. and Co., Hanover Street Mill	221	100
Gillibrand, Thomas and Sons, Hollins Grove Mill	1300	550

	Looms	Wkpple
Greenfield Mill Co., Greenfield Mill, Spring Vale	952	479
Grime, William and Co., Hampden Mill	462	200
Halliwell, James, George-street Mill	706	300
Harwood Bros., New Bridge Mill	387	190
Hindle, E. and G., Hollinshead Mill, Tockholes	318	120
Holden, Preston, and Martin, Hindle Street Mill	300	120
Knowles, E. Hillside Mill	448	220
Leach, Robert, Barley Bank Mill	308	110
Lightbown, Leach, and Catlow, Springfield Mill	212	100
Lightbown, Leach, and Catlow, Radford Mill	216	100
Munroe, M., and Co., Springfield Mill, Guide	550	300
Oddie, John and Sons, Syke Mill, Belthorn	320	102
Pickup and Holden, Bank Top Mill	750	200
Shorrock, Christopher and Co., Bowling Green Mill	842	450
Shorrock and Whewell, Progress Shed	500	234
Shuttleworth and Co., Queen Street Mill	220	100
Shuttleworth and Co., Lower Wood Mill	200	90
Walsh, George, Ellenshaw Mill	300	120
Walmsley, William, Industry Mill	192	100
Walmsley, John and Sons, Vale Mill	354	180
Walmsley, John and Sons, Holme Mill	400	200
Wardleworth, John, Primrose Mill	280	100
Whipp, Bros., Cotton Hall Mill	500	200
	23,586	12,398

CALICO-PRINTING AND BLEACHING.

Calico-printing was commenced in Lancashire in the year 1764, on the banks of the River Darwen in Walton-le-Dale, and in 1776 it was introduced into Darwen by Mr. James Greenway. The antiquary Pennant, after his visit to Blackburn in 1773, wrote :—" The manufactures are cottons ; considerable quantities are printed here ; others are sent to London. The fields around are whitened with the materials which are bleached from them. The thread, which must be ranked with them, is brought from Ireland." At first the bleached calico had the coloured pattern printed on it by means of blocks of wood engraved by hand, but so early as 1784 block-printing was succeeded by cylinder-printing at Mosney, near Walton-le-Dale. Mr. James Greenway, who established calico-printing in Darwen in 1776, is believed to have come from the south of England. He commenced business at Livesey Fold—a homestead once occupied by the Livesey family,—and extended it in 1808 to Dob Meadows. At this time Mr. Greenway took into partnership his relatives Mr. Charles Potter and Mr. Maude, and soon afterwards retired, when the firm became known as Potter, Maude, and Co., and existed as such until about 1830. This firm also built the Print Shop on Bury Fold Brook, which is now used as cottage dwellings. In 1832 the Dob Meadow Works were leased by Mr. Greenway, junior, to Messrs. Charles Potter and William Ross, but in 1841 Mr. Charles Potter retired from this firm, and, along with his brother Harold, founded the prosperous paper-making and printing business now carried on by Messrs. Potter and Co. at Hollins Mill in Lower Darwen and at Belgrave and Livesey Mills in Over Darwen. Mr. Ross continued the calico-printing business alone for five years, and in 1847 retired in favour of Messrs. Heron, Baron, and Eddlestone, who continued the business as co-partners until 1872, when Mr. Eddlestone died. The business was then carried on by Messrs. Heron and Baron, who gave up business in 1878 and had their machinery sold by auction and removed. The success with which the business of Messrs. Greenway, Potter, and Co. was carried on was not alone due to the partners in the firm, for they were greatly aided by Mr. W. Henrey, their superintendent or manager. On his death in August, 1823, the *Blackburn Mail* published an extremely laudatory article, stating that he was distinguished for his scientific knowledge and its application to the art of calico-printing. He was followed to his grave in St. Peter's Churchyard, Blackburn, by his employers, many friends, and a large concourse of people. Two of Mr. Henrey's daughters married into old and well-known Darwen families, now represented by Mr. Christopher Shorrock and Mr. Richard Henrey Smalley.

Mr. Greenway, the founder of the Livesey Fold and Dob Meadow business resided at Livesey Fold. He was a shrewd, persevering man, exceedingly plain in manners and habits, but much esteemed by his friends. Many curious anecdotes are told of him, one of which is well worth preserving. Being about to undertake some large operations, requiring many out-door labourers, he engaged several men for one day in removing stones from one side of a road to the other. He stood by all day watching the work, which went on with great spirit and was finished in the evening. On its conclusion he expressed himself dissatisfied with what had been done and told the men to begin in the morning and carry the stones back to their original position. The men began on the following day as directed, but Mr. Greenway did not appear on the scene until the day's work was nearly over, and then he found that only half the stones had been carried back. He thereupon paid the men three days' wages, and dismissed them, saying that "men who only did half the work when left to themselves that they would do when overlooked would not suit him."[1] He was succeeded in his

[1] *The Heart of Lancashire*, chap. vii.

business and in his Darwen property by his son, the late James Greenway, Esq., who built and for many years resided at Darwen Bank. His gentlemanly bearing, handsome appearance, and quiet retiring habits will be well rembered. He died without issue, in the 90th year of his age, on July 8th, 1866, leaving the bulk of his property to his nephew, the Rev. Charles Greenway, M.A., J.P., of Darwen Bank (at one time incumbent of St. James's Church), who in 1878 sold the old bleaching croft and adjoining property to the Corporation for the site of a Town Hall and Market House.

The following prices of cattle and manufactured goods are culled from a stock-taking account of Mr. James Greenway, dated 1795:—Horses, £17 17s. 0d., £15. £12 12s. 0d., £10, £7, £5, £4 10s.; cows, from £6 to £7 7s. 0d; calico prints, 32 inches wide by 95 yards in length, one piece of 9·8ths. chintz print, £2 8s. 4d.; one piece of black and purple, £2 3s. 4d.; one piece of light chintz, £2 5s. 11d.

Calico bleaching was introduced into the township before the year 1800 by Mr. Richard Hilton, a native of Blackburn, and one of his bleaching works was rented, in 1812, by Mr. Samuel Crompton. The Hiltons were still engaged in bleaching in 1818, but soon afterward gave it up and embarked in paper-making. With the £5,000 granted by Parliament in June 1812, Samuel Crompton, the inventor of the spinning mule, came to Darwen from Bolton and began bleaching at Hilton's Higher Works, now known as Spring Vale Paper Works. He took into partnership his eldest and youngest sons, George and James. Many circumstances conspired to make Crompton's Darwen business unsuccessful, especially the conduct of his sons. George left his father and made an unsuccessful attempt to carry on the business of bleacher at Hoddlesden, where Vale Rock Mill now stands, and soon afterward both places were given up and the family left the town. Crompton was also crippled by a costly lawsuit arising out of the sinking of coal-pits near his works, which diverted the supply of spring water on which his business was dependent. That "pleasant dwelling place," Low Hill House, was built by Mr. Crompton, and occupied by him for five years. He was an industrious, kindly man; thoughtful, unobtrusive, and fond of music. The late Mr. G. H. Openshaw remembered that when he was a little boy his father came home late one evening, accompanied by Mr. Crompton and another friend, and he (the boy Openshaw) was roused from bed in order to join them in a new quartette which Crompton had just received, and the friends were anxious to perform.[1] George Crompton, Samuel's eldest son, resided when an old man in Blackburn, and was for some years cashier at Messrs. Yates's Foundry. Crompton's unselfish genius and lifelong disappointments are matters

[1] *The Heart of Lancashire*, chap. ii.

of history. Others have reaped the benefit of his inventions. In 1834 the Rev. Gilmour Robinson, M.A., Vicar of Tockholes, with the aid of Sir Robert Peel, was instrumental in obtaining a grant of £200 from the Royal Bounty fund for division between George Crompton and his brother and sister, as a reward for their father's meritorious invention of the spinning mule. George at that time lived at Fearnhurst, Lower Darwen; the brother and sister resided in Bolton.

Sir Robert Peel, the statesman upon whose recommendation this grant was made, was the chief representative of a family intimately connected with the development both of the cotton trade and of calico-printing in this part of Lancashire, and the grandson of "William Peel, of Darwen," who in 1713 married Jane, daughter of Lawrence Walmsley, of Over Darwen, gent., and subsequently inherited Peel Fold.

The trades of calico-printing and bleaching in Darwen are now extinct.

PAPER-MAKING AND PAPER-STAINING.

Hilton's Paper Works, erected by Mr. Richard Hilton shortly before his death in 1836, were in their day the largest in the world, but the very magnitude of the concern involved the firm in financial difficulties. The elder Hilton was a native of Blackburn, who came to Darwen and set up business as a calico-bleacher at Spring Vale a few years before the end of the eighteenth century. He also had works on the River Darwen where Darwen Mill now stands, and here he built his extensive Paper Works, surrounded by a chain of reservoirs and connected by tramways. Between 1836 and 1843 Messrs. Richard Hilton and Sons were the principal employers of labour in the town. Their failure in the last-mentioned year took place while the works were under the management of Mr. Henry Hilton, second son of the founder of the firm—"an accomplished and energetic man, who did more than any other resident to improve the external appearance of this district." The Hiltons for two generations possessed commanding influence in the town and lived in the oldest mansion of the district, Whitehall. Mr. Henry Hilton planted woods and laid out some beautiful walks on the hill-sides. After his failure in business he set sail for Natal, to try his hand at cotton planting, but died there, shortly after his arrival, in 1850. Hilton's Paper Works were run by Mr. Edmondstone in 1847, and by other parties, but they were eventually demolished, and the bulk of the paper trade of the town passed into the hands of Messrs. Potter and Co., founded at Belgrave Works and Livesey Fold in 1841. While the paper trade of the Hiltons originated in calico-bleaching, that of the Potters sprang from calico-printing, and at one time their Belgrave Works were used for carpet-weaving. With paper-making Messrs.

C. P. HUNTINGTON, Esq., J.P.

Potter and Co. combined paper-staining, and these two important branches of local industry are second only to the cotton trade in extent and in the number of operatives employed. The stained wall-papers of Messrs. C. and J. G. Potter are noted all over the world, and the business has been so successful that several men have made ample fortunes in it. Mr. John Gerald Potter, J.P., who has four times been a candidate for Parliamentary honours, is the senior member of the firm, but Mr. W. B. Huntington, J.P., and Mr. C. P. Huntington, J.P., are the active superintending partners at the present time. Mr. John Charles Potter, son of Mr. J. G. Potter, was admitted into the firm, on attaining his majority, in September, 1884. The Belgrave Paper-Staining Works are the oldest and largest in the world, and the firm have resident representatives both in Europe and the British Colonies. The manager is Mr. Edward Gregson, and 500 workpeople are employed—all men and boys. The staining of paper by machinery was invented by Mr. Walmsley Preston, who was an ordinary workman employed by the firm, soon after paper-staining was commenced. Preston had been a calico-printer at Dob Meadows, under Messrs. Potter and Ross, and he took the idea of printing wall-paper from the process in use in calico-printing. He eventually became manager, and, afterwards, managing-partner of the firm of C. & J. G. Potter, paper-stainers. The principle he introduced has since been much developed, and it is still employed. The Darwen Paper-Staining Co., of Livesey Mills, Belgrave Road, is connected with the firm of C. & J. G. Potter, but the mill is worked separately, under the management of Mr. John Heald, and it employs between 150 and 200 workpeople. This business was transferred from the works of Messrs. Wm. Snape & Co., Livesey Fold, to the new works erected in Belgrave Road and called Livesey Mills. Messrs. Potter & Co.'s paper-mill at Hollins Grove employs 200 workpeople, and is under the management of Mr. George Hitchen. It contains five machines, and the goods manufactured include "stainers" (for the Belgrave Works and the Livesey Mills), writing, printing, enamel and chromo papers.

There are nine paper-mills in Darwen, but two are at present stopped. The seven that were running at the end of 1888 find employment for 930 men and boys, whose average weekly wages are about 23/6. In the paper-staining trade, both males and females being employed, the average wages are not more than £1 per head.

MINING AND QUARRYING.

The coal trade of Darwen, which has been shown to have flourished in centuries past, is now subsidiary to other branches of mining. Three collieries have been turned into flag pits, and five into pits for the production of fire-clay. At the fire-clay pits coal is still got, not for sale, but for use in the manufacture on the spot of sewage pipes, chimney-pots, tiles, and various other coarse kinds of earthenware. Messrs. Joseph Place and Sons, Hoddlesden, are the largest firm engaged in this trade. They employ in all 300 workpeople. Altogether there are 770 men and boys engaged in the excavation and manufacture of fire-clay and its subsidiary industry, coal-mining, and they turn out yearly 70,000 tons of manufactured goods, valued at £53,000. Their weekly wages average 28/- per head. There are three flag-pits and five quarries in Darwen, the former being worked by shafts like collieries, and being, in fact disused collieries. The Entwisle family are the principal employers of labour in this branch of mining and quarrying. Before the days of railways it was no uncommon thing for a string of thirty farmers' carts to come like a caravan to the collieries of the Entwisles from various parts of the Ribble Valley, for coal, and the colliers had often to work night and day in order to supply the demand. The flag-pits and quarries of Darwen find employment for 430 men and boys, whose wages average 25/- weekly, and produce 132,000 tons of flags and stones per annum.

THE IRON TRADE.

The Darwen and Mostyn Iron Co., Limited, have extensive smelting works in Eccleshill, adjoining the railway, about midway between Over and Lower Darwen. They have a locomotive engine to do their own shunting, and their works and railway sidings cover a large area. They employ some 110 workmen, who earn about £1 a week each on the average. The engineering and machine trade of Darwen is a very important one, the principal firm being that of Messrs. J. & R. Shorrock, who have large foundries on the Lea, and in Bolton Road, employing about three-fourths of the ironworkers of the town The total number of engineers, mechanics, moulders, and others employed in this trade is 485, and their weekly wages per head average about 24/-.

WORKS IN OVER DARWEN IN 1867.

For comparison with the more modern statistics collated in the preceding pages, I append a table showing the state of trade in Darwen in 1867. The particulars in it were compiled by the Local Board for the purpose of showing Parliament the importance of the town on the occasion of an application for the enfranchisement of Over Darwen under the Great Reform Bill.

Description.	No. of works	Work-people	Annual Production.	Approximate Annual Value
Tileries	1	80	....	£7,280
Quarries...............	6	142	....	12,715
Foundries	6	196	....	31,200
Collieries	5	477	101,290 tons	42,568
Paper-Making	4	440	5,720 ,,	169,936
Paper-Staining	2	350	8,000,000 doz. yds.	130,000
Calico-Printing	2	220		120,000
Cotton-Spinning ...	4	800	6,060,000lbs. of yarn	400,000
Cotton-Weaving ...	32	6,950	28,550,000lbs. of cloth	2,141,250
Total	62	9,655		£3,054,969

THE RAILWAY.

An Act of Parliament was obtained in 1845, authorising the construction of a line called "The Blackburn, Darwen and Bolton Railway," and the first portion of this, from Blackburn to Sough, was opened on the 3rd of August, 1847. For the next ten months passengers from Blackburn for Bolton and Manchester had to leave the train at Sough station, and proceed by Birch's stage-coach to Bolton; but Sough Tunnel was in the course of construction, and the complete line was opened on June 12th, 1848. This section now belongs to the Lancashire and Yorkshire Railway, and forms part of the Lancashire and Yorkshire and Midland express route from Manchester to the North. For the purpose of allowing the passage of sleeping cars, Sough Tunnel, which is about a mile in length, was, in 1880, enlarged by the lowering of its bed. The new Darwen Station was built in 1883-4, its name being change from "Over Darwen" to Darwen with the approval of the Over Darwen Corporation, who have since changed the name of the borough in like manner. Lower Darwen Station was included within the borough of Blackburn on the extension of the borough in 1879. Near it there is a large engine shed used for storing and cleaning the engines stationed at Blackburn. A branch line from Darwen to Hoddlesden was opened in 1876. It is used solely for goods traffic in connection with the works of Messrs. Place, Bullough, and Carus.

In August, 1887, a subsidence of land took place at Spring Vale Station while a passenger train was going through, but the train passed safely along with a wave-like motion. Part of the stone platforms and the iron rails sank into the ground to the depth of two or three feet, and the buildings on both sides the line were so cracked that it was wonderful how they held together. The subsidence was found to be due to old mining works underneath the line.

Darwen is dependent on the Lancashire and Yorkshire Railway for all its supplies both from north and south, and many attempts have

1. While Sough Tunnel connects Darwen with Bolton and Manchester, the hill through which it is cut is the natural boundary of the Darwen valley on the southern side, and divides the water shed of the River Darwen from that of various small tributaries of the Irwell.

been made in vain to obtain additional accommodation and healthy competition. The Corporation have, at various times within the last ten years, petitioned the Midland Railway Company and the London and North-Western Railway Company to bring a line into Darwen, and have even gone so far as to suggest to the latter Company that a line should be brought either through Egerton from Bolton, or through Tockholes from Chorley.

THE LOCAL BOARD OF HEALTH.

Local government may be said to have begun in the year 1854, when the now-extinct Local Board of Health was formed, with Mr. Charles Potter as chairman. The subsequent chairmen of the Board were Messrs. James Shorrock (1857), Eccles Shorrock (two years), Nathaniel Walsh, James Wardley, Joshua Baron (two years), and Mr. G. H. Openshaw; the Rev. Philip Graham, Mr. R. S. Ashton, the Rev. Philip Graham again (two more years), Mr. James Shorrock again, Messrs. Henry Green, Joseph Eccles (two years), Thos. Grime, J. T. Kenyon (two years), and Wm. Snape (from 1875 until the incorporation of the borough). The establishment of the Cemetery and of the Free Library took place during the reign of the Local Board., and in 1873 the Board promoted a Bill in Parliament which enabled them to purchase the Gas and Waterworks. In 1874, on the petition of the Local Board, the district of Over Darwen was divided into wards. The original proposition was that there should be six wards, called South-East, Central, West End, St. James's, Trinity, and St. John's, but at the Government Inquiry in February, 1874, an objection was taken to the ecclesiastical names, and ultimately the Local Government Board decided to divide the town into six wards, each to have three representatives, the names respectively to be South-West, West-Central, North-West, North-East, Central and South-East.

A very serious epidemic of typhoid fever occurred in the year 1874, and the Local Board of Health, whose primary duty it was to take care of the sanitary condition of the town, had a very arduous and thankless task to perform under unusual circumstances of difficulty. The first case occurred on the 25th of September, at Woodside Bank, the house of the Rev. Thomas Davies, whose daughter was stricken with it. Three weeks later, the newly-appointed Medical Officer of Health, Dr. George Hindle, of Holker House, reported to the Local Government Board that there were then between 500 and 600 cases of typhoid or enteric fever in the district, and that the epidemic was almost precisely similar to one that occurred in 1861. He attributed the epidemic primarily to the defective sanitary condition of the town, adding—" It is simply dirt fever, arising from bad drainage; nightsoil lodged in imperfect cesspools, and a large amount of filth and organic matter in other parts of the town." Dr. Stevens, an Inspector under the Local Government Board, immediately came down to Darwen, and going direct to the house where the first case occurred, discovered by pulling up the drains that the water-supply of the town was polluted. Addressing the Local Board at a special meeting the same day (Oct. 31) he remarked that since the 8th of October they had lost 44 lives, and that on the lowest computation there were then 1200 cases of fever in the town. He said he had traced the sewage of Mr. Davies's house until it "sucked itself into the pure water" running through a porous stone drain from one reservoir to another, and "there was as much dirty black matter as any one of them could be steeped in." "Hence," he said, "they had this sudden flash of fever, which had broken out in all parts of the town," and "the town was prepared for the distribution of any kind of disease," by its bad sanitary condition. He described the scavenging system then carried out in Darwen as "a farce, a delusion, and a snare," and said that "an enormous amount of work must be done in the way of drainage." It subsequently transpired that the pollution of the water by the drains of Woodside Bank was suspected in 1861, on the occasion of the former epidemic, and that the authorities at that time, as they believed, effectually stopped the sewage from getting into the conduit, but did not connect the iron pipe which they put in to carry it safely across! The Rev. H. H. Moore, M.A., Vicar of St, John's, wrote a long letter in *The Times*, (London) on November 2nd, severely criticising the neglect of the Local Board to put the town into a proper sanitary condition, and Darwen obtained an unenviable notoriety by the vivid pictures of its benighted condition which were drawn by the leader-writers of the London and provincial Press. In November, the filtering-lodge of the town's water-supply was cleaned out, for the first time for 20 years, and more evidences of contamination were brought to light. The Local Board at once laid a line of earthenware pipes along the porous stone conduit of the water-supply, where the pollution had taken place, the cost being £544. They also had the water analysed, and Mr. R. Railton, F.C.S., of Blackburn, twice reported emphatically that there was not the slightest evidence in the samples submitted to him of animal or sewage pollution. He said, "You must look nearer to your river side for the cause of the fever which is now raging in your town, rather than to your water-supply."

The first annual report of the Medical Officer showed that during the year 1874 there were 839 deaths in Darwen, the death-rate being 36·9 per 1000 of the population, against an average for the previous five years of 25·3. The death-rate of the United Kingdom for 1874 was 21·6. More than one-third of the total number of deaths in Darwen were due to the zymotic diseases; the zymotic death-rate being 12·9 per 1000 of the population, whilst for the whole of England and Wales it was only 3·6. This was chiefly due to the epidemic, there being 114 deaths from enteric fever during the last three months of the year. The Medical Officer added that in 222 cases the cause of death was not certified by any legally qualified medical practitioner.

About this time Mr. John Gerald Potter, J.P.; Mr. J. B. Deakin, and other influential ratepayers, sent a memorial to the Local Government Board, alleging default of duty on the part of the Over Darwen Local Board, in not enforcing the provisions of the Nuisances Removal Acts, and in not providing the district with sufficient sewers. An inquiry was instituted by the Government and conducted by Colonel Cox and Mr. H. Basil Caine, on January 20th and 25th, 1875. The Local Board, in reply to the allegations of the memorialists, presented a "Concise Statement," in which they admitted "that much remains to be done to improve the sanitary condition of the town by (amongst other things, the carrying out of additional sewerage works) the alteration of the present cesspool and ashpit system, the paving of new streets, and other matters." The default of the Local Board was alleged to have commenced at the election of members in March, 1872, but the Board replied that the period between that date and the present (Jan., 1875) had been "one of great activity on the part of the Board, as shown by the increased number of the Board's meetings." In summarising the work they had done they stated that they had won "an arduous and expensive lawsuit, brought by Sir Willam Henry Feilden against the Board for an alleged fouling of the River Darwen with sewage; purchased the Gas and Water nearly completed a high-level Water Reservoir, at a cost of £30,000; grappled with the tangled state of the Board's accounts and the unsatisfactory state of the Surveyor's and Gas Departments, dismissing both the Collector and Surveyor, and changing Managers at the Gasworks; and remodelled the Bye-Laws, in order to extend the powers of the Board over the drainage and ventilation of new buildings, the cleansing of cesspools and ashpits, the keeping of slaughterhouses, the sewering and levelling of new streets, and the removal of nuisances." Explaining "how such nuisances as undoubtedly exist in the Board's district have been permitted to grow up there," the Board pleaded that Over Darwen had "shot up from a mere hamlet to a large commercial town in an incredibly short space of time," and that with a limited staff it was "utterly impossible to carry out the sewerage works required," with sufficient speed; that the first Local Board, in 1884, had "committed themselves to the cesspool and ashpit system," which had clung to the town and been an interminable nuisance, and that until the present Board took the matter in their own hands the removal of nightsoil and ashes had been neglected. As to the alleged default in providing sufficient sewers, the Board contended that the responsibility rested with the property owners and not with the Board, remarking that "the Board are prepared to show that they have provided sufficient main sewers for draining their district, having provided the main sewer right through the town, the Darwen Chapel main sewer in an easterly direction from Duckworth Street, and the Hoddlesden main sewer for draining Hoddlesden, and that, therefore, all that is wanted to sewer the streets named by the memorialists is for the owners of the newly-built properties abutting upon such streets to construct branch sewers into these main sewers which the Board have provided for the purpose." The reason why the Board had not been able to execute more public works was "that the money borrowed by their predecessors for the express purpose of executing such works, to the extent of £7,000, . . . had been applied in the payment of the ordinary expenses of the Board, which ought to have been satisfied out of the General District Rate." They complained also that the action of the Board in relation to public works had often been thwarted by the conduct of owners of property." Summarising what they had done "to improve the health of the town," since their election in 1872, the Board stated that they had sewered and paved fourteen streets, endeavoured to improve the state of the river, cleaned out Scholes Fold Brook (a covered watercourse), and resolved to apply to Parliament in 1876 for increased powers to improve the river; improved the sewage settling tanks; examined the highways; improved the slaughterhouses; and paid particular attention to the effectiveness of all new drains. A Medical Officer of Health, one of the first in Lancashire, was appointed in December, 1873, and, on his recommendation, the Board now contemplated adopting the tub system, so as to do away with the objectionable ashpits, and it was whilst engaged in these deliberations that "the Epidemic which has occasioned the present Inquiry suddenly made its appearance, and spread with incredible swiftness throughout the district." During this epidemic labourers refused to work at the drains, and the Board stopped the emptying of cesspools for fear of spreading infection. It was therefore "manifestly unfair" to take the existing condition of the town as a basis for a charge of neglect on the part of the Board. At the end of 1874 the water pipes were improved, ashpits were condemned, and the tub system was adopted. Insanitary dwellings and outhouses were closed or demolished, and other measures were taken to promote health and prevent the spread of disease. The Board summed up their position as follows :—

As the matter stands at present, the Board's position is shortly this :—That through the easy-going indifference of former Boards a rotten system pervaded every department of the Board's affairs : the present Board has rectified these abuses, and has replaced the Officials who committed or suffered them to exist. They have had large undertakings of gas manufacture and water supply to manage, and have done so with advantage to health, and profit to the public purse. They have struggled to correct a pernicious system of dealing with the nightsoil and ashes, and have spared no efforts to ensure that cesspools, where unavoidable, should be rendered as little mischievous as possible. They have protected the water supply from contamination, closed unhealthy dwellings, resolved upon a new system of dealing with their sewage, and not been unmindful of what is wanted to improve the river. They have directed the removal and abatement of all nuisances reported to them, or which have come under their notice, but that they have not done all that might have been done is simply admitting that the members of the Board are but human the same as other people.

At the close of the Board's existence, in 1878, the acreage of the town was 5135 acres ; length of highways, 13 miles ; and length of sewers 14 miles. The length of streets paved and sewered in the last three years of the Board's existence was 3039 lineal yards, or about 1¾ miles, at a cost of 9757 ; and the length of new streets unpaved and unsewered, was about three miles. One of the chief undertakings of the Local Board was the purchase and enlargement of the Gas and Waterworks. For this purpose they promoted a Bill in Parliament, in 1873, which enabled them to acquire, on behalf of the ratepayers, the works, plant, and monopolies belonging to the Over Darwen Gas Light Company and the Darwen Waterworks Company, of which some account is given in a subsequent section of this chapter.

In the year 1873 the *Blackburn Times* was full of correspondence on public events connected with Over Darwen, and among other things there was an agitation proceeding for the incorporation of the town. It was argued that a corporation would be less expensive and more effective than a local board, and that the affairs of the town would be more under the direct control of the burgesses. Over Darwen at that time had a population of 24,000, and a property rate of over £50,000. One correspondent showed that there were 150 boroughs in England and Wales with a less population and ratable value than Over Darwen, many of which, including four Lancashire boroughs, had obtained their charters of incorporation within the past ten years. The best men on the Local Board, including the chairman, Mr. William Snape, after stamping out the epidemic of 1874 devoted their energies to a remodelling of the system of local government and the formation of Over Darwen into a corporate borough.

The offices of the Local Board at the time of its dissolution were in the front portion of the building now devoted exclusively to the purposes of the Free Library, and the Local Board meetings were held in the one room then available for lending, reference, and newsroom purposes, as well as for the storage of books.

INCORPORATION OF THE BOROUGH.

The borough of "Over Darwen," now called "Darwen," was incorporated by Royal Charter, dated March 22nd, 41 Victoria (1878), in accordance with the provisions of the Municipal Corporations (New Charters) Act, 1877, and in response to a petition of the "inhabitant householders" of the district. The resolution to apply for a Charter of Incorporation was passed at a public meeting in the Co-operative Hall, on March 20th, 1877, and within ten days a petition to the Queen was signed by 670 ratepayers. On the 7th of September, in the same year, Major Donnelly held a public inquiry relating to the subject-matter of the petition, and the prayer of the inhabitants was shortly afterwards acceded to. Mr. William Snape, J.P., Chairman of the Local Board, and Mayor-designate, arrived in Darwen with the Charter in his possession on the afternoon of March 25th, 1878. He was met at the railway station by a procession consisting of the members and officials of the Local Board, and a number of tradesmen, who escorted him to the Free Library, where the meetings of the Board were usually held. Fog signals were exploded on the railway, the bells of Holy Trinity Church rang out a joyous peal, and the crowd in the streets cheered lustily. The Library was crowded with townsmen while Mr. Charles Costeker, Clerk to the Board, read the Charter, and after several humorous and congratulatory speeches the meeting dispersed with three ringing cheers for the Queen. The following is a summary of the Charter:—

The inhabitants of the district of Over Darwen shall be one body politic and corporate by the name of the Mayor, Alderman, and Burgesses of the Borough of Over Darwen, with perpetual succession and a common seal, and may assume armorial bearings, and may take and hold land and buildings within the borough, for the official purposes of the Corporation. The Corporation shall have the powers, authorities, immunities, and priveleges usually vested in such Corporations. The number of Councillors shall be eighteen; the borough shall be divided into six wards, each ward electing three Councillors. The offices of the Local Board shall serve for the present in lieu of a Town Hall; Charles Costeker shall act as Town Clerk; and William Snape as Mayor. The first meeting of the Town Council shall be held on the 9th of July, 1878. The first burgess list shall be made out and the first municipal election shall take place as directed by the Municipal Corporations Act. Two Schedules annexed to the Charter give the names and define the boundaries of the six wards and settle all dates and conditions relating to the first election of councillors and aldermen.

The first municipal election passed off without a contest, eighteen townsmen—all Liberal in politics—being nominated and returned unopposed. The first meeting of the Town Council was held in the Free Library on July 9th, 1878. Councillor William Snape was elected Mayor; Councillors William Snape, William Pickup, Henry Green, William Entwisle, John Walmsley and Ralph Pearson were elected Aldermen; Messrs. Pickup, Pearson, and Walmsley being elected for three years only, the three others for six years. For the various purposes contemplated in the Charter of Incorporation, the period from July 1st, to November 1st, 1878, was reckoned a complete year. An extraordinary election of councillors to fill the vacancies caused by the promotions to aldermanic rank, took place on July 13th; no contest. A burgess list, published on the 6th of May, 1878, showed the total number of householders in Darwen to be 5,500; divided as follows:—North-East Ward, 953; North-West Ward, 766; South-West Ward, 1,045; South-East Ward, 850; West-Central Ward, 851; and Central Ward, 1,035. There was no contest at the first election, in July, 1878, nor at the November elections of 1878, 1879, and 1880. On November 9th, 1880, Messrs. William Pickup, John Walmsley, and Ralph Pearson were re-elected Aldermen. In November 1881 there were contests in four of the six wards and the voting was as follows:—North-East Ward,—James Halliwell (L), 350; Thomas Wade (C), 74. Central Ward,—Henry Yates (L), 325; William Grimshaw (L), 255. West-Central Ward,—David Ainsworth (L), 356; John Gettins (L), 118. South-West Ward,—David Raine (L), 251; William Grimshaw (C), 167. The polling was light, as the streets were made almost impassable by snow, the tramway traffic being completely stopped. In November, 1882, there was a contest only in Central Ward, when the retiring Councillor, Thomas Harwood Marsden, was defeated by Dr. W. H. Armitage by 24 votes; the polling being—Armitage, 322; Marsden, 298. There was no contest in 1883, and in 1884 the only contest was in North-West Ward, when Mr. R. W. Holgate polled 308 votes, against 205 for Mr. W. Almond. There was no contest in 1885 or 1886. In November, 1887, the Conservative Party contested five of the six wards, but were defeated all round, the aggregate Liberal majority being 776. In the following year, however, they renewed their attack and won their first seat on the Council, Mr. J. W. Gillibrand (C.) defeating Mr. J. Haworth (L.) in

ALDERMAN WILLIAM SNAPE, J.P.,
FIRST MAYOR OF OVER DARWEN.

North-East Ward by a majority of four votes. In the four other contested wards the aggregate Liberal majority was 255.

Alderman William Snape, J.P., the first Mayor of Darwen, deserves the chief credit for the marked progress that was made in the good government of the town during the first few years of its existence as a corporate borough. He was four times in succession elected Mayor and not only during his prolonged mayoralty but for years afterward he devoted nearly the whole of his time and energies to the welfare of the borough. Though not a native of Darwen, he had made Darwen his home and by his assiduous attention to the town's welfare he attained a position of prominence that has not been exceeded by any other man who figures in local history. Born at Walton-le-Dale in 1819, the youngest of the eight children of a builder, he received only a rudimentary education, but developed a talent for art and was bound apprentice to the designing department of calico-printing. He came to Darwen in 1846 as chief designer for Messrs. C. and J. G. Potter, paper stainers, and nine years later he commenced business on his own account at Livesey Fold, a business which has since been absorbed by the Potters. He retired with an ample fortune in 1875, but in his declining years he lost a great deal of money by investments in the cotton and chemical trades. His career as a public man began with his election to the Over Darwen Local Board in 1859, but he did not take a leading position until after the outbreak of the fever epidemic in 1874. He then sought re-election to the Board, and in 1875 became its chairman. Remaining at the helm of the town's affairs for seven years he was principally responsible for the rigorous attention paid during that period to sanitary improvements, for the elevation of the town to the status of a corporate borough, the extension of the gas and waterworks, the improvement of the highways, the erection of the Market House and Municipal Offices, and the reform of the financial system of the borough. His speeches at the Council meetings were always based on sound information, and they bore evidence of having been carefully thought out. As a politician Mr. Snape became proprietor of *The Darwen News*, Chairman of the Liberal Executive of North-East Lancashire and afterwards of the Darwen Division, and one of the foremost organizers of his day. It was on his affidavit that an application was made to the Court of Queen's Bench for a scrutiny for the purpose of unseating Lord Cranborne in 1885. In religion he was a Baptist. He was a strong upholder of all Nonconformist principles, and a good supporter of chapels and schools in various parts of the country. During the last few years of his life he was afflicted with partial blindness but, he bore this and his financial losses alike with Christian fortitude and stuck to his public work to the last. He died on March 31st, 1888, in his 69th year.

Councillor Alex. T. Eccles, the present Mayor of Darwen, was about 35 years of age when chosen to fill the civic chair, in November, 1887. He is the youngest son of Mr. Joseph Eccles, J.P., of High Lawn, and resides at The Cottage, Darwen. He is a partner with his father and brother in the cotton trade. His first appearance in public life was in 1883, when he succeeded his uncle, the late Mr. Thomas Eccles, J.P., as a representative on the Town Council of North-West Ward. He is a Liberal and a Congregationalist, and one of the principal supporters of Hollins Grove Congregational Church. On March 20th, 1888, he was presented by the Members of the Town Council with a silver cradle, to commemorate the birth of his first-born child. He was re-elected Mayor in November, 1888.

LIST OF MAYORS.

Date of Election.	Name.	Residence.	Occupation.
1878, July 9th.—Ald.	William Snape, J.P.,	Lynwood,	Gentleman.
,, Nov. 9th.—	,,	,,	,,
1879, ,, 10th.—	,,	,,	,,
1880, ,, 9th.—	,,	,,	,,
1881, ,, 9th.—Ald.	Henry Green, J.P.,	Woodbine Cottage,	Cotton Manufacturer.
1882, ,, 9th.—Ald.	William Entwisle,	Rosehill,	Quarry Owner.
1883, ,, 9th.—	,,	,,	,, ,,
1884, ,, 10th.—Coun.	Timothy Lightbown,	Falcon House,	Cotton Manufacturer.
1885, ,, 9th.—	,, J.P.,	,,	,, ,,
1886, ,, 9th.—Coun.	Thomas Grime,	Heatherby,	Paper Manufacturer.
1887, ,, 9th.—Coun.	Alex. T. Eccles,	The Cottage,	Cotton Manufacturer.
1888, ,, 9th.—	,,	,,	,, ,,

LOCAL ACTS OF PARLIAMENT.

One of the first duties of the Corporation was to promote a Bill in Parliament setting forth the nature of the work they intended to perform and seeking borrowing powers on the security of the rates for carrying out this work. The only Act obtained by the Local Board was the Over Darwen Waterworks and Gasworks Act, of 1873. A bill seeking various powers was drafted by the Corporation, and on the 11th of August, 1879, it received the Royal Assent. This "Over Darwen Improvement Act, 1879," had for its object the extension of the borough boundaries; the improvement of the River Darwen at a cost of £15,000; street improvements, £20,000; cemetery improvements, £1,200; erection of a town hall, £40,000; erection of a market house,

Councillor ALEX. T. ECCLES,
Mayor of Darwen, 1889.

£25,000; construction of a park, £1,600; purchase of part of the gas and water undertakings of the Blackburn Corporation, £13,500. In regard to the extension of the borough boundaries so as to include portions of Lower Darwen and Eccleshill serious opposition was encountered. Messrs. Potter & Co., of Hollins Paper Mill, Lower Darwen, threatened opposition on their own account, and the ratepayers of Lower Darwen, in public meeting assembled, decided also to oppose the Bill. The chief opposition from Eccleshill came from the Darwen Ironworks Company, and eventually the Corporation agreed not to include their land within the borough boundaries. After negotiations extending over a period of four months, the opposition from Lower Darwen ended in a compromise, the ratepayers, on February 20th, 1879, agreeing to accept the terms offered by the Corporation, namely, half-rates for six years. The portions of Lower Darwen which it was agreed should be included in the borough of Over Darwen extend from a line drawn from the Peak, near Birch Farm, to a point in Sandy Lane, a little to the southern side of Edwards' farm buildings, and then in a direct line past Oakenhurst; so as to take in all Oakenhurst, and on till the boundary line meets Darwen at the brook. The portion of Lower Darwen not taken into Over Darwen was added to the Borough of Blackburn, and considerable excitement was caused in November, 1879, by the seizure of 171 gas meters in the portion of Lower Darwen newly joined to the Borough of Over Darwen. These were removed by order of the Blackburn Corporation, and the householders were left without gas for nearly five days. The Over Darwen Corporation claimed compensation and on the 5th of January, 1886, they received a letter of apology from Blackburn accompanied by a cheque for £275 in settlement of the dispute. Within eight years the Corporation found it necessary to apply for fresh borrowing powers, so again promoted a Bill in Parliament, the principal object of which was to extend the gasworks. This local Act received the Royal Assent on the 8th of August, 1887. Its object was to alter the name of the borough and corporation from "Over Darwen" to "Darwen," to extend the limits of the gas supply, and to confer upon the corporation further powers in relation to their water and gas undertakings, to make further provisions for the improvement and good government of the borough, to authorise the creation of corporation stock, &c. The Act sanctioned the borrowing of £100,000 for the following purposes:—Purchase of additional land for the cemetery, fencing and draining the same, £2,000; extension and improvement of the waterworks, £10,000; extension of the gasworks, £70,000.

PUBLIC BUILDINGS.

A proposition to purchase land for the erection of a Market House and a Town Hall was made at the last meeting of the Local Board, held in the Free Library on June 3rd, 1878. The site chosen was a piece of low-lying land in Railway Road, occupied by some old saw mills, a bleach works, nearly a century old, some cottages and other higgledy-piggledy property, and part of it was a croft containing a lodge of dirty water. This land was fenced off from Railway Road by a wooden railing, the road being on a higher level than the site. From its first meeting the new Town Council pushed forward the work of providing suitable municipal buildings; but only one, the Market House, has yet been erected. On the 21st of June, 1882, the new Market House was opened by Mr. F. W. Grafton, M.P., with a golden Key, and the occasion was one of great public rejoicing. After the doors had been opened, speeches were delivered from the balcony in the market, and there was subsequently a public banquet in the Co-operative Hall and a ball in the Market Hall. The architecture is a modification of the Queen Anne style. Inclusive of the site, which cost over £11,000, the erection of this building entailed an exepnditure of £31,000. The principal frontage is to the new Market Square, which was constructed at the same time, and there is another frontage on the opposite side, in School Street. There are four entrances—one from School Street, one from the Market Square, and two from the small, covered, wholesale market on the west side. The area of the Market Hall proper is 60 feet by 120 feet. On the north side of the building, in School Street, there are six butchers' shops, and on the south side there are six other shops. At the west end, near the entrances from the wholesale market, are six fish stalls. Over the shops on the south and west sides there are extensive suites of rooms, including a Council Chamber 55 feet long by 18 feet wide and and 13 feet high, and all the municipal offices except those of the Town Clerk, who still occupies his old offices in Church Street. Above the principal entrance to the hall there towers a lofty gable, the ridge of which is surmounted by a turret, rising to the height of 80 feet from the ground. The contractors for the stonework and building were Messrs. J. Orrell and Sons, of Darwen; and the ironwork was supplied by Messrs. Handyside, of Derby, and Messrs. Goddard and Massey, of Nottingham. The foundation stone was laid by Alderman Snape, during his mayoralty, on the 2nd of October, 1881; and the opening ceremony took place during the mayoralty of Alderman Green. It was not at first intended to make this building into a *quasi* Town Hall,

MARKET HALL AND MUNICIPAL OFFICES, 1882.

a site adjoining that of the Market having been already obtained for the larger building, and a most desirable plan for it selected in an open competition. Mr. Chas. Bell, F.R.I.B.A., of London, is the architect whose plans were accepted, both for the present Market House and the future Town Hall.

Adjoining the site of the Market House, a plot of land measuring 5,365 square yards was secured for the purpose of erecting a Town Hall. This is rented at 11d. per yard from the Rev. Chas. Greenway, the yearly ground rent being about £245. Another plot adjoining, and measuring 197 square yards, was taken from the Knott Paper Mill Co. at 10d. per yard, or a yearly ground rent of about £8. Owing to the large expenditure which the erection of a Town Hall will entail, a scheme was brought forward at the end of 1888 for improvising a Town Hall by purchasing the Theatre Royal from the executors of the late Alderman Snape. Messrs. Maxwell and Tuke, of Manchester and Bury, architects, were employed to devise a plan for the conversion of the Theatre into a Town Hall. They reported that the building, which could be purchased for £3,000 from the executors of Mr. Snape, would require an additional £6,000 to adapt it for municipal purposes. Plans were submitted, showing that an assembly room could be formed capable of accommodating 1,300 people; and a Council Chamber, reception room, and municipal offices, &c., provided. The cost of the scheme being so great, the Corporation rejected it, and about Christmas, 1887, the Theatre was sold to Mr. J. Pitt Hardacre for £3,250. It originally cost £9,000.

The only other public buildings of note belonging to the ratepayers are the Peel Baths and the Free Library, which stand together in Church Street. The Baths were erected, at a cost of £1,300, in 1853, partly by public subscription. They have since been enlarged by the Town Council. The Free Library, established in 1871, is governed by a body of eight Commissioners, half of whom are elected annually at a small meeting of ratepayers held in the Library. They levy a rate of 1d. in the £ annually, which is collected by the Librarian, Mr. Ephraim Neville. It realises £300. Prior to the adoption of the Free Libraries Act, there had existed in Darwen, for a period of 32 years, a very successful Mechanics' Institution, and the books of that institution, numbering 4.000, were presented to the town to form the nucleus of the new Free Library. The business of the Post Office is conducted in the shop of Mr. H. T. Timperley, stationer, photographer, and postmaster. It is situated exactly in the centre of the town, on one side of the open space called the Circus, where five of the principal roads of the borough converge. The Police Court, in Duckworth Street, is the property of the County Authority. Among other buildings of note are the Liberal Club, Market Street; the Working Men's Reform Club, William Street; the Conservative Club and Public Hall, in Church Street; the Co-operative Hall, School Street, erected in 1866; the Old Market House (private property), in Market Street, erected in 1845; and the Theatre Royal, Railway Road, 1877.

THE GAS AND WATER WORKS.

An Act for the better lighting with gas of the village of Over Darwen received the Royal Assent on June 15th, 1855, whereby the Over Darwen Gas Light Company was incorporated and authorised to raise £6,000 by the creation of shares of £10 each, and £2,000 by a mortgage on their undertaking, for the purpose of manufacturing the supply of gas within the village. The gasworks were constructed and gas was supplied in the following year. In 1873 the Local Board obtained an Act of Parliament authorising the purchase of the works by them on behalf of the ratepayers, the shareholders having their interest valued at £73,500 payable in annuities. A new gasholder was erected in 1874, and in 1888 the gasworks were entirely rebuilt. To extend and improve these works the Corporation have borrowed on mortgage £78,500, and they have power to borrow a further sum of £42,700. The Corporation Fire Brigade is composed of workmen employed at the gasworks.

The Waterworks were originated by a private company called the Darwen Waterworks and Reservoirs Company in 1847. The Darwen Waterworks Act was passed in 1869, dissolving and reincorporating the company, and enabling them to execute additional works and raise further capital, and by the Waterworks and Gasworks Act of the Over Darwen Local Board, dated June 16th, 1873, the Board were empowered to acquire the undertakings at a cost of £63,750. The original reservoir of the Company was the Dean or Earnsdale Reservoir, which lies 705ft. above the sea level, and holds 97 million gallons. The Sunnyhurst Hey Reservoir was in course of construction when the Local Board purchased the Waterworks. It is 914ft. above the level of the sea, and has a capacity of 95 million gallons. It was opened in April, 1875. The cost of its construction was between £30,000 and £40,000.

An unexpected evidence of the former wooded state of this district was discovered close to the Stepback Clough by the excavators for the Sunnyhurst Hey Reservoir. The surface of this plateau was quite bare and treeless, covered with heath like the adjoining moorland, but the excavators brought to light an ancient wood buried underneath the heather. Beneath a surface of peat averaging about two feet in thickness, lay roots, trunks and branches of trees, principally oaks and silver birch, the latter with the bark almost as perfect as when the trees were alive. Under the trees came four or five feet of clay, and below that three or four feet of clayey gravel, then clayey shale, and next sandstone rock. Hundreds of trees were removed in the course of the excavation, and the discovery formed an interesting theme for the local geologists. A tenant of Lower Trees Farm once told Mr. W. T. Ashton that in his father's time it was a tradition that a great wood extended from Woodhead in Darwen to Woodhead in Pickup Bank, and many old men have spoken of the great size of the oaks, sycamores, and beeches which formerly existed in the neighbourhood.[1]

In 1874, while searching for evidences of sewage, Mr. R. Railton, F.C.S., of Blackburn, found traces of lead in the town's water, and since the incorporation of the borough there have been several serious cases of lead poisoning in the town. The Corporation have at various times experimented with the view of neutralising the undoubted property the town's water possesses of dissolving lead from the service pipes.

The water from the Lower Reservoir has practically no action on metallic lead, but that from Sunnyhurst has. Dr. Frankland, in 1888, recommended three methods of combatting this property :—(1) Filtration through sand, flints, and limestone ; (2) treatment with carbonate of soda ; (3) mixture with drift water. In a report to the Gas and Water Committee, Dr. Frankland remarked that the existence of an abundant supply of drift water in the immediate neighbourhood would appear to afford a peculiarly advantageous means of combatting the lead difficulty, for his experiments had abundantly shown that an admixture of this water, in suitable proportions, neutralised the activity of the Sunnyhurst water, whilst, by the same means, the supply would be largely increased, the double benefit being obtainable at a reasonable cost. The one drawback attaching to this project was that the hardness of the water would be very materially increased ; but this would not interfere with its fitness for drinking, and the drift water might be softened before admixture. For the information of the inhabitants, he pointed out the principal means of avoiding the consumption of lead-contaminated water on a small scale as follows :—(1) No water drawn for drinking purposes should be collected until after the tap has been allowed to run for such a length of time as will presumably clear the service pipe (say, one minute). (2) The filtration of the water through any form of animal charcoal filter practically guarantees its absolute freedom from lead. (3) Hot water acts more powerfully on lead than cold, and, therefore, metal teapots and other soldered vessels for holding hot water should be especially avoided.

At the present time (1889), the Corporation are engaged in preparing for an important extension of the waterworks, which are inadequate in dry seasons for the rapidly increasing needs of the town. The Town Council have four schemes under consideration—(1.) The purchase of Jack's Kay Reservoir and drainage area ; (2) the purchase of that part of the Blackburn Waterworks and drainage area known as the Daisy Green and Pickup Bank Reservoirs ; (3) the purchase of that part of the Liverpool Waterworks and drainage area known as the Upper Roddlesworth Reservoir ; and (4) the raising of water by pumping. The present drainage area is 604 acres, and there are 25 inches of available rainfall annually on the average, one inch being equal to 22,651 gallons

[1] *The Heart of Lancashire*, chap. vii.

per acre. Compensation water has to be given every working day to the extent of 400,000 gallons.

PARKS AND RECREATION GROUNDS

There are two public parks on the westerly side of the town, both occupying hilly situations of natural beauty. The one at Whitehall was opened in 1887, and it has cost upwards of £4,000. It covers 15½ acres of land. The fountain in the little lake was the gift of Mrs. Timothy Lightbown. Another park is being laid out at Bold Venture, as part of the scheme originated in 1887 in commemoration of the Queen's Jubilee. It covers 15 acres of ground, and its main feature is a chain of three lakes at the bottom of a deep ravine. From either of the parks the public may walk direct on to the breezy heights of Darwen Moor, where there are nearly 30 miles of footpaths set apart for their use, furnished here and their with seats given by Mrs. Timothy Lightbown. The old Fair Ground was in 1888 enclosed and fitted up with gymnastic appliances as a public Recreation Ground.

Independent of any artificial parks the people of Darwen have an immense recreation ground, extending over the whole of Darwen Moor. During the first five or six years after the incorporation of the borough, there was a great public agitation respecting the right of road over the moors. Mr. W. T. Ashton had commenced the agitation long anterior to this time, and had always maintained the right of riding over bridle paths and walking over footpaths in every part of the township, in accordance with the traditions of the old inhabitants. On the 31st of July, 1878, writs were issued by Mr. Edmund Ashworth the younger, who owned the shooting rights over the moor, and the Rev. W. A. Duckworth, lord of the manor, against Richard Ainsworth, Joseph Kay, James Fish, Ellis Gibson, and John Oldman, all inhabitants of Darwen, for trespass, and the case was heard in the Chancery Court, London, on August 2nd, 1878. The Master of the Rolls, Sir George Jessel, refused to grant an injunction against the defendants, and the case came on again on February 22nd, 1879, when the following order was agreed to, each party paying its own costs :—" By consent it is ordered that a perpetual injunction be awarded to restrain the defendants respectively from sporting over Darwen Moor at Over Darwen, wherein certain private rights of common are alleged to exist, and from infringing upon any right or rights of sporting belonging to the plaintiff, Edmund Ashworth the younger, exercisable upon the said Darwen Moor, and from inciting any other person to sport upon the said moor, or to infringe the said right or rights of sporting upon the said Darwen Moor, but without prejudice to such rights of highway and common respec-

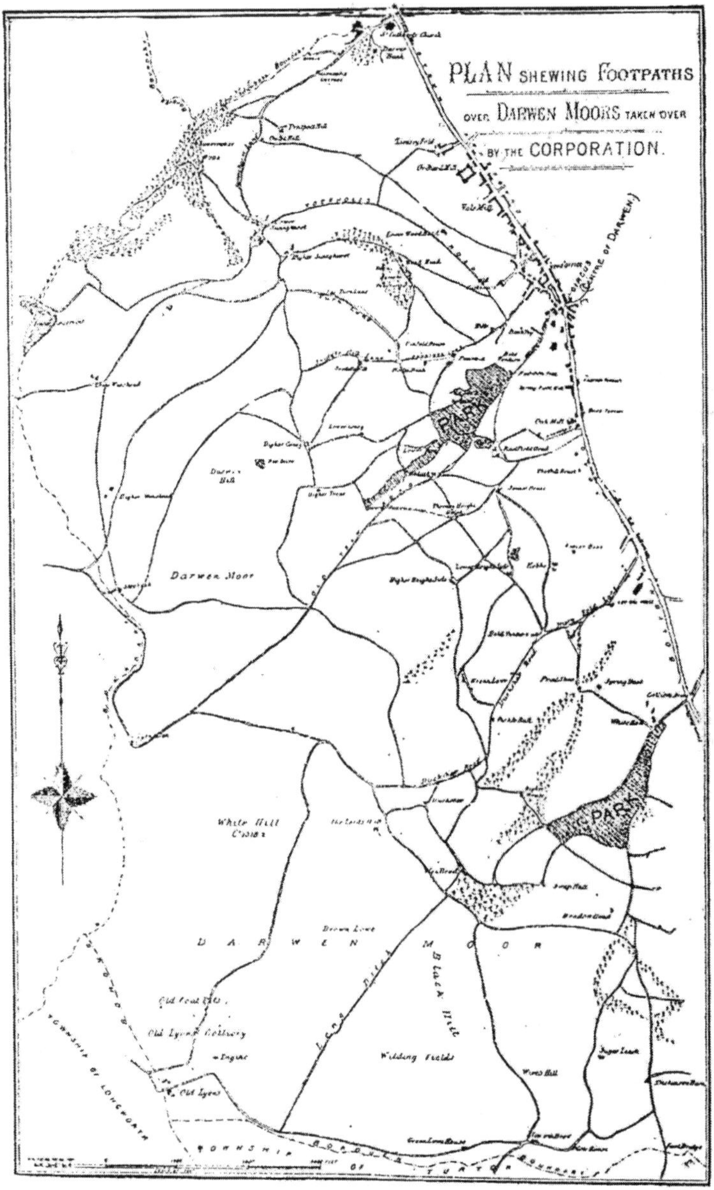

PLAN SHEWING FOOTPATHS
OVER DARWEN MOORS TAKEN OVER
BY THE CORPORATION.
PARK
PARK
Darwen Moor
White Hill
D A R W E N   M O O R
Black Hill
Old Coal Pits
Old Lyons Colliery
Old Lyons
Wilding Fields
TOWNSHIP OF LONGWORTH
TOWNSHIP BOUNDARY
OF TURTON

FOUNTAIN IN THE WHITEHALL PARK.
THE GIFT OF MRS. TIMOTHY LIGHTBOWN.

tively, if any, exercisable over the said moor." This compromise was arrived at by the mediation of the Mayor (Alderman Snape), on behalf of the Corporation, on the understanding being arrived at that the Corporation should map out upwards of 29 miles of roads to be taken over by them for the use of the inhabitants, and about five miles of the same put and kept in good repair at a cost to the rates of the borough of not more than £100 per year. Darwen Moor consists of a common of 296 acres, intersected with a network of footpaths 29 miles 7 furlongs and five yards in length. On the 11th of July, 1881, Mr. William Thomas Ashton, the prime mover of the footpaths' agitation, contributed a letter to the *Darwen News*, urging the people to "go up and possess the land" reclaimed for them by the Corporation. In it he observed :—

> Our town has not many advantages compared with other places. York's mighty minster, Ely's towers, and Salisbury's soaring spire, are far away. Trent and Severn reflect many a fair city and town, but the beauty of our historic stream is gone. Our lofty moorland, with its sweeping lines and breezy heights, still remains as lovely as ever. From the street corners its slopes rise upwards till they mingle with the grey and purple summits. Even at night the Moor is interesting, as it lifts its dark mass above the sleeping town against the starry sky. Over its wide rolling summits there is a tract of land almost unchanged in a country where everything else is changing. As we see it now it was seen and loved by our Saxon fathers, who made some of their most stubborn fights for freedom under its western shadows. The Ancient Britons, of whom we know so little and have lost so much, found it as we see it now. Before the unknown scholar took up his pen to tell us that old and wondrous story of the man of Uz, before men wrote on Ninevite tablets or Egyptian papyrus, these moorland tops were much as they are now. From these "tops" we can see from the Peak of Derbyshire to the Langdale Pikes, from Snowdon to Ingleborough; while, near at hand, all that renders his native county dear to the heart of the Lancastrian lies clustered round ; and from here, if anywhere, is visible our "historic grounds." From these "tops" nearly all our inhabitants can see the fields and lanes where they spent their early days—where their fathers and mothers were born, and the graveyards where nearly all that is dear to them in the past lies buried. These feelings are not confined to any class of the community. One of my old workpeople wrote, many years ago, from Queensland :—"I am always thinking of Darwen Moors, and the little brooks running down the moor side, with the throstles singing in the trees." An old friend of mine, who left this country more then twenty years ago, wrote to me from Sydney :—"I take a swim in the bay at Sydney every morning, winter and summer, and I often fancy I can see Darwen Moor rising across the water, but I fear I shall never see it again in this world." Nor shall I commit a breach of confidence by repeating that an old and highly-esteemed townsman, lately dead, told his wife that he built his house where he did because from its windows he could see the cottage and room where his mother died.

HEALTH OF THE BOROUGH.

Notwithstanding two or three circumstances which exert a real or supposed influence prejudicial to the health of the borough—including the humid climate, the conditions of labour under the factory system, and the occasional epidemics of zymotic diseases to which all towns are subject,—the death-rate of Darwen is comparatively low. The number of deaths in the town during the year 1888 was 600 (290 males and 310 females), equal to 17·9 for every 1,000 of the population, estimating the population at 33,500. Of these deaths 35 were attributed to zymotic diseases. The highest death-rate in the borough for the last nine years was 24 per 1,000 in 1880, and the lowest 15·4 per 1,000 in 1885; average 19·5. As a precaution against epidemics the Corporation in 1888 erected on Bull Hill a permanent hospital for infectious diseases at a cost of £4,000.

A public Cemetery was constructed by the Local Board at Whitehall in 1861. It has three mortuary chapels. The total number of interments there up to the end of 1888 was 15,514. The Cemetery is under the control of a Burial Board consisting of the whole of the members of the Town Council. Mr. J. Ridge is the registrar. Up to the present the cost of the Cemetery (land and buildings) has been £9,650. It is now being extended at an estimated cost of £15,000.

THE RIVER DARWEN.

The "rapid Darwent" has been turned to great account in bleaching, paper-making, paper-staining, and in running cotton factories. By long usage the property owners on its banks have acquired certain rights the extent of which has never been satisfactorily settled, and they have not merely destroyed the natural beauty of the stream, but have made it little better than a common drain. So long ago as 1852 Whittle, in his *Blackburn as it Is*, mentioned that "Some of the residents who live near the stream deposit in it the refuse, which settles at the first fall it reaches, to the detriment of the adjoining owners of property." It has been alleged that the Over Darwen Local Board not only neglected to suppress the pollution of the river, but contributed to its pollution themselves, but in a famous action at law, in which the Local Board were the defendants, the Court held that there was not sufficient evidence to prove this.

In the Court of Queen's Bench, on February 1st, 1873, before Justices Mellor, Lush, and Archibald, the case of Feilden *v.* the Over Darwen Local Board of Health was heard. Sir Wm. Hy. Feilden, Bart., had taken proceedings against the Over Darwen Local Board of Health for polluting the river Darwen with town sewage. The case had previously been heard at the Liverpool Assizes, before Mr. Justice Lush, when the jury returned a verdict for the defendants. A rule was afterwards obtained calling upon them to show cause why a new trial should not be had on the ground of misdirection, and that the verdict was against the evidence. It appeared from the arguments before the Queen's Bench that Sir William H. Feilden was the owner of an ancient house known as Feniscowles Hall, about five or six miles below Over Darwen, on the banks of the River Darwen, but in consequence of the river being in such a polluted state, from the drainage of the town of Over Darwen, the house had become uninhabitable and the property had in consequence materially depreciated. The plaintiff had also taken proceedings against the authorities of Blackburn for polluting the river Blakewater, a tributary of the Darwen. He obtained an injunction against the Blackburn Corporation, who were directed to erect tanks for the reception of the sewage, and on their declining to do so, the plaintiff recovered £1,250 damages. The reply of the Over Darwen Local Board to the action was that other towns contributed towards the pollution, and that the nuisance attributable to Over Darwen was of an inappreciable character. The Court, in giving judgment against Sir William, said there was not sufficient evidence to show that Over Darwen had caused the nuisance, and as the Blackburn nuisance would in a short time be entirely discontinued, there would then be an opportunity of ascertaining whether really any nuisance was caused by Over Darwen, in which case another action could be brought against the authorities. At a meeting of the Local Board on February 3rd, a vote of thanks was given to the Clerk, Mr. Charles Costeker, for having twice brought this case to a successful issue.

Having cleared themselves of the charge, the Local Board at once took steps to prevent the riparian owners within their district from polluting the river, and the Corporation, which succeeded the Local Board a few years later, followed up the work of improvement. Under the Rivers Pollution Act, 1876, the Corporation have prosecuted several mill owners for putting ashes in the river, and having cleaned out the numerous culverts, they have mitigated the risk of damage in flood times caused by overflow. By the local Act of 1879 the Corporation obtained powers to borrow £15,000 for the improvement of the river, but none of this has been expended. As the stream flows for two miles through Darwen, the town has been subjected to disastrous consequences in flood times, and it was stated by the Mayor, on the occasion of a great flood in 1880, that within the last ten years, independent of that occurrence, the overflow of the river had caused a greater outlay of money by damage to property, &c., than would be necessary to reconstruct the whole channel. The stream is a very impetuous one, having a considerable fall and many obstructions, and it is fed by rivulets from the hill sides which become mountain torrents in rainy weather. From the Watery Lane Bridge, Sough, to the large weir at Hollins Grove, the river—3,702 yards long—has a fall of 1 in 71; and the total fall from one end of the town to the other is 155 feet. The result of the stream's rapidity is to wash down a vast quantity of earth and stones, which lodge and accumulate in the channel; not to mention tons of ashes and refuse which are tipped over the banks in the vicinity of mills and other works. There are no fewer than 60 arches over the river from one end of the town to the other, without reckoning the small footbridges, and considering each of the long culverts only as one arch, and the majority of these spans are much too small. The volume of the water coming down during the flood of 1880 was almost, though not quite, a hundred square feet, and the result of this swollen stream trying to force its way through culverts measuring only thirty or forty square feet was to flood the town and wash down property. Underneath India Mill and the adjoining land there is a culvert 500 yards long, which will only take 33 square feet of water, and that subject to the obstruction of 29 iron pillars which support the fabric of the mill. The tunnels under the centre of the town, which open in Bridge Street, and again near Knott Mill, after passing under the new Market House, are of ample capacity, and one of them, a barrel culvert, which skirts the foundations of the Manchester and County Bank, is admirably constructed. About this point underground the river rushes onward with an impetus gained from the rapids in Bridge Street, and tumbles over a fall of 4 feet 6 inches. The new square culvert with a girder roof, upon which the Market House is built, measures about 13 feet by 17 feet, and will take three times the quantity of water ever likely to come down the course. Brookside Mill, Woodfold Mill, and other large buildings stand over culverts of insufficient capacity.

PUBLIC WORKS.

The borough now (1889) contains 7,300 houses, and a population of 38,000. Roughly speaking the population doubles itself in 20 years. There are nearly 33 miles of public highways within the borough boundaries, and the main roads contain 4 miles 70 yards, of public works, which have cost £28,770. Over eight miles of streets have been paved and sewered as private improvements, at a cost of £24,980.

FINANCIAL

The Corporation have the authority of Parliament to borrow on the security of the rates and the public works and buildings money amounting to £387,000. Of this amount £238,000 has been borrowed, and £43,000 has been paid off by means of a sinking fund. The unexercised borrowing powers on March 31st, 1889, amounted to nearly £111,000. The rates levied by the Local Board for the nine years preceding the incorporation averaged 2s. 10d. in the £ ; for nine years after incorporation the rates levied by the Town Council averaged 2s. 7½d.

POPULATION AND RATABLE VALUE

The estimated population of the Borough of Darwen at the end of 1888 was 38,000. The four townships dealt with in this History comprise the Registration Sub-District of Darwen, which at the Census of 1881 contained a population of 33,555 persons, of whom only three were over 90 years of age, and 10 over 85 but under 90. The statistics appended are collated from the Census Returns and other official sources.

DARWEN REGISTRATION SUB-DISTRICT.

	Acres.	Houses. In-habited.	Houses. Unin-habited.	Build-ings.	Popula-tion.	Males.	Females.
Darwen, Lower	2667	920	105	—	4531	2160	2371
Darwen, Over	5134	5557	494	48	27626	12990	14636
Eccleshill	797	146	22	—	716	350	366
Yate & Pickup Bank	850	143	64	—	682	336	346
Total	9448	6766	685	48	33555	15836	17719

BOROUGH OF OVER DARWEN.

	Acres.	In-habited.	Unin-habited.	Build-ings.	Popula-tion.	Males.	Females.
Darwen, Lr., part of	657	363	38	—	1819	837	982
Darwen, Over	5134	5557	494	48	27626	12990	14636
Eccleshill, part of	127	63	14	—	299	150	149
WARDS:							
Central	—	1036	123	22	5206	2415	2791
North-East	—	1291	143	7	6577	3117	3460
North-West	—	859	31	10	4181	1940	2241
South-East	—	925	104	5	4482	2147	2335
South-West	—	1071	95	4	5418	2526	2892
West-Central	—	801	50	—	3880	1832	2048
Total	5918	5983	546	48	29744	13977	15767

POLICE DIVISIONS.

Darwen Petty Sessional Division 9426 ... 6316 ... 642 ... 48 ... 31327 ... 14740 ... 16587
Blackburn Lower Lieut'cy Sub-Div. 84270 ...40538 ...3259 ...477 ...206528 ... 98398 ...108130

ECCLESIASTICAL PARISHES.

	Date of Formation.	Inhabited Houses.	Population.
Darwen, Over, Holy Trinity	1830	2344	11441
Darwen, Over, St. James	1842	846	4343
Darwen, Lower, St. James	1842	402	1907
Hoddlesden, St. Paul	1863	334	1619
Darwen, Over, St. John Evangelist	1865	1831	9103
Darwen, St. Cuthbert	1874	900	4608

GROWTH OF POPULATION SINCE 1801.

	1801.	1811.	1821.	1831.	1841.	1851.	1861.	1871.	1881.
Darwen, Lower	1646	1805	2328	2667	1996	3521	3301	3876	4531
Darwen, Over	3587	4411	6711	6972	9348	11702	16492	21277	27589
Eccleshill	346	374	456	715	510	598	543	633	755
Yate & Pickup Bank	1045	1230	1359	1209	1068	1208	1111	767	682

VALUATIONS OF PROPERTY.

	Estimated Ann. Val. 1821. £	Ratable Value.					
		1854. £	1866. £	1872. £	1877. £	1884. £	1888. £
Darwen, Lower	4329	8203	11126	17232	21580	21225	23714
Darwen, Over	6629	20143	44215	62916	82714	85755	97910
Eccleshill	1048	1634	2463	2840	3926	3300	3402
Yate and Pickup Bank	1358	1664	1776	1544	2278	2165	1874

POLITICAL ANNALS.

Viscount Cranborne, M.P., son and heir of the Marquis of Salisbury, present Prime Minister of England, was the first representative of Darwen in Parliament, and he represents not merely the town and district of Darwen, but a large county constituency called the Darwen Division. This Division was formed during the Redistribution of Seats in 1885, as one of the four single-member constituencies created to take the place of the North-East Lancashire Division. Prior to this Darwen was very inadequately represented in Parliament, as only forty-shilling freeholders and occupants of houses worth £12 a year could vote. A great Reform Demonstration took place in Darwen in 1867, and the Local Board petitioned Parliament for the enfranchisement of the borough. The prayer of the petitioners was not acceded to, but in the following year the electors of Darwen took part in the first election for the new county division called North-East Lancashire, at which Mr. J. Maden Holt and Mr. J. P. Chamberlain Starkie (Conservatives) were returned. The open voting of this election disclosed the fact that in a total electorate of 1,200 voters in the Darwen polling district there was a majority of 100 on the Liberal side. The first election under the Ballot Act took place on February 7th, 1874. The voters for the township of Over Darwen polled at Duckworth Street School and St. John's School, and the Duckworth Street School was also the polling place for Lower Darwen, Eccleshill, Tockholes, and Yate-and-Pickup Bank. Sixty Liberal voters in the Darwen polling district had been struck off the register at the previous revision on an objection to their properties being held on under-leases. North-East Lancashire continued to be represented by Messrs. Holt and Starkie until 1880, when the Marquis of Hartington and Mr. F. W. Grafton (Liberals) carried the seats. Alderman William Snape, Mayor of Darwen, was Chairman of the Executive for the Division, and he entertained Lord Hartington at his house at Lynwood. Darwen did its full share of work at that election, 1,000 Darwen electors having signed a petition inviting Lord Hartington to contest the Division, and pledging their hearty support. The total number of voters in the

THE RIGHT HON. VISCOUNT CRANBORNE,
FIRST M.P. FOR DARWEN DIVISION.

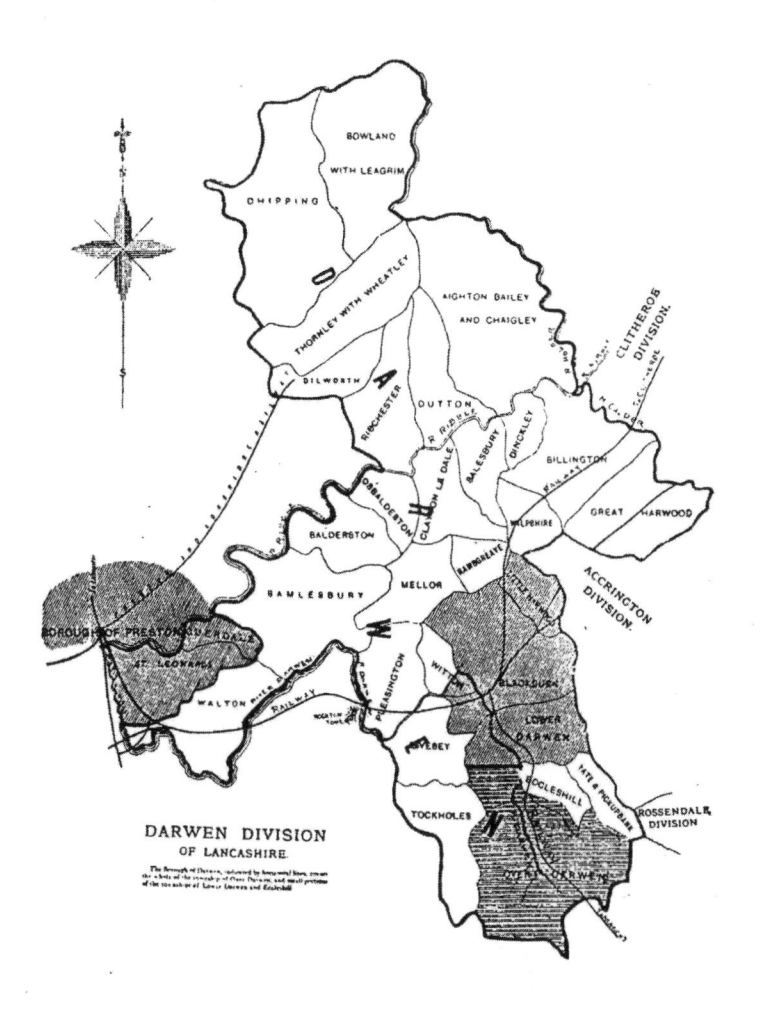

DARWEN DIVISION
OF LANCASHIRE.

Darwen polling district was 1,726 in 1880, compared with 1,580 in the previous year, and 1,222 in 1874. The total electorate of the Division was 12,991. The Liberal victory was complete and decisive, the result of the election being—Hartington (L) 6,682, Grafton (L) 6,513 ; Ecroyd (C) 5,231, Starkie (C) 5,185. The poll was declared at Blackburn at 10 p.m. on the 9th of April, 1880, and as soon as the news reached Darwen a torchlight procession was formed in front of the Liberal Club, Market Street. Proceeding along the road to Blackburn, the exulting Liberals met Mr. Snape's carriage (containing Mr. Snape and Lord Hartington) in Craven Brow. The horses were taken out, and the carriage and its occupants were drawn by the people to the Liberal Club, from the windows of which Lord Hartington addressed the crowd in the street shortly after midnight. He and Mr. Snape were then taken in the carriage to Lynwood, hundreds of willing men taking the place of the horses by pulling at the ropes attached to the shafts.

In February, 1879, a motion was brought forward in the Town Council demanding separate Parliamentary representation for the borough, but was rejected. Subsequently the agitation for the enfranchisement of the borough became more pronounced, and when the question of Redistribution was occupying the attention of Parliament and the country in October, 1884, the Town Council, on the motion of Alderman Snape, petitioned Parliament in favour of separate and independent representation being granted to Darwen in any Redistribution Bill that might be brought forward by the Government. The people of Darwen were disappointed with the result of that Redistribution, for the Radical borough had the Conservative freeholders of Blackburn and the new electorate of a large agricultural area in the Ribble Valley attached to it. Strong protests were made in the Town Council, and by representatives of the Council appearing before the Boundary Commissioners, but when the Commissioners had finished their work it was found that the Darwen Division would contain a population of 168,717 (according to the census of 1881), including the Borough of Blackburn. Its total area is 76,694 acres, or 120 square miles, and its ratable value £720,894. It extends from Bamber Bridge in the west to Great Harwood in the east, and from Bowland-with-Leagram in the north to Darwen in the south, the length from north to south being 20 miles. In the Parliamentary borough of Blackburn the county suffrage is confined to freeholders, of whom, in 1885, there were 2,133 ; but in the rest of the Division there is household suffrage, householders, freeholders, leaseholders and lodgers all having votes. The following is a list of the townships in the Division, with their population according to an official return :—Darwen, 29,445 ; Eccleshill, 716 ; part of Yate-and-Pickup Bank, 682 ; Tockholes, 484 ; Livesey, 1,616 ; these are in Darwen and the immediate neighbourhood. Borough of Blackburn, 105,000 ; Pleasington, 459 ; Witton, 176 ; Mellor, 1,096 ; Walton-le-Dale, 9,286 ; Samlesbury, 752 ; Balderstone, 487 ; Osbaldeston, 154 ; Ramsgreave, 240 ; Clayton-le-Dale, 295 ; Salesbury, 184 ; Dinckley, 123 ; Billington, 1410 ; Wilpshire, 280 ; Great Harwood, 6,287 ; these are between Blackburn and the Ribble. Beyond the Ribble :—Ribchester, 1,282 ; Dutton, 259 ; Dilworth, 2,116 ; Aighton, Bailey, and Chaigley, 1,663 ; Thornley-with-Wheatley, 349 ; Chipping, 987 ; Bowland-with-Leagram, 206.

Lord Cranborne, who had been previously announced as a candidate for the old Division of North-East Lancashire,[1] was invited on the 13th of February, 1885, to champion the Conservative cause in the new Darwen Division. On the 23rd of March he made the acquaintance of his future constituents by opening a bazaar at Blackburn, and on the 16th of May he appeared in Darwen as a candidate for election, and opened a Conservative club in Grimshaw Street. Mr. John Gerald Potter, J.P., had been adopted as the Liberal candidate on May 2nd, but he did not begin his campaign until July 4th. In August, and again in October, the Irish voters had meetings and decided to hold aloof from both political parties, pending the receipt of instructions from Mr. Parnell, who eventually gave the word that the Irish vote all over the kingdom must go against Mr. Gladstone in order to equalise the parties in the House of Commons and give the Nationalists the balance of power. There being some hundreds of Irish electors in the borough of Darwen alone this attitude of the Nationalist Party resulted in a Liberal defeat. The election was a memorable one, and its result equally so. The Liberal Party was in a decided majority in the town of Darwen, but the rest of the Division, except Great Harwood and Bamber Bridge, was largely Conservative, and with the Irish vote against them in addition the Liberals knew they had a hazardous task before them. They never despaired of the result, however, until the poll was declared on December 3rd, when it was found that Lord Cranborne had won by five votes. The counting took place in the Co-operative Hall, Darwen, on December 3rd, and the result was declared at 2-15 p.m., as follows :—Lord Cranborne (C), 5,878 ; John Gerald Potter (L), 5,873 ; Conservative majority FIVE. The excitement consequent upon this close contest was intense, and the

[1] The announcement that Lord Cranborne would contest North-East Lancashire against Lord Hartington at the next General Election was made by the Rev. Philip Graham, J.P., at a Conservative meeting in the Public Hall, Darwen, on October 9th, 1884, and it caused a sensation throughout Lancashire.

JOHN GERALD POTTER, Esq., J.P.

Liberals were thoroughly dissatisfied with the method of counting which had been adopted by the Sheriff's officers. Mr. Snape on behalf of the Party made an application upon affidavit to the Court of Queen's Bench for permission to inspect the voting papers, his object being to have the whole recounted, and some doubtful ones rejected. The application was made before Justices Denman, Field, and Day, on December 21st, and they dismissed it on the ground that there was no reason to allow an inspection of the papers in the absence of any petition complaining of undue return or of corrupt or illegal practices. Mr. Justice Day dubbed it a "fishing application."

The affidavit made by Mr. Snape, "as a voter in Over Darwen, and Chairman of Mr. Potter's Election Committee," was as follows :—" The counting of the votes took place at Darwen the day after the voting (Dec. 2nd), when the Returning Officer declared the numbers to be Cranborne 5,878, Potter, 5,873, with 42 spoiled papers and eight tendered votes ; and he certified that there was one ballot paper short in two of the boxes and one too many in another. There were 11 officials appointed by the Under-Sheriff to conduct the counting, but he refused to allow more than six agents for each candidate to remain in the room to check them, notwithstanding that the election agents for both candidates contended that there ought to be at least one agent on each side to each official counter, and entered a formal protest against the Returning Officer's refusal to allow this. I and the other five agents appointed on behalf of Mr. Potter were allowed to count the voting papers once, and we made out that there was a majority in Mr. Potter's favour, but the Returning Officer refused to allow us to recount the papers after he had stated that he made out the majority to be in Lord Cranborne's favour, although a formal request for permission to do so was made to him by Mr. Potter's election agent. Under the circumstances it was impossible for Mr. Potter's agents properly to verify the result which was arrived at by the Returning Officer. This result, however, cannot be accurate, because the total number of votes counted and rejected is one more than the number of voting papers actually found in the ballot boxes, according to the Returning Officer's report. Certain votes were also objected to by Mr. Potter's election agent on the ground that the ballot papers were improperly marked, some of them being marked only by a dot instead of a cross, others having a cross on the wrong side of the paper, and others having marks in addition to the cross, by which the voters might possibly be identified. The objections taken to these papers, however, were overruled and the votes allowed and counted, several ballot papers being counted for Lord Cranborne which the Returning officer had at first disallowed, and endorsed 'rejected' accordingly. I desire to have an order under section 40 of the Ballot Act, 1872, permitting an inspection of the rejected and counted papers to be made by my solicitors and counsel, in the presence of the Clerk of the Crown, in order that I may be advised whether the votes were correctly counted, and whether the ballot papers objected to were properly allowed, all proper precautions being taken by the Clerk of the Crown to see that no opportunity is given for ascertaining by whom any particular votes have been given."

On the 17th of June, 1886, Lord Cranborne, M.P., commenced his second campaign in the Darwen Division. The circumstances attending this election were very different from those of the last. Mr. Gladstone's

Home Rule Bill had been rejected, and while the Irish vote was now bodily transferred to the Liberal side the Conservative ranks were greatly augmented by the addition of the Liberal Unionists. Among the Liberal Unionists of Darwen were Mr. J. Gerald Potter, J.P., who now openly supported his former opponent. The Liberals, on June 24th, adopted Mr. John Slagg as their candidate, and two days later Mr. Slagg commenced his campaign. The election took place on July 7th, Lord Cranborne was returned with a greatly increased majority, the result being :—Cranborne (Conservative and Unionist), 6,085 ; Slagg (Gladstonian Liberal), 5,359 ; majority, 726.[1] Lord Salisbury became Prime Minister, and the Marchioness of Salisbury visited Darwen on the 1st of December in the same year to help her son to establish the Conservative cause firmly in the Division for which he was the first Member.

James Edward Hubert Cecil, commonly called Viscount Cranborne, is the eldest son of the Marquis of Salisbury. He was born in 1861 ; educated at Eton and the University College, Oxford ; elected M.P. for the Darwen Division of Lancashire in 1885 and 1886 ; and made private secretary to his father, who became Prime Minister of England in 1886. In 1887 he married Lady Cicely Alice Gore, second daughter of the Earl of Arran. He holds the rank of Major in the Yeomanry. Address, Hatfield House, Herts ; 30, St. James's Place, London, S.W. ; Carlton Club.

THE COUNTY COUNCIL.

On the formation of the Lancashire County Council in January, 1889, Mr. Timothy Lightbown, J.P., and Mr. Graham Fish, J.P. (both Liberals), were elected unopposed as representatives of the two polling districts of the Borough of Darwen. Mr. Charles Costeker, Town Clerk of Darwen, took the leading part among the representatives of boroughs having populations under 50,000, in the action to secure due consideration in the distribution of the new powers and privileges conferred by the Local Government Act, 1888. The result of this action was section 32, providing for an equitable adjustment of the financial relations between counties and county boroughs.

POLICE ARRANGEMENTS.

The Darwen Petty Sessional Division formerly included the townships of Over Darwen, Lower Darwen, Eccleshill, Yate-and-Pickup Bank, and Tockholes, and the police arrangements under the Inspector stationed at Darwen still cover the same district, though the Darwen county magistrates, since the formation of the Borough Bench, have jurisdiction only over Tockholes, Yate-and-Pickup Bank, and the rural portion of Eccleshill. The surviving county justices are :—John Gerald Potter, Earnsdale, Darwen, qualified April 7th, 1852 ; Eccles Shorrock, Low

[1] The number of electors on the register was 12,629.

GRAHAM FISH, Esq., J.P.

TIMOTHY LIGHTBOWN, Esq., J.P.

MEMBERS OF THE COUNTY COUNCIL.

Hill House, Darwen, July 4th, 1855; Ralph Shorrock Ashton, Blackburn, July 4th, 1885; Rev. Charles Greenway, Darwen Bank, February 19th, 1868; James Dimmock, Radfield Hall, Darwen, July 3rd, 1872; Lawrence H. Wraith, Lower Darwen, January 9th, 1879; Charles Philip Huntington, Astley Bank, Darwen, January 14th, 1879; William Balle Huntington, Woodlands, Darwen, April 19th, 1886. Clerk: Charles Costeker. A Borough Bench was formed in September, 1881, through the exertions of the Mayor, Alderman Snape. Appended is a list of the borough magistrates living at the present day, with the dates of their qualification :—Chief Magistrate, Alex. T. Eccles, The Cottage (Mayor), qualified November 10th, 1887; James Dimmock, Radfield Hall; Charles Philip Huntington, Astley Bank; Henry Green, Woodbine House; Christopher Shorrock, Moss Bridge; William T. Ashton, Ashdale; Dr. Thomas Aspinall, Turton Tower; Robert Smalley Entwisle, Southport; James Walsh, Prospect; qualified September 1st, 1881. Timothy Lightbown, Falcon House; William Entwisle, Rosehill; Joseph Eccles, High Lawn; Graham Fish, Woodside House; Robert Thomas Gillibrand, Hollins House; Eccles Shorrock, junior, Low Hill; qualified January 16th, 1885. Richard Herbert Eccles, Lynwood; William Walmsley, Corncliffe; Alexander Carus, Hoddlesden; Robert Gillibrand, Whitehall; William Grimshaw, The Rookery; Thomas Baynes-Taylor, Radley Fold; qualified April 19th, 1886. Dr. J. H. Wraith, Lower Bank; J. H. Shorrock, 9, Trinity Terrace; E. M. Davies, Cranberry Cottage; J. W. Gillibrand, Earlswood, Hollins Grove; qualified December 7th, 1887. Clerk: F. G. Hindle.

A FAMOUS LICENSING CASE.

The annual Licensing Sessions held on the 24th of August, 1882, are memorable as having furnished a precedent for the sweeping away of beer off-licenses. A fortnight before that day the "Off Licensing Act of 1882" received the Royal assent. Being of opinion that this Act of Parliament authorised them to refuse the renewal of existing beer off-licenses where they considered them unnecessary, the magistrates, acting under the advice of their clerk, Mr. F. G. Hindle, sanctioned the issue by Mr. Bryning, the local superintendent of police, of notices intimating that the renewal of their licenses would be opposed on the ground that there was no necessity for them. At the adjourned sessions, on the 14th of September, the Bench refused the renewal of 34 out of 72 existing licenses, on the ground that they were not required in the district. Twenty-five of the applicants gave notice of appeal, and at the Preston Quarter Sessions, Mr. Higgin, Q.C., the chairman, said he was strongly in favour of the view taken by the magistrates—namely, that the new Act gave them exactly the same power over the renewal of existing off-licenses, that they always had over the renewal of existing public-house licenses, and that these latter were now, and always had been, held simply from year to year at the discretion of the licensing justices. The decision of the court was to select a test case for the Court of Queen's Bench to be consulted upon this point of law. The question came before JJ. Field and Stephen, in the Court of Queen's Bench, on the 24th November, 1882, the test case being "Kay v. the Justices of Over Darwen," and the judges, without hesitation, confirmed the ruling of Mr. Higgin. An attempt was made to carry the case further—to the Lords Justices of Appeal, but this was strongly discountenanced by Lord Chief Justice Coleridge, who refused on the 12th December to grant any facilities for having the case re-heard. On the 15th of December the appellants gave notice withdrawing the appeal, which was subsequently dismissed, with costs against the appellants, as were the other 24 appeals depending on it. This case settled the point of law, so far as off-licenses are concerned, that licensing justices have power to refuse the renewal of licenses, and in the following year many towns followed the example of Over Darwen and swept away a large number of these licenses. Since then a test case has been taken from Westmoreland, proving that magistrates can also refuse the renewal of public-house licenses, contrary to the popular opinion regarding vested interests. Mr. F. G. Hindle in March, 1883, published a work entitled "The Legal Status of Licensed Victuallers," giving full details of the Darwen appeals; and this handbook is now accepted as an authority on some knotty points of licensing law. In 1888, after the decision of the Court of Queen's Bench regarding the vested interest of innkeepers or publicans, Mr. Hindle issued a fourth edition of his book interleaved with some additional matter.

The borough of Darwen contains 52 public-houses, 24 beerhouses, 37 off-licensed beerhouses, and 8 houses licensed to sell wine to be consumed off the premises. In the district of the Darwen county magistrates there are eight public-houses and six beerhouses.

POOR-LAW ADMINISTRATION.

The "Old Workhouse," which for fifty years has been applied to various purposes, but still bears the name of workhouse, was erected and maintained for the use of the poor of the township of Over Darwen prior to the formation in 1836 of the Blackburn Union, of which Over Darwen forms a part. Shortly after the formation of the Over Darwen Local Board in 1855, the workhouse land and buildings were conveyed by the Overseers of the Poor to the Local Board for the use of the town. Over Darwen elects four guardians, Lower Darwen, Eccleshill, and Yate-and-Pickup Bank each one. Four assistant overseers are chosen for Over Darwen, two for Lower Darwen, three for Eccleshill, and two for Yate-and-Pickup Bank. There is one registrar of births, marriages, and deaths, also one vaccination officer, and one relieving officer for the whole of the Darwen district, urban and rural. Over Darwen has an assistant overseer, and so has Yate-and-Pickup Bank, and the townships of Lower Darwen and Eccleshill are united under a third. Yate-and-Pickup Bank and the rural portion of Eccleshill have each a representative on the Rural Sanitary Authority of the Union, and each a surveyor of highways. Darwen has no School Board, but there is a School Attendance Committee for the borough of Darwen having the oversight of 20 day schools, 16 of which are in Over

Darwen and four in Lower Darwen. There is one school in Yate-and-Pickup Bank under the supervision of the School Attendance Committee of the Blackburn Union, sitting at Blackburn, but no day school in either the urban or rural portion of the township of Eccleshill. The portion of Lower Darwen incorporated into the borough of Blackburn contains three schools, which come under the supervision of the Blackburn School Board.

BLACKBURN AND DARWEN STEAM TRAMWAY

On the 14th of April, 1881, there was opened between Darwen and Blackburn the first tramway in the kingdom worked entirely by steam. Prior to this steam engines had only been used on tramways in an experimental way, but the Mayor and other members of the Darwen Corporation having witnessed the results of these experiments, consented to the passing of an Act of Parliament authorising the construction of the Black burn and Over Darwen Tramway to be worked entirely by steam. The headquarters of the tramway, including offices, store rooms, and commodious sheds for the engines and cars, were built in Lorne-street, Darwen. The tramway is five miles long, and the rails are of steel, laid upon Barker's patent system, with loops at frequent intervals, to enable cars travelling in opposite directions to pass each other, and triangles at the termini for reversing the engines and cars without uncoupling. Up to the 30th of June, 1887, the capital expenditure of the Company amounted to £46,450, including all costs of construction and the purchase of nine locomotive engines, eight cars carrying passengers both inside and out, and four open workmen's cars. Subjoined are some official statistics of the working of the line up to the end of 1888:—

Half-year ending	No. of Passengers.	Miles run.	Dividends paid.	Traffic receipts.
1881—June 30	————	15,200	7%	1164 17 0
Decr. 31	312,813	68,290	7%	3798 11 3
1882—June 30	337,616	67,428	6%	3412 10 7
Decr. 31	396,637	64.876	—	3558 19 10
1883—June 30	375,709	65 264	—	3353 18 4
Decr. 31	419,357	67,558	—	3599 6 8
1884—June 30	402,506	68,002	—	3351 5 9
Decr. 31	467 494	70,676	10%	3797 19 10
1885—June 30	432,407	71,500	4%	3499 14 1
Decr. 31	452 554	67,650	4%	3627 15 11
1886—June 30	432,079	66,154	2%	3490 18 5
Decr. 31	545,901	78,000	4%	4392 2 11
1887—June 30	516,647	72,512	4%	4203 9 7
Decr. 31	572,272	79,110	5%	4572 12 8
1888—June 30	555,898	79,441	5%	4496 4 8
Decr. 31	607,084	79,791	5%	4874 4 7

From the middle of 1882 until the end of 1884 there was no dividend paid, as the Company had a big law-suit on hand arising out of the overturning of a car on Ewood Bridge, Blackburn, on July 7th, 1882, resulting in the death of one person and injuries to 28 others. Among the advantages of this line is the warming of the cars in winter time by the waste steam from the engines.

CO-OPERATION.

The co-operative principle of trading, originated by the "Pioneers" of Rochdale in 1844, was adopted in Darwen in 1860, and it has since exercised a potent influence among the thrifty inhabitants. Premises for a co-operative store were first taken in Green Street—the shop now occupied by Mr. Ireland, saddler,—and in January, 1861, the Over Darwen Industrial Co-operative Society was established. At that time the right to hold property in their corporate capacity had not been extended by the legislature to co-operative societies, so the license to sell snuff, tobacco, tea, &c., was taken out on behalf of the new society in the name of Richard Ainsworth, one of its founders. Scarce had the business of the society been started (on the ready-money system which is one of the fundamental principles of co-operation) when it was threatened with sudden extinction by the outbreak of the American War and the Cotton Famine which resulted from it, but it safely weathered the storm. One of the immediate effects of the establishment of this society was a general lowering of prices among all the shopkeepers of the town, whose object was to nip the new venture in the bud. But year by year the society struck deeper its roots and spread wider its branches. The central stores in Green Street became totally inadequate to meet the requirements of the growing trade, so towards the close of 1866 the members set themselves the arduous task of erecting the first portion of the present stores in School Street. In June, 1868, this building, which had cost £9,000, was opened, free from debt, and besides this the society's capital was found to have increased by £7,000 during the 18 months occupied in the work. One of the first acts of the society on removing to its new premises was to set aside 2½ per cent. of its profits for educational purposes—a practice which has been followed without intermission to the present day. A few months later the party strife generated by the warmth of the General Election of 1868 led to a division among the members, and a new society was formed which is still in existence, making progress year by year relatively as great as that of the parent society.

The Provident Co-operative Society, formed by political seceders from the Industrial Society in 1868, has its central stores in Green Street and five branches in different parts of the town. Its 1000 members have subscribed a share capital of £10,000, and the annual turnover is now over £30,000. This society owns cottage property in the town to the value of nearly £3,000.

Recovering from the temporary check caused by this division the Industrial Society continued to prosper until the joint-stock mania of 1873-4, when some heavy investments which the directors had made in one or two joint-stock companies of were lost. Many of its members individually lost money also in joint-stock transactions, and there was a run on the society's capital in addition to a new-born feeling of distrust in co-operative principles. But all financial demands were met, and the society stood firm despite the withdrawal of its more timid members. In more recent years it has had to cope with competition unparalleled in its previous history, and in order to hold its own against the shops which began to be planted at every street corner it had to build branch stores in all parts of the town. Thus moving with the times it has gained both capital and custom, until to-day it numbers over 3,200 members, with an aggregate capital of nearly £100,000. The annual turnover amounts to £104,000, and brings £13,000 in profits to its customers after paying interest on capital. The total profits made since the establishment of the society amount to nearly £200,000, of which £5,000 has been spent in education. In addition to its central stores, offices, public assembly-room, reading-room and class-rooms in School Street, extended in 1876, the society has eleven branch stores, all its own property. It has two newsrooms and a circulating library of 5,500 volumes. Science and art classes, under Government inspection, form the chief of its educational arrangements. It owns 50 cottages in the town, built at a cost of over £8,000, and some £32,000 of its capital has been advanced on security to various members to enable them to become the possessors of their own dwellings. A Penny Bank has been founded which has now 4,000 depositors, and a weaving shed has been built out of the society's funds. There are several smaller co-operative societies in the borough, and some of the joint-stock companies, engaged in the cotton and paper trades, have survived, and are fairly prosperous.

MISCELLANEOUS.

The public spirit of the inhabitants of Darwen has been shown in many respects. Lectures and concerts, cricket and football, exhibitions and the like are taken up as town's affairs. The Darwen Temperance Society, formed in 1834, is in existence at the present day, though temperance work is now extensively carried out by numerous societies and clubs of modern growth. Two companies of Rifle Volunteers have been enrolled and officered by local gentlemen. The Peel Baths were erected partly by public subscription, and the public clock in Holy Trinity Church tower was likewise subscribed for by the inhabitants. Educationally the town occupies a high position, and the science lectures given under the auspicies of the Gilchrist Trustees and through the munificence of Mr. W. B. Huntington, J.P., are greatly appreciated. Two newspapers are published in the town—the *Darwen News*, established in 1874, and the *Darwen Post*, 1885. Twice during the last 20 years have extensive exhibitions of art treasures been held, which have attracted thousands of visitors from all parts of Lancashire and the neighbouring counties. Both were promoted in connection with the Belgrave Congregational Schools, projected chiefly by the Rev. James Mc.Dougall, and opened by the Marquis of Hartington. The first, in 1868, was held in the India Mills, then newly built. It realised the sum of £1,115, which was added to the fund for the erection of the Bolton Road Congregational School, but the one in 1879, which was held in the Belgrave Schools, entailed a financial loss, although visited by about 40,000 persons, in addition to the 800 season ticket-holders.

INDEX TO BOOK I.

ACTS of Parliament, Local, 172-3, 176
Ancient Landowners in Darwen, 56-9
Art Treasures Exhibitions, 194
Ashton, W. T., a local Antiquary, 10-11, 16-18, 20, 24, 26-7, 45

BERRY, House of William and Henry, 31, 76, 97
Blacksnape, Roman Road through, 23-5, 27-8
—— Sunday School, 28
Bold Venture Park, 178
—— Reservoir, 31
Borough Boundaries, 173
—— of Darwen (see Darwen)
British Burial Ground at Whitehall, 11-12
Bury Fold, 27, 31, 46

CALICO-PRINTING and Bleaching, 157-60, 163
Celtic of Invasion of Britain, 8
—— Place-Names, 9-10
Cemetery at Whitehall, 180
Census Returns, 183-4
—— of Churches, Chapels and Schools, 128-32
Chapel in Over Darwen, The, 49
—— Darwen (St. James's Church), 71 *et seq.*; its endowment, 73-4, 88-9; its early ministers, 73, 75, 80-3, 90; used under a Presbyterian license, 76, 97; seized by the Nonconformists and restored to the Vicar of Blackburn by the King, 76, 80, 98; ruinous condition of the fabric, 79; church-rate levied for repairs, 80, 83; rebuilt, 84-5; restored, 85-8; graveyard, 88; list of curates, &c., 90-1; parsonage and schools, 92.
Chapel, Yates's, 105, 112-14
Chapel, Lower, 84, *et seq.*; origin of Congregationalism in Darwen, 96-101; Presbyterian licenses, 97; early Nonconformist preachers, 97-101; Nonconformist worship on the moors, 98-9; tramping from Haslingden to Darwen to worship, 99-100; Charles Sagar, 100-1; building of Lower Chapel, 102, 111-12; the trust deeds, 102-4; ministers of Lower Chapel, 102-12; schools, 112
Chapel on Pendle Hill, Ruins of Jollie's, 99
Chapels, the Place-Name, 49-71
Chapels, Nonconformist. Lower Chapel (see Chapel); Pole Lane, Ebenezer and Belgrave, 107, 114-17; Bolton Road, 117; Duckworth Street, 110, 117-21; Hollins Grove, 121; Pickup Bank, Belthorn and Lower Darwen, 121-2; other Nonconformist chapels, 126-7 (see Methodism); revenues, 129
Charter of Incorporation, 169-70
Church, The Roman Catholic, 72-127
Church of England. St. James's Church, Over Darwen (see Darwen Chapel); Holy Trinity, 92-3; St. James's, Lower Darwen, 93-4; St. Paul's, Hoddlesden, 94; St. John's, 94-5; St. Cuthbert's, 95-6
Churches and Chapels, Census of, 128-9.
Civil War, 62-7
Climate, 4, 147, 179-80
Coal Getting, 134, 162-3
—— Measures, 3-6
Commonwealth, Seizure of Land by the, 67-70
Conquest to the Revolution, From the, 33-70
Constable of Over Darwen, 135
Co-operation, 192-3
Corporation, Darwen (see Darwen)
Cotton Trade, its origin, 145; introduction of the factory system, 146; Samuel Crompton, 146; early Darwen chapmen, 146, 148; the old mill in Lower Darwen, 146; Lower Darwen factory school, 132, 146; first twenty-spindle bobbin wheel in Darwen, 147; atmospheric conditions, 147; the top factory, 148; loom-breaking riots, 148; Eccles Shorrock, the eminent merchant and manufacturer, 149-50; India Mill, 31, 150, 194; the Great Strike, 150-3; strike riots, 151-2; wages, 150-6; the

Ten Weeks' Strike, 153-4; statistics, 154-7, 163; cotton mills in the district, 156-7
County Council, Lancashire, 188
Cranborne, Rt. Hon. Viscount, M.P., 184-8; attempt to unseat, 187
Crompton, Samuel, 146, 159-60

DARWEN Chapel (see Chapel and Chapels)
—— Corporation of, 169, 84; incorporation of the borough, 169-70; municipal elections, 170-1; William Snape, first Mayor, 171-2; list of Mayors, 172; local Acts of Parliament, 172-3: public buildings, 174-6; gas and waterworks, 176-8; parks and recreation grounds, 178-9; health of the borough, 179-80; cemetery, 180; the river, 180-2; public works, 182; corporation finances, 182; population and ratable value, 182-4
—— Directory of, for 1824, 143-5
—— Division of Lancashire, 184-8
—— Manor of Over, 35-9
—— Manor of Nether, 40-1
—— Moor, highest point of, 2; public footpaths, 2, 178-9; view from summit, 2, 179; common rights on, 36 7
—— Name of the Borough of, 1, 169, 173; physical features and earliest inhabitants, 1-20; its condition in 1688, 133; in 1795, 138; in 1806-24, 143; modern progress, 133-194; first mentioned in history, 33; Green, 15-16; Valley in the past, 10-11, 17-18
—— River, its source and course, 2; its name, 8-9; Saxon settlements on the, 12-13; noted by Camden, 48; battles on Darwen Bridge, 64, 65-7; Union Street Bridge, 26, 140; fords, 140; floods, 139, 181-2; pollution, 180-2
Darwynd Hall, 37, 45
De Lacy Inquisition, 35

ECCLES, Alex. T., Mayor of Darwen, 172
Eccleshill, Manor of, 41-2
—— Sale of an Estate in, 138
Ecclesiastical History, 71-132 (see Churches and Chapels)
Elections, Municipal, 170-1
—— Parliamentary, 184-8
Elizabethan Buildings, 27, 45-7
Exhibitions of Art Treasures, 194

FAMILY History, 43-59
Fernhurst, Manor House of Lower Darwen, 40-1, 44, 46, 134
Feudalism. 33 *et seq*.

Fever Epidemic, 164-8
—— in Eccleshill, 135
Fire-Clay, 5, 162-3
Five Children at a Birth, 136-7
Flag-Rock (see Quarries)
Forests, Evidence of Primeval, 17-18, 176
Free Library, 175

GAS and Waterworks, 176-8 (see Waterworks and Water Supply)
Geology of the Darwen Valley, 1-8
Greenway, James 157-9
Grime, James, of Bobbin Hall, 139
Grimshaw Family, of Eccleshill, 41, 47, 67-70

HARWOOD, Rev. Edward, D.D., 137-8
Haworth, Giles, outlawed for murder, 49-51
Health of the Borough, 179-80
Hilton, Richard and Henry, 160
Hoddlesden, 27, 35, 44-6
Hoghton Estates in Darwen, 36
—— Tower, 59-65
Holker House, Hoddlesden, 27, 45-6

INCORPORATION of the Borough of Over Darwen, 168-70
India Mill, 31, 150, 194
Industries, Local, 5, 145-163
Inhabitants of the Darwen Valley, 1-20 (see Family)
Inquisitions Post Mortem, 55-9
Iron Trade, 162-3

KNIGHTHOOD declined by John Crosse, 54

LANDOWNERS in Darwen, Ancient, 56-9
Licensing Case, A Famous Darwen, 189-90
Local Board of Health, 164-9; chairmen of the Local Board, 164; division of the town into wards. 164; the fever epidemic, 164-8
Lord's Hall, 32, 38
Lyon's Den, 19-20

MANOR of Over Darwen, 35-9; Lord's Hall, 32, 38; Manor Court, 39
—— of Nether Darwen, 40-1; Fernhurst, 40-1, 44, 46
—— of Eccleshill, 41-2; Grimshaw family, 41, 47, 67, 70
Mansions of the Gentry, 30, 141
Mayors of Over Darwen, 172
Market Hall and Municipal Offices, 174-5
Mechanics' Institution, 175
Methodism in Darwen, 122-6; visits of John Wesley, 122-3; the Blackburn-Darwen Wesleyan Methodist Circuit,

DARWEN AND ITS PEOPLE. 197

124-5; Primitive Methodist Chapels. 125-6; U.M.F C . 126
Mining and Quarrying, 161-3 (see Coal, Quarries, &c.)
Modern History, 133-194
Moor, Darwen (see Darwen)
—— Allotment of Lower Darwen, 136
Municipal Affairs (see Darwen Corporation)

NINETEENTH Century Progress, 141-3

OAKENHURST, 46, 135-6
Old Darwen Families, 43-59 (see Book II., Jeremy Hunt's Recollections of Old Darwen Families)
—— Inhabitants of Darwen tempus Henry VIII., 44; Queen Elizabeth, 46-8; James I., 49-53; Charles I, 53-5; list of prominent Churchmen in 1719, 85

PAPER-MAKING and Paper-Staining, 160-1, 163
Parks and Recreation Grounds, 178-9
Parliament, Local Acts of, 172-3, 176
Parliamentary Elections, 184-8
Patriotic Inhabitants of Lower Darwen, 138-9
Physical Features of the Darwen Valley, 1-8
Pin Fold, The, 31. 45
Place-Names, Celtic, 9-10; Saxon, 12-20; Scandinavian, 19
Pole Lane Chapel and Graveyard, 28-30, 107, 114-17
Police Arrangements, 188-9
Political Annals, 184-8; petitions for enfranchisement, 162, 184-5
Poor-Law Administration, 190-1
Population and Ratable Value, 182-4
Potter and Co., 157-8, 161
—— C. and J. G., 161
—— John Gerald, 161, 166, 186-8
Pre-historic Man, 7-8
Print Shop on Bury Fold Brook, 30-1, 157-8
Public Buildings, 174-6
—— Works, 182

QUARRIES, Stone and Flag, 7, 162, 163

RAILWAYS, 163-4
Recreation Grounds, Public, 178-9
Reservoir, Bursting of Bold Venture. 31
Revolution, The, 70
River Darwen (see Darwen)

Roads, Old, 21-32; Roman road through Darwen, 22-5, 27-8; pack-horse roads, 26, 32, 134, 139-41; first wheeled vehicle coming into Darwen, 139; the new road from Blackburn to Bolton, 141 (see Tramways and Railways)
Roadside Town, Darwen a, 21
Roman Road from Manchester to Ribchester, 22-5, 27 8

SAXON Bridle Road, An Old, 25-32
—— Burial Grounds, Supposed, 14
—— Place-Names, 12-20
—— Settlements on the River Darwen, 12-13
Scandinavian Place-Names, 19
Schools, Statistics of Day and Sunday, 129 32 (see Churches and Chapels)
Smalley's Charity, 138
Snape, Alderman William, J.P., First Mayor of Darwen, 171-2, 184-5, 187
Sough, 26, 30, 140; land subsidence at Spring Vale Station, 163; Sough Tunnel, 163

TEMPERANCE Society, Darwen, 193
Tockholes Road, 31
Township Administration, 190-1
—— History (see Manor)
—— of Yate-and-Pickup Bank, 42-3
Town Hall, Site for a, 174-5
Tramway from Darwen to Blackburn, Steam, 191-2

UNION Street Bridge, 26, 140

VALLEY, Darwen, 1-20

WALKDEN'S Diary, Peter, 134
Water Supply, 4-5, 165-6, 168, 176-8
Waterworks, Blackburn, 177
—— Darwen, 176-8
—— Liverpool, 3, 177
Welshe, Rev. Edward, a deposed Vicar of Blackburn, 49, 53
Wesley, John, Visits of, 122-3
White Hall, the oldest house in Darwen, 27, 30, 46, 138
Whitehall, British Burial Ground at, 11-12; estate sold, 139; park, 178; cemetery, 180
Witchcraft, Display of Supposed, 51-2
Works in Over Darwen in 1867, 162-3

YATE-AND-PICKUP Bank, Township of, 42-3
—— Tradition of a Serpent at, 42-3
Yates's Chapel, 105, 112-14

INDEX TO BOOK II.

ADDITIONAL Families, Note on, 132
Author's Own Life, The, 5
Conclusion, 131
Genealogical Tables, 14, 22
—— Note on the, 31
Introductory, 1
The Briggses, 63
  „ Burys, 136
  „ Duxburys, 137
  „ Eccleses, 48
  „ Entwisles, 133
  „ Fishes, 118
  „ Grimes, or Grahams, 106
  „ Harwoods, 37
  „ Hindles, 79

The Holdens, 22
  „ Hunts, 5 and 86
  „ Jepsons 95
  „ Kays, 136
  „ Kirkhams, 135
  „ Leaches, 73
  „ Lightbowns, 140
  „ Marsdens, 14
  „ Pickups, 46
  „ Shorrocks, 59
  „ Smalleys, 33
  „ Thompsons, 142
  „ Walmsleys, 139
  „ Walshes, 113
  „ Watsons, 102

₊ For further reference see the summaries printed at the head of each chapter.

JEREMY HUNT.
BORN FEBRUARY 27th, 1806; DIED JULY 20th, 1887.

OLD DARWEN FAMILIES.

DARWEN AND ITS PEOPLE.

BOOK II.—OLD DARWEN FAMILIES.

Introductory.

Population of Darwen—Jeremy Hunt's Unique Position—Description of Darwen at the time of Jeremy's Birth—Jeremy's Authorities on Ancient History—His "Grandmother Marsden"—Preparation of Jeremy's "Recollections" for *The Blackburn Times*.

AMONG the crowded manufacturing towns of Lancashire there is none which has sprung up within a century with such vigorous and healthy growth as that of Darwen. Out of a few hillside hamlets of quaint but thrifty British workmen there has arisen a large town of 30,000 inhabitants, nearly all more or less directly dependent upon the Cotton Trade or the Paper Trade for their daily bread. One of the 30,000, Mr. Jeremy Hunt, aged 80 years,[1] is a man with a most remarkable memory for names, dates, and trifling historical incidents. He can sort out the remaining 29,999 of his fellow-townsmen, arrange them into families and clans, distinguish the adventitious from the aborigines, supply a list of births, marriages, and deaths, with correct dates and full details, and bring to light the girlish escapades of nearly everybody's great-great-grandmother. If the Vicar of Wakefield had happened to be a "Darruner" he need have had no fear of being imposed upon by pretenders claiming without title to be fortieth cousins, for Jeremy would have speedily ascertained the exact relationship which everybody bore to him. Without exaggeration, Jeremy can give, out of the deep recesses of his wonderfully acute and retentive memory, the pedigree of most of the old families belonging to the neighbourhood, and show that people who have no idea of their mutual relationship sprang, five or six

---

[1] Jeremy completed his 80th year on February 27th, 1886.

generations ago, from the same father or mother. The enormous multiplication of the *genus homo* in the town during his long lifetime has not puzzled Jeremy so much as the changing of names by marriage —a practice peculiar to the female sex. But even this has not thrown him off his track, for at lectures which he has given, when young people —total strangers to him—have come forward to learn their family history, the mere mention of the maiden name of their mother or their grandmother has been sufficient to open his mind and let out the treasures of his knowledge.

Jeremy's personal recollection carries him back to a time when the only public buildings in the neighbourhood were two Nonconformist Meeting-Houses, one Wesleyan Chapel, one Church of the Establishment, and a Printworks at Livesey Fold. The inhabitants at that time were occupied in handloom weaving, coal-getting, calico-printing, and the tilling of the soil. He was a young man when the first cotton factory was erected, and used as a handloom weaving warehouse. From calico-printing sprang paper-staining and paper-making, and from handloom weaving the factory system of the present day. Jeremy remembers both the paper trade and the cotton trade in their incipient stage, and, excepting one church and one chapel, he can, from his own recollections, trace back every place of worship in the town to its infancy. The situation of the public buildings at the time of Jeremy's birth will give to readers of the present generation an indication of what Darwen was like. The road from Blackburn to Bolton, which now forms the backbone of the town, was then quite a new thing, and the only public buildings near it were the Livesey Fold Printworks and the old Wesleyan Chapel. "Chapels," as it is called, must have been the headquarters of the locality, for there were situated both the Lower and the Higher Chapels, each boasting of some antiquity and interesting historic associations. Darwen is a great place for "chapel folks," and it is a remarkable fact that even the ancient church of the town was once claimed as the property of the Nonconformists, and even yet is well known by the name of "Higher *Chapel*," whereas its proper name is "St. James's Church." Next to Chapels comes Sough, for when Jeremy's father and a number of other old "Non-Cons." seceded from the Lower Chapel in 1792-3 they pitched upon Sough as the site for a new chapel, called by the name of "Pole Lane Chapel." On the opposite hill-side, very near the centre of the present town, there was a Wesleyan Chapel, built in 1791. Later we find the Blackburn and Bolton road developing, for when Jeremy was in his fifteenth year the oldest portion of Bowling Green Mill was built. Meanwhile Dob

Meadows Printworks had been erected at Earnsdale, and thus, while the church and the chapels were up on the hill-tops, in the old centres of the population, the workshops were beginning to spring up in the valley, and draw people down to the banks of the river and the edge of the new road. In the end business prevailed over other considerations, and the population gravitated towards the river side, for the next chapel that was built occupied the site of the present Belgrave Chapel, and the next church was Trinity Church, which stands close to it, and from its central position and commanding appearance often gives strangers the impression that it is the Parish Church of Darwen. The town, however, is too modern to have such a luxury as an ancient Parish Church of its own, for its oldest place of worship was originally a chapel-of-ease for Blackburn Parish Church, which is the mother church of all this neighbourhood.

It is quite evident from the above analysis of the state of the town at the beginning of this century that the town of Darwen, as we at present conceive it, had no existence at the time of Jeremy's birth, but that the elements out of which it has been formed were getting ripe for coalescence. And if the town did not exist neither did the people. The population, during Jeremy's lifetime, has increased tenfold, and when he was a boy it was quite possible for one to have a personal acquaintance with nearly everybody residing on the hill-sides and in the valley. Jeremy's father and mother had this extensive personal acquaintance. They were actually related, either by blood or marriage, to three-fourths of the population, and Jeremy's "Grandmother Marsden," with whom he lived in his boyhood, could take them back in her recollection to a time when the population numbered not 30,000 as at present, nor 3,000 as then, but merely a few hundreds of people whom she could classify into clans or families so few in number that she could reckon them up on her fingers. These were the aborigines of Darwen, and Jeremy's traditions concerning them come direct to him from his grandmother, or indirect, through his mother. His immediate ancestors, like himself, had a *penchant* for tradition, and among them they have handed down some very useful information for the benefit of the present generation and posterity. When Jeremy dies[1] his traditions will die with him, unless they are committed to writing, for there is no one man who can take his place when he is dead. For some years he has been anxious to have a portion of his store of knowledge preserved for posterity, and to this end a member of the staff of this journal[2] has taken down in shorthand from the old man's own lips various long

[1] He died July 20th, 1887.
[2] J. G. Shaw, Editor of *The Blackburn Times*, and Author of this Volume of History and Traditions

accounts of what he knows concerning the past. The history of the town, as a town, has already been written by the [late] Editor of this journal[1] in his "History of Blackburn Town and Parish" (Darwen being a portion of Blackburn Parish), and it has therefore been decided, with Jeremy's full concurrence, to write a series of articles, of which this is the introduction, as a sort of traditional history not so much of the town as of the people who form it. Any old Darwen family is worthy of a place in this history, no matter whether the members of it belong to the highest or the lowest grade of society. If they are "Darruners" that is a sufficient qualification to find them a place here. At the same time it has been thought desirable to eliminate from Jeremy's traditions certain stories showing the kinship of great men of the present day with poor rag-gatherers or notorious felons of the past, to pass lightly over the wickedness of men and the weakness of women, and to preserve chiefly traditions of the good qualities which distinguished the forefathers of the present generation and of the interesting connection of one family with another. Our representative's shorthand notes have been transcribed, as far as possible, so as to let Jeremy tell his own story in his own language, and Jeremy himself has revised the "copy" before its appearance in print. We shall first reprint an account of Jeremy's own life from *The Blackburn Times* of March 6th, 1886, and then proceed to publish a series of articles giving his traditions. The series will have a special interest inasmuch as the whole of the matter has been dictated from memory, without reference to records of any kind whatever.[2]

[1] Mr. W. A. Abram, J.P., Editor of *The Blackburn Times*, from 1867 to 1887.
[2] *The Blackburn Times*, November 6th, 1886.

The Author's Own Life.

Jeremy's Birth—Pickup Bank Mill—Longevity of the Hunt Family—The Hunts 200 years ago—The Marsdens 200 years ago—Jeremy's Immediate Ancestors—His Childhood—"Owd Timothy o'th' Looms"—The Hunts Churchmen—Conversion of Jeremy's Grandfather to Nonconformity—Secession of the Pole Laners—Jeremy's Marriage—Pickup Bank Day School Established 1843—Hoddlesden Church School Built, 1851—Jeremy's Occupation for 70 years—Jeremy as a Singing Master and Sunday School Teacher—No Sunday's Dinner for 11 years—A New School-Chapel Built with 3s. 3d.—Handloom Weavers' Wages in 1834—Jeremy introduces Chanting into Nonconformist Chapels—Trade Ruined after the Battle of Waterloo.

THE substance of the following sketch of Mr. Hunt's life has been previously published by us,[1] but it is here inserted in its proper place in these "Recollections:"—Born on the 27th of February, 1806, the subject of our sketch will soon complete his 81st year. He first saw the light of day in an old corn mill, close to the brook at Waterside, now superseded by a block of cottages, which are known to this day as Pickup Bank Mill. The old mill was used for grinding corn by water power two hundred years ago, but at the time of Jeremy's birth it was the residence of his father, who kept in it six handlooms, a spinning wheel, and a large family. Two of the large millstones lay in the brook for many a year in Jeremy's recollection, and another formed part of the pavement of the floor of the house where he was born. Jeremy was the youngest of nine children, having five sisters and three brothers, all older than himself. He alone survives, for the last of his brothers, James, died in 1868, aged 69 years, and the last of his sisters, Hannah, died in America about two years ago, aged nearly 82. Two others of the family, besides the father and mother, lived to an old age, namely, Jeremy's sister Mary, born in 1787, died in 1862, aged 75; and Ellen, born in 1796, died in 1870, aged 74.

Jeremy's father, Nathaniel Hunt, was a great-grandson of one Hunt of Samlesbury, who came to Darwen about 200 years ago, and settled at Eccleshill with his two sons, John and Robert, but on his mother's side Jeremy claims to be a "Darruner" of eight of nine hundred years

[1] *The Blackburn Times* of March 6th, 1886, when an account was given of the celebration of his 80th birthday.

standing, and consequently he sets great store on his "Grandmother Marsden," who connects him with the Marsdens (or "Marsdynes") of Hoddlesden, a family of yeomen of considerable repute and ancient settlement in the neighbourhood. Mr. Abram's "History of Blackburn" records the existence of a Henry Marsden, of Over Darwen, freeholder, who lived in 1637, and of James Marsden, of Hoddlesden, yeoman, born in 1686, who became a governor of Blackburn Grammar School; but the earliest Marsden of whom Jeremy Hunt has any knowledge is his great-grandfather, James Marsden, who was born in 1700, and lived until the summer of 1792. This James Marsden had two sons and three daughters, and Jeremy cherishes a personal recollection of one of the sons and two of the daughters—one of the daughters, in fact, being his grandmother. Old Jeremy belongs to a long-lived family. When he was twelve years of age his maternal grandmother before alluded to died at the ripe old age of 83 years, and she chatted with him many a long twilight hour about the old fogeys of the neighbourhood, including her own father, the nonagenarian, whose personal history goes back to the year 1700. The old dame's husband died in March, 1809, aged 84, but Jeremy has not yet forgotten his face and his figure, nor the incidents which as a child he noticed at the funeral. Jeremy's mother lived to be 77, and from her "our hero" imbibed a great deal of the tradition of the neighbourhood. Among other things he carries in his memory a faithful record of births, marriages and deaths, names, dates and ages, many of which can be tested by reference to registers in Blackburn and Darwen, and other parts of the kingdom. His father was born in 1757, and lived to be 87. From him Jeremy learned the history of a most prolific old-timer, "Owd Timothy o'th' Looms," surnamed Holden, a man born two hundred years ago, and from whom there have descended a mayor, a member of Parliament, and a very large section of the present population of Darwen. In fact, Darwen people who have heard old Jeremy unfold his recollections of how the Holdens are intermarried with many of the most numerous families of the town look back upon "Owd Timothy o'th' Looms" much as the world in general looks back to Adam. "Owd Timothy" possesses a special interest for Jeremy Hunt, for, says Jeremy, "My wife's great grandmother and my own great grandmother were both sisters of "Owd Timothy o'th' Looms."

The Hunts of Samlesbury were Churchmen, and every important branch of the family, except the one formed by Jeremy's father has stuck to the Church and State. For instance, there is a Richard Hunt well-known in Darwen, who has been a churchwarden at St. James's. His great-great grandfather and old Jeremy's father were brothers—

descendants of the John Hunt who came from Samlesbury as a lad with his father. Connected with the same church there is another family of Hunts, but these are descended from the other lad from Samlesbury, Robert Hunt, and wherever the Hunts are found about Darwen or Blackburn they are generally Churchmen. But the subject of this sketch is a strong " Non-Con," and the story of the conversion of his branch of the family is interesting. Let Jeremy tell it in his own words. He says:—My grandfather, Nathaniel Hunt, was the son of John Hunt, one of the lads from Samlesbury. John, though a Churchman, had married a very strong Dissenter, Rachael Ratcliffe, of Whitehall, Darwen, and they split their differences by bringing up their lads to th' Higher Chapel (St. James's Church), and their lasses to th' Lower Chapel, the lads going with their father and the lasses with their mother. Consequently, my grandfather, Nathaniel, was brought up a Churchman. I have heard my father laugh and tell what a strong Dissenter his grandmother, Rachael, was. When the children were reading their lessons out of the Bible, at home, she would not let them read verse by verse in turns, because she said it sounded "too much like th' parson and th' clerk." About 150 years since, my grandfather, Nathaniel, married a wife, and she was a Dissenter. They went to the Lower Chapel on the first Sunday after their marriage, and to the Higher Chapel on the next Sunday, but on the third Sunday they each went to their own. They lived in Eccleshill, and on the fourth Sunday they walked together as far as Holden Fold, where they came to a spot at which two paths met, one leading to the Higher Chapel and the other (now blocked up) leading to the Lower Chapel. When the time came for parting company, my grandmother looked into her husband's face and said, "Nay, 'Thannel, we're wed, and we hev to live together o week; we'll never part o' th' Sunday. Go to th' chapel as yo'n a mind an' aw'll follow." My grandfather looked over his shoulder and smiled, and then walked down to the Lower Chapel. There the matter ended, and our branch of the Hunts have been Dissenters ever since.

Jeremy Hunt's father was brought up to attend the Lower Chapel, and he became an important member of the church worshipping there. But in 1791, when Richard Smalley was chosen to be the pastor, in succession to his father, Robert Smalley, Jeremy's father was one of the seceders who banded themselves together and built Pole Lane Chapel at Sough. All that remains of Pole Lane Chapel to-day is a graveyard, but the old place is represented by its grandchild, Belgrave Chapel, the leading Nonconformist place of worship in the town. Following the track of the growing population, the Pole Lane congregation removed to the centre of the rising town of Darwen in 1822, and built Ebenezer Chapel on the plot of land which is now the graveyard of Belgrave Chapel, and Jeremy's father was an active worker and a liberal giver at this place until his death, which occured 22 years later.

By trade Mr. Jeremy Hunt is a handloom weaver, but he has spent a portion of his life in the exalted position of a village schoolmaster, and in his latter days has been an "odd hand" in various cotton mills. His father was a handloom weaver before him, and his mother, prior to her marriage, was in the strictest sense of the word a spinster. She took her spinning wheel with her to her new home when she got married, and occasionally added to the family income by its means after doing her household work. At the age of eight or nine years Jeremy was put to the handloom, and he followed the occupation of his father until the year 1843. Two years before this he married Hannah Kirkham, a half-cousin, at Ebenezer Chapel, but in 1846 his wife died, leaving him with three young children, two of whom still survive. He says he has not had time to marry again. In the year 1843 the inhabitants of Pickup Bank set their minds on having a day school on their hill-side, with Jeremy Hunt for its master. He advised them to establish a school in the neighbouring village of Hoddlesden, where it would pay better, but they were bent on having one all to themselves. They subscribed among themselves and paid Jeremy £25 a year besides what he could make out of fees of the children. The half-timers came to his school in the morning with their day's food in their handkerchiefs, going straight from school at dinner time to their work at Hoddlesden Mill. A night school was also opened, and the adults came in to be taught by Jeremy after a long day's work in the fields or at the mill. In 1846 the school was transferred to Hoddlesden Mill, and conducted in a room at the mill until 1852. Hoddlesden Church School was then built, and Jeremy's unpretentious institution died a natural death. Our friend then found work under the proprietor, Mr. Place, in the warehouse of the mill, as a bundler, and next year he became an "odd hand" in the warehouse of Brookside Mill, Darwen, under Mr. Eccles Shorrock. He had spent nearly thirty years as a handloom weaver, and ten as a schoolmaster, and now he had a spell of sixteen years as an "odd hand" with Mr. Eccles Shorrock. In 1870 he went to Cotton and Slater's, King Street and Hollin Bank, Blackburn, in the same capacity; then, in 1874, he returned to Darwen, and filled a similar position at Mr. Lightbown's Dove Mill, spending in all about twenty-five years in this sort of work. Up to this time he had worked for his living for a period of 65 years, and he completed a life's labour of three score and ten years by taking a situation in Mr. Nuttall's coal office at the Darwen railway station, until Christmas, 1884. For two years now he has lived the life of a partially retired gentleman, residing with his son Nathaniel, and trusting to the savings of his frugal life to carry him through the rest of his days.[1]

From early childhood Jeremy was brought up to attend the Pole Lane Sunday School, and in 1822 he went over, with the rest of the Pole Lane congregation, to the new Ebenezer Chapel. In 1822 he had begun to assist his eldest brother, John, to teach a singing class at Pole Lane, and there is not one member of that class except himself now [1886] living. When the congregation went over to Ebenezer, Jeremy was a very active member. He became teacher of a singing class there in 1825, and for eleven years went without his Sunday's dinner in order to contribute to the funds of the Church. Having to walk all the way from Pickup Bank to the centre of modern Darwen, he was allowed three-halfpence a week to buy a bun and a "parkin" for his Sunday's dinner, but as there was a debt on the Church, he did what he could to remove it by saving up his halfpence and giving them at the periodic collections. This he did for no less than eleven years, never having a dinner on a Sunday for the whole of that long period. In 1828 the Lower Chapel people began a school at Pickup Bank. All the chapel folks on Pickup Bank belonged to Lower Chapel, at that time, except Jeremy's family, but Jeremy soon became the leading man of the branch school. The school was held at first in a cottage on the moor side, nearly opposite the present school, and it was chiefly intended to teach adults who could not read. Jeremy's brother John was asked to be the teacher, and he consented, but as he was taken ill Jeremy went in his place. Jeremy taught the class at this cottage-school by candle-light at eight o'clock on Sunday morning during the winter and by daylight at the same time in summer. He did this for several years. It took him twenty minutes to go to the cottage up the hill side, and fifteen minutes to get back home after the lesson. Then he had to cross another hill and get into the Darwen Valley to the Ebenezer Chapel, some three miles distant, but he was always to be seen in the singing-pew before the morning service began, looking as "spick and span" as if he had just come out of a bandbox. (The expression is his own.) In 1834 a regular service was begun at the Pickup Bank cottage-school, conducted by two or three volunteers, on Sunday afternoons. The natives clubbed together and bought a pulpit, but they were short of a Bible and hymn-book with which to furnish it. Jeremy said that if they would make

[1] I have heard Jeremy say that he never earned more 16s. a week at any period of his life. — J.G.S.

another collection for the Bible and hymn-book he would form and teach a singing-class for them. The books were got, and a balance of 3s. 3d. remained in hand. The subscribers wanted to give it Jeremy, but he would not have it. However, after some discussion, he said, "Well, give it to me, and we'll build a new school with it!" The idea of the new school was received with great gusto, and from that day the project was looked upon as possible, although there was not a hand-loom weaver on the hill-side earning 10s. a week. This happened in the spring of 1834, and in eighteen months the new school was opened. Week by week the people put their money together, Jeremy, who now remained in the village on Sunday, acting as treasurer. The men collected the stone and flags on the hill-side, and in fact all the material except the slate and wood. They built the school on a common and paid for nothing that they could do themselves. Everybody lent a helping hand. On the afternoon of the 5th of November, 1835, Dr. Skinner, of Mount Street, Blackburn, preached the opening sermon, and the Rev. Samuel Nichols, of Lower Chapel, preached by candle-light in the evening. Jeremy attended Pickup Bank School from 1834 to 1847, and then accepted the post of singing-master at Ebenezer Chapel, six months before the opening of Belgrave, and at Belgrave he laboured for eleven years. Even while coming to Darwen every Sunday he kept up his connection with the Pickup Bank School from 1847 to 1852. The pulpit at Pickup Bank was supplied by students from the Blackburn Independent Academy, an institution in Ainsworth Street, which has since become the Lancashire Independent College (Manchester). But about twenty-five years ago Mr. Unwin, of Belthorn, was engaged to preach every Sunday night, and once a month on a Sunday afternoon. Then Mr. Harrison, schoolmaster, from William Street, Darwen, became a regular preacher there, and twenty years ago the Rev. J. Clyde was installed as the first resident pastor in charge of the place.[1]

One of Mr. Hunt's greatest hobbies has been singing. He is a singer of the old school, and revels in nothing more than in hearty congregational singing. He began learning to sing 72 years ago, and he can sing to-day[2] in a manner which shows what a rich, flexible cultivated voice he was once possessed of. He began to teach a clas of singers at Ebenezer Chapel in 1825, but not one of the pupils is living to-day. By the taste and ability for singing which he infused into the people of Pickup Bank he contributed largely to the establishment o a Congregational Church on their hill-side, and to the making of their

[1] Rev. Clyde died January 10th, 1886.
[2] He sang a song at Furthergate School, Blackburn, on February 19th, 1887.

services hearty and enjoyable. More than 50 years ago he used to collect the hand-loom weavers of the neighbourhood together at four o'clock every Monday afternoon—lazy Monday—and teach them to sing hymns. In 1847 he was sent for to become the singing-master at Belgrave, and he continued there until the church became wealthy and fashionable enough to engage a paid choir and choirmaster. Jeremy claims that he had some of the best singing in Pickup Bank School ever heard in a place of worship, and he also claims that he was the first to introduce the chanting of the psalms into Nonconformist chapels. It was about the year 1838 that his country choir began to chant the psalms for variety on their practice nights, and then to sing them in their school-chapel at the charity sermons and on other special occasions. At first, some of the preachers stood aghast at this step towards going over to the Established Church, but they soon began to like the change, and the students from the Blackburn Academy used to say to Jeremy "When we get places of our own we'll have chanting." In this way the system spread from the obscure country school to all parts of the world, and its originator says he does not believe there can be found a chapel anywhere where it was introduced earlier than 1838. He prophesied from the first that in less than twenty years chanting would become popular, if not universal, and his prophecy has proved true. The psalms were chanted direct from the Bible, and the first ever given in the chapel was the 34th, "I will bless the Lord at all times." In 1843 Jeremy received an invitation to become the singing-master at Mount Street Presbyterian Church, Blackburn, under Dr. Skinner, and though very reluctant to leave his native place, he accepted the engagement for three months. He had not been at Mount Street many weeks before he told Dr. Skinner that they had talent enough in Blackburn without him, and he recommended the appointment of Wm. Baron, a young fellow of 21, to the post of singing-master. This was agreed to on condition that Jeremy should remain in charge for six months. Baron proved a good singing master, but, after holding the office for 26 years, he died, an old man of 47, and Jeremy, a young man of 64, was again sent for. He found them another singing-master, George Harwood, from Pickup Bank, remarking in his quaint way, "Now, when yo'n worn that out, if you'll send for me, I'll come again." Harwood is still in harness, but Jeremy says he is prepared to fulfil his promise. Our friend still teaches singing, having a class at Belgrave School every Wednesday evening.

Handloom weaving was the staple trade at the time of Jeremy's birth, and during the wars on the continent, when England had a monopoly of trade, a handloom weaver could earn 33s. in four days. But after the Battle of Waterloo prices came down with a rush, the weavers having to submit to a reduction of as much as 7s. per cut, without the slightest notice, time after time, until, when Jeremy began to be a full-fledged weaver they were getting less that one-fourth of the former prices. In all his life Jeremy never earned more than 10s. a week off his loom, and all the necessaries of life were much dearer in those days than they are now. The hours of labour were from about six in the morning until late at night, according to a man's necessities or inclination.

The following observations on "Mr. Jeremy Hunt as a Singing-master" were contributed to *The Blackburn Times* a week or two after Mr. Hunt's death, by Mr A. Taylor, of London, who knew Mr. Hunt at Mount Street, in 1843 :— There are not a few people *outside* Darwen and Blackburn who will read the announcement of Mr. Jeremy Hunt's death with sincere regret. The life of an octogenarian must always be very uncertain, but Jeremy's temperate habits, sound constitution, and recent expression of "feeling like a young man" naturally led us to believe that his useful life would be spared for years to come. I first saw him at a "practice" in Mount Street Chapel, Blackburn, just after he became singing-master, and remember being as much pleased with his genial manner as with his musical ability. I often attended the week-night practice while Jeremy was leader, esteeming it a treat to be present. I have heard him pour out his stores of local knowledge upwards of forty years ago, and relate racy anecdotes in his rare, quaint style. He was then in the prime and vigour of life, and apparently as happy as a man could possibly be in his position. I was a youth then, and when listening to him often wondered

How one small head could carry all he knew.

Jeremy's reputation as an active Nonconformist had reached Blackburn some time before his engagement with Mount Street. We had heard of the psalm-chanting at Pickup Bank, and on one occasion when it was the topic of conversation, Mr. Henry Mc.Cave, who was then the singing master at James Street Chapel, expressed his determination to try the experiment. He selected the 103rd Psalm, and after a practice of several hours, it was chanted on the following Sunday in chapel, and, as it happened, "took remarkably well." Such an innovation seems simple and trivial now, but to the Nonconformists of that day it was an event of some importance. That the minister and congregation did not stand aghast at the change, was probably owing to the fact that their minds had been somewhat prepared for it by the chanting at Pickup Bank.

Conservative as is human nature in such matters, one cannot help thinking o the difference in the reception of psalm-chanting fifty years ago, when introduced by Jeremy Hunt, and the reception of hymn-singing in the beginning of last century, when its introduction was stoutly opposed by Independents, Baptists, and Presbyterians Thomas Bradbury, one of the most popular ministers in London in the reign of Queen Anne, refused to have Watts's version of the Psalms sung in his congregation, and when, after much opposition to the doctor's hymns, he allowed them to be sung, he would announce them by saying, "Let us sing one of Watts's *whims.*" A fierce controversy arose on the question of hymn-singing in public worship, and a minister deemed it necessary to write a book in its defence. Popular as Watts's hymns have been during the past hundred years or so, the churches that first used them were suspected of heresy, and some forty or fifty years elapsed before their general adoption. But Watts's hymns were no "whims" to Jeremy Hunt. They were sacred lyrics which he sang with fervour and earnestness, and may it not be said that by his introduction of chanting an additional means of grace was added to Nonconformist worship?

"Singing pews" are proverbially bad to manage, but fractious indeed would be the singers that Jeremy could not control. He was a great favourite with every one of the singers at Mount Street. In short, he was altogether a remarkable man; endowed with a memory as retentive, I believe, as Macaulay's. What he would have been with Macaulay's intellectual training it is, of course, impossible to say. That such a man should have worked sixteen years as an "odd hand," and thirty years as a hand-loom weaver in receipt of *less* than 10s. a week, is nothing less than a condemnation of the present order of things.

The Marsdens.

The Oldest Family in Darwen—A Nonagenarian—Jeremy's Connecting Link—A "Prop" of the Church—The Act of the Uniformity—Seizure of the Higher Chapel, 1687—James Marsden, of Liverpool, a Musician—Liverpool Musical Festivals about 1826—Cottage Concerts at Hoddlesden—Councillor T. H. Marsden—Sick Society at Chapels—A Tragic Incident—"Owd Nine Penn'orth"—No Steamers on the Mersey—The Marsdens of Blacksnape—"Owd Jem o' Isaacs" and the Haslingden Fair Bully, 1801—A Boggart at Blacksnape—Wellington, Nelson, and Blucher—Timothy Marsden o' th' Oakenhurst—Timothy Marsden, Cotton Manufacturer, Blackburn.

THE MARSDENS are reputed to be the oldest family in Darwen. They have lived about these parts for hundreds of years, and I am told that their name (sometimes spelt "Marsdyne") can be found in old deeds and other documents, showing that they flourished on the borders of Lancashire and Yorkshire near this village centuries ago. The oldest member of the Marsden family of whom I have any knowledge is old James Marsden, my great grandfather, a man who lived nearly a hundred years himself, and whose birth dates back nearly two centuries. He was born in the year 1700, in the neighbourhood of Hoddlesden, just over the little hill forming the eastern boundary of the Darwen Valley. Hoddlesden belongs naturally to Darwen, and now forms part of the borough, so that the oldest Marsden of whom I have any knowledge was a "Darruner" "bred and born." He died in 1792, eaving two sons and three daughters, and I myself have lived long enough to know two of the daughters and one of the sons; in fact, one of the daughters was my grandmother, and, as I knew my grandmother very well, I am thus connected by a single link with one of the most ancient of the known citizens of this important town. Old James Marsden's sons were called James and Joseph. I never knew James, but I knew Joseph. Joseph was a little older than my grandmother, who was born in April, 1735, and as near as I can ascertain he was born about the year 1733.

Joseph Marsden, born about 1733, was one of the great "props of the church"—not of the Established Church, but the Free Church

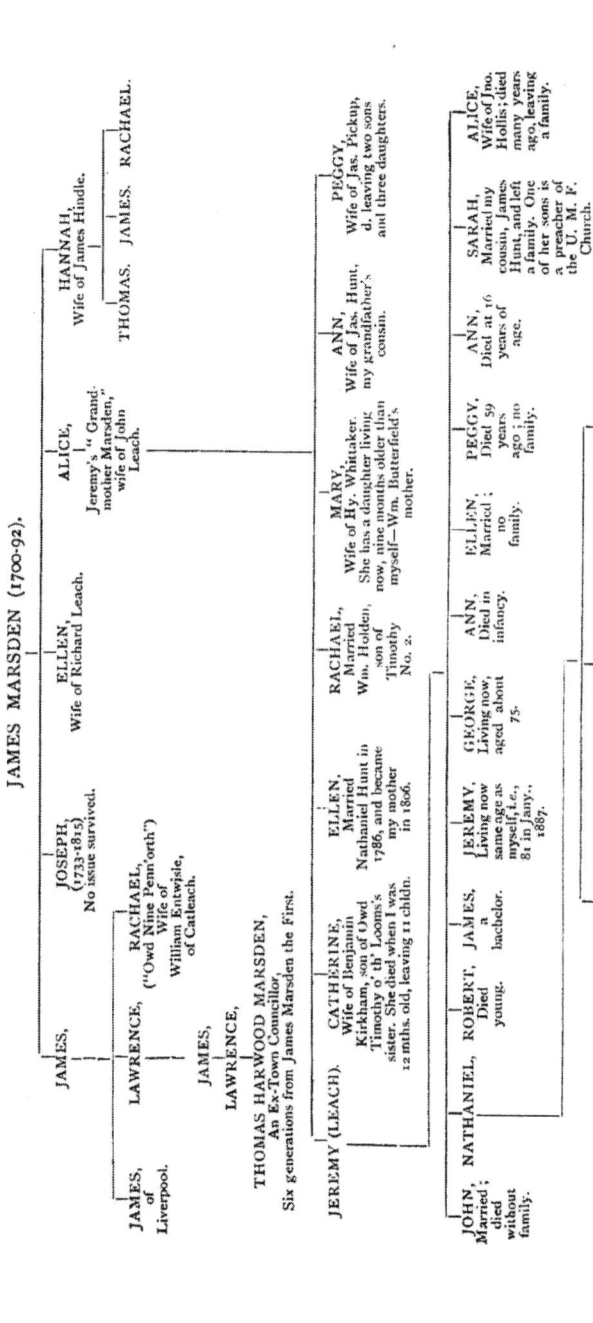

JAMES MARSDEN (1700-92).

Children of James Marsden:

JOSEPH (1733-1815)
No issue survived.

ELLEN, Wife of Richard Leach.

Children:
- **LAWRENCE**
- **RACHAEL** ("Owd Nine Penn'orth") Wife of William Entwisle, of Catleach.
- **JAMES**
- **LAWRENCE**
- **THOMAS HARWOOD MARSDEN**, An Ex-Town Councillor. Six generations from James Marsden the First.
- **JEREMY (LEACH)**
- **CATHERINE**, Wife of Benjamin Kirkham, son of Owd Timothy o' th' Looms's sister. She died when I was 12 mths. old, leaving 11 chldn.
- **ELLEN**, Married Nathaniel Hunt in 1786, and became my mother in 1806.
- **RACHAEL**, Married Wm. Holden, son of Timothy No. 2.
- **MARY**, Wife of Hy. Whittaker. She has a daughter living now, nine months older than myself—Wm. Butterfield's mother.

Children of Ellen (Hunt):
- **JOHN**, Married; died without family.
- **NATHANIEL**
- **ROBERT**, Died young.
- **JAMES**, a bachelor.
- **JEREMY**, Living now same age as myself, i.e., 81 in Jany., 1887.
- **GEORGE**, Living now, aged about 75.
- **ANN**, Died in infancy.
- **ELLEN**, Married; no family.
- **PEGGY**, Died 59 years ago; no family.

Children of Nathaniel:
- **JEREMY**
- **JOHN F. LEACH**, Manager at Graham Fish's; six generations from James Marsden the First.
- **ELI**, Cotton Manufacturer.
- **NATHANIEL LEACH**, Printer, Bolton-road; six generations from James Marsden the First.
- **THREE DAUGHTERS**.

ALICE, Jeremy's "Grandmother Marsden," wife of John Leach.

- **ANN**, Wife of Jas. Hunt, my grandfather's cousin.
- **PEGGY**, Wife of Jas. Pickup, d. leaving two sons and three daughters.
- **SARAH**, Married my cousin, James Hunt, and left a family. One of her sons is a preacher of the U. M. F. Church.
- **ANN**, Died at 16 years of age.
- **ALICE**, Wife of Jno. Hollis; died many years ago, leaving a family.

HANNAH, Wife of James Hindle.
- **THOMAS.**
- **JAMES.**
- **RACHAEL.**

JAMES, of Liverpool.

[See Note on pp. 31-2.]

which the people of this valley have so staunchly supported from the earliest times to the present day. He was one of the leading men of his day, and a great supporter of the old Lower Chapel. My grandmother lived next door to us, and I remember him coming to see her many a time. I was nine years of age when he died. He was rather an eccentric character, and one of the things I noticed about his personal appearance was that he had remarkably big knuckles, which, to my childish eyes, seemed like ducks' heads. He lived at Scotland, just on the other side of Hoddlesden. His wife I never knew, but he had been married, and his children, I learned, had died in infancy. An uncommon strong "Non-Con." was Joseph Marsden. In his days the Act of Uniformity had not been passed long, and the Non-Cons. of Darwen knew something about persecution. They had taken possession of the Higher Chapel in 1687 and had been turned out by the Church parson, and naturally the irritation between Churchmen and Nonconformists was stronger in Joseph Marsden's days than in these ; but Joseph stuck faithfully to the religion of his fathers and became noted as one of the chief men connected with Lower Chapel. He was not exactly a Puritan, for among other eccentric notions he held unique views on the question of keeping the Sabbath. When I knew him as an old man he used to occupy his time by making birch besoms and such like things. If he were going to chapel on Sunday and chanced to see in the lane or the hedge a nice stick for making a broom handle he would stop to get it, and then put it on one side out of sight and go on to his devotions. On his return home at night he would not forget the stick, but pick it up and take it home. He used to say, "It is lawful to do well on the Sabbath day," and if any of the stricter "Non-Cons." said a word to him about picking sticks on the Sunday he always had a ready answer. I fancy he died about 1815 ; I know he was living in 1814.

As I said before, I never knew Joseph's brother, James Marsden the Second. But I knew James the Third, son of James the Second and grandson of Old James Marsden. This James the Third, as I have called him, was a brushmaker. He was brought up in Hoddlesden, but served an apprenticeship to a brushmaker in Liverpool. He afterwards settled in Liverpool, and being of a musical turn of mind he became singing master at Great George Street Chapel. He was there before Dr. Raffles, and also in Dr. Raffles's days. I remember him coming round this neighbourhood getting orders for brushes, and I have a clothes brush o-day that he gave my mother before I was born. My mother and he were cousins. He had one son called Joseph and another called James (James the Fourth). They were all great singers in Liverpool. About

60 years ago there used to be gigantic musical festivals at Liverpool, in which a number of singers from Darwen took part—old Richard Entwisle, William Fish, Joseph Walmsley, John Peel, and others. I know a good story about these Liverpool festivals which brings credit to Darwen as a musical town. Old Joseph Walmsley was one of the alto singers on a particular occasion when they were rehearsing " And the glory of the Lord " from the " Messiah." Gratrix was the conductor. In one part of the chorus the whole body of the singers went off a beat too soon. But Joseph Walmsley was an exception. He would not be dragged wrong, but all alone chimed in his solitary voice in the proper time, and did his best to pull the others right. Gratrix stopped the singing, went up to him and said, "Young man, you stand here and lead these altos," and stand there Joe did, two inches taller than ever he stood before, every day of the festival, and nobody was prouder or more pleased with the incident than James Marsden, of Liverpool, who did not forget to tell everybody that Darwen was his native town. Joseph Walmsley was remarkably prompt in time, and a thorough-going musician, just as James Marsden himself was. I have heard my mother tell about James coming over from Liverpool and spending his holidays among his friends about Hoddlesden, singing all the time. On one occasion when the party had been singing far into the night James declared that he was tired and would not sing another note. Nothing that the others could plead or urge would induce him to stay up any longer, so he went upstairs to bed. The company sat quiet until he had just got into bed, and then they broke the stillness of the night by " brasting off " with one of Old James's favourite choruses. They had not got through more than a bar or two when they heard James's feet on the room floor, and down stairs he marched again, beating time with each step, and singing as briskly as the best of them, to the great merriment of the company. These cottage concerts marked all the visits of the Marsdens of Liverpool to their native town, and attracted all the singers in the neighbourhood who had the opportunity of joining in them. Some of the descendants of this branch of the Marsdens were living on the Cheshire side of the Mersey a few years back.

James Marsden, of Liverpool, had a brother named Lawrence, and through him Mr. Thomas Harwood Marsden, an ex-Town Councillor of the present day, is descended from the first James Marsden, born in 1700. Thomas Harwood Marsden is six generations removed from the first of his line of whom I have any knowledge. Lawrence, the great grandfather of Thomas Harwood Marsden, married Ann Peel. I don't know where she came from, but she died at Ellison Fold more than sixty years ago. There used to be a Male Sick Society at Chapels, held at a public-house. My brother James and a number of his companions were going home to Hoddlesden from Chapels one dark March night through a storm of sleet and snow. It was the 25th of March. As they were going across the fields they heard a cry which seemed to come out of the clouds. They followed the cry until they got into a ploughed field. Who should they drop across in this out-of-the-way place but Ann Peel, as they called her—Old Lawrence Marsden's wife. She had lost one shoe, and was half dead with cold. They took her home to her son's house at Ellison Fold, and she was so frantic with cold that she seized the top bar of the fire-grate and was so badly burned that she could hardly loose her fingers. She never recovered from the shock, but died about six weeks afterwards. They found her shoe when they harrowed the field.

Lawrence had sons named James, Baron, and Robert, Baron was a collier. Robert ("Bob o' Lol's") married James Eccles, daughter of old Richard Eccles, and sister to the mother of Joseph and Thomas Eccles, magistrates of the borough of Darwen to-day. Robert died, and his widow then married another Marsden.

James and Lawrence had a sister named Rachael. She was married to a man named William Entwisle, of Catleach, and I knew her well. Sometime in her girlish days she had gone to a dancing school, for which she had to pay a penny a week, and Old Rachael had gone until she had got nine penn'orth. Whenever she was in a merry mood, she had a trick of giving an exhibition of her dancing powers, and she always wound up with saying, "That's some o' my nine penn'orth." She got the nickname of "Nine Penn'orth," and was never called anything else. Her brother James, of Liverpool, granted her an allowance of five shillings a week as long as she lived. She used to go over to Liverpool occasionally, and being a very broad-spoken "Darruner" she amused them highly. James's servants used to get her into the kitchen, and get her to talk for them. One day they were going over to Birkenhead in one of the old-fashioned ferry-boats—there was no steam on the Mersey in those days—and as the river was rather lumpy Old Rachael got nervous and cried out, "Eh, fooak! we'st o be i' th' hoyle." That expression was kept up in Liverpool, by people who knew the Marsdens, for many a year, it tickled their fancy so. Rachael was a great favourite of my father's. She used to visit our house, and I remember my father often saying that Old Rachael was the most thoroughly honest woman he ever met with. Her husband, William

Entwisle, was better known as " Owd Billy o' Ralph's," and as Billy was the "father of seven sons " a lot of the Entwisles are descended from her.

James Marsden (the first) had three daughters. Two of them, Ellen and Alice, married two brothers named Richard and John Leach, and from them are descended the two main branches of the Leach family living at the present day.

The second daughter, Alice, who, as I have said, married Richard Leach's brother John, happened in the course of events to be my grandmother. Through my grandmother, Alice Marsden (afterwards Leach), I am one of the descendants of Old James Marsden, one of the earliest inhabitants of these parts of whom we have any knowledge. My Grandmother Marsden, as I sometimes call her, was born in April, 1735, and she died on the 23rd of September, 1818.

Hannah Marsden, the third of Old James number One's daughters, married a man named James Hindle, of the Holker House Hindles— the Hoddlesden Hindles. I knew all three of them very well.

My Grandmother Marsden always told us that all the Marsdens in Darwen belonged to the same family. Old James Marsden of 1700 must have had several brothers, though I don't know their names, for I can trace the descendants of two of his brothers. One of these brothers of James the First settled at Blacksnape, and fifty or sixty years back there were a good number of his descendants there. If the Marsdens of Blacksnape were sorted out to-day, I believe a good many of them could be traced back to this line. There was one old fellow of the name of James Marsden living at Blacksnape when I was a lad, and he had sprung from one of the brothers of James the First. He was rather a notorious character. They called him " Owd Jem o' Isaac's." His chief forte was fighting—fighting and drinking. In those days fighting didn't mean boxing or fencing and striking only above the belt, but dashing in anyhow with fists and feet alike. Owd Jem was ready with both, and he didn't care which. Neither did he care whether he fell under or over his adversaries ; he could always " lick 'em." If he were on the top he gave them a good pummelling, and if he were underneath he had a trick of gripping them in his arms like a Russian bear and squeezing the breath out of them, while, at the same time, he brought down his heels upon their legs like sledge hammers. They used to say that to get in Owd Jem's embrace was like getting into an hydraulic press. I remember he once went to Haslingden Fair, and Haslington Fair 70 or 80 years back was as noted for fighting as Turton Fair used to be not long ago. The rough characters for miles round used to go to

Haslingden Fair for a spree and a fight, and, of course, Owd Jem went too. On this particular occasion there was a man there who had come for a fight, and he kept getting on the top of the horse block, or "riding stone," as we called it, at the Roebuck Inn, Dearden Gate, just going into Haslingden from this end. From the top of this stone he kept swaggering that he would fight any man in Haslingden. A great crowd gathered round him, but nobody durst take up his challenge until Owd Jem came up. Jem sneeringly said—"Whod ar' ta mekkin thi noise abeawt? Con *ta* feight onny?" "Why, con yo'?" replied the other in a somewhat milder tone. "Come off thooase steps, and aw'll let thi' see," says Jem. The man came down and squared up for a fight, but before he could make any use of his fists Owd Jem flew at him and threw him down, and as the bully turned tail he punched him all the way down the street. The crowd followed, and ginger bread stalls and toy stalls were scattered in all directions. When Jem had finished with him, and the defeated bully had fairly run away, the crowd made a collection to reward the "Darruner" for licking the fellow who had terrorised over them so much. I should say it is quite 85 years since that happened. There is another lively incident in the history of this representative of the Marsden family to relate. When he was in liquor, Jem had a habit of muttering to himself all the way home, and this drew the attention of the young men of Blacksnape to him. One of these, for a lark, dressed himself up in a sheet and waylaid Jem one dark Saturday night, and, standing in the middle of the lane, waved his ghostly arms dramatically as Jem came muttering along. As sudden as a gunshot Jem stopped talking and took a good look at the ghost which blocked his path. But drunk as he was he twigged the joke, and exclaimed—"Oh! is thad thee, boggart? Aw'll be at thi." The boggart kept up the arm-waving performance, but backed as rapidly as possible down the road, so as to keep at a respectful distance. Jem, rolling along at his drunken gait, gained on his tormentor, until the apparition turned and fled. Then ensued a race for life, the ghost being in the undignified position of having its back to the foe. The young fellow thought to elude his pursuer by slipping into a porch by the road side, and divesting himself of his spiritualistic garment, but Jem followed him in and pummelled him till he cried hard for mercy. When Jem left him half dead with fright and pain, he said, "Aw'll tek thee off playin' boggart ageeon."

Owd Jem o' Isaac's had a son called John. I knew him very well. John had three sons called respectively Wellington, Nelson, and Blucher. One of the three used to keep a beershop in Back Lane.

We used to call them "Wellington o' Owd Jack's o' Owd Jem's o Isaac's;" "Nelson o' Owd Jack's o' Owd Jem's o' Isaac's;" and "Blucher o' Owd Jack's o' Owd Jem's o' Isaac's." These new-fangled soldiery names didn't seem to hitch up with the good old Scripture names which the "Non-Cons." of Darwen were accustomed to give their children.

Old Timothy Marsden o' th' Oakenhurst, born in 1760, came from another of the brothers of the James Marsden of 1700, and I was told that Timothy had an elder brother who settled as a cotton manufacturer (handloom) in Manchester, where his descendants are to this day, occupying very good positions. Timothy was rather younger than my father. He married Jane Ainsworth, of Eccleshill, my father's cousin, and his family consisted of five sons and two daughters. In the next chapter I shall mention "Owd Timothy o'th' Looms," surnamed Holden, the most distinguished patriarch of this neighbourhood, and I may as well state here that all the Timothys of Darwen seemed to be connected with this ancient Timothy. Timothy Marsden o' th' Oakenhurst, for instance, was his grandson, and inherited the Christian name of his maternal grandfather. Timothy o' th' Oakenhurst died about 1827. His sons were John, William, Timothy, Edmund, and James, and his daughters Ellen and Grace. Edmund had three sons and two daughters, but John Marsden, agent for the Clifton and Kearsley Coal Company, is the only one of the five now living. The families of William and John are living in Darwen, but I don't know them particularly well. Timothy (son of Timothy o' th' Oakenhurst) had a son called Timothy, who is a cotton manufacturer at Bánk Top, Blackburn, to-day, the only male descendant of that generation now living. James was the "father of seven sons" and also of two daughters. William Henry Marsden, Inspector of Nuisances, is one of the seven, and Edward Marsden, Tailor and Draper, Duckworth Street, is another.

MARSDEN OF OVER DARWEN.

Henry Marsden, of Over Darwen, a freeholder, died in 1637. Escheat inquisition taken Nov. 8th in that year showed that he died seized of 5 messuages, 5 gardens, 30 acres of land, meadow and pasture, in Chorley; and 2 messuages, 3 gardens, 60 acres of land, meadow and pasture, in Over Darwen, the latter held of Sir Gilbert Hoghton, Knt. and Bart., as of Walton Manor in socage, worth 40s. yearly. Ralph Marsden, his son, was then aged 16 years.

James Marsden married, in 1682, Alice Rothwell, of Haslingden Chapelry. Mr. James Marsden, of Upper Darwen, buried sons George and James, March 3rd, 1717.

Mr. James Marsden, of Over Darwen, elected Governor of Blackburn Grammar School in 1731, would be the James Marsden of Hoddlesden, yeoman, born Jan. 8th, 1686, who died May 8th, 1733, in his 47th year, leaving by Mary his wife, daughters Ann and Mary. Mary Marsden, his widow, died Nov. 16th, 1771, in her 82nd year. Mary, the daughter, married George Hargreave, Esq., of Haslingden, and died, aged 75, in 1796.—From W. A. Abram's *History of Blackburn*, p. 508.

OLD DARWEN FAMILIES.

MARSDEN OF OKENHURST, &c.

William Mersden is assessed on lands in Lower Darwen to the Subsidy of 1523. Henry Mersden is named as a first Governor of Blackburn Grammar School in 1567. Christopher Mersden was assessed for lands in Lower Darwen to a Subsidy in 1570.

Henry Marsden, who died April 12th, 1619, possessed, as shown by inquisition taken Sept. 14th, 1620 (at Blackburn), half a messuage, 10 acres of land, 2 of meadow, 10 of pasture, 5 of wood, and 40 of moor and moss in Lower Darwen. Alice, widow of the same, was living in 1620. Christopher Marsden, his son and heir, was then aged 40 years and upwards.

Christopher Marsden succeeded, and dying June 11th, 1631, the inq. post mort. was taken at Blackburn, April 25th, 9th Charles I., when it was found that he had held of the King as of the Duchy of Lancaster, by a yearly payment of 5s., one messuage, and 16 acres of land, meadow and pasture, in Lower Darwen. Henry Marsden was his son and heir, then aged 25 years.

Henry Marsden, of Okenhurst, yeoman, occurs as a trustee of James Piccop in 1657.

Ralph Marsden, of Okenhurst, was father of James Marsden, of Lower Darwen, yeoman, who died April 14th, 1630; and on inquisition taken Sept. 7th, 1630, his estate was found to consist of 1 messuage, 1 garden, 8 acres of land, 4 of meadow, and 6 of pasture, in Lower Darwen. William Marsden, son of James, being dead before his father, James Marsden, the latter had conveyed the estate to William Marsden, of Tockholes, yeoman, and Christopher Marsden, of Okenhurst, yeoman, in trust to the use of himself and his heirs. James Marsden, son of the late William, son of James, was found next heir, aged 15 years.

James Marsden, yeoman, grandson of the above James, held the property several years. He was dead before 1637. June 23rd, 13th Charles I., an inquisition taken at Bolton returned that James Marsden had been seized of 1 messuage, called Okenhurst, in Lower Darwen, with 1 garden, 8 acres of land, 2 of meadow, and 8 of pasture appurtenant to the said messuage of Okenhurst, William Marsden was son and heir, aged 9 months and 7 days.

Concerning this infant heir I have no particulars. The following names occur later:—John Marsden, of Lower Darwen, yeoman, died in 1698. Henry Marsden, yeoman, of this township, buried Elizabeth, his wife, in 1699. Another Henry Marsden, yeoman, married, April 13th, 1701, Ann Ainsworth, of Blackburn. Nicholas Marsden, of Lower Darwen, yeoman, who died in 1756, had sons Thomas and John, with other issue, by his wife Hannah.—Abram's *History of Blackburn*, p. 484.

The Holdens.

"Owd Timothy o'th' Looms"—Numerous Relationships of the Holdens—Timothy Lightbown, Mayor, 1884-6—W. E. Briggs, M.P. for Blackburn 1874-85—Immigration of the Holdens from Holden Hall, Haslingden Grane—Dissenting Meeting House on Pendle Hill—Eluding the King's Scouts—John Lightbown, a Nonagenarian—James Holden, Conjuror and Astrologer—"Ralph o'th' Back o'th' Heights "—" Owd Timothy o'th' Looms's " Uncle—Cornfields at Waterside in 1820—The Old Lower Chapel Built in Timothy's Cornfield—"Th' Looms" in Ruin —Timothy's School—Garsden Fold—James Holden, Overseer—Rev. Henry Townsend, First Minister at Pole Lane—Timothy the Second and the Landlord—His Personal Appearance—Holden and Martin, Cotton Manufacturers—"Jack John."

TIMOTHY HOLDEN, nick-named "Owd Timothy o'th' Looms," is the first prominent figure in the history of the second family in my programme. The Holden family enter into more relationships with other families of the district than any other I know,[1] and consequently the history of Owd Timothy is bound up with that of many noted families of the present day, including the Lightbowns, of whom comes one of our ex-Mayors, and the Briggses, from whom comes the late senior Member of Parliament for Blackburn. I have called the Marsdens the oldest family in Darwen, because I believe that they have lived longer in this valley than any other, but Owd Timothy o'th' Looms's personal history takes us back nearly twenty years further than that of James Marsden's did, and I know something of Timothy's grandfather which takes us back further still. The Holdens came to Darwen from Holden Hall, in Haslingden Grane, between 300 and 400 years ago. The earliest of their stock that I have heard about is Timothy's grandfather. I do not know his name, but Timothy, who was my father's great uncle, told my father that he lived at Scotland

[1] In this chapter Jeremy incidentally mentions the names of no fewer than forty families connected with the Holdens by marriage, namely :—Ainsworth, Beckett, Brandwood, Briggs, Butcher, Duxbury, Eccles, Egerton, Elliott, Ellison, Fish, Harrison, Harwood, Haworth, Heyes, Hollis, Howorth, Hunt, Garstang, Jepson, Kershaw, Kirkham, Leach, Lightbown, Marsden, Morris, Neville, Nuttall, Parkinson, Shorrock, Slinger, Southworth, Taylor, Townend, Townsend, Walsh, West, Whalley, Wild, and Yates ;—and half of these were " Old Darwen Families."

HOLDEN,
A man named Holden, of Darwen, used to worship on Pendle Hill when Nonconformists were hunted down.

HOLDEN,

TIMOTHY HOLDEN, "Owd Timothy o' th' Looms;" b. abt. 1684; d. abt. 1774.

(SISTER), Married a Thompson.

THOMAS, His descendants are legion.

MARY, Married a Kirkham.

TIMOTHY, A famous character; married twice; large family; strong Nonconformist.

ELLEN, Married Wm. Watson.

(SISTER), No record.

(SISTER), Married a Yates; some of the Yateses of Lelthorn are her descendants.

(SISTER), Married a man named Ellison.

JAMES, Two daughters; one married Jas. Lightbown, father of John, the nonagenarian, and grandfather of the ex-Mayor, Timothy Lightbown.

JOHN, Head of a very prolific family.

(SISTER), Married a Marsden.

TITUS,

MARY, Wife of Wm. Leach; d. half a century ago.

ANN, Wife of Edward Jepson.

LETTICE, Wife of James Briggs.

EDWARD BRIGGS.

WILLIAM EDWARD BRIGGS, M.P. for Blackburn, 1874-85; Six generations from "Owd Timothy o' th Looms.

TIMOTHY MARSDEN, (o' th' Oakenhurst).

[See Note on pp. 31-2.

Farm, just beyond Hoddlesden. My father was seventeen years of age when Owd Timothy died, and he got a good deal of information from him. It was either at the latter end of 1774 or the beginning of 1775 that Timothy died, and my father always represented him as being a very old man, so I imagine he got to be about 90. In this case Owd Timothy's birth dates back fully 200 years, and through a single link (my own father) I am connected with the recollections of a man which go back so far into the obscurity of unwritten history.

A good story used to be told by Owd Timothy o' th' Looms about his grandfather. In the days of Timothy's grandfather the Nonconformists were hunted down by the King's scouts, and their preachers expounded the Word of God at the risk of their liberty and their lives. There was a small Dissenting Chapel on Pendle Hill which existed until a few years ago, and many people living in Darwen to-day have seen it. But, between 200 and 300 years ago, the inhabitants of Darwen went to Pendle Hill, not for sight-seeing, but for worship, and Owd Timothy used to tell that his grandfather was a member of the congregation who worshipped in that place amid the wilds of Pendle. Men would be thought strong Nonconformists to-day if they walked, or rode, all the way to Pendle Hill to chapel—a distance of twenty-six miles there and back. The congregation used to meet in the large room of the little chapel, and the minister occupied a little vestry like a pantry. There was a square hole in the wall connecting one place with the other, and through this the minister poured forth the inspired Word of God in a manner that attracted devout worshippers from all parts of the district. Whenever the King's scouts came near, the little hole was quickly closed by means of a trap door, and the minister slipped out at the back and fled over Pendle Hill. I remember that services were kept up in this interesting little chapel, until quite recently, every Easter Sunday.

Owd Timothy o'th' Looms never had a brother that I heard of, but he had four sisters. One of them married a man named Thompson, but there are very few Thompsons in Darwen descended from her. Some of her descendants settled in Harwood and spread there. Another of the sisters became the wife of a man named Kirkham, and a great many of the Kirkhams in Darwen are descended from her. There are other Kirkhams in Darwen that are not descended from Old Timothy's sister, but they are all related to her on her husband's side. There were two other sisters. My wife's great-grandmother and my own great-grandmother were sisters, Owd Timothy o' th' Looms's sisters. One of them was married to a Kirkham and the other to a Watson. I come from the Watsons on my mother's side, and my wife comes from the Kirkhams. Her maiden name was Hannah Kirkham; I changed it to Hannah Hunt. She has been dead now for forty years. If ever I knew what became of the fourth sister I have forgotten, but I don't think I ever knew.

The population of Darwen springs very largely from Owd Timothy and his sisters. Timothy himself had five sons and three daughters. His sons were Titus, James, John, Thomas, and Timothy; the daughters respectively married a Yates, a Marsden, and an Ellison.

Titus was the first son. I never knew any family that he had except a daughter called Mary. She married a man named William Leach.

James, the second son of Owd Timothy o'th' Looms, went off to be a soldier, leaving a wife and two girls behind him. James Lightbown married one of the girls, and the late John Lightbown (father of the ex-Mayor), who died recently at the patriarchal age of 92, was his son.

Owd Timothy o'th' Looms's third son, John, had three sons and three daughters—James, Ralph, and Timothy; Mary, Ann, and Phœbe —and this branch of Owd Timothy's family has been very prolific. James married a young woman whom I knew very well by sight, but I cannot tell who she was, and I have enquired of her descendants in vain. Her name was Fish. He had two sons, James and John, and six or seven daughters. James was a very eccentric character. He never wore a cap or hat, and I remember many curious things he used to do. When he left Darwen he set up business in Birmingham as a conjuror and astrologer, and afterwards he turned quack doctor. What became of him I never knew, but he was older than me, and no doubt is dead and buried before this. John's sons are living in Darwen, but I don't know them personally. One of the seven daughters married a man named Elliott, of Westmorland, who went abroad at the Queen's expense. Two of the other girls were married respectively to John Shorrock and Thomas Wild, but left no families. Another married Ralph Morris. Ralph (son of John Holden) lived at Blacksnape, and was well known by the cognomen "Ralph o' th' Back o'th' Heights." His two sons, John and Nathaniel, were never married so far as I know, and one of his two daughters was never married. The other daughter, Phœbe, was married to John Taylor. The late James Taylor, of the George Inn, is one of her sons, and another, Joseph, keeps a pawnshop at the bottom of Green Street. A third son named John is dead.

Timothy (son of John Holden) had four daughters by his first wife—Mary, Alice, Phœbe, and Betty. Mary was married to a man named John Haworth. She died and left one son, who is living now, aged 75. Alice was married to Henry Southworth, and they had a number of daughters, but only one son. Southworth died about two years ago. His daughter Ann was married to a George Walsh, and they have a numerous family, mostly living in Blackburn. Alice, another daughter, was married to John Townend (their descendants are living at Pickup Bank), and a third, Mary (still living at Hoddlesden Fold), married James West. The son (Timothy Southworth) is dead, but he has left two sons and a daughter. Phœbe, the third daughter of Timothy Holden, was well known as "Phœbe o' Owd Timothy's." She became the second wife of the late John Lightbown, and mother of the ex-Mayor of Darwen. Betty o' Owd Timothy's became William Fish's second wife, but never had a family. By his second wife Old Timothy Holden (son of John) had two sons, John and James. John died unmarried, and James died last November [1885] over 80 years of age—the great-grandson of Owd Timothy o'th' Looms. He was about eleven months older than me. James's daughters were Mary, who married a man from Hoddlesden named Haworth, and Phœbe, who married John Eccles and went to live in Audley, Blackburn. Her husband died a year or two ago. Eli Southworth married a third and Jeremy Yates a fourth. There were five or six lasses altogether, and four sons—Fish, Nicholas, John, and Timothy. Fish Holden is living at Rishton. "Tim." went off to be a soldier and died. John, I think, is unmarried, but Nicholas married and has a family. Mary, daughter of John of Owd Timothy o'th' Looms, married Robert Townend (Bob o' Jeremy's), and her descendants are living in Darwen to-day. Ann, Mary's sister, was married to Thomas Fish. Phœbe, daughter of John of Owd Timothy o'th' Looms, married a James Briggs, of Bull Hill.

I have given here some account of "Owd Timothy o'th' Looms" and three of his sons. Before passing on to the two remaining sons and the three daughters, I should like to tell a little more about the old stock. Owd Timothy o'th' Looms used to tell my father about one of his (Timothy's) uncles weaving all day on Sunday, while his father was away, to fetch up for lost time. There used to be a lot of corn grown in Darwen, and I have a mark on the little finger of my left hand to this day caused by shearing corn at Waterside, in 1820. That seems a long time ago, but Owd Timothy o'th' Looms sheared corn on the site of the Old Lower Chapel, which was built above a hundred years before that, and when they took the corn-field off him to build the old chapel he lent his cart for nothing to cart the stone on to the ground. He kept a sort of school did Owd Timothy. He was a hand-loom weaver, and every day at noon the children of the neighbourhood used to go and learn their lessons from him, the shuttle flying all the while. My father got his bit of learning there, and so did his brothers. "Th' Looms," as Timothy's house was called, is an old house in Eccleshill Row, the lowest house in front of the Hoddlesden railway. It has stood empty now for many years, and the windows are boarded up.[1] There is another old house at Garsden Fold, Pickup Bank, supposed to have been built by the Holdens. Over the door there is an inscription in bold relief "R. H., 1601." I should think that "R. H." stands for Ralph Holden, for Ralph was a common name among them.

Thomas, fourth son of Owd Timothy o'th' Looms, had three sons and three daughters. Briggs Holden, the eldest son, lived and died at Awshaw, near Grimehills. He married Alice Leach, daughter of Richard Leach, and cousin to my mother. They had sons—Thomas, Richard, Titus, James, and Jeremy; daughters—Ellen, Nancy, Rachael, Peggy, and Alice.[2] They used to sit next to us in Pole Lane Chapel 70 years ago, and I knew them well; but then, everybody knew everybody else in those days. There is not one of them living now. Their descendants are living all over the town, "thick and three-fold," as we used to say. James Holden, whose body lies in Belgrave Churchyard, was the second son. He died in 1832, after being overseer for the township of Over Darwen for more than twenty years. He had one son and one daughter. His son, James Green Holden, married Rachael, daughter of John Holden, of Cotton Hall, but had no family. His daughter Alice was married to Henry Townsend, son of the Rev. Henry Townsend, first minister of Pole Lane Chapel. She died and left one daughter, Miss Jane Townsend, now living at Eccles, near Manchester. Henry married again, and had a son, Samuel Townsend, of Blackburn, who married a daughter of James Kershaw, of Darwen. Titus, the third son of Old Thomas, married Nancy Harwood, of Hoddlesden. His sons were Thomas, Timothy, and Briggs—"Tom o' Titus's," "Tim o' Titus's," and "Briggs o' Titus's." Tom married Betty Briggs (Betty o' Owd James o' Briggs's). Timothy married twice. His first wife was one of Old John Holden's lasses, of Jack's Kay, who died in 1810, and the second was a Briggs. He had one child (a daughter) by his first wife, and lots by his second—John Thomas, David, Timothy, and

---

[1] On another occasion Jeremy remarked to the writer, "I think the place called 'Th' Looms' is now used as a hencote. What an end for the ancient family seat of our most distinguished ancestor to come to!"

[2] The whole of these ten children were married, and the name of their descendants is legion.

others. One of them went to New Zealand, the rest are living in Darwen. Briggs Holden, son of Titus, married Peggy Kirkham, of Pickup Bank. His children were—Thomas, Titus, Benjamin, Kate (wife of William Thompson), Ellen (only lately married), and another one, I think, who died. Old Titus had only one daughter, Jane. She married Richard Kirkham (Dick o' Sally's). Ann, daughter of Thomas o' Owd Timothy's, was married to Edward Jepson. Edward died and left her with three daughters, but Ann followed him home six months later, and the three orphan daughters were left to the care of their relatives. One of this interesting trio was christened by the old-fashioned name of Lettice. She became the wife of the late James Briggs, of Blackburn, mother of Edward Briggs, cotton manufacturer, and grandmother of William Edward Briggs, ex-M.P. for Blackburn, who is thus six generations removed from Owd Timothy o'th' Looms. Jane, another of the three orphan girls, married Michael Holden. Joseph Slinger, [late] organist of Belgrave Chapel, is her grandson. Betty, the third of the trio, was married to James Beckett, father of William Beckett, of Cross Street, Sudell Road, represented to-day by J. J. Beckett and W. E. Beckett, two well-known local gentlemen. There were also four girls, sisters of J. J. and W. E. Beckett, but they are all dead. One of them became the wife of J. F. Leach. Betty, a third daughter of old Thomas Holden, was married to Samuel Jepson, of Marsh House. About the year 1825, she fell through the floor of her house, through a flag breaking. She alighted on the top of an old-fashioned press in the cellar, and broke her thigh. Her injuries were so severe that she died in a few days. Her husband died about the end of June, 1827. Jane, another daughter of old Thomas Holden, was married to Christopher Duxbury, of Hoddlesden. They had a numerous family, and I knew them all.

Timothy, fifth son of Owd Timothy o' th' Looms, married a Miss Duxbury. She died, leaving him two sons and a daughter—Timothy, William, and Catherine. He married a second time, taking for his wife Ellen Hunt, my grandfather's sister, and by his second marriage he had three sons and a daughter—John, Robert, James, and Rachael Timothy No. 3 married Hester Jepson, sister of the Samuel Jepson before-mentioned. He has a numerous progeny—Samuel, Timothy, Edward, George, Thomas, William, and John, besides two daughters, Ellen and another. George was killed in a stone delph. William, brother of Timothy and Catherine, married Rachael Leach, daughter of John Leach, my mother's sister. They had sons—John, Timothy, and William; daughters—Ellen, Catherine, Alice, Mary, Ann, and Rachael.

Ellen was married to a man named James Shorrock; Thurston Briggs, of Hoddlesden, married Catherine; Alice never was married; Mary was married to James Briggs; Ann to Micah Jepson; and Rachael to Thomas Parkinson. Alderman Roger Howorth's wife (Blackburn) is one of Micah's daughters. Of the three sons, John only left one male representative—James—who married a daughter of William Holden, of Shaw Fold, Eccleshill, and they never had a family, so the male branch died out. But John had several girls. Rachael was married to James Holden, of the old overseer's family, but had no issue. Ann was married to John Beckett, and her branch is represented by J. J. and W. E. Beckett. John Marsden, coal dealer, married another of the girls. She died and left one daughter, who married a man named Holden There was another girl still. She was married to Thomas Jepson, but I am not aware that she ever had any family. William's family consisted of four sons—William, Timothy, Lawrence, and John; and four daughters—one married to a Brandwood, another to an Eccles, a third to Nathaniel Fish, and a fourth to man named Neville. Lawrence and William went to America; the former is dead, but I am not sure about the latter. Timothy is living in Darwen with a numerous family; he has been married twice. Timothy (brother of John and William, sons of William o' Owd Timothy's o' Owd Timothy's) married a Miss Harrison, a Roman Catholic. They are both dead, their only son is dead also, and the branch is extinct. Catherine, daughter of Timothy o' Owd Timothy's was married to James Yates, and had a numerous family, but they are every one dead. We were neighbours. Their children were Timothy, Mary, James, Ellen, Joseph, Catherine, Rachael, Peggy, Robert, and John. Joseph and Catherine were twins. Joseph married a Miss Hollis, who lived to be over 80 years of age, and then died. Catherine, the other twin, was married to Nathaniel Leach, and became the grandmother of J. F. Leach.

I will now give the progeny of Timothy, fifth son of Owd Timothy o' th' Looms, by his second wife, Helen Hunt; but first I must tell a story about him. He was a strong Non-Con. was Timothy the Second, and he lived under the Hargreaveses, of Hoddlesden. Now old Hargreaves was a strong Churchman, and on rent days he and Timothy used to have many a cavil about Church and Dissent. Timothy bought a work called "Towgood on Dissent," and used to read it up diligently just before rent day. Hargreaves kept a pack of hounds, and during the summer he would give them to his tenants to keep for him. One rent day while cavilling with old Timothy, he told him he would send him a hound to keep, and see if he could turn that into a Dissenter.

Timothy retorted "Aw think th' owd bias 'll be rayther to' strong in id." That remark cost Timothy his shop, for he got notice to quit the farm soon after. He got hold of Towgood's book and said "Tha med me flit, and aw'll keep thi while aw live." Keep it he did, and I believe the old book is in existence to this day, for I have seen it myself. It will be more than 100 years since this incident occurred. He was a rather eccentric old character was Timothy. He used to come to Pole Lane Chapel in a curious costume, and he always had his clogs greased with a bit of fresh butter. He used to sit and stand in a pew at the angle of the gallery, and to my eyes he looked like some old image that we sometimes see in churches. He died at his daughter's house at Brocklehead in 1816, aged 81 or 82. I was ten years old then, but I have impressions of his character and appearance as strongly imprinted on my mind as if it were only yesterday. Now for Timothy's progeny by his second wife. John married a Miss Butcher, of Bolton, and went to live that way. His children are scattered, but there is a grandson named William Henry living in Kay Street, a daughter named Alice, wife of David Ellison, living in Duckworth Street, while Mary (who married a man named Ainsworth) has died without issue. Timothy, who married a woman from Egerton, has died and left one daughter; James has died lately; another son died when quite a young man many years ago, and Ellen died young. The family are scattered over Bolton and Darwen, and there are some branches in America. Robert married a Miss Garstang, from Moss (near Moss Bridge), Lower Darwen, but his family has nearly died out. He had two sons and two daughters— Thomas, Timothy, Ellen and Betty. Thomas married a Miss Whalley, and their only surviving son, Robert, is a tradesman in Duckworth Street. Their other children were James, who died unmarried; Thomas, who married a Miss Holden, and dying, left two children; Ellen, still living, unmarried; and another daughter. Robert, the surviving son, married a Miss Heyes, but has no family. Timothy married Betsy Shorrock, my sister Mary's daughter. He died on the 12th October, 1857, leaving a widow and five little children. His widow died on the 22nd of the following November, the youngest child then being 15 months old, and the eldest 14 years. There is only one of the five now living, John Holden. He is the senior partner in the firm of Holden and Martin, cotton manufacturers. Ellen was married to Ralph Nuttall, and they are both living, still, old Ralph being over 86 years of age. They are without issue. Betty was married to James Briggs, son of Thurston Briggs, of Hoddlesden. He only lived six week after their marriage, but she is living yet, a widow, aged 73, but childless. James Holden (brother of

Robert) married a Miss Harrison. What has become of his family I don't know. They are nowhere in this neighbourhood, and I have lost all trace of them. Rachel (sister of Robert and James), the youngest daughter of Owd Timothy No. 2, was married to John Beckett, of an old Darwen family. She died in 1814, and left nine sons and one daughter. There is not one living to-day.

Of the three daughters of Owd Timothy o' th' Looms I have not much to tell. One married a Marsden, and became the mother of Timothy Marsden o' th' Oakenhurst, whose history I have already given; another married a man named Yates, and their descendants are living about Belthorn. Timothy Yates Nuttall is one of the chief representatives of this branch. The third married a man named Ellison, and I don't know what has become of the family. I knew John and Timothy of the Yates family. John's progeny are spread about Belthorn, and one of Timothy's daughters was the first wife of old Ralph Nuttall, on The Lee, who afterwards married Ellen Holden, his present wife. One of Timothy's sons went to America, and another into the Egerton district, where Timothy himself went. Darwen is noted for its peculiar nicknames, but one of the lads of this family had a most unusual appellation. He was always called "Jack John," meaning Jack, the son of John.

There are many families of the name of Holden in Darwen that I cannot trace to have any connection with Owd Timothy o' th' Looms, although there may have been a connection in the dim distance of the past. Holden is a very common name in Darwen, and the more I think about it the more am I convinced that the great majority of families of that name are connected with Owd Timothy, and that the rest, with very few exceptions, are distant relatives, whose connecting link I either never knew or have forgotten.

HOLDEN OF HODDLESDEN.

Mr. Abram mentions a Thos. Holden of Hoddlesden, whose Will dated October 9th, 1647, names his wife Alice; sons William and Robert; and daughters Jane, Elizabeth, Isabel, and Ann Yate, then a widow.

HOLDEN OF PICKUP BANK.

George Holden, first of Pickup Bank, was a younger son of Ralph Holden of Holden Hall, gent. On the wall of the old house of the Holdens at Pickup Bank are inscribed with the date "1602" the initials "G H" (George Holden.) He had sons, Robert; George; and Thomas; and daughters, Alice, wife of Lawrence Haworth of Th'urcroft, gent.; and Elizabeth, who died unmarried in Oct., 1624. George Holden, the father, was living in 1626, when his son—

"George Holden of Pickup Bank, junior," died, in May, 1626. He had been made a Governor of Blackburn Grammar School in 1625. His wife had died in June, 1619. In his Will, dated May 30th, 1626, testator names sons, Robert (a minor); George; and Thomas; daughter Anne (born in 1604); brothers, Thomas and Robert Holden, who are made executors; and his kinsman Andrew Holden of Todd Hall, to be supervisor.

"Thomas Holden of Pickup Bank, son of George," had a son, William, bapt. Jan. 21st, 1626-7.

OLD DARWEN FAMILIES.

Robert Holden of Piccop Bank, Greave of Rossendale in 1591, was Robert son of the first-named George Holden. "Ellen Holden of Pickup Bank, widow," relict, I think, of this Robert, in her Will, dated May 19th, 1637, names her five sons, James (who had sons, George and Thomas); Thomas (who had George, and Ellen); Robert; John; and William.

James Holden of Pickup Bank (eldest son of Robert and Ellen above), served as Greave of Rossendale in 1644. He had sons, George; Thomas, born in 1634; Robert, born in 1637; and John, died in 1656. James Holden of Pickup Bank died in Oct., 1689.

George Holden of Pickup Bank, yeoman, eldest son of James, married, Aug. 6th, 1655, Agnes, daughter of Edward Pilling of Pickup Bank (she died in Feb. 1678-9), and had a son, James Holden, bapt. Sept. 21st, 1657; and daughters, Anne, born and died in 1656; and a second Anne, born in 1668.

Thomas Holden of Pickup Bank (second son of James above), died in 1673, and had sons, James, died in 1662; Jeremiah, born in 1662; and a second James, born in 1665.

Robert Holden, youngest son of James, had issue, sons, born in 1663, William, born in 1665; Andrew, born in 1667; and Thomas; and daughters, Margaret, born in 1656; and Ellen, born in 1659.

Of the younger sons of Ellen Holden, widow, who died in 1637, were, John Holden of Pickup Bank, who died in 1673, and his wife Margery in 1670; and William Holden of Pickup Bank, who had a son Andrew, born in 1654; a daughter Ellen, died in 1663; and [———] died in 1675.

A later Robert Holden of Pickup Bank had sons, Miles, died in 1685; and Robert, born in 1695.—*History of Blackburn*, p. 762.

HOLDEN OF YATE BANK.

William Holden of Yate Bank was buried March 30th, 1685. Thomas Holden of Yate Bank, yeoman, died in 1691. His Will is dated Feb. 20th, 1691; and names his sons, William, John, Thomas, and James; and a daughter Margaret. Robert Holden of Yate Bank died in September, 1710. John Holden of Yate Bank, had a son Thomas, born in 1701, and other issue. John Holden of Yate Bank, yeoman, died in his 96th year, in 1796. William Holden, living recently, had a small estate in Yate Bank, left to him by his great-uncle John Holden, who died in 1796.—*History of Blackburn*, p. 762.

NOTE ON THE GENEALOGICAL TABLES.

In the early stages of our work we had a notion of compiling genealogical tables showing the connection of the old families of the town one with another and the exact line of descent of all the principal characters mentioned in Jeremy's "Recollections." But I soon discovered that I should seriously hamper Jeremy in his work if I persisted in my endeavours to keep him at work in a straight line, as he liked to talk on about men and things just as they came into his head. Whenever I mapped out a line of discourse for him, and tried to keep him to it, he would overlook some of the more important episodes, which, in his garrulous way, he would dilate upon when left to himself, and the history of Darwen families would have become tame and insipid if he had kept to a strictly genealogical record. Now that my friend is dead and gone, I have no reason to regret that, after the first few weeks of ur work, I let him chatter away uninterrupted, in his own style, for I am able, in onsequence, to glean from my shorthand notes much important matter relating to other families than those he was primarily speaking of—notably in the case of the Lightbowns, the Duxburys, and the Entwisles — which I have been able to add to his Recollections, together with other jottings of a more fragmentary nature.

I have found among my papers some incomplete genealogical tables compiled in the early days of our work, and two of them I have considered worth giving as a faint illustration of the complication of the task of compilation which we found it inadvisable to continue. I could easily fill out, or fill in, the tables, to a much greater extent, from Jeremy's "Recollections," but I prefer to give them to the public in the unfinished state in which they were left when we agreed to abandon the tabular system and stick to the gossipy style which pervades the "Recollections" as they are now printed. Persons whose family connection gives them a special interest in the work will be able to trace out genealogical trees for themselves.

The first of these tables has for its head the nonagenarian James Marsden, born in 1700. Of his two sons, only one had issue that survived, and this branch includes some notable characters, besides introducing the Entwisles by the marriage of Rachael Marsden to "Owd Billy o' Ralph's." Of the three female branches of Old James the First's family, two develop into Leaches, and one into the name of Hindle, so that two more "Old Darwen Families" are thus early introduced. In the table which I here publish, Jeremy only traces out the descent of one of these three branches, which is that of his famous "Grandmother Marsden," from whom he derived so much of his information, and his taste for folk-lore, when a child. This "Grandmother Marsden" of his, was Alice, daughter of Old James of 1700, and wife of John Leach. She is shown in the table to have had one son and six daughters, and the marriage of the six daughters leads us to four more "Old Darwen Families," viz:— the Kirkhams, the Hunts, the Holdens and the Pickups. Leaving those families to be dealt with separately, Jeremy traces the family of his grandmother's only son, Jeremy Leach, who had six sons and six daughters. The sons have extended their race, and some of the best-known Leaches of Darwen of the present day belong to this group. The families of the daughters are not followed up.

In the seond genealogical tree (Holden) we go still further back into obscurity, for "Owd Timothy o' th' Looms" is shown to have been born about 1684, and Timothy's grandfather, about whom Jeremy tells an interesting anecdote, is put at the head of the list. Timothy's sisters, by their marriage, bring in the name of another important old Darwen family, Watson, beside the Kirkhams, already named, and the Thompsons, who are not now very numerous in the town. His five sons spread the name of Holden far and wide, and through their progeny we speedily came across early representatives of the Lightbowns and the Briggses, while one of their sisters married one of the ancient Yateses, and a host of other families are introduced in later generations. These tables, brief and fragmentary though they be, are valuable as showing how the "Old Darwen Families" are related one to another by an interminable chain of inter-marriages, and how the people of Darwen are one people, welded together as firmly as any highland clan or Israelitish tribe.

J. G. S

The Smalleys.

Thomas Smalley Cotton Manufacturer and Musical Composer, in the Eighteenth Century—The Rev. Robert Smalley, Astrologer—An Ill-fated Child—"Young Parson Smalley"—The Pole Lane Secession—Blackburn and Bolton Railway—A Stubborn Old Man—The Local Aristocracy—Smalley's Hotel.

IN his "History of Blackburn," Mr. Abram mentions the Smalleys as possessors of a small freehold estate in Darwen, and names several members of the family, carrying their history back 200 years. The members of the Smalley family that I heard most talked about by old people, two or three generations ago, were two brothers, Thomas and Robert, the sons of one Richard Smalley by his second wife. Thomas was born in 1726, and Robert in 1729. Thomas was a hand-loom manufacturer of what at that time were called "Blackburn checks." He was also a musician, and he composed several hymn tunes that were very popular sixty or seventy years ago. Among them were the "New Darwen," the "New Blackburn," the "Newcastle," and the "Durham," besides others, the names of which I cannot recall at the present moment. "Durham" is the only one I ever saw in print. In the Bristol Tune Book it is called "Huddersfield." The others are probably in existence in old MS. music books possessed by some of his descendants. Thomas Smalley's descendants, I have been told, settled in Blackburn. His brother, the Rev. Robert Smalley, was minister of the Old Lower Chapel from 1751 to 1791. He died January 26th, 1791, leaving two sons, Richard and Robert. Richard was born in 1760, and died in 1800.

I have just borrowed, for the purpose of this sketch, a small pamphlet, which was "printed by request" so recently as 1858. It is entitled "Some thoughts upon the death, and over the grave of my dear child, Yates Robert Smalley, who was drowned September 25th, 1765, about noon, aged 2 years, 4 months and 8 days." It concludes with a quotation from one of Pope's Essays, "Chance is direction which thou canst not see," and it is signed "Robert Smalley," "Ann Smalley" There is a most remarkable but thoroughly authentic tradition concerning the drowning of this child. In my younger days I often heard old people relate that the Rev. Robert Smalley was not only an astronomer but an astrologer, and could read the meaning of the planets. Soon after this child's birth he predicted that it would be drowned on a certain day. When the fatal day arrived the anxious father watched that child like a cat watching a mouse, or a bird its young, determined in his own mind not to lose sight of it for a single instant. He lived at Princes, on the top of the hill going towards Hoddlesden, and about noon, as he sat at the door, intent on the child, and fully occupied with his own thoughts, a man came riding up on horseback. The traveller reined up to speak to the parson, and during the conversation the child slipped away unobserved. He was, however, missed in a few minutes, and on a search being instituted he was found drowned in a well, the father's prediction being thus fulfilled despite all his precautions to prevent it.

Richard Smalley (" Young Parson Smalley ") married Ann, daughter of Richard Kershaw, of Astley Bank. He died in June, 1800, aged 40, leaving two sons—Richard Kershaw Smalley and Robert Kershaw Smalley, the former born in 1795, the latter in 1797. They died in 1839 and 1841 respectively, one at Astley Bank, Darwen, and the other in Liverpool. Richard Kershaw Smalley (who built Astley Bank House) had two sons—Robert and John. Robert is still living at Sydney, in New South Wales. He had five daughters—Ann, Sarah, Catherine, Jane, and Maria. Ann, Sarah, and Jane are dead. Maria is in India, and Catherine, who married the late Dr. Payne's son, is living in London. Robert Kershaw Smalley was a surgeon. He married Maria Henrey, and had three daughters and one son. One of the daughters is still living, and the son keeps the Millstone Inn.

Richard Smalley, before mentioned, was always called "Young Parson Smalley." He was elected minister of Lower Chapel on his father's death in 1791, but a large section of the congregation were strongly opposed to his election, and a secession took place which resulted in the building of Pole Lane Chapel, opened on the 6th of May, 1793. Richard was only a minister for a little over twelve months. My father used to say that he was a rollicking young gentleman, educated for the ministry, but not fitted in any way for his calling. When he came home from college he used to play all sorts of pranks and larks, even in the chapel itself, while his father was in the pulpit. My father was a singer at that time at Lower Chapel, and he used to watch young Dick amuse himself by pinning girls' hair to the backs of the pews, during the service, and cutting the stitches of their dress pleats behind, for a lark. When my father used to tell of these pranks, he would add, "An' th' craytur were preyching for his fayther at t' same time!" for Dick was always called upon to fill a vacancy when necessary.

Coming back to old Robert (son of the Rev. Robert who died in 1791) I remember that he died in 1824, aged 61, but that his widow, who was formerly a Miss Yates, lived until 1832, and then died, aged 87. I knew them very well. They lived at Hey Fold, and had four sons and three daughters—Robert, Richard, Thomas, Lawrence Yates Smalley, Kitty, Betty, and Mary. Betty became the wife of William Entwisle, of Sough, and mother of the present Robert Smalley Enwisle, J.P., of Southport; also of Alderman William Entwisle, J.P., ex-Mayor. Kitty married John Pickup, of Marsh House. Robert and Thomas were never married; but Richard did double duty, for he married twice, and had three sons, Robert and Thomas, by his first wife, and one by his second.

The Smalleys owned an estate at Hey Fold, which was cut in two by the making of the railway from Blackburn to Bolton. Now Old Robert Smalley (son of Robert and grandson of the Rev. Robert), no matter what he was in politics, was a Conservative by nature, for he refused persistently to let anything be altered or touched, and even after the Railway Company had got an Act of Parliament for the compulsory purchase of his land, he would have no dealings with them. The Company sent men to cut through the estate, and Old Robert ran at them with a spade to try and drive them away. He could not stop the work, so he did the next most stubborn thing by refusing to accept the money which the Railway Company had to pay for his land and by way of compensation. It was, however, paid into the bank, and I have no doubt it came in very handy for his relatives after his death.

The Smalleys were always a sort of local aristocracy, and they are well connected yet, though there are not many of them left now. There for is Robert Smalley, son of Richard the son of Robert, managing a mill Mr. Joseph Eccles. He has a brother, Thomas, living, and two sisters. One of the sisters is the wife of James Lightbown, of Pendleton, of whom I shall have something to say in a future article; and the other, Catherine, is the wife of William Shorrock, of Cranberry Fold, who had a child drowned during the fog the other week, aged 15 years. I have mentioned Lawrence Yates Smalley. He kept the New Inn, as it is sometimes called, and gave his name to it. It is best known to-day as

"Smalley's Hotel." It is a very old hostelry, for it stood in its present place long before the Blackburn and Bolton Road was made, and what is now the front of it used to be the back. Lawrence Yates Smalley had two sons—George and Robert, and I believe both are in Australia. He had another called Lawrence, who died. Mrs. Eli Walsh, Mrs. Gregg, and Mrs. Alexander Milner Briggs are all his daughters. .

SMALLEY OF HEY FOLD, ASTLEY BANK, &c.

A small estate at Hey Fold, near Darwen Chapels, was the early freehold of this family. Richard Smalley, of Upper Darwen, died in 1709, and another Richard Smalley died in 1715.

Richard Smalley, of Upper Darwen, chapman, married, first, Oct. 22nd, 1717, Jane Marsden of Clayton, and had issue Richard, bapt. Feb. 18th. 1718-19. Jane, wife of Richard Smalley, was buried Jan. 10th, 1720-1. By his second wife, Mary, Richard Smalley had sons, Thomas (see · Smalley of Blackburn, ante), born in 1726 ; and Robert, bapt. May 25th. 1729.

Richard Smalley of Eccleshill and Blackburn, chapman, first son of Richard, died in August, 1773. By Margaret his wife he had sons, Richard, William, Robert, and Thomas ; and a daughter, Margaret. His brother—

Robert Smalley, of Princes, younger son of Richard, was minister of the Lower (Independent) Chapel in Darwen, from 1751 to 1791.—*History of Blackburn*, pp. 509-10.

The Harwoods.

"*We mun spend some labbur o'th' Harruds*"—Various Branches of the Harwood Family—Joseph and Thomas Harwood, Cotton Manufacturers—"'Merica Joe"—The Harwoods Leaders of Thought—The Great Reform Bill—The Pole Lane Secession—Origin of Blacksnape Sunday School—Seth Harwood's Cottage Library—The First Registrar for Darwen—The Rev. Edward Harwood, D.D.—Edmund Harwood, Composer of "Vital Spark"—His Anthems and Hymn Tunes—Miss Molly Harwood, a Famous *Prima Donna*—The Handel Jubilee, 1785, and Centenary, 1835—Musical Services at the Higher Chapel—"I know that my Redeemer liveth"—"Sing me an old Darwen Tune"—"A gradely owd Darrun Tune" in Westminster Abbey.

AFTER our Christmas holidays and our Christmas geese and turkeys, for which the proprietors of *The Times* have our best thanks, we resume our work like giants refreshed, and it is with great satisfaction that we find the Harwood family next on the list for dissection.[1] We wish those time-honoured "Darruners," the Marsdens, that most numerous clan, the Holdens, and those local aristocrats, the Smalleys, a very Happy New Year, and we have also the best of wishes for all the other important Darwen families whose records have yet to be put down in black and white; but we cannot help being gratified that at this stage of our genealogical labours we stumble in the most natural manner possible across such a distinguished family as that of the Harwoods. As the author of these curious genealogical records remarked to his collaborateur, "We mun spend some labbur o' th' Harruds," and "labbur" the "Harruds" certainly deserve, for their forefathers were not only leaders of thought among the homely inhabitants of the "Peaceful Valley," but men of such mental solidity and ability that several of the most prominent have acquired national fame, especially in the musical line. Let Jeremy now give their history in his own words.

The Harwoods are rather a numerous family in Darwen and district, and they are split up into several distinct branches. There are the Pickup Bank Harwoods, the Hoddlesden Harwoods, the Blacksnape

[1] This chapter appeared in *The Blackburn Times* of January 8th, 1887.

Harwoods, the Marsh House Harwoods, and the Darwen Harwoods, all sprung from the same stock. One of the ancestors of the Pickup Bank Harwoods I knew very well. His name was Edmund Harwood. He died, upwards of 70 years of age, at t' Top o' th' Meadow, Pickup Bank, in May, 1832. He left six sons—Thomas, John, Christopher, James, Edmund, and William. William, the last of the family, died in Blackburn in the spring of last year [1886], aged 68; his widow and two of his sons, Edmund and George, are still living in Blackburn. There are living in Pickup Bank at the present time 17 householders of the name of Harwood, all descendants of old Edmund Harwood of t' Top o' th' Meadow, and a number of the same name and family in Blackburn.[1] Next, I place the Hoddlesden family. Old James Harwood, of Hoddlesden, had six sons—John, Michael, Seth, Richard, Elijah, and William. John and Michael are dead; the others are living, all old men, with families. He had also six daughters; four are dead and two living. He had fourteen children altogether, eight sons and six daughters, but four of them died young. The present Seth Harwood, joiner and builder, is one of the fourteen. His son, Baron Harwood, is a well-known cricketer. The Blacksnape and Marsh House Harwoods are the same family. Old Thomas Harwood, of Blacksnape, lived at "t' Pantry," at the bottom end of Blacksnape, when I knew him. His only son was James Harwood, who built the Dun Horse Inn, Hacking Street. James also had an only son called Thomas, who died, leaving a daughter or two, but no one to perpetuate his name. There were several other members of the same family, but I am not well up in the Blacksnape branch. James Harwood, of the Marsh House lot, was the first Chapel-keeper at the Duckworth Street Chapel. He has been dead many years, but he has four sons living—Joseph, James, Michael, and Lawrence; and a daughter who married Ralph Taylor, of Duckworth Street. Joseph and Lawrence are both cotton manufacturers in Darwen, the former at Bridge Mill, and the latter at Two Gates; James is a rope maker on the hill-side; and Michael is living in Preston, employed as a book-keeper by the Eccleses. There are a good many members of this branch, but I am not well acquainted with them.

Coming to the Darwen Harwoods, I have a great deal to tell about three brothers—Joseph, John, and Ebenezer—and a cousin of theirs, John Harwood. Two of the brothers (Joe and Eben) and the cousin John were men of note in the town. They were only common working-

[1] "A Blackburn relative of the Harwoods of Darwen, informs us that there are 94 Harwoods on the Register at Darwen, of whom 92 are Liberals and only two Conservatives. Our contributor, Mr. Jeremy Hunt, mentioned 17 of them living at Pickup Bank; and he now says there are 19 there, all Liberal voters."—*The Blackburn Times*, Feb. 12th, 1887.

men, however,—hand-loom weavers. I knew the eldest of the lot, Joseph, 75 years ago, and he was an old man then, when I had scarcely got out of my petticoats. (They wore them longer[2] in those days than they do now.) He was the sexton and chapel-keeper at Pole Lane Chapel, and lived at Sough. He was rather a remarkable man, was Joe, and what was considered in those benighted days a "dangerous Radical." He got the name of "'Merica Joe," for advocating the cause of the Americans during the struggle for independence, more than a hundred years ago. I have heard my father say that he was a very strong partisan of the Yankees, and would go from place to place on purpose to have a cavil about the great political question of the day. He was both a politician and a theologian, but more of the former than the latter. One night he was noticed to be very excitable and bad-tempered, and some of his friends remarked, "Whatever's to do wi' thee to-neet, Joe? Thou'rt so bad tempered." "Why," says he, "they're brunning me o' Darrun Green, un aw cornd abide." They were burning his effigy! He had two sons that I knew, John and Robert; and the only male descendants that I know in Darwen at the present time are Joseph Harwood, insurance agent,[2] and his two

[1] Jeremy used the word "longer" in a double sense.

[2] Mr. Joseph Harwood, Insurance Agent, is one of the two Conservative members of the family mentioned in the previous foot-note. From *The Darwen News* of January 8th, 1881, I transcribe the following paragraph relating to him:—

"*A Reward for Bravery:*—Mr. Joseph Harwood, of Heys-lane, in this town, but who formerly resided at Preston, has just had presented to him the sum of £5, and the certificate of the Royal Society for the Protection of Life, as a reward for the bravery he displayed on the occasion of a fire at Ashton Mills, Preston, where he was then employed on the 22nd January, 1879. The address is beautifully written and illuminated, and is also illustrated with copies of the Society's Medals. The certificate is as follows:—" Royal Society for the Protection of Life. established 1836 and 1843, for providing public fire escapes with men duly qualified to attend with the same, instructing others in the use of such escapes, also for rewarding persons for saving life from fire. Patron: Her Most Gracious Majesty the Queen. Testimonial, on Vellum, to Mr. Joseph Harwood, of 47, Heys-lane, Darwen, Lancashire, to record the intrepid and judicious services rendered by him on the occasion of a fire at the Ashton Mills, Preston, Lancashire, on the 22nd of January, 1879; a fire which broke out about four o'clock in the afternoon, and spread with great rapidity, compelling many of the operatives to seek refuge upon the roof of the premises. Joseph Harwood, who was among the men thus circumstanced, rendered valuable aid in securing the safety of a lad, also of two men, who, stupefied by the smoke, had given up all hope of escaping from the burning building.—Thos. O. Finnis (Chairman); Chas. Wright (Secretary). Presented at the Quarterly Meeting, 66, Ludgate Hill, October 21st. 1879.

The "dauntless bravery" of the spinning master was the town's talk at Preston when the conflagration occurred, but, as he was thrown out of work by the fire, he returned home to Darwen, and it took the Royal Society two years to discover his whereabouts and reward him. " His own modest account " of what he did is given in *The Preston Guardian* of January 25th, 1879, in the following terms:—" Joseph Harwood, of Wellington-road, Ashton, Spinning Master, states—At the time of the outbreak of the fire I was in my cabin giving a spinner a strap. I heard some boys shouting, but did not hear what they said. Then the engine stopped, and I went into the top room; that is the room opposite my cabin. They did not seem to know anything about a fire there; indeed I did not know myself that there was one, but thought there was some one hurt. I then went into the second room, but they knew nothing there of what had happened. In the third room I heard a shout of "Fire," and when I got to No. 2 the fire was raging. I went back to order the people out of the rooms above.

brothers. They come from Robert. John had a lot of lasses, but I never knew any lads. 'Merica Joe must have been dead something like 75 years, but I recollect him very well. He had a perfectly white head, and his form was rather tall and spare. He had four daughters—Ann, who became the wife of Thomas Kershaw; Esther, who married Timothy Yates; Sarah, wife of George Haworth; and Mary, wife of Edward Whewell.

John Harwood, brother of 'Merica Joe, settled in Bolton, and some of his descendants are living there now in good positions.

Ebenezer, the third brother, had three sons and three daughters. The sons were—Michael, Samuel, and Edward. Michael died in 1827. He has a son and two grandsons in America at the present time, and one grandson, Peter Harwood, in Darwen. Sam o' owd Eben's married my sister, Ellen Hunt, and had four sons, who grew up. Two of them died young men, unmarried; the other two, Ellen and James, are living now in New Zealand, with families. Sam's daughters are Mary, widow of William Harwood, of Wood Street; Hannah, widow of the late Nicholas Fish; Alice, unmarried; and Ellen, unmarried; all living in Darwen, except Hannah, who was killed in a tramway accident at Bury in 1885. Betsy, the youngest daughter, died, a young woman, about 20 years back. Owd Eben himself died in 1834, aged about 73. Edward, the third son of Ebenezer (Neddy o' Owd Eben's), had three sons—Ebenezer, Edward, and Thomas. Young Edward died in 1846, unmarried, and Thomas died in 1883, leaving two sons and a daughter, all married. Neddy had three daughters—Mary and Phœbe, unmarried,

When I came down, communication was cut off by the fire, which was rapidly extending to the rooms above. With two assistants, I got the winders out of the winding-room. I shouted into the other rooms that all must come out. I went to my cabin for books and other things belonging to me. In coming down the second landing, I found a boy on the steps, unconscious, or pretty nearly so. I afterwards learned that he had been in the room where the fire had broken out, and that he had gone to one of the upper rooms to tell his father of the fire. I dropped the books and carried the lad to a window, for we could not get down in consequence of the smoke and flame. Six spinners came rushing to me from the upper room, and we tried several times to get through the fire, but could not. I then broke the staircase window, and got on the top of the winding-room slates, and I assisted the boy and the other men to get through. A ladder was put up by some men below, but it was too short. Some banding was then thrown up, and by means of it we drew a rope up, and I told a spinner to fasten it. Prior to this a man had fainted, but on a window being broken, and fresh air admitted, he recovered. A man, in his excitement, jumped from the third storey on to the cotton shed, off which he rolled on to the ground, where he was found unconscious with his leg and an arm broken. As a spinner was sliding down a rope it broke, and he fell to the ground and hurt himself. Whilst this was going on I broke through the skylight of the winding-room and got down thereby, and the men followed. I carried the boy across the room to the window-sill. The window was fastened, and I smashed the frame. We then threw some of the workpeople's things out of the window. A ladder was put against the window, and we escaped. Some of the people in the upper rooms escaped by the hoist. The boy whom I found on the staircase was the son of the man who fainted. Whilst we were on the winding-room slates, part of the roof of the main block fell. We were the last that came out of the mill." I gather that he was instrumental in saving no fewer than nine ives.—J.G.S.

and Ann, widow of George Fish, who lives in Hindle-street. That's old Edward ("Neddy o' Owd Eben's") who died in December 1844. Eben, son of Neddy o' Owd Eben's, is living in Olive Lane. He has four sons—Edward, Thomas, John, and Ebenezer—and two daughters. Edward died a few weeks ago, leaving a widow and one child; Thomas and John are living, with families; and Ebenezer is alive, unmarried. Owd Eben's daughters were Lettice and Esther by his first wife and Mary by his second. A man named John Oldham—that's an Oswaldtwistle name—married Lettice, and Titus Leach married Esther; while Mary became the wife of John Duxbury.

John Harwood, cousin of old Joe, John, and Eben, never had either brother or sister that I ever heard of, and I have inquired of his relatives, who confirm my recollection that he was an only child. I knew three of his sons—Thomas, Amos, and Seth—but no daughters. I think he had had a daughter who died young. Thomas married a woman who, being called Harwood like himself, never changed her name, and he was not by any means the only Harwood who married a woman of the same name as himself. He had two daughters; one died unmarried, and the other went to Liverpool, got married, and left children, whose families are in Liverpool to-day. But let me tell you something about Owd John. He died so lately as May, 1831, so that I knew him very well. Like his cousin 'Merica Joe, he was both a theologian and a politician, very strong in his convictions, and a remarkable man for his day. They were leaders of thought were these Harwoods, all of them, as Darwen stood then. I will give you a simple but characteristic illustration of the strength of Owd John's strong political opinions. He lay on his deathbed in April, 1831, when the glorious Reform Bill, which became law in 1832, had passed the second reading in the House of Commons by a majority of one. There was some rejoicing in Radical Darwen, I can tell you, and the town was ablaze with illuminations. Owd John was lying in bed as near death as he could well be without losing consciousness, but knowing of all that was going on in the streets, he insisted on having his candle put in the bedroom window that his light might shine before men, and both he and they could see how he rejoiced in the success of the People's cause. He died on the 4th of the next month, full of years and honours. His age was 79. This same John Harwood was one of the leading men of the group who seceded from the Lower Chapel, and built Pole Lane Chapel. My father was another of that lot, and he and Owd John were close friends and associates. John was a man of very strong mind and firm principle. There were several old men living when I was a lad to whom the

Darwen of to-day owes a great deal. They were men of strong convictions, men of principle, men who would walk up to the canon's mouth in a righteous cause. Darwen Nonconformity and Darwen Liberalism owe a great debt to half-a-dozen old men of this stamp, whom I knew when quite a lad, men who were born about the middle of last century, whose conversation I listened to with interest sixty and seventy years ago, and who have left the impress of their strong minds on the town and people of Darwen of the year 1887. Among these leading men of my boyhood's days, the Harwoods were probably the foremost.

Old John Harwood, cousin to Eben, Joe, and John, lived at Blacksnape nearly 70 years ago, and began a Sunday School there in an old empty building. After a while he resolved to have a school built, and he set to work to collect subscriptions. The result was that the present Blacksnape School was built in 1823, and opened in October that year by the Rev. J. Fox, of Duke's Alley Chapel, Bolton. I recollect the event well enough. The school is now a very flourishing day and Sunday school. It has about 120 day scholars, drawn from the country district covered by a radius of about four miles, and William Jepson is the head teacher. Over the door there is this inscription cut in stone—" Jehovah Jireh. Built by subscription, through the exertions of John Harwood, 1823." I was appointed one of the teaching staff of the school in 1824, and my eldest brother was another. We used to go in turns to take charge of the school on Sundays—once in six weeks. This same John Harwood (cousin to Eben, Joe, and John) had three sons—Thomas, Amos, and Seth. Thomas had two daughters; one died unmarried, the other went to Liverpool, and some of her family are living there now. Amos and Thomas went to America nearly 60 years ago, and I don't know what has become of them. Now Seth was a great authority in Darwen on almost every subject under the sun. He was married to Sarah Briggs, and about half a century ago his cottage library was the largest possessed by any man in Darwen. He was a very intelligent man, although only brought up as a hand-loom weaver. He became the assistant of old James Holden, who was overseer for twenty years, and after old James's death Seth was appointed the first Registrar of Marriages and Deaths in Darwen. He died, aged 84, in 1868.

Continuing my account of the Harwoods, I shall now leave the region of the politics altogether, get deeper into theology, and lay open one of the brightest pages of musical history with which Darwen has any connection. In the branch of the Harwoods which I have classified as belonging to Darwen proper, I come next to the Rev. Edward Harwood, D.D. This old "Darruner" was a Nonconformist minister at the end of last century, and that is about all I know of him, except that he was a doctor of divinity, but an interesting autobiography of him is given in Mr. Abram's "History of Blackburn."

Edmund Harwood, musician, and his sister "Molly" are probably as prominent in history as any "Darruner" ever was. I don't know what their father's name was, but they belonged to the Darwen Harwoods, and were brought up in Hoddlesden. Edmund was an alto singer of some repute, and his name will be handed down to posterity as the composer of that lovely funeral anthem "Vital Spark," as well as as of a number of good hymn tunes and other anthems. My father had a copy of the first edition of Edmund Harwood's anthems and hymn tunes, and I have sung from the old copy many a time. But that time is more than 60 years since, and the book got quite worn out or I should have had it yet. The "Vital Spark" was originally written in three parts instead of four, and so were all Edmund Harwood's anthems. But his hymn tunes were written for four voices. Harwood's masterpiece has been imitated many a time, but never equalled. I think a lot of old Edmund Harwood, for I am an alto singer myself, and only this Christmas [1886] I was singing alto in the Messiah in the Co-operative Hall, Darwen, while a grandson of mine was singing bass behind me.[1] Edmund went to Liverpool to sing in one of the churches there, and he sang until he burst a blood vessel. That is more than a century ago. He would be a handloom weaver, sure enough, would Edmund. At any rate his sister Molly was, and she gained even more repute as a singer than her brother, for she became one of England's prima donnas, and talent fetched its price both in the case of Edmund and Molly. They are excellent instances of a great man and a great woman having risen from among the looms, but there are many more instances to be found by anyone who will take the trouble to inquire; for nobody can deny that there is much sterling worth among our Lancashire factory workers, who many a time make their way in the world, despite their humble beginnings.[2] Molly Harwood was brought

[1] Mr. Geo. Thompson, alto singer, of Blackburn, informs me that when he and my father, and other Blackburn musicians of the old school, went to assist at a concert in Darwen, ten or a dozen years ago, he and Jeremy Hunt sang side by side. Immediately in front of them sat a euphonium player. The great bell-mouth of the instrument was gaping before them, and Jeremy remarked —" It's no good of us singing down that tunnel; it's like a red robin singing in a thunderstorm ! " —J.G.S.

[2] ANOTHER LANCASHIRE SONGSTRESS OF THE EIGHTEENTH CENTURY.—In illustration of Jeremy's remarks, and as a parallel case to that of Miss Harwood, I quote the following from the "Gentleman's Magazine," for 1781 :—*Anecdotes of the Late Miss Harrop, now Mrs. Bates.*— This English musical phenomenon was born in an obscure place in Lancashire, of poor though industrious parents, who bred their daughter, as most poor people do in that part of England, to the female

up in Hoddlesden as a handloom weaver. The Hargreaveses were at that time the landlords of the Hoddlesden estate, and the house now known as the Griffin Inn was the family seat. The landowners knew of Molly's habit of sitting singing so sweetly over her loom, and one day they took some of their fashionable friends in to hear her. The party of ladies and gentlemen were so much pleased that they sent the girl to London to be educated at a College of Music, and took such a personal interest in her that she rose to the top of the tree as a professional musician. In 1785—nearly 102 years ago—she sang *as a principal* at the Handel Jubilee Festival, in Westminster Abbey. I have seen the programme of the 1785 Jubilee, and also that of the Centenary in 1835. There is the name of a bass singer named Bellamy appearing in both, and it may be the same man. Miss Mary Harwood's name appears only in the first, though she may have been living fifty years later.[1] I knew several of Molly's cousins who lived in Darwen. Old Edmund Harwood, of Top o' th' Meadows, was one of them. One of his great-granddaughters called Molly has a very promising voice. Miss Molly used to come over to Darwen to see her relatives, and whenever she came it was the signal for a tip-top musical service at the Higher Chapel—the only place in the town with an organ. Though they

branch of the occupation of the loom and spinning. Our heroine was, at a very early period, as is common in Lancashire, put to a publick school, where church and other vocal music is taught; but however she might be admired, as other girls in the first musical form are, she was never distinguished for a pre-eminence in natural taste, voice, and execution, till discovered by the celebrated Dr. Howard, who heard her in publick at Leicester. The Doctor was so struck with her vast natural abilities that he exclaimed on the spot to some friends, "that the female he had just heard would one day surpass all the English, nay, even Italian female singers; for he had never heard such a natural delicacy of taste, and such surprising musical excellence, in any Englishwoman, and but very few foreigners." The Doctor, after the performance was over, was introduced to her; and although he complimented Miss Harrop with all the enthusiasm that any musical connoisseur would do on discovering a prodigy in vocal music, yet it very little affected her, as in a few days she returned into Lancashire to her parents, where, for some time after, she unambitiously chanted at her work, as the other girls do in the country. Dr. Howard, however, much to his honour as a man, to elevate such talents to their proper sphere, and much to his critical judgment as one of the cognoscenti, spread the fame of the Lancashire St. Cecilia wherever he went, till, at length, on its reaching the Sandwich Catch Club, one of their members, we believe her present husband, was deputed to wait on her, and bring her to London. Here, soon discovering the invaluable ore they had acquired, her natural abilities where polished by the best writers, and she continued to enrapture and astonish the musical world for several years, till Hymen snatched her from the ear and the eye of the public by a marriage with Joah Bates, Esq., one of the Commissioners of the Victualling Office. The success of Miss Harrop, who acquired (like Mrs. Sheridan) a very considerable fortune by her amazing vocal powers, has had the same effect in Lancashire and Leicestershire as a twenty-thousand pound prize falling to the lot of the poor labourer would have upon the people of the village where he resided; everyone there, who has a daughter, being emulous of having her instructed in vocal music; and Miss Harrop's first master, who is still alive, and follows his profession, holds up his pupil Harrop, as well he may, to his young scholars as a pattern to imitate, which has proved a very great stimulative to the females in that part of England, who have since attained to great perfection in executing the most difficult pieces of music with taste and correctness. It is delightful to observe them at work, with their musical tasks stuck up before them, where they practise all day with indefatigable zeal and attention; and many of them can sing at sight the most difficult pieces of music. At eve you may see them trudging along in their stuff gowns, singing all the way what they are to perform before their masters, where, if the traveller with a fine taste should chance to pop in, he will be convinced that the Lancashire Witches are not more remarkable for their beauty than for their astonishing vocal powers, as they may well vie with the rural nymphs in the most musical provinces of Italy.—H.

1. In looking over an old score copy of "Handel's Songs, &c.," belonging to my father, I have come across the one "In Sweetest Harmony," inscribed "As sung by Miss HARWOOD, in *Saul*." Its range is from E to G. sharp. The same book contains two songs inscribed "As sung by Mr. Bellamy, Junr."—J.G.S.

were Dissenters to the backbone the Harwoods and other musical Nonconformists used to go to church at such times for the sake of the organ. I have seen my father get into raptures when relating how Miss Molly sang "I know that my Redeemer liveth" on such occasions as these. On one of her visits more than a century ago, she brought a number of little presents for her friends, and my mother, who was among the number, came in for a little piece of blue and yellow ribbon as her share. My mother kept this little relic until her death in 1839, and then it came into the possession of one of my sisters. I believe Miss Molly died in Liverpool. An old friend of mine, who was half cousin to her, once went over to Liverpool with another Darwen man to find her. That will be more than fifty years ago, and Miss Molly was then an old maid, having seen more than eighty summers and never been wedded, except to her music. They had given up their search as futile, and were about to return home when they heard of her by a mere accident. Despite her four-score years she was still following her profession as a teacher of singing and the pianoforte. When they found her they told her who they were and whence they came, and one of the first things she said to them, after bidding them welcome, was— "Sing me an old Darwen tune." They sang one and the tears rolled down the old lady's face at the recollections of home and childhood which it recalled. When they took their leave Miss Molly walked with them as far as the street corner, gave them a sovereign out of the fulness of her heart, with an excuse that it would pay their expenses home, remarking as she watched them off "I may never look on a Darwen face again." She did not live long after this affecting incident. Having shown the tender side of her nature I will now relate an incident to show what a brave-hearted woman Molly was. She once had a leg broken in a carriage accident, and the bones were set so badly that she was lame for a long time, but in order to have a cure effected she bravely went to the celebrated Whitworth doctors to have the leg broken again, and re-set in a proper manner.

One of the most popular of "Harrud's" tunes is a long metre in three sharps called "St. Peter's." I have seen it printed somewhere. Old William Hutchinson, of Darwen, was once in Westminster Abbey when this tune was sung. He never tired of telling how surprised and delighted he was, and he used to wind up with the remark, "Eh! I wish Harrud could have heard it sung as I heard it sung in Westminster Abbey—a gradely owd Darrun tune."

The Pickups.

John Pickup, of Sunnyhurst— Richard Eccles, J.P.—William Pickup, son of John—James Pickup— Robert Smalley Entwisle, J.P.—James Halliwell, J.P.—Alderman William Pickup—A Fifty Years' Courtship.

THE first Pickup that I have any recollection of was old John Pickup, of Sunnyhurst, who married Hannah, the daughter of old Thomas Eccles, of Pickup Bank. Old Richard Eccles, J.P., of Lower Darwen, Chairman of the Blackburn Board of Guardians, is a grandson of Hannah's brother. This old John Pickup had two sons, William and James, and, I think, six daughters—Betty, Ann, Sarah, Mary, Jane, and Ellen. Betty became the wife of James Shorrock, of Chapels; Ann, the wife of James Green, of Chapels; Sarah, the wife of Richard Watson, Hey Fold; Mary, the wife of Daniel Gregory; Jane, the wife of William Shorrock, Sough; and Ellen, the wife of Joshua Watson, Chapels.

William, the first of old John's sons, had sons, John, George, James, and William—and daughters, Hannah, who became the wife of James Pickup No. 2, of Sough; Sarah, Martha, and Betty, who all died unmarried. John, the first of the family, married Kitty Smalley, and had only one son, William, and he is living at Marsh House. William Pickup, of Marsh House, has one daughter, who his married to Mr. Yates, surveyor. But John, though he had only one son, had five daughters. Pilkington Shorrock married one, Robert Smalley Entwisle, J.P., took another as his second wife; the late James Halliwell, J.P., cotton manufacturer, married a third; and two others died unmarried. George, the second son of William o' old John's, had six sons—William (an alderman of the borough to-day), James, John, Christopher, Robert and George. All are living except John. Alderman William Pickup has one son and a daughter. The son, John, is married and living at Marsh House; the daughter is unmarried.

In addition to six sons, George had five daughters. Sarah married Joseph Walmsley, of Eccleshill; Hannah became the wife of James

Holden, of Bank Top Mill, Darwen; Martha died unmarried; and Eliza and Betsy are living unmarried. James, the third son of old William, died a young man, and William, the fourth, died a bachelor, over 50 years of age.

James Pickup, brother of William, and son of Old John, married a Miss Shorrock, sister of old William Shorrock, of Sough. He had two sons and one daughter. One of the sons, John, was never married. He lived to the age of three score years and ten, and courted one woman more than half-a-century, but both he and his sweetheart died single. The woman was Alice Duxbury. The other son, James Pickup, married his cousin Hannah, the daughter of William Pickup, of Marsh House. This is the man I have spoken of as James Pickup No 2. He had one son and one daughter. The daughter, Sarah, became the first wife of Mr. Robert Smalley Entwisle, J.P., who married two cousins. Sarah, Robert Smalley Entwisle's first wife, had an only son, the present James Pickup Entwisle. I said that old James had two sons and one daughter. The daughter, Hannah, was married to Ralph Walsh, and had three sons and a daughter. James, Ralph, and John were the sons; the daughter died unmarried. James was killed by falling off a building of his own, near Bolton, while repairing it. He left a family. Ralph was killed in a coal pit. A rope that was being wound round the winch slipped off, caught the lad under the chin, knocked his neck out and threw him up into the air. That is more than 60 years ago. John is living at Bull Hill. He has two sons and two daughters.[1]

[1]. Jeremy mentions a James Pickup who married his (Jeremy's) Aunt Peggy youngest daughter of John Leach), and had two sons and three daughters. George Pickup, clogger, of King Street, is one of his descendants.

The Pickups in Tockholes and Darwen belong to the same stock.—J. H.

The Eccleses.

Mill Barn, Pickup Bank—Edmund Eccles's endowment o the Higher Chapel—"Old Sapling Bough"—John Pickup, of Sunnyhurst—Edward Eccles, steward to the first Sir Robert Peel—Mill Barn House built 1770 —John Leach, of Mill Barn—The Hunts at Mill Barn—"Grandmother Marsden's" China—Eccles Shorrock, J.P.—A specimen of "Blackburn Checks"—Ichabod—Scriptural names—"Thomas, o' Owd Sapling Bough's" family—Descendants of Joseph Eccles, of Lower Darwen—Eighty-six Years' Tenancy—Dr. Skinner's Marriage—A Legacy of £80,000—Migration of the Eccleses from Clitheroe—Garsden or Eccles Fold—Thomas and Martha—The first cotton factory in Darwen built 1820—George Eccles, singer—Thomas and Joseph Eccles, magistrates—Marrying a deceased Wife's Sister—Love among Cousins—The Coldest Day of this Century—Mrs. Muncaster—The Peninsular War—Marrying a deceased Husband's Brother—The Eccleses of Walton-le-Dale—Curtailing Watts's Hymns at the Lower Chapel—"Lime Dick"—Harwood and Eccles, cotton manufacturers—Richard Eccles, choirmaster—James Eccles Professor of Music.

THERE are two distinct families of the name of Eccles in Darwen. In the principal family, the first man I know anything about is Thomas Eccles, of Mill Barn, Pickup Bank, who flourished at the beginning of last century. This Old Thomas Eccles, of Mill Barn, owned a bit of property that we used to live on at Pickup Bank. It was a farm that the Eccleses had had in their possession at least 200 years. He had a brother called Edmund, who owned two farms higher up, called Garsden Fold by the old inhabitants, but put down in the rate books as Eccles Fold and Shorrock Fold respectively. I could never glean a fragment of tradition as to what became of the decendants of Edmund Eccles, but Mr. Abram, in his history, states that Edmund and two or three more gave £200 as an endowment to the Higher Chapel, on Christmas Day, 1718.

"Old Sapling Bough" was the common appellation of the Thomas Eccles, of Mill Barn, whom I have mentioned above, and he got the name from a very trivial circumstance. There was an oak sapling growing in the fence which separated his land from that of the next peasant proprietor, and around this Thomas one day constructed a wicker fence. His neighbour from across the fence said "Art ta beawn to own thad, Tom?" "Ay," says Tom. "Well, then," rejoined the other, "Aw'll co thee 'Saplin Bough' whel aw live." And all the descendants of old Thomas Eccles are best known to old people to this very day as the Sapling Bough Eccleses. I was talking some years ago to an old lawyer in Blackburn who is connected with the Eccleses by marriage, and when I was mentioning some member of the Eccles family he said, "Oh, you mean old Sapling Bough Eccleses."

Sapling Bough had three sons and one daughter. The daughter married old John Pickup, of Sunnyhurst. Two of the sons were called John and Thomas. I knew them both. Mr. Abram mentions a third called Edward, who was steward to the first Sir Robert Peel. One of Thomas's grandsons has told me that Thomas died in 1819, aged 75; Mr. Abram gives the date as September 11th, 1818. Thomas Eccles No. 2, son of Sapling Bough, used to live at Waterside, just across the brook from the old mill barn, and his cattle were turned out to graze on the Mill Barn farm. He had an odd custom, every time he crossed the brook to attend to his cattle, of picking up a stone or two out of the bed of the stream and carrying it with him. Out of the stones thus collected he built the modern portion of Mill Barn house, in 1770, and there it stands to this day. If you examine the stone you will find it is sandstone, like the stones in the bed of the stream, while the barn itself is built of flag rock from Pickup Bank Heights. Thomas removed from Waterside to his new house at Mill Barn in 1771, and lived there twelve months. He then removed to Lower Darwen, and my grandfather, John Leach, became the tenant in 1772. Our family lived on that farm until 1858. I have another curious story to tell about old Thomas's family. My "Grandmother Marsden" (or Leach) had an infant about the same time as Thomas Eccles's wife presented her lord with twins. The child of my grandmother died, and it was arranged that my grandmother should nurse one of the twins, Jane, for twelve months. This child afterwards became the mother of the late Eccles Shorrock. At the end of the twelve months the child was taken back to its mother, who made my grandmother a present of a set of blue and white china cups, &c., which were dearly prized and only brought out on state occasions. When my grandmother died, in 1818, her goods were divided, and the much-prized china fell to the lot of my mother's sister Rachael, and only the other week I saw one of these very cups—more than 100 years old—at the house of her granddaughter.

Just another story about old Thomas, and then I will go on with names and dates. Thomas was brought up a handloom weaver, and I have seen an apron made out of a piece of cloth woven by him at least 150 years ago. It was a blue and white check of the kind so well known as "Blackburn checks," and it was shown to me, about 40 years ago, by an old woman whose mother had had the cloth given her by old Thomas himself, when he lived at Waterside. It was so old that it almost dropped in pieces and it was darned all over. Old Martha Boardman, the daughter of Thomas Eccles, with her daughter, Mrs. Towers, went over from Blackburn to Pickup Bank with me to look at it, at least 40 years ago, and it was affecting to see with what reverence the old woman looked upon a sample of her father's weaving. I will now go on with my history, but there is just one more story about old Thomas, of Waterside. He was very intimate with my father, and once told him that he had been three times over worth no more money than he could put into the bowl of his pipe. One of these periods of adversity happened at the time his second son was born, and he called him Ichabod, "because," he said, "the glory is departed." (I. Sam. iv., 21.) I have remarked before about Scriptural names being common among old Darwen families, and this is a capital instance illustrating the fact that Darwen people in the last century were familiar with their Bibles.

Now for Thomas o' Owd Sapling Bough's family. I believe Joseph was the eldest—(Joseph, of Lower Darwen, father of Richard Eccles, J.P., chairman of the Board of Guardians,[1] and Thomas). There was another son called Ichabod, a third called Thomas, who died a young man, leaving two children, and a fourth called William. There was also a fifth son of Thomas o' Owd Sapling Bough's, called John, besides three daughters—Jane, wife of Ralph Shorrock, and mother of the late Eccles Shorrock; Mary, the wife of a man named East; Martha, the wife of Robert Boardman, of King Street, Blackburn. I have mentioned Mrs. Boardman as going with me to see a piece of her father's weaving. A generation ago she and her husband lived a retired life in King-street, Blackburn, next door to the Vicarage, and I have had my tea there many a time. Her only daughter, Mary, married a man named George Towers, and afterwards became the wife of the Rev. H. Cameron, late of Blackburn. She is now dead.

The descendants of Joseph, son of Thomas o' Owd Sapling Bough's are given in Mr. Abram's history, as follows:—"Joseph Eccles, Esq., of Lower Darwen, cotton spinner (eldest son of Thomas), married Mary Livesey, of Darwen, and had issue, sons, Thomas, born in May [April] 1806; Richard, born in 1808;[1] Joseph, of Liverpool; William Eccles, of Blackburn; and Edward Eccles, who died July 2nd, 1872, aged 47, within a week of his marriage [I saw him married at Chapel-street, Blackburn]; and daughters Mary, born in the year 1805, and was killed

[1] Richard Eccles, J.P., died February 26th, 1888, in his 80th year.

by a fall at Matlock, May 18th, 1835; and Ellen, married August 18th, 1831, Christopher Shorrock." There was another daughter, Betty, who grew up to womanhood, but was never married. Richard Eccles, aged 80, is the only one of Joseph's sons now living. His brother, Thomas Eccles, went to Torquay, and married Miss Mitchell. Mr. Abram gives his family as follows:—"Alexander Eccles, of Liverpool; Thomas Mitchell Eccles, of Blackburn; Rd. Eccles, jun., of Lower, died aged 38, in 1875; Eccles Shorrock Eccles, Esq., of Liverpool; and several daughters."

William had a son called Thomas, who died a young man; another called William, who became a cotton manufacturer, and settled towards Bamber Bridge, where he may be living yet; a third called Edward, who married a sister of old James Pilkington, cotton broker, Liverpool, and died some years ago; and a fourth called John, who died at Wellfield, Leyland. This John married his cousin, Miss Ainsworth, and had no family. He was our last landlord at Pickup Bank. We lived under the Eccleses 86 years, three generations of our family being tenants of Pickup Bank mill, while three generations of the Eccleses were the landlords. In addition to these four sons, William had one daughter, Mary Jane, who married Bannister Eccles, her cousin.

John, brother of Joseph and William, I never knew much about, but he had two sons, Bannister and Joseph, and two daughters—one became the wife of the Rev. Francis Skinner, of Mount-street, and the other married the Rev. Mr. Smith, a student at Blackburn Academy, and afterwards a missionary. Joseph settled at Mill Hill, Blackburn, and I saw from the *Blackburn Times*, last year [1886], that Bannister Eccles's son, a lawyer, died in London, leaving about £80,000 for his heirs. Unfortunately I wasn't one of them.

Ichabod died at the age of 23 years, leaving one or two children whom I lost sight of, and Thomas, the remaining son of Thomas No. 2, also died a young man, as mentioned above.

I have been told by one of the family that the Eccleses came to Darwen from Clitheroe, and I reckon that that must be at least 300 years ago, because the Eccleses have owned three little estates at Pickup Bank more than 200 years. One of these estates is called Garsden Fold, from a John Garsden who lived there more than a century ago, but in the town's book it is Eccles Fold, which is an older name. Old Garsden died in 1820, aged 82. He has a great great grandson working at the *Blackburn Times* office as an apprentice to the printing trade.

Sapling Bough's son John was married twice. By his first wife— a Miss Walsh—he had two children, Thomas and Martha. In Mr.

Abram's history they are called Thomas and Matthew, but this must be a misprint or a clerical error, for I knew this "Matthew" very well, and *he was a woman!* Martha was a woman of rather weak intellect, and also somewhat of a cripple. I call attention to this merely in order to chronicle the peculiar circumstances attending her death. All her life she had a mortal dread of horses and carts, and as she could not hurry across the street, owing to her deformity, she had a habit of standing still and setting up a shrill scream of terror whenever she saw a vehicle approaching. Notwithstanding all the dangers to which she was thus exposed she lived to be nearly 70 years of age, and then, singular to say, she was knocked down by a cart, and injured to such an extent that death resulted six weeks afterwards. The late Eccles Shorrrock allowed her five shillings a week for several years before her death.

Old Thomas Eccles, brother of Martha, and son of John by his first wife, used to live neighbour to our folks at Pickup Bank Mill. He was a warper in Bowling Green Mill, and he let a weight fall on his big toe, which caused his death. Mr. Abram's History gives the date of his death as 1824, but it must have been 1825, because he died a few weeks after his daughter, whose tombstone, dated October, 1825, is to be seen in Belgrave Chapel yard. I remember Thomas burying his daughter (Ann, the wife of Thomas Briggs, of Sunnyhurst), and, the very Sunday after, my father remarked to me, after he came home from Ebenezer Chapel, that he had never seen old Thomas look as calm and composed for many a year as he looked that morning. His daughter's death seemed to have a great effect on him, and he said he was going to go regularly to chapel now, but he never went again, for the same week he let a weight fall on his big toe, and died from inflammation a few weeks later. He sat in the next pew to us. This Thomas Eccles, son of John by his first wife, married a Miss Walsh, of Pickup Bank. His sons were John, William, Joseph, George, and Thomas, and his daughters Ann, Alice, Mary, and Betsy. John and William built the first portion of Bowling Green Mill about 1820, as a handloom weaving warehouse. This was the first cotton mill in Darwen. It was originally a kind of warehouse for handloom weavers, but it was afterwards enlarged and furnished with power looms. John married Miss Bury, daughter of Andrew Bury, of Bury fold, and had two sons, Andrew and John, but both are dead. He has a daughter living towards Tyldesley. William married Ann, the daughter of old Ralph Entwisle, and aunt of the present Robert Smalley Entwisle, J.P. She died, and he then married Mrs. Leach, formerly Miss Cocker, daughter of John Cocker, of Tockholes. His only male representative that I know is William T.

Eccles, of White Coppice, near Chorley. George married Miss Harwood, of Darwen. He was a very eccentric man was George, but nevertheless he was one of the best singers Darwen ever produced. If he had kept steady I believe he would have ranked with such men as Santley and Hilton, but he was a fool to himself, and died in the Workhouse. Thomas, brother of John, William, Joseph, and George, died unmarried, at Edenfield, near Haslingden, aged 69. Joseph married Mary Eccles, daughter of old Richard Eccles, of Pole Lane, and left her with one boy, Thomas, now a J.P., and another son, Joseph, who has also become a magistrate, was born to him two or three months after he had died. These two, Thomas and Joseph, are manufacturers at Bottomcroft Mill. Thomas was a member of the Local Board, and, subsequently, a member of the Town Council from 1878 to 1883.[1] Young Joseph's son, Alexander Thomas, is a Town Councillor, and his daughter is the wife of William E. Bickerdike, of Blackburn. Ann, the eldest daughter, married Thomas Briggs, farmer, of Sunnyhurst. She died in 1825, as mentioned above. Alice, the second daughter, married James Harwood, half-cousin to Miss Molly Harwood, and became mother of the late James Harwood, organist at Park Road, Blackburn, who married Miss Sefton, of Blackburn. Mrs. Harwood is well known in Blackburn, having been one of the leading singers of the town for many years. She is now the wife of Mr. J. S. Scott, solicitor. Mary and Betty were successively the wives of Richard Harwood, of Heys Lane, son of James Harwood, of Hoddlesden. The law about marrying a deceased wife's sister didn't trouble these old "Darruners." Betty, the second wife of Richard Harwood, is the only one of nine brothers and sisters now living.

Old John's second wife was a Miss Haworth. By her he had issue —Robert, John, Edmund, Ephraim, Ann, and Mary.

Robert married Isabella Scholes, of Pickup Bank, and had two sons and nine daughters. Of the sons, Joseph married a Miss Walsh, of Holden Fold, and he has two sons living in Pickup Bank. The other, James, was married, but I never knew his family; he went abroad. These daughters seemed to set their affections pretty much in the same direction, for two of them married two cousins of the name of Thomas Grime, and two of them married two more cousins called Lomax. That disposed of nearly half of them, and I daresay many an unhappy father who "has his quiver full of them" would be glad to get rid of his marriageable daughters as easily. I knew eight of them. Isabella I did not know; she died at the age of 12. They were called Betty, Ellen, Peggy,

[1] Thomas Eccles died on the 10th of March, 1888, aged 63 years.

Ann, Nancy, Mary, another Betty, Isabella, and Susannah. There were two Bettys, and "thereby hangs a tale." Betty the elder became the wife of Edward Harwood (Neddy o' Owd Eben's), in October, 1813, and died about the 2nd of January, 1814. She was buried on the first Saturday of January in that year, a day which I remember well, as it was one of the coldest, if not the coldest day of the nineteenth century. Here's where the story comes in. They had a burying and a christening on the same day, the christening having reference to poor Betty's younger sister, who was only a few weeks old. Pole Lane was the place where the "double event" "came off;" they left one Betty in the chapel-yard, and brought another home with them, and thus it happened that there were two Bettys (sisters) in the same family, and for a week or two, both living at the same time. Of these nine interesting girls there is only one now left, namely, the youngest, Susannah. She first married John Harwood, grocer, of Bolton-road, and afterwards became the wife of a man named Muncaster. Everybody knows Mrs. Muncaster. She is a widow now, and noted for her open-handed charity. She has built a school-chapel at Sough, for the Primitive Methodists, with which body she is connected. She never had a family.

John has two sons, Richard and Joseph, living at Chapels, and a daughter, who is the wife of John Eccles, of Tithebarn Street. She belongs to the Lower Darwen Eccleses, but her husband represents another family of the same name.

The third of old John's sons, Edmund, was never married. He went to be a soldier, and after serving in the Peninsular War, under Wellington, came back with a pension, and passed his days in peace.

Ephraim had three sons, John, Joseph, and William, and one daughter, who married Joseph Entwisle, of Blacksnape. John and Joseph both married the same woman—not at the same time, but one after the other. She was Elizabeth, daughter of Thomas Kirkham, of "Harruds," near Hoddlesden. She outlived both her husbands, but is now dead. By her first marriage she had a son, John, who keeps a shop in the Market House.

Mary, daughter of old John, by his second wife, married Samuel Jepson, whose family will come under our notice at some future time. I cannot for the life of me recall who Ann married, but I did know.

I believe I have already said that there are several distinct families of the name of Eccles in Darwen. Having given particulars of one important family, I will now deal with another, and leave the rest untouched. The Lower Darwen Eccleses, of whom I have spoken, came, I am told, from Clitheroe ; the next lot of Eccleses came, as I

OLD DARWEN FAMILIES.

know well, from Walton-le-dale. Whether there was any connection between the Darwen Eccleses and the Walton Eccleses "nobody knows and nobody cares." A child named Richard Eccles was born at Walton, in March, 1758, and brought to Darwen by his parents in 1760. From this child there springs a very important Darwen family. Richard lived to be a good age and had eight children—William, Robert, John, Nathaniel, James, Ann, Mary, and Jane. His wife was Mary Hunt, daughter of Nathaniel Hunt, of Harwood Fold, and cousin to my grandfather, Nathaniel Hunt. Old Richard was a very earnest man in all he said or did. Whether he knew anything about music or not I don't know, but he was one of the most vigorous singers that ever shook the timbers of the old Lower Chapel. They used Dr. Watts's hymns in those days. One Sunday the parson on giving out the hymn announced that two verses would be omitted. But old Richard was not going to have his enjoyment curtailed, so he went on singing the whole of the hymn, and carried both choir and congregation with him. When he was spoken to about it afterwards, he said—"Dr. Watts never med no bits o' hymns, and aw'm nod beawn to leeave ony verses eawt." When old Richard died I don't know, but I knew his children very well, and I will tell you something about them.

William Eccles, eldest son of Richard, had no issue by his first wife. For his second spouse he betrothed Miss Marsden, of Pole Lane, and had four sons—Richard, Marsden, John, and William. He had also a daughter, who, I believe, is living still.

Robert, second son of old Richard, married first Kitty Fish, of Blacksnape, daughter of William Fish, and sister of Fish Fish. His second wife was Alice Kirkham. He had a family of both sons and daughters, but I did not know them well enough to sort them out without making enquiries. Robert and his wife are both dead. I know one of their sons, Dick, and also one of their daughters, both living.

John, third son of Richard, married my cousin, Ellen Hunt, daughter of Robert Hunt, of Chapels, my father's brother. His family consisted of five sons—Robert, Richard, Nathaniel, William and James. Robert's family is extinct. He married Mary Ann Walkden, who died, leaving him with one son, John. This John married Phœbe Holden, of Hoddlesden, but died in Audley, Blackburn, a year or two ago, leaving two grown-up sons and three daughters. Richard is living in Audley to this day, aged 81. He was always best known as "Lime Dick," because he dealt in lime. He married Miss Lightbown, daughter of James Lightbown, of "Brigg End," Grimshaw, Eccleshill. She is dead, but she has left him some children, both sons and daughters, who are living in Blackburn. Nathaniel, the third son of John, died unmarried over 50 years ago. William, the next, is living. He first married Miss Hindle, of Prince's, and afterward Miss Waddicor. He resides at Sunnyfield, near Hoddlesden. The last son of old "John o' Owd Richard's" was James. He married his cousin, a daughter of Nathaniel Eccles, and died, leaving her with seven children. Two of his sons, John and Nathaniel, and two or three of his daughters are living. Still keeping to the family of old John, third son of old Richard, I next come to his three daughters. One married a man named Pickering, another married a man named Marsden—"Jim Monk" they always called him,—and the third, Rachael, is in America.

Nathaniel, fourth son of old Richard, was married, and had a family of three sons and eight or nine daughters. I am sure about eight of the daughters, but not about the ninth, for eight grew up to woman's estate, and four of them are living now—one a widow, one a wife, and two spinsters. The three sons were Richard, Christopher, and John. Richard married Martha Whittaker, daughter of John Whittaker, of Hoddlesden, and has two sons—Nathaniel, of the firm of Harwood and Eccles, Bridge Mill, and John, waste dealer. Christopher married Agnes, daughter of John Whittaker, of Hoddlesden, and has seven daughters, but no sons. John married Miss Eccles, of the Lower Darwen lot, but has no family.

James, fifth son of old Richard, had three sons, Richard, Thomas, and John, and two daughters. Richard, the eldest has been choirmaster at Duckworth-street Chapel for the last thirty years. He is not only a musician himself, but the head of a musical family. James Eccles, professor of music, who has organised and conducted such excellent concerts in Darwen, is one of his sons, and Ralph Eccles, who assists his brother James in the music business, is another. Another son, John, is in America, and I know he used to play the fiddle, so it is quite evident that music runs in the family. There are also four daughters of Richard, sisters to these musicians. Thomas, brother of the choirmaster, and second son of old James died on the 1st of February, 1887. The third, John, died a young man. Old James had two daughters. One of them, Catherine, is living yet.

As to the daughters of old Richard Eccles—Richard the first—Ann became the wife of Ralph Holden ; Mary, the wife of Joseph Eccles, son of Thomas Eccles, of Prince's; and Jane, the wife first of Robert Marsden, and then of Thomas Marsden, both Darwen Marsdens, but not near relatives.

OLD DARWEN FAMILIES.

Messrs. Joseph and Thomas[1] Eccles, magistrates, are representatives of both the Lower Darwen Eccleses and the Walton-le-Dale Eccleses, for they are the sons of Joseph son of Thomas Eccles, of Princes, who belongs to the first family, and of his wife Mary Eccles, daughter of old Richard the first, of Walton-le-Dale.

ECCLES OF LOWER DARWEN, BLACKBURN, &c.

The Eccles family is stated to have had an estate at Eccles Fold, Garsden Fold, and Shorrock Fold in Pickup Bank for about two centuries. Edmund Eccles of Pickup Bank, yeoman, died in March, 1734. Joseph Eccles, of Lower Darwen, webster, married, Aug. 24th, 1702, Ann Cowburne, of Blackburn.

Thomas Eccles and Elizabeth Shorrock, both of Pickup Bank, married Oct. 8th, 1717, and had issue a son Thomas; a daughter Elizabeth, born in 1726, &c.

Thomas Eccles, yeoman, of Pickup Bank and Ecclesbill, resided at Mill Barn farm, his freehold, where the house has initials upon its chimney-piece "T E" (Thomas Eccles), with the date '1737." He married, Oct. 31st, 1739, Martha Haworth, of Pickup Bank, who died July 17th, 1777, by whom Thomas Eccles had sons, Edward, Thomas, and   ; also twin daughters Martha and Mary, bapt. at Over Darwen Chapel, April 28th, 1740. "Thomas Eccles of Pickup Bank, yeoman," was buried at Blackburn, Sept. 18th, 1769.

Mr. Edward Eccles, son of Thomas, was steward to the first Sir Robert Peel for his local estates.

Thomas Eccles, the other son of Thomas, of Pickup Bank in 1771, subsequently settled in Lower Darwen. He engaged in the manufacture of "Blackburn Checks," and he built, about 1774, the "Old Mill" in Lower Darwen for a cotton spinning mill. Mr. Thomas Eccles was also steward to the Sudells of Blackburn. By his wife Mary (who died April 23rd, 1799, aged 58), he had sons, Joseph; Ichabod, died June 6th, 1803, aged 23; William; Thomas, who died in 1791, and whose sons, Edward and Richard, died in infancy; and John; his daughters were, Martha, born in 1778, married to Mr. Robert Boardman, of Blackburn; and Jane, married to Mr. Ralph Shorrock, of Lower Darwen. The father, Mr. Thomas Eccles, died Sept. 11th, 1818, aged 75.

Joseph Eccles, Esq., of Lower Darwen, cotton spinner (eldest son of Thomas), married Mary Livesey, of Darwen, and had issue, sons, Thomas, born in May [April], 1806; Richard, born in 1807; Joseph, of Liverpool; William Eccles, of Blackburn; and Edward Eccles, who died July 2nd, 1872, aged 47, within a week of his marriage; and daughters, Mary, born in 1805, and was killed by a fall at Matlock, May 18th, 1835; and Ellen, married Aug. 18th, 1831, Christopher Shorrock, Esq.

The two eldest sons of Mr. Joseph Eccles, Thomas Eccles and Richard Eccles, Esqrs., are the living chief representatives of this old local family; and are commercially connected in the firm of Messrs. T. and R. Eccles, cotton spinners, of Lower Darwen and Bamber Bridge. Thomas Eccles, Esq., who resides at Torquay, married Miss Mitchell, by whom he has had issue, sons, Alexander Eccles, of Liverpool; Thomas Mitchell Eccles, of Blackburn; Richard Eccles, junior, of Lower Darwen, died, aged 38, in 1875; Eccles Shorrock Eccles, Esq., of Liverpool: and several daughters. His brother, Richard Eccles, Esq., of Highercroft House, has long filled the office of Chairman of the Guardians of the Blackburn Union.

Wm. Eccles, Esq., son of Thomas who died in 1818, had sons, Edward Eccles, Esq., of Liverpool (who married, May 18th, 1837, Mary, second daughter of the late James Pilkington, Esq., of Blackburn, and died in 1875, and whose eldest son is James Eccles, Esq., of London, late of Blackburn); John Eccles, Esq., of Leyland, who married, Aug. 12th, 1824, Elizabeth, daughter of Thomas Ainsworth, Esq., of Preston, and died in 1868; William Eccles, of Bamber Bridge, cotton spinner; and Joseph, who died young.

John Eccles, of Lower Darwen, yeoman (brother of Thomas and William), who had to wife a daughter of Mr. Bannister Pickop, of Tockholes, was father of Bannister Eccles, Esq., of Blackburn, and Joseph Eccles, Esq., of Mill Hill, Livesey. Mr. John Eccles also had two daughters; Martha, the eldest, married Rev. Francis Skinner, M.A., of Blackburn, March 29th, 1837, and died April 16th, 1838, aged 39; the other daughter married Rev. Mr. Smith, a missionary.

Bannister Eccles, Esq., of Blackburn, cotton spinner, &c., eldest son of Mr. John Eccles, married Oct. 13th, 1825, Mary Jane, only daughter of Mr. William Eccles, of Blackburn (she died Decr. 3rd, 1859, aged 61); and had issue, daughters, Sophia, born 1831, died 1832; Elizabeth, born

---

1 Since deceased (see *ante*).

1833, died at Golden Hill, Leyland, Aug. 2nd, 1852; and Harriet Maria, born Oct. 30th, 1838, died in London, aged 34, May 11th, 1873. Bannister Eccles, Esq., died April 17th, 1849, in his 49th year.

Joseph Eccles, Esq., of Blackburn and Mill Hill, Livesey, brother of Bannister, married April 12th, 1831, Frances Coates Parsons, third daughter of Rev. Edward Parsons, and had issue, a son Joseph, born June, died Aug., 1841; and daughters, Catherine, born June, died Dec., 1836; Frances Parsons, married, in 1854, Captain W. B. Elgee, and died Feb. 28th, 1858, aged 24; and Margaret, married, Rev. J. D. Kelly, Vicar of Christ Church, Ashton. Joseph Eccles, Esq., purchased the Mill Hill Estate in Livesey, in 1844; and died aged 60, May 3rd, 1861.

I add some particulars of a branch of this family settled in Over Darwen:—John Eccles, of Pole Lane, Over Darwen (a son of Thomas Eccles of Pickup Bank, who died in 1769), married, first, a Miss Walsh, and by her had issue, sons, Thomas and Matthew [Martha]; and, secondly, Miss Haworth, by whom he had five children. His eldest son, Thomas Eccles, of Princes, Over Darwen, hand-loom manufacturer, born in 1766, died in November, 1824, aged 58 years. By Alice his wife, he had issue, sons, John, who died, aged 68, May 10th, 1859; William, of Low Hill House, Over Darwen, died in Dec., 1829; Joseph; George, died, aged 71, in 1872; and Thomas, died at Edenfield, aged 69, Oct. 9th, 1875. The third son, Mr. Joseph Eccles, of Princes, died, in his 24th year, Dec. 21st, 1822; his wife was Mary Eccles, of Pole, and he was father of Mr. Thomas Eccles, of Hollins, Lower Darwen and of Mr. Joseph Eccles, of High Lawn, Over Darwen, cotton spinner in Darwen and Preston.— *History of Blackburn*, p 475-7.

The Shorrocks.

Shorrocks of Eccleshill, Lower Darwen, and Over Darwen—The Subsidy Roll, 1663—Eccles Shorrock, Merchant and Cotton Spinner—New Mill—Price of Flour in 1817—Alderman Christopher Shorrock, J.P.—Other Shorrocks.

THE Shorrocks of Darwen are a very important local family, and for brevity I cannot do better than quote the following genealogical records from Mr. Abram's History. The family are connected with the townships of Eccleshill, Lower Darwen, and Over Darwen, and Mr. Abram gives the following particulars concerning one branch :—

William Shorrock, of Eccleshill in 1651, was assessed to a subsidy in 1663. He had sons Thomas and James. Thomas Shorrock, of Eccleshill, yeoman, died in 1728. He had sons, Robert and William. William Shorrock, of Eccleshill, born in 1690, died, aged 73, in May, 1764. Thomas Shorrock, of Eccleshill, married, in 1741, Ann Thompson, of Lower Darwen.

William Shorrock, of Lower Darwen, had a son James, born in 1701. I think James Shorrock was father of the next-named Ralph Shorrock, and of James Shorrock.

Ralph Shorrock, of Low Hill, Lower Darwen, yeoman, by Nancy, his wife (she died April 17th, 1817, aged 74), had sons, Ralph ; James, born in 1771 ; John, born in 1775 : and William, born in 1781, died, aged 62, August 22nd, 1843 ; daughters, Jane, Mary, Nancy and Sally. Ralph Shorrock died, in his 87th year, Sept. 28th, 1818.

Ralph Shorrock, of Lower Darwen, yeoman, son of Ralph, married Jane, daughter of Mr. Thomas Eccles, of Lower Darwen, and by her (who died Nov. 1838) had issue ; sons, Ralph, born in 1798, died, unmarried, aged 18, May 8th, 1817 ; Thomas, died, unmarried, in 1832 ; George, born in 1801, died in 1802 ; and Eccles, born in 1804 ; and a daughter Mary, wife of Thomas Ashton.

Eccles Shorrock, Esq., a younger son of Ralph, was the eminent merchant and cotton-spinner of Blackburn and Over Darwen. Mr. Eccles Shorrock acquired a landed estate in Over Darwen, and resided at Low Hill House. He also purchased the Hollinshead Hall and manorial estate in Tockholes. His first wife was Eliza, daughter of Mr. James Bailey, of Witton (she died, aged 46, October 10th, 1850). Eccles Shorrock, Esq., married, secondly, Jane, daughter of John Brandwood, Esq., of Turncroft, by whom he had no issue. He died, aged 49, July 17th, 1853, having made his nephew, Eccles Shorrock, eldest son of Thomas Ashton, Esq., his heir.

JEREMY HUNT'S RECOLLECTIONS OF

I knew Ralph, the son of Ralph, and his brother James, born in 1771. Their brother John I knew also. He had a family, and he worked as a warehouseman at New Mill,[1] but afterwards went to America. The next brother, William (who lived until 1843), I did not know personally, though I knew of his existence. Old Ralph, father of these, I did not know, except as being the grandfather of the late Eccles Shorrock. He would probably live at Lower Darwen, which was rather out of my way. I recollect Thomas, son of Ralph No. 2, very well. He died with his brother, at Low Hill House, and the fourth son of Ralph No. 1, the late Eccles Shorrock, was well known in Darwen. He was born in 1804, and died in 1853. The present Eccles Shorrock (whose real name is Eccles Shorrock Ashton) was his adopted son—the son of his sister Mary, who married Thomas Ashton. He was adopted when quite young, educated by his foster father, and became his heir. Mr. Eccles Shorrock, Junr., is son of Eccles Shorrock (Ashton).

You will observe that the second Ralph Shorrock (son of Ralph) was the father of the late Eccles Shorrock, and it will soon appear that Eccles Shorrock's father was cousin to James Shorrock, great grandfather of Christopher Shorrock, J.P. Mr. Abram continues :—

Another branch of the Shorrocks descends from James Shorrock, of Lower Darwen, brother of the first Ralph Shorrock named above. James Shorrock had sons, Ralph, James, and William Shorrock, of Sough (who by his wife, a daughter of Pickup, of Sough, had a son, William Shorrock, of Sough); and a daughter, wife of James Pickup, of Sough.

James Shorrock, of Chapels, son of James, married Betty Pickup, and by her had sons, James, born in 1776; and Ralph; and daughters, Sarah and Ann. Mr. James Shorrock died in November, 1819.

James Shorrock, of Lower Darwen, was the brother of the first Ralph Shorrock. I knew his sons—Ralph, James, and William Shorrock, of Sough. This James was James of Chapels. William died, I believe, in 1826. James and William married two sisters, Betty and Jane Pickup, and their sister married James Pickup, brother of Betty and Jane—three of one family marrying three of another. William Shorrock, of Sough, had three sons, but I never knew any daughters. The sons were John, Michael, and William. John had four sons and four daughters, but I never knew them. Michael had two sons and five daughters, and I never knew them. William was married, but never had a family.

Now, James Shorrock, of Chapels, had five sons—James, of Princes, born in 1776; John, Michael, Ralph, and William; and two daughters—Ann and Sally. I knew them all very well. Ann became

[1] New Mill was built by the late Eccles Shorrock, in 1835.

the wife of George Briggs. Sarah, who was never married, died at the age of 82 in the house where she was born. James Shorrock, of Princes, is the fourth James in succession from the James born in 1701, mentioned by Mr. Abram. His family is given in Mr. Abram's History as follows, but I remember that he had also a son William, who died when quite a lad, and a daughter Hannah, coming between Sarah and Nancy.

Mr. James Shorrock, of Princes, was eldest son of the last-named James. He married, in 1797, Nancy, daughter of Mr. Christopher Hindle, and by her (who died, aged 71, December 5th, 1849), had issue, sons, Christopher, born Sept. 6th, 1804; James, born April 7th, 1806; and George, born in 1822, died in 1859; and daughters, Betsy, Sarah, [Hannah] Nancy, Mary, Ann and Jane. Mr. James Shorrock died Dec. 28th, 1861.

Christopher Shorrock, Esq., of Manchester, eldest son of James, married, in 1831, Helen, daughter of Joseph Eccles, Esq., of Lower Darwen, and by her (she died in 1837), had sons, Eccles, born in 1832; James, born in 1833 (James Shorrock, Esq., of the Beeches, Bowden, Cheshire, who married Miss Good, of Bowden, but has no issue); and Joseph Shorrock, born in 1834, married Nancy, daughter of Mr. James Shorrock, of Astley Bank; has no issue. Christopher Shorrock, Esq., died March 28th, 1862. His next brother—

James Shorrock, Esq., J.P (of Astley Bank, married, in 1831, Miss Rachel Henrey, and by her (who is yet living) had issue, sons, Christopher, William Henry, Peter, James, Peter; and daughters, Betsy, Nancy, Sarah Maria, wife of Edward Elworthy. Esq.; and Rachel Henrey. James Shorrock, Esq., died April 11th, 1869.

John, son of James of Chapels, had sons—Ralph, Joseph, Michael, and William; and three daughters—Sarah, Jane, and another. Ralph, Michael, and William died unmarried. Their brother James married the daughter of James Shorrock, of Baron Mill, and he has left two sons and a daughter, both living yet. Another daughter grew up, but died. His sons are—John Shorrock, clogger, of Chapels, and Ralph Shorrock, accountant, of Olive-lane. They have each families.

Michael Shorrock, son of James of Chapels, married my sister Mary in 1814, and died in 1817, leaving two daughters. Their second daughter married Timothy Holden, grocer, Duckworth-street, in April, 1839. Timothy died in October, 1857, and she died next month, leaving five children, the eldest 14 years, and the youngest 15 months old. The only one of the five now living is John Holden, of the firm of Holden and Martin, cotton manufacturers. When my sister Mary's husband lay dead in the house in April, 1817, flour was selling at sixpence a pound, for she went out and gave 7s. 6d. for fifteen pounds of flour, to bake bread for the funeral.

Ralph and William, sons of James of Chapels, died unmarried.

As to the daughters of James Shorrock, of Princes, Betsy married Thomas Haydock, of Bolton; Sarah died a young woman; Hannah was the second wife of Thomas Ashton; Nancy married Edward Moore; Mary Ann and Jane died unmarried. An engineer, named Bates, who had a great deal to do with railways and waterworks about here, married Christopher Shorrock's daughter Ellen.

Betsy, daughter of James Shorrock, of Astley Bank, is the wife of Ralph Shorrock Ashton. Nancy married her cousin, Joseph Shorrock, son of Christopher Shorrock. Sarah Maria became the wife of Edward Elworthy, who went to New Zealand; and Rachael Henrey married William Cheetham, now in India.

Mr. Abram concludes his record of the Shorrocks by the following reference to the present Christopher Shorrock, J.P. :—

Christopher Shorrock, Esq., of the Moss, Lower Darwen, eldest son of James, married, in 1863, Jane, daughter of James Chetham, Esq , of Chadderton, and has issue.

Mr. Christopher Shorrock has five sons and two daughters.

There are other branches of the Shorrocks. Ralph Shorrock No. 2 had a brother James whom I knew, at Baron Mill, and there were other brothers too, as I know from descendants they have left. This James Shorrock, who was uncle to the late Eccles Shorrock, had fourteen children, but I only knew twelve—Thomas, William, John, James, Robert, Hannah, Mary, Alice, Jane, Peggy, Nancy, and Ellen. The two others died young. Of the fourteen there are only two living now— Robert and Hannah. Hannah is the widow of George Croft, Mary was never married, Peggy was Mrs. Procter, Nancy the wife of James Marsden, of Union Street, and Ellen the wife of John Worsley.

Ralph Shorrock, druggist, is the representative of another lot of Shorrocks, and the foundry masters represent yet another—all " Darrun " Shorrocks. The Eccleshill Shorrocks are represented by Thomas Shorrock, of the firm of Shorrock and Whewell, Highfield Mill, and James Shorrock, shopkeeper, Railway Road.

The Briggses.

W. E. Briggs, M.P.—Four Brothers and their numerous Descendants—Removal of Two Coffins from Pole Lane Graveyard—Fighting Bill—An Old Inhabitant—George Briggs, of Chapels—Thomas Briggs, of Sunnyhurst—Thurston Briggs, of Hoddlesden—His Fatal Sprint—Drowning of his brother James—"Money Ned's Lot"—Jas. Briggs, fire beater—" Little Tot," alias " Blackburn Times"—Henry Briggs, of Cranberry Fold—John Briggs, of Moss Gap—A. M. Briggs, the Borough Accountant—Noah, the Nonagenarian—John Briggs, of the White Bull, Blackburn—James Briggs, of Bull Hill—The Blackburn Briggses—Three Brothers Marry Three Sisters—George Briggs, of Sunnyhurst—James Briggs, of Blackburn—"Willie" Briggs's Descent—George, of Sunnyhurst's, Funeral—John Slagg, M.P. for Burnley—Cobden and Bright at Blackburn—" Old Lettice."

DARWEN is well stocked with families of the name of Briggs. Mr. W. E. Briggs, ex-M.P. for Blackburn, comes from one branch, but I was once told by a member of the family (who is now 86 years of age) that that branch came out of Yorkshire. All the rest I feel sure are old " Darruners," and I think that " Willie " Briggs's lot are old " Darruners," too. I can trace a lot of the Briggses back to four brothers, named George, Thurston, John, and James, only one of whom (James) I ever knew, as the others died before I was born. The descendants of these brothers, for number, are about on a par with those of the patriarch, " Owd Timothy o'th' Looms "—their name is legion.

George Briggs, the first of the four brothers, lived and died at Ellison-fold, and his body lies in Belgrave Church-yard. He was born in 1731, and died in 1796. He was buried inside Pole Lane Chapel, just at the foot of the pulpit stairs, but when the Pole Lane congregation built Ebenezer Chapel and removed to a spot which has since become the centre of modern Darwen, one of his grandsons got his coffin taken up and transferred to the grave where it now lies in Belgrave Church-yard. His wife died in 1794, and her body was also removed to Belgrave. The gravestone was transferred at the same time. I have walked over it many a time in Pole Lane Chapel, and now it is in Belgrave yard, near the side gate leading into Belgrave Square. Old George had two sons and two daughters. His sons were Robert and James—which was the elder I don't know. Robert married the sister of "Fighting Bill" (Wm. Aspden). Bill didn't play at boxing, he knocked his opponents down, and punched them, too. Robert has a family, but they live towards Whittlestone head now, and a number of the Yateses are descended from him, one of his daughters having married a Yates, while another married a man named Aspden, towards Edgeworth. Another daughter, Sarah, married Henry Livesey, and went to America, where she died. His sons were never married, so far as I recollect, but I am not very sure about Robert, so the name of Briggs died out in old Robert's branch. He had two other sons, Thurston and another, old bachelors, who lived at Bull Hill, so recently as a quarter of a century ago. James (son of Old George) married a woman named Watson, of the Darwen Watsons, and had sons,—George, who died in March, 1853; Thomas, who died, aged 82, on the 4th of February, 1871, and whose memory is perpetuated by a monument in Belgrave Chapel-yard; and James, the youngest, who died before Thomas; besides a number of daughters, among whom I remember Betty, Sarah, Susannah, and Jane. Betty married Thomas Holden (Tum o' Titus's; Sarah married Seth Harwood, and never had a family; Susannah married Nicholas Fish, uncle to the present Nicholas Fish, cabinet maker; and Jane married Michael Whittaker, of Blackburn, whose family are living in Blackburn now. Both Robert and James (sons of Old George) lived in Ellison Fold in my days, one after the other. Old George Briggs had two daughters—Betty and Sarah. William Pickup, of Marsh House, grandfather of Alderman Pickup, married Sarah, and Betty became the wife of Thomas Hindle.

Thurston Briggs (one of the four brothers) had two sons, James and Thurston. I knew James. Thurston, I think, was the elder, but I did not know him personally, although I knew his family. He left two lads. One of them went off for a soldier in 1826, and died in Mauritius, and the other, who died in a decline, was buried, as I remember well, on Holy Thursday, 1828. The soldier, John, had married Alice, daughter of Thomas Grime, of Pole Lane, and he left his wife with two children —a boy and a girl. The "boy" died lately, at a good age, unmarried, and the girl is living in Ashton, married to George Fish. John's brother Thomas was never married, so the name of Briggs died out in Thurston of old Thurston's branch.

John (the third of the four brothers) has a grandson, James, living in Darwen now, aged 86 years and seven days.[1] There were several sons of old John. I never knew them except George. Old James, who is now one of the oldest inhabitants of Darwen, was born before this

[1] This remark first appeared in print on February 26th, 1887.

nineteenth century was two months old. He is the son of George and grandson of John George had another son called Thurston, and a daughter, who is living yet, aged 83.

James (the fourth of the four brothers) was the only one of the four that I knew. He was the youngest, and he was living when I was a boy, which the others were not. He had three lads and two lasses. The lasses both died unmarried. The lads were James, John, and George, and some of their families are living towards Egerton. I met one of old James's great grand-daughters at the Darwen Exhibition, in 1879.

I will now take the families of the "old original" four brothers and trace them down to the present time. We will first take old George who died in 1796. He had two sons, Robert and James. James had a son called George, of Chapels, who died in 1853; and George of Chapels has a son George, living in Blackburn; and George, of Blackburn, leather currier, has two sons, Walter and Richard Henry, who are both married and have families, their children being the sixth generation from George the first. George Briggs, of Chapels, had another son besides George of Blackburn. He was called James, and he died young. George of Chapels had also seven daughters—Betty, who married John Pickup (George Pickup, clogger, Blackburn, is her son); Ann, who married James Watson; Sally, who died unmarried; Nancy, who married James Briggs, of Hoddlesden, and left one son, Thurston Briggs, agent, of Blackburn; another, who married and died, and two others whom I don't recollect. Of the nine children of George Briggs, of Chapels (grandson of George the first), George the third, leather currier, Blackburn, is the only one living. The wife of Old George, of Chapels, was Ann, daughter of James Shorrock, of Chapels, whom I have mentioned before.

Old George, of Chapels, had a brother, Thomas Briggs, of Sunnyhurst. Thomas, had four sons—James, George, John, and Thomas.

James was killed with a cart in 1834, aged 20. George is living in Bolton Road, where his daughters conduct a well-known Ladies' School. John married Hannah Shorrock ("Hannah o' Owd William's"), but afterwards ran away and left her. The old woman is living yet in the same street as me. She has three sons living, James Briggs, commission agent; William Briggs, accountant; and John Shorrock Briggs, plumber. A fourth went to sea, and died at Sydney, a bonny lad of 16 or 17. He was a perfect picture. Thomas, fourth son of old Thomas Briggs, of Sunnyhurst, has four sons, all living, namely, Thomas, who formerly kept the Millstone Inn, James, George, and Thurston. He had also two daughters, Catherine, wife of John Fish ; and Ann (dead), wife of Benjamin Fish. Old Thomas, of Sunnyhurst, had two daughters. One died unmarried, and another married John Smith, a cattle dealer. They are both dead, but they left a son and a daughter. The son is dead, but the daughter, Sarah Ann Smith, keeps a lodging-house in Blackpool.

George, of Chapels, and Thomas, of Sunnyhurst, had another brother called James. He married my cousin Mary, daughter of William Holden, of Cotton Hall. They are both dead, but they left two daughters, who are married and have families.

Continuing my account of the Briggses who are descended from the four brothers who flourished at the end of last century, I will take up again the thread of Old Thurston's lot, because I have finished with George, and have nothing of importance to tell about James and John, except that James Briggs, organist of Bolton-road School, is son of the late James Briggs, bandmaster, grandson of Old James, now living, aged 86, and great-great-grandson of Old John, the third of the original four brothers. Old Thurston had two sons, James and Thurston, and a daughter.

Now, James, the son of Thurston, one of the original four, had four sons, Thurston, James, Thomas and George. I will take up their families in order. Thurston lived to be a good age, and died suddenly on his way from Hoddlesden to Belgrave Chapel one Sunday afternoon. He had been to the morning service and home again to dinner, and was returning to chapel after dinner, when he saw some lads in his meadow. Making a " sprint " after them, he exerted himself too much, dropped down in the road, and died there. He was twice married was old Thurston. His first wife was Kitty Holden, a cousin of mine, who accompanied him to the altar in 1813, and by her he had three children, James, Alice and William. James I have already mentioned as marrying one of old George Briggs's daughters, and leaving a son, Thurston, who is an agent in Blackburn ; so that on his father's side the present Thurston Briggs, of Blackburn, comes from one of the four brothers, and on his mother's side from another of the four. This James, the father of Thurston, married a second time, but died six weeks later, and his widow is still living, childless, on the Lee. Alice married Thomas Briggs, and became the mother of Thomas Briggs, of the Millstone, who is also descended from two of the original four brothers. William died unmarried. Now, Thurston Briggs, of Hoddlesden, the man who dropped down dead in the road, was married twice, as I have already said. His second wife was Alice Duxbury, of Hoddlesden. The descendants of this marriage were Christopher, Ann, Jane, Sarah and Thurston. Christopher has been married twice, but never had a family, He keeps a public-house in Shorrock Fold. Ann and Sarah are dead. Jane is living, twice widowed. Thurston, the youngest, is a commission agent, in Rochdale-road, Manchester. He married Elizabeth Grime, of Darwen, and has a family.

James, second son of James, and brother of the Thurston who dropped down dead, was drowned in the Knott Mill lodge between thirty and forty years ago. His eldest son, James, has been married three times, and, as you might expect, he has a family. He lives on a farm at Edgeworth. Thomas, another son of James of Old James's is also living at Edgeworth. He is married, and has a large family, and some of his children are married, too. Ambrose, another son, was married and had one child, but his wife would not live with him, and he went to America, where he has since died. A fourth son of James of Old James's was Thurston, and a fifth son was John, who died a year or two back. John was married twice. Both his wives came of a family named Entwisle, which supplied half the neighbourhood with wives. Their mother and father (Edmund Entwisle) had both large families when they married each other, and after the marriage there sprang up a third lot. The whole three lots of children were brought up together, and it would puzzle anybody to "sunder 'em out." They were chiefly girls, and they were best known as "Money Ned's lot." There was such a "squad" of them altogether that it became a matter of common talk what a lot of wives came out of that family. John Briggs's family are mostly living about Bury. Christopher J. Beckett's wife is the daughter of John's second wife and John's step-daughter. In addition to his five sons—James, Thomas, Ambrose, Thurston and John—James of Old James's had also four daughters, namely, Alice, who married Timothy Yates; Ann, who married Joseph West, and is now a widow; Mary, who married Moses Neville; and Nancy, who married John Catlow, cotton manufacturer.

The third son of Old James was Thomas, who married a daughter of John Kay, of Grimehills, and had six sons—James, John, Briggs Briggs, Thurston, Henry, Thomas, and four daughters, James, the eldest of the six lads, was a big strong young man, and he used to pick up the lads like dolls. He was married, but died, leaving a family. By occupation he was a fire-beater, at Sough, and one day, when he was cleaning to get off in hurry, he got his hand chopped off in a cog wheel. But he was a brave man, was James, as well as strong, and picking up his hand he walked into the factory with it, and showed his fellow workmen what had happened. He followed his occupation as a firebeater at Guide for many years after he had lost one hand. John, the second of the six, has died lately, at Bury, leaving a family. Briggs Briggs died a young fellow. Thurston is dead. Harry is married, and Thomas married a Miss Duxbury, but is now a widower. Of the four daughters of Thomas of Old James's, two are living on the Lee, unmarried, and the other two are married respectively to a Fish, of London, and a Wood, of Great Harwood. There are four lasses and two of the six lads living yet.

Lastly, there comes George, the fourth son of Old James. He died last year at Farnworth, leaving one son and two daughters, all living at Farnworth. All have been married, but one of the daughters is a widow.

I have said in the introduction to this article that Old Thurston the first had two sons and a daughter. The daughter married a man named Fish. She died and left him with a son, Thurston, and a daughter, Mary. The son was called "Little Tot." He was the first man, so far as I recollect, who went round in Darwen hawking *The Blackburn Times*. He then got the name of "Blackburn Times," and his old *nom de plume* of "Little Tot" was dropped. He had a very large family. Some are dead and some are living. Little Tot's sister Mary was the first wife of John Duxbury, of Huddlesden. She died and left him with a son and a daughter. The daughter is dead, but the son is living at Ashton-under-Lyne, an old man over seventy.

The next lot of the Briggses in importance is the lot that springs from old Henry Briggs, of Cranberry Fold, and his brother, old John Briggs, of Moss Gap. I knew Henry as an old man 70 or 71 years ago. His wife was one of the Kays, of Hill Top, Turton,—an old Turton family. In his younger days Henry was reckoned to be rather a rough and ready character, always at home in a frolic. One night while sitting in a public-house chatting with his friends, one of the company deliberately tried to irritate him, but Henry, to the surprise of the company, pocketed the insult quite composedly, without even a sharp retort. One of his friends afterwards said, " Henry, how happened it tha didn'd ged up and lick yon craytur?" "Eh, mon!" replied Henry, "Awd bin eawt this foornoon wi' t' cart, an getten gradely ill weet, an' aw' wer bun to strip me an' put t' wife's shift on, an' aw' couldn'd forshame t' poo mi cooat off !"

Old Henry had five sons and two daughters—John, Jonathan, Thomas, Henry, Arthur, Ann and Betty.

John, the eldest son of Old Henry, had three sons and six

daughters. The sons were named John, Henry, and Joseph. John married a daughter of Edmund Holden, of Grimehills, and had six sons and three daughters. The only one of the sons I know is a stonemason who lives in Green-street. Henry had three sons and two daughters. Joseph died a young man in May, 1833. Three of the six daughters married three sons of old Thomas Fish, of "Harrud's;" one of them married William Beckett, and another (the eldest) married James Marsden. The youngest of the six is living now in the same street as me, aged about 68. She is the widow of John Longworth. Ann, widow of Thomas Fish the younger, is also living yet.

Jonathan, second son of old Henry Briggs, had three sons—William, Thomas, and Henry, and one daughter. I believe the daughter is dead. William married, but both he and his wife are dead. They left one son and a daughter, who are both in New Zealand. The daughter is the wife of Joseph Maudsley, who was a draper in Market-street, until he went to New Zealand a few years ago.

Henry went to America, and I don't know what became of him.

Thomas, third son, of Old Henry, had five sons—Andrew, Henry, Michael, John, and William; and four daughters. Alexander Milner Briggs, Borough Accountant, and Organist at Duckworth-street Chapel, is the only son of Andrew.

Henry and Arthur, sons of Old Henry, went to a place beyond Manchester, and though they afterwards came back, I have lost sight of their families.

As for Ann and Betty, daughters of Old Henry—Ann married Thomas Duxbury, of Hoddlesden (Tummas o' Owd Kester's), and Betty married Timothy Holden, of Brocklehead. They have each a large family scattered about Darwen.

Old John Briggs, of Moss Gap, was brother to Old Henry, of Cranberry Fold. He had four sons and two daughters—Noah, James, John, and Lot; Deborah and Mary.

Noah lived to be over 90 years of age. He was the oldest of the family, and lived to see all his brothers and sisters buried.

James had a large family of both sons and daughters, but I never knew much of them.

John, third son of John of Moss Gap, died in Blackburn. He used to keep the White Bull Hotel, on Salford Bridge, half-a-century ago. It has been re-built since. One Saturday afternoon, more than 40 years ago, I happened to walk into the porch of Ebenezer Chapel, when I saw a bier with a coffin upon it, standing in the vestibule, as the bearers could not get it inside. I suppose I must have inherited a fair share of curiosity from my ancestress "Mother Eve," for I lifted up the pall to have a peep at the coffin plate, and what should I find there but the name of this John Briggs, of the White Bull, Blackburn.

Deborah married John Harwood. They went to America, and John Harwood was drowned there. Married a man named Bury.

Old James Briggs, of Bull Hill, cousin to John o' Owd Henry's, had two sons, John and James, and they were both married, but I don't know where their families are, though they're somewhere in Darwen. He had five daughters—Jane, Ann, Alice, Phœbe, and another. Three of the daughters were married to three of old Arthur Kay's sons, of Cranberry Fold. I knew them all very well, both lads and lasses.

Now for the Blackburn Briggses, "Willie" Briggs and his relatives. I had some doubts about their relationship with the old Darwen families, so I went to the old woman in our street, who was formerly a Miss Briggs, as mentioned above, and I said to her—"Was Old James Briggs, of Blackburn, anything related to your father?" "Ay," she said, "they were some relation; he used to come up to our house and have a chat did old James, of Blackburn." I "sperred" her a bit more, and as far as I could gather from her, Old George Briggs, of Sunnyhurst, and Old Henry Briggs, of Cranberry Fold, were cousins. Now Old George, of Sunnyhurst, married a Miss Eccles, a descendant of Richard Eccles, who came from Walton-le-Dale in 1760. He had two sons, George and James, and two daughters, Betty and Dorothy. The son James was the James of Blackburn, to whom I have referred. James married Lettice Jepson, daughter of Edward Jepson, of Darwen, and had three sons, George, Edward, and William. George was born in 1806, at Waterside, Eccleshill, and I was born in the same neighbourhood six weeks later. Then his father, James, removed to Blackburn, where his other sons, Edward and William were born. George was married, and had one son and two or three daughters. The son died young, and where the daughters are I don't know. George's wife was a Catholic, and I am told the daughters are in a convent. Their mother, I believe, is still living in Blackburn, a widow. The next son of Old James, of Blackburn (formerly of Waterside), was the late Edward Briggs, cotton manufacturer, of Blackburn, and father of James and William Edward Briggs. Everybody knows "Willie." He represented Blackburn in Parliament nearly a dozen years. A few days ago I was having a chat with Mr. Christopher Shorrock, who said, "I dined with 'Willie' Briggs in Liverpool last Monday. He says he gets *The Blackburn Times* every week, and reads your articles. He also said, 'I see Old Jeremy is on the Briggses next week. I wonder whether he'll give our family or not?'" I told Mr. Christopher Shorrock that they would not come in the first lot of the Briggses, but that they would come in before I had done, and here they are now. I once gave William Edward Briggs his pedigree, showing him to be six generations removed from "Owd Timothy o' th' Looms" (Timothy Holden). I will now show that he is the distinguished representative of two old Darwen families. First, I will take the Briggses.

William Edward was the son of Edward; Edward was the son of James, of Blackburn; James was the son of George, of Sunnyhurst; George, of Sunnyhurst, was an old "Darruner," who died in 1827.

Now take it another way.

William Edward is the son of Edward.

Edward was the son of James, of Blackburn, and of his wife Lettice (formerly Jepson)

Lettice was the daughter of Edward Jepson and his wife Ann (formerly Holden).

Ann Holden was the daughter of Thomas.

Thomas Holden was the son of "Owd Timothy o'th' Looms," who flourished in the oldest portion of Darwen, 200 years ago.

Old James Briggs, of Blackburn, had seven daughters. Four of them are living yet—Mrs. Bruce, wife of Dr. Bruce, of Huddersfield; Mrs. Dewslip, of Lytham, widow of the late Rev. Mr. Dewslip; Mrs. Samuels, of Blackburn, a widow; and Emma, who has never been married.

Old George Briggs, of Sunnyhurst, great-grandfather of William Edward, was buried at Ebenezer Chapel, in 1827, as I said before. I remember his funeral sermon very well. He had selected the text himself, " Let me die the death of the righteous," and I can picture to myself, as well as if it were yesterday, the Rev. Richard Fletcher preaching from it. Old George has no gravestone to perpetuate his memory, but I think, from his appearance, he would be between 70 and 80 years of age, so that his life takes us back to the middle of last century.

Edward Briggs, father of William Edward, married a Miss Slagg, and William Edward is cousin to the present M.P. for Burnley. I remember seeing Edward Briggs's wife at an Anti-Corn Law tea party, in James Street School, Blackburn (Cobden and Bright were there), 42 years since, and having a long chat with her mother-in-law, Old Lettice, about her, and about the family in general. I was on the best of terms with Old Lettice. My eldest sister had been her bridesmaid, and her son George was born at Waterside six weeks before me. We reaped up many an old story, one relating to myself. I was a little bit of a fellow, the son of an old woman, and her son, George, six weeks my senior, was a well-built man, the first-born son of a healthy and blooming couple. Lettice said she could remember well that they used to put her child and me together to show the contrast between us. Be that as it may, George has been dead something like a quarter of a century, and I am well and hearty yet, although 81 years of age.[1]

George, son of old George Briggs, of Sunnyhurst, had one son—George—and three daughters. The son died a young man. One of the daughters is living somewhere about Mill Hill, Blackburn. Another married William Holden, of Cotton Hall, and went to America, but returned. The third died unmarried. George's wife was a Miss Halliwell. I remember their marriage about 70 years since. They sang the wedding anthem for them at Pole Lane on the following Sunday, according to the old-established custom—" Blessed are all they that fear the Lord," set to music by Knapp. George gave the singers five shillings.

The daughters of Old George, of Sunnyhurst, were Betty and Dorothy. Betty married James Entwisle, and Dorothy became the second wife of a man named Bradshaw.

1. Jeremy died July 20th, 1887.

The Leaches.

Richard and John Leach—James Marsden of 1700—"Grandmother Marsden" again—"Billy Go-Deeper"—"Thi feyther spoiled thee"—"Dick o' Jim's o' Harry's"—First Conductor of the Darwen Choral Society—The "King Maker" of the Blackburn Town Council—My Grandfather: his birth and his funeral—Lightbown, Leach, and Catlow—Jeremy Leach, of Portland Street—My Three Cousins—More Mixed Marriages—The Leaches all of one stock.

THE LEACHES are a very old Darwen family, but not a very numerous one. They are all of one stock, and the majority of the Leaches that I know are the descendants of two brothers, Richard and John Leach, who married two sisters, Ellen and Alice, daughters of old James Marsden, of 1700. I never knew Richard Leach nor his wife, for the very good reason that they both died before I was born, and my personal recollections do not take me back further than that important stage of my life. But I knew John Leach, and his wife too. His wife, in fact, happened in the course of events to become my grandmother, and she is no less a personage than my "Grandmother Marsden," on whom I set so great store, because it is through her and not through the Hunts that I claim to be an old "Darruner."

Richard, the eldest of the two brothers, had three sons, James, Jeremy, and Joseph, and five daughters, Catherine, Rachael, Alice, Mary, and Peggy.

James, son of Richard, had four sons, Richard, Jeremy, James, and Edward, and several daughters, but I never knew them. The youngest son, Edward, was the father of Christopher Leach, iron-monger, of Market Street. He (Edward) married Mary Hindle, of Langshaw Head. I never knew whom James or Jeremy married, but the eldest of the brothers, Richard, married a daughter of John Whittaker, of Pickup Bank. This lot of the Leaches lived at "Th' Top o' th' Meadow" farm, Whittlestone Head, at the other end of Sough Tunnel. The tunnel was not there then, but the farm was.

Jeremy, second son of Richard, lived at Langshaw Head, near Hoddlesden, and died there, I believe. He had only one son, Robert, but five daughters. Robert married Ann, daughter of Thomas Fish, of Meadow Head, near Hoddlesden. They had a family, some of whom are living yet. One of Robert's sons was killed one dark night while getting off a train at Accrington. Of the daughters, Mary became the wife of John Holden; Hannah, the wife of William Hutchinson, nicknamed "Billy Go-Deeper;" another married William Thompson, and her grandson, William Thompson, a one-armed man, is clerk at Entwisle's, at Sough; the fourth married Henry Mather; and the fifth, Ann, married an adventitious citizen named Walton, who came to live at Hoddlesden, when Hoddlesden was a bleaching place. "Billy Go-Deeper" (pronounced "Good-eeper") built the Greenway Arms, and got his nickname while the men were digging out the foundation for the cellar walls. He was a shrewd fellow was Billy, a wise man of sterling merit. That includes a good deal, though I don't mean to say he was faultless. He got it into his head that there was a spring on his land, and he kept urging on his workmen to "go deeper," "go deeper," and go deeper they did until they found a spring. He was a Conservative and a Churchman, but a very sensible man, and we could always agree about everything but politics. He once said to me,—"Aw con do no good wi' thee; thi feyther spoiled thee." "Heaw did he spoil me?" I asked, "He med thi think for thisel, and theau's never gi'n o'er!"

Joseph, third son of Old Richard, had seven sons and two daughters. They were my playmates, for we lived under the same roof for twenty years. The sons were Richard, Thomas, John, Benjamin, Joseph, Jeremy, and William; and the daughters, Hannah and Ellen; and there are only two of them, named Jeremy and William, living now.[1] Richard married Miss Aspinall, and he has descendants in Darwen. Aspinall Leach and Joseph Leach are his sons. Thomas married Peggy Isherwood, sister of the late John Isherwood, contractor, and has left a family in the town. One of his daughters is the wife of Mr. Thompson, cotton manufacturer, Woodfold Mill, and I met one of his (Thomas's) sons, Harry, at a concert in Furthergate School, Blackburn, a few weeks ago.[2] John never had a family, though he was married. Benjamin has a family about Waterside. Joseph married a Miss Hurst, from Bank Fold, and his family are spread about Waterside. Jeremy, who is still living, aged three score years and ten, married the daughter of Rothwell Yates, of Jackson House. She is dead, but her children and grandchildren are living in the town. William is also living, aged about 65. He married Nanny Yates, of Belthorn, daughter

---

[1] Jeremy lives in Nancy Street, and William at Waterside.
[2] At this concert Jeremy sang a song.

of Dick o' Jim's o' Harry's, and she is also living yet. That disposes of the seven sons of Joe o' Owd Richards.

Old Richard, as I have said, had five daughters; the first, Catherine, married Thomas Walkden, who died and left her with two sons—Richard and Thomas—and four daughters, who all died young women. I remember them very well. The sons lived at Dewhurst's, at the top of Blacksnape, but were never married, and consequently Catherine's branch is extinct. They were best known as Dick o' Catherine's and Tom o' Catherine's. Rachael o' Old Richard's became the wife of Thomas Duxbury, and they lived at Stand, near Hoddlesden, 70 years back or more. She had several sons, who will be heard of again under the head of the Duxburys. Alice married Briggs Holden, of Aushaw Farm, Entwistle, mentioned in a previous chapter. Mary was never married. Peggy had a son, James Leach, who was organist at the Higher Chapel for more than 20 years, and first conductor of the Darwen Choral Society, formed in 1828, with me and my brother John as two of its original members. This James Leach married Betty, only daughter of John Hutchinson, of Holden Fold, and only sister of "Billy Go-Deeper." She has a nephew in the person of Robert Hopwood Hutchinson, J.P., the "King Maker" of the Blackburn Town Council, whose father, Richard Hutchinson, I knew before he was married.

John Leach, brother of Old Richard the First, as I have mentioned before, was my grandfather. He was born on the 4th of September, 1724, when there were only 699 people in Darwen besides himself, and he died on March 23rd, 1809, when I was three years and a month old. I recollect his appearance and his movements for about twelve months before his death, and his funeral I remember very well. I can call to mind the fact of his dying, and all the bustle of the funeral, and I have yet in my mind's eye a general view of the appearance of the people who attended the funeral. There was one young man in particular. The place where he sat in the house, and the colour of his necktie—red and yellow—are as distinctly imprinted on my memory as if my grandfather had only been buried yesterday instead of seventy-eight years ago. I don't know who he was, but as he sat on one side of the house on a three-legged stool his red and yellow tie attracted my childish attention, and made me take more notice of him than any other person at the funeral. I had a very good eye for colour, and the first sensation I ever recollect was produced by colours. John Leach's family consisted of an only son, Jeremy, and six daughters, Catherine, Ellen, Rachael, Mary, Ann, and Peggy.

Jeremy, the son of John, married Sarah, daughter of Nathaniel

Hunt, of Harwood Fold, Eccleshill, cousin to my grandfather, who was also a Nathaniel Hunt. He (Jeremy Leach) had six sons and six daughters—John, Nathaniel, James, Robert, Jeremy, and George; Alice, Ann, Ellen, Peggy, another Ann, and Sarah. John, the first of the dozen, got married, but both he and his wife died without issue. Nathaniel married Kitty, daughter of James Yates, and died in November, 1830, leaving her with two sons and three daughters. Kitty died a year or two later. James died unmarried. Robert died a child. Jeremy and George, the two youngest of the six lads, are living now. Alice, the first daughter of Old Jeremy of Old John's, married John Hollis, whose family are living in Darwen. Ann died a child. Ellen married John Shorrock, but died without family. Peggy married George Pilkington—both are dead, and they have left no family. The second Ann died a young woman, unmarried, more than sixty years ago. Sarah married James Hunt. She has died lately, leaving a family, some of whom are living about Mill Hill, Blackburn.

Let us trace the descendants of these twelve children a little further. The second of them, Nathaniel, had a son, Jeremy, born in 1819, and this Jeremy is living on the Lee. This Jeremy, grandson of Jeremy of Old John's, has had two sons and two daughters. His eldest son Nathaniel, died a young man. The other, John Frederick Leach, is manager at Graham Fish's cotton mill. The two daughters are living, unmarried. Nathaniel left another son, Eli, who is a member of the firm of Lightbown, Leach, and Catlow, cotton manufacturers. The fifth of the six sons of Jeremy o' Owd John's was Jeremy. He was born on January 26th, 1806, just a month before me, and he is living yet, in Portland-street, off Bolton-road. I was born on the 27th February in the same year. We were both christened on the same day, and we were both christened alike. My mother says I was christened Jeremy, but sometimes, for fear of offending an old man's feelings, people send letters to me addressed "Jeremiah Hunt, Esq.," and in writing back I sometimes sign my name "Jeremiah," for fear of wounding their sensitive feelings. This Jeremy Leach is uncle to Old Jeremy Leach on the Lee. He married Alice, daughter of Thomas Kirkham, of Harrud's, and has two sons and two daughters living. Both his sons are married and have families. George, the sixth of the sons of Jeremy of Old John's, is living in Vernon-street with one of his daughters.

Turning back to the six daughters of Old John the First, who must not be confounded with the six daughters of Old John's son Jeremy, I will take first Catherine. She married Benjamin Kirkham, and died in 1807, leaving him a legacy of five sons and six daughters.

OLD DARWEN FAMILIES.

Ellen, the second daughter of Old John, had the distinguished honour of being my mother. She married Nathaniel Hunt, of Eccleshill, grandson of the John Hunt who came from Samlesbury, and she had a family of four sons and five daughters. I happened to be the youngest of the nine, and though I could never gain a day on my brothers and sisters, I have outlived them all, and if I live a year longer I shall be the oldest as well as the youngest.[1]

Rachael, third daughter of Old John, married William Holden, whose family of three sons and six daughters I have given in a previous chapter.

Mary, fourth daughter of Old John, married Henry Whittaker, of Darwen, and had three sons and five daughters. One of the daughters is Mary, widow of Richard Butterfield, and mother of Mr. Butterfield, druggist, Nova Scotia, Blackburn. She is a cousin of mine. I have had a lot of uncles and aunts, and a swarm of cousins, but I have only three cousins left, and she is one of then. The other two are Jeremy and George Leach, sons of Jeremy.

Ann, fifth daughter of Old John, married James Hunt, the only son who grew up of Nathaniel Hunt, of Harwood Fold. My uncle Jeremy married his sister, and he returned the compliment by marrying my uncle Jeremy's sister. She (Ann) had two sons and three daughters.

My aunt Peggy, the last of Old John's daughters, died 80 years ago. She was the wife of James Pickup, natural son of old John Pickup, of Sunnyhurst, and had two sons, John and James, and three daughters. John married Betty, daughter of George Pickup, of Chapels, who died and left one son, George Pickup, clogger, King-street, Blackburn. James married twice, and has left a family in Darwen. Of Peggy's daughters, Alice, the eldest, was married to James Aspden, of Sough, and she died three years ago, aged 85. She was the oldest in the family, and lived the longest. Her family are living in Darwen. Margaret, her next sister, was blind. She lived to be an old maid of four score summers. Martha, the third, was brought up with me. My father took her "to play with me" when her mother died, and, when she grew too old for playing, she was married from our house, to John Holden, who died in 1831, leaving her with two daughters and one son, Jabez Holden, who lives in Railway-road. Both the daughters are dead. but have left families. One of them I mentioned before, as being the mother of Mrs. Joseph Maudsley, who went to New Zealand.

My grandfather, John Leach, had two sisters, and I think there was a third. One of them married a man named Knowles, and the

[1] He did not live a year longer.

other a man named Woodcock. David Knowles, of Blacksnape, a well-known Darwen man who died a few years ago, was a grandson of the Knowles who married my grandfather's sister. The Woodcocks are still to be found in the town.

I will soon sum up the rest of the Leaches, and show that they all sprung from the same stock. There is an old man named John Leach, at Chapels. His grandfather and mine were cousins. The late Robert Leach, of Prospect House and Barley Bank Mill, had a grandfather who was also cousin to my grandfather. Robert's sister married the late Pickup Hartley, grocer, of Blackburn, and I believe her sons now run the Barley Bank Mill. There was an old man named Robert Leach who lived at Pickering Fold 70 years back. He was another of my grandfather's cousins. He had a son called George, but I never knew what became of him, and he had also three daughters. One of them became Mrs. Dugdale, of Pickering Fold; another was the wife of Ralph Shorrock, of the Darwen Shorrocks; and the third was the second wife of Joseph Scholes, of Pickup Bank. I knew all the three very well. There are a number of Leaches at Pickup Bank, who are descended from yet another of my grandfather's cousins, and there is a William Leach in Union-street, whose great-grandfather was cousin to my grandfather. There is a gravestone in Pole Lane Chapel-yard showing that this William Leach died in 1817. His wife was Mary, daughter of Old Titus Holden, and she died in 1825. Their sons were named Titus, Timothy and Robert. The last was never married. Titus was married and had a family; he went to a place beyond Manchester in 1826; what became of the family I do not know, but I think there are none of them living in Darwen. I knew one of the daughters named Mary, and a son named Richard, but they have passed out of the range of my observation. Timothy, the other son of Old Titus, buried some of his sons, but there are two living now—William, by his first wife, and Joseph, by his second,—and their families are living in Darwen. Joseph has only one daughter living, but William has both sons and daughters. If I could only go a bit further back and sort out these cousins we should soon bring all the Leaches in Darwen back to one common father.[1]

[1]. My friend, Mr. W. Hulme, of Blackburn, has kindly copied for me, from an old family Bible, the following list of the "children of T. Leach, of Dee Eye Farm":—Betty, born April 8th, 1802; John, born March 23rd, 1807; Mary Ann, born January 24th, 1813; Rebecca, born May 30th, 1815; Thomas, born January 22nd, 1818; Matthew, born October 17th, 1821; James, born April 14th, 1825; Alice, born January 13th, 1827.—J.G.S.

The Hindles.

Christopher Hindle of Cowbarrows and Holker House—Holker House, Hoddlesden, 1591—Shorey Bank Farm—"Th' Duke o' Darrun"—Local Horse Races—Cock Fight at Chapels, under the patronage of the Earl of Derby—The Hindles of Blackburn—George Hindle, Organist—His Violent Death—James Walsh, a noted local preacher—Tragic Event 99 years ago—Old James of 1700 again—"Owd Billy o' Ralph's"—"Little Tot"—Peace-Egging 60 years ago—New-foundland—Lively Times in Australia—"Owd Triangle"—Conversion of a Catholic Chapel into an Inn—Dr. Geo. Hindle, Medical Officer for the Borough—Fred. G. Hindle Magistrates' Clerk—Thos. Hindle, founder of the Lancashire Football Association.

MOST of the Hindles of Darwen—I may say all,—are descended from a Christopher Hindle, of Cowbarrows and Holker House, Hoddlesden, yeoman, who was born probably about the reign of Charles II. I have lately seen a deed dated 1744, by which the Cowbarrows farm was conveyed to this Christopher Hindle, towards the close of his life, and Holker House, at Hoddlesden, belonged, until very lately, to his descendants. He would be the great great-grandfather of Dr. Hindle, our Medical Officer of Health, who, when he built his present residence, about twenty years ago, named it Holker House, after the old place at Hoddlesden. This is described by Mr. Abram in his "History of Blackburn Parish," as "an old messuage standing at the upper end of the hamlet of Hoddlesden, having a gabled porch, over which is a stone dated 1591." The Thomas Hindle mentioned by Mr. Abram as having been born in 1758, was Dr. Hindle's grandfather. He resided at Shorey Bank, which he sold with the farm to the late Mr. James Greenway, about a year before I was born—1805. Shorey Bank Farm at that time included the fields on which the present Market House and the greater part of Market Street have since been built. His son George, who was born in 1791, married Betty, the daughter of John Duxbury, of "The Knowle," Darwen Chapels, who was then a "putter-out" of pieces to handloom weavers, and locally known as "Th' Duke o' Darrun." He was a well known character in his time, and I remember him very well. He was a great patron, indeed, he was the starter, of the local horse races, which were

JEREMY HUNT'S RECOLLECTIONS OF

then held in a large open field, on part of which Duckworth Street Chapel has since been built, and a pair of silver spurs won in one of these races are still preserved in the family. He was also very fond of cockfighting, which was a very popular sport in Darwen about the beginning of this century. I remember on one occasion there was a great "main" fought in a field at Darwen Chapels, at which the Earl of Derby, the grandfather of the present Earl, and other sporting characters from Preston, attended, some of the Darwen birds being widely celebrated for their "gameness" and courage. Nancy Hindle, who was born in 1778, married Mr. James Shorrock, of Princes, grandfather to Alderman Christopher Shorrock, J.P.

Christopher Hindle, the head of the family, had four sons—John (born in 1745), Christopher, James, and Thomas. The first son, John, of 1745, whom I will call John the first, had four sons—Robert, John, Christopher, and William.

Robert, son of John the first, removed to beyond Blackburn, and I fancy some of the Hindles of Blackburn are his descendants, but more than this I cannot say with certainty.

John, son of John the first, was married twice. His first wife was Rachael Scholes, of Pickup Bank, by whom he had two sons and six daughters; and his second wife was a cousin of mine, Miss Pernall Hunt, daughter of Robert Hunt, who increased his family, in course of time, by the introduction of four more sons and four more daughters—total, sixteen children.

George was the eldest of John the second's sixteen children. He was married three times—first to Alice, daughter of James Kay, of Pike Low, who died in 1837, leaving him a son and two daughters. The daughters both died unmarried, and the son, John, died about six months ago without family. John's wife was a sister of Joseph Slinger. George's second wife left him two or three children, of whom there is one living, and he had no children, so far as I am aware, by his third wife. The descendants of this triple marriage are therefore reduced to one. One off-shoot of his second marriage, George Hindle, was organist of Withnell Church. By trade old George was a street pavior, in the latter part of his life, though he was brought up, like most other folks, as a handloom weaver. He was a remarkable man was old George. For more than twenty years he was choirmaster at the United Methodist Free Church, Duckworth Street, which is now about to be pulled down and rebuilt. He was a rough-and-ready chap, with no French polish about his manners, but for all that he was one of the best trainers of a choir I ever knew. He was an old pupil of mine, and used to lead the singing class trained by me at Pickup Bank. He met with a violent death in the spring of 1864. He had taken a farm in Withnell, and, in the spring of the above-named year, he was leading a young cow when he got his feet entangled in the rope and was dragged along the ground for a considerable distance, and so injured that he died without recovering consciousness.

John the Third, brother of old George, and son of John the second, married Jane Wood, of Pickup Bank, and died before her, leaving her with three or four children, some of whom are still living.

The five daughters of John the Second, by his first wife, were Mally (Mary), who became the wife of the late John Whalley, fish-monger; Martha, wife of Thomas Duerden, of Ellison Fold-lane; Betty, wife of Edmund Harwood, who is still living in Audley, Blackburn, with some children; Ann, living in Blackburn, widow of Thomas Thompson; Ellen, who married, first, George Wood, and secondly John Walsh; and Rachael, who became the wife of John Jepson.

The remaining eight of John the Second's sixteen children can be summed up easily. William married the daughter of Marsden Hindle, of Hoddlesden, and both are dead. Robert died without family, and his widow is married again. Jeremy is living unmarried. Nathaniel died a child. Hephzibah became the wife of a man named Barlow. She has died lately, leaving a family in Blackburn. Esther is the widow of John Wood, of Hoddlesden, and has five or six children. Mary Ann, wife of James Waddicor, of Redearth-road, has a family; and Peggy, who was brought up beyond Manchester, is also married, I believe, and has a family. One of her aunts, living beyond Manchester, adopted her when her mother died.

Christopher, third son of John the First, married Miss Aspden, sister of " Owd Feightin' Bill," and had five sons and two daughters—Robert, Andrew, Thomas, James, and Christopher: Alice and Nancy. Robert was the eldest, and he was never married. Thomas has died this month [March, 1887], unmarried. James Hindle, late of Hindle-street, to which he gave the name, married Miss Richardson, and she is living, with a family. Christopher married Mrs. Yates, of the Griffin Inn, Hoddlesden, but had no family. Alice died unmarried, and Mary married Edward Leach, mentioned in a previous chapter as the father of Christopher Leach.

William, fourth son of John the First, married a daughter of James Walsh, who was a noted local preacher amongst the Methodists, about 60 years ago, but I believe he died without issue.

These four sons of John the First had an only sister, Betty. She became the wife of George Duxbury, who used to play the organ at the Higher Chapel, nearly a hundred years ago.

Christopher, brother of John the First, and second son of Christopher the First, had two sons, James and Ralph, and a daughter, Nancy. His eldest son, James, married four times. His first wife was Ann Beckett, of Yate and Pickup Bank, by whom, I believe, he had six sons and four daughters. His second wife added one son, Andrew, who is living yet, but his third and fourth only increased the family by their own presence. While old James was enjoying the society of his fourth wife, he used to say he would be wed again when she died, but she outlived him. Without going into particulars of Old James's descendants, I may mention that his grandson, Joseph Hindle, violinist, of Redearth-road, is his principal representative.

Old Christopher, son of Christopher, came by a violent death, just 99 years ago last Saturday, by the ecclesiastical mode of reckoning. You know that Mid Lent Sunday is Fig Pie Sunday; a hundred years ago everybody had fig pie on that day. Well, on the day before Fig Pie Sunday, in the year 1788, Old Christopher's wife was making fig pies, and her husband went out to fetch her some turf from the barn to put under the oven. They lived at Princes. When he got outside Old Kess saw some lads setting his field on fire, and set off at a run after them. Owing to the smoke and the glare of the fire, he ran headlong into a pit and was drowned. He left his wife with two children, James and Nancy, mentioned above, and a third, Ralph, was born a few weeks after his death. Ralph enlisted when a young man, and while soldiering in Manchester he married a wife. After her death, and when he had returned home from the wars, he settled down in his native place and married Mary, widow of Joseph Eccles, of Princes, and daughter of that old Richard Eccles who came out of Walton-le-Dale. Ralph had sons named Ralph and James. Both had families. Ralph, who has been a "great talking chap" in his day, is living yet. By his second wife Ralph the First had one daughter, who married William Whewell, but died a few weeks after marriage. One of Ralph's daughters married Robert Smalley, manager at Bottomcroft Mill; another married Joseph Duxbury; a third, Nancy, married John Kirkham; and, I think, there is another somewhere.

I have next to deal with the descendants of two old "Darruners," James and Thomas Hindle, the third and fourth sons of old Christopher the First. James married Hannah Marsden, daughter of Old James of 1700, and sister to my grandmother. He had three sons, James, Thomas, and Marsden; and one daughter, Rachael.

OLD DARWEN FAMILIES.

James, the son of James, married Miss Entwisle, daughter of old William Entwisle, of Catleach, best known as "Owd Billy o' Ralph's." He had two sons and five daughters. His sons were Marsden and Seth. Marsden went to America and died there; Seth died in Darwen some years ago. Of the five daughters, two married two cousins of the name of Bury; two others married two brothers of the name of Lightbown, sons of old Henry Lightbown, collier, of Dandy-row, best known as "Owd Harry Dep;" and the fifth died unmarried. Nancy, who married Jack Bury, is living yet, and one of her sisters is living with her.

Thomas, son of James, married Miss Walsh, of Blacksnape, and had five sons and six daughters. The sons were named James, John, Blake, Thomas, and Henry. James died young, and left one son, who is also dead, but has left a family. John was married three times. His first wife was Betty, daughter of Christopher Duxbury, of Hoddlesden. She died young, and left one son, Thomas Hindle, a well-known cornet-player of the Darwen Rifle Band, who is now living at Witton, Blackburn. John's second wife was Elizabeth, daughter of Thurston Fish, best known as "Little Tot," or "Blackburn Times," and his third wife was the widow of Aaron Hunt, of Eccleshill. She is living yet, but John is dead. I cannot exactly sort out John's descendants, but I believe he had three families by his three marriages. Blake, the third son of Thomas of old James's, is dead, but he has left a family. Thomas, the next, I never knew, but I believe he married and left a family. Henry never was married. The eldest of old Thomas's daughters was Hannah, who became the wife of of old James Eccles, a well-known character, mentioned before. Of the whole six girls, in fact of the whole eleven children, there is only one living—the youngest. She is over 70 years of age.

Marsden Hindle, third son of Old James, married as his first wife the daughter of Henry Jepson, of Hoddlesden,—a man unknown to the present generation—and as his second wife, Peggy Duxbury—"Peggy o' Owd Kester's." By his two wives he had three sons and three daughters—I don't know which belonged to which. The sons were James, John, and Timothy, and the daughters—Jane, Alice and Rachael. James married Martha, daughter of Thomas Kirkham, of Harwood Farm, and he is now living at 101, Ribbleton-lane, Preston. James died a young man, unmarried. Timothy married a daughter of Joseph Leach of Hoddlesden. He died some years ago, but left a family. Jane married Benjamin Walsh, best known locally as "Cotty." They are both dead, but have left a family. Alice became the wife of William Hindle, son of John Hindle No. 2; their fathers were cousins. They are both dead, but they have left about two children behind them. Rachael is the wife of Christopher Harwood, of Pickup Bank, farmer.

Rachael, daughter of Old James, married a man named Entwisle. One of her sons, Anyon, was a well-known local character, particularly notable for composing peace-egg songs, and for going a peace-egging 60 years ago. When he got tired of peace-egging, he went to Australia, with his two lads, in 1827. Australia was then commonly spoken of as the New-found-land. Australia didn't agree with him, for he was killed there by the aborigines, and one of his lads, who was bound apprentice over there, was so ill-punished by his master that he died. The other lad came back to Darwen, and said they might go to a new found land as would, but he'd stop in one as were hard worn before he'd go again. Old Anyon used to be called "Pigeon Anyon" in Darwen. He was a regular blade, full of all kind of tricks and mischief, but he couldn' stand the tricks of the native Australians. His son used to tell when he came back that when the natives attacked their cabin he hid under the bed, but his father stood his ground and was killed. The natives, having killed his father, probed the bed with their spears to see if there was anyone there, but he crouched in a corner and escaped unhurt. Old Rachael had other sons beside Anyon. I remember Marsden and Caleb, but no more.

Old Thomas Hindle, one of the four sons of Christopher the First, married for his first wife a daughter of George Briggs, of Ellison Fold. I didn't know his second wife. Thomas died at Linswithins Bar, on the Blackburn and Haslingden-road. He was a curious old character was Thomas, and from the three-nooked answers he used to give to questions that were put to him he got the nickname of "Owd Triangle." He had four sons—George, John, James, and Christopher, and two daughters that I knew.

George, son of Thomas, was a farmer at Sunnybank, but afterwards kept the Black Horse Inn in Redearth Road, which he purchased about 40 years ago, when it was a Catholic Chapel, and got the license for it. The Catholics for many years afterwards conducted their religious services in an upper room of this Inn. His wife was Betty, daughter of John Duxbury, of the Knowle Farm, whom I have referred to. He had two sons, George Hindle, surgeon, of Holker House, Railway-road, Medical Officer of Health for Darwen, and John Hindle. Dr. Hindle married Miss Ingham, daughter of a paper manufacturer near Bury. He has two children, a daughter named Janet, and a son named James.[1] John married a Miss Alice Chadwick, and has six sons and one daughter. Fred. George Hindle, the lawyer and magistrates' clerk, is the eldest of his sons. Another, Joseph, qualified as a doctor, went to Canada, and, I believe, died there. Thomas Hindle, accountant, the founder of the Lancashire Football Association, is a third. William, who is articled in the office of his brother the lawyer,[2] is another; another, Edwin, is a wholesale cattle dealer; and yet another, John, is in Australia. Janet, the only sister of these six brothers, is living unmarried, with her parents.

John Hindle, son of Thomas, had four sons and six daughters. Dr. George Hindle, junr., of Green-street East, is one of the sons; the others are Thomas, Peter, and John. There are four of John's daughters living and two dead. One of the four is unmarried, and lives with her mother in Green-street East; another is the wife of Joshua Watson, grocer, Market-street. Old John's widow is living in Green-street East, just opposite me, aged about 79 years.

There is a James Hindle, cousin of William Hindle, mentioned above, and he married William's widow (formerly Miss Walsh). I said I thought he had no family, but I have since discovered from the old lady who lives opposite me that he left one son, who went to Manchester. He is dead. James, the second husband of Miss Walsh, had one daughter, who is the wife of Park Hacking, newsagent.

Christopher was the fourth son of "Old Triangle." Joshua Hindle, clogger, Nova Scotia, Blackburn, is the only one of his family that I know.

One of "Old Triangle's" daughters was the wife of Richard Smalley, of Hey Fold, and the other was the wife of Joseph Bentley, wheelwright.

1.—He died in June, 1888.
2.—William, in 1888, obtained a practice in London.

The Hunts.

Migration of the Hunts from Samlesbury—Death of my Grandfather, 128 years ago—My Grandmother's Dream—Family Names: "Nathaniel" and "Jeremy"—Fifty-two Turton Fairs—Poachers in a Funeral Procession—Nancy's Feat of Strength—A faint-hearted Recruit—"Owd Dinner Bag"—My Brothers and Sisters—Another old woman's Superstition—Bitten by a Mad Dog.

MY great-great grandfather, Nathaniel Hunt, who migrated from Salmesbury into Eccleshill, something like 200 years ago, was the first Hunt of Darwen. He brought with him his wife and two sons—John and Robert. I imagine John was the elder. John married Rachael Ratcliffe, of Whitehall, and had two sons and three daughters—Nathaniel, John; Margaret, Ellen, and Ann. Ann, the youngest, was the only one of the family I knew, although Nathaniel, the eldest, was my grandfather. Both my grandfather and his brother John died in 1759. I never knew whether John had a family or not, but I suppose he hadn't, or I should have heard something about his descendants.

Nathaniel Hunt, grandson of Nathaniel, from Samlesbury, and my grandfather, had five sons and one daughter, the daughter being born in September, 1759, about three weeks after his death. When the girl was born, my grandmother, Nathaniel Hunt's wife, had a fever, and during her convalescence she dreamed that she had just 21 years to live. My father was then a year and eight months old, having been born in 1757, and of course he was a man at the expiration of 21 years. Towards the end of the term allotted to my grandmother's life she began to show symptoms of decay and my father fetched the doctor to her. But the old woman had thoroughly made up her mind that doctors could do her no good, and repeatedly told my father it was no use, as her time was up. Singularly enough she pined away and died at the end of the twenty-one years, and so her dream was fulfilled. I am a great lover of folk-lore and tradition, but I have never given much credit to the superstitions which were so common among the primitive inhabitants of this valley. In the case of my grandmother I do not believe she would have died if the superstitious feeling had not taken such a hold of her mind and assisted her to "shuffle off this mortal coil," when a more healthy and hopeful mind would probably have pulled her round. My grandfather's five sons were John, Robert, Nicholas, James, and Nathaniel, and his only daughter was named Rachael. Rachael became the wife of Joshua Beswick, of Chapels. I will deal with her five brothers more fully.

John, eldest son of Nathaniel, was twice married. His first wife was a Miss Galloway, from Grimshaw Park, by whom he had one son called Nathaniel. "Nathaniel" is the principal name among the Hunts, and I don't think you can find a Nathaniel in Darwen that I cannot trace back to some member of our family. On the other hand "Jeremy" comes from the Leaches, and I should think every Jeremy in Darwen is a relation of mine through my connection with the Leaches. To resume, the second wife of my uncle John was Ann Holmes, of Lower Darwen, by whom he had two sons and three daughters—James and John; Mary, Nancy, and Betty.

Nathaniel, eldest son of my uncle John married a woman from Belthorn and had eight sons—John, James, William, Andrew, George, Nathaniel, Doctor, and Aaron—and two daughters. The only one of the ten children living is Nancy, who is the wife of Thomas Nowell, quarrymaster and builder, of Tockholes. John, Andrew, and Nathaniel died old men, unmarried, and were all buried in St. James's Churchyard, at Chapels. James was killed at Belthorn many years ago, but he has left a family in Blackburn. Jacob Hunt who used to work at Harrison's, in "Novas," was one of his sons; and John, another son, was engineer for Coddington's, at Crossfield Mill, Blackburn, and was killed there; and George, another son, kept the Duke of York, at Eccleshill, Waterside. William is the man about whom I have received a letter, printed below. George, who died twenty-six years ago, left a family, and Nathaniel Hunt, grocer, Heys lane, and James Hunt and William Hunt, both overlookers at Bamber Bridge, and Mary Ann Dorsett, wife of John Dorsett, overlooker, of Olive lane, Darwen, are the only children living. Doctor married a daughter of John Yates, better known as "Cock o' Nancy's." He has a son, John, who has now settled down in Blackburn, after spending sixteen years in Bombay, India. Aaron married a daughter of Nathaniel Baron, of Brick House, near Black-a-Moor. He died and left a family, and his widow became the third wife of John Hindle, who is now living in Park-road, Darwen.

Mary married Andrew Lomax, died and left a family; James, a collier, living at Burnley; and Nathaniel, a collier, living at Holden Fold, Darwen; and Nancy (Mrs. Nowell) is living at Tockholes at the present time, an old woman. I have received the following interesting letter from a granddaughter of William Hunt, mentioned above. I print it here with a few remarks thrown in.

24, Walsh street, Blackburn, April 4th, 1887.

SIR,—After reading *The Blackburn Times* I find you are going on to the Hunts next week, and, being a descendant from the Hunt family, I wish to make a few remarks. My mother was the daughter of William Hunt, formerly of Eccleshill, and late of Black-a-moor, who died about 15 years ago, and was buried at St. James's, Black-a-moor, aged 73 years. He was better known as Old Billy Woods, or Billy for Turton, through going to Turton fair for 52 years together. My mother's name was Peggy Ann. She was the daughter of William Hunt, and was christened at St. James's, Chapels, by a minister called Dunderdale, who would not christen her name Peggy without Ann to it. She died in April last year, and was buried at St. James's, Black-a-moor, aged 65 years, She was the wife of Andrew Bury, who died in December, last year. When my mother was living she heard us read one of your first sketches in the paper, and she often wondered whether you were present or not when Joseph Hague preached his farewell sermon at Belgrave. [It was the *funeral* sermon of Joseph Hague, and, as he couldn't very well preach it himself, it was preached by a parson named Jones, from Bolton.] She was present with two of Gillibrand's daughters, from Grimshaw Bridge—[I know the Gillibrand lasses very well]—she being living there at that time, and she wondered if you could remember where he took his text from in the Bible. She said the place was so full that everybody could not get inside, and that he preached outside in a cart—[It was a bit of a scaffold that he preached from; they could not get a cart in Belgrave yard]—and took his text from the 1st Book of Chronicles, 4th chapter and 9th verse, and I have heard her repeat the words in the verse. She also said that the minister was a very delicate man, and that sweat dropped from his brow while he was preaching. [It was a terribly hot day.] We have often thought of writing to you since her death, to see what you thought of it. My mother had one brother, who is living yet at Black-a-moor; his name is Nathaniel Hunt, and he is living with his sister, both of them being unmarried. Another sister, Alice Baron, wife of James Baron, is living in Blackburn, and one sister died quite young. That was all Old Billy's family.—I remain, yours truly,   ESTHER ANN BURY.

To Mr. Jeremy Hunt.

James, half-brother of my cousin Nathaniel, and second son of my uncle John, has been dead many years. He left a son, Nathaniel, farmer, at Waterside, who has died lately; another son, James, who married Sarah Leach, my cousin, and was killed some years ago by falling off a hay-mow at Black-a-moor. James's family are living at Mill Hill. I met one of his daughters the other Sunday. She came to me in the street, saying, "You don't know me, though I'm akin to you." She is living in Victoria-street, Mill Hill, and belongs to a lot that I have previously mentioned as having settled at Mill Hill. My cousin

James had also a son John, who has died lately; and another, Henry, who only lived to be ten years of age. I remember his funeral taking place sixty years ago My brother was there, and there were also in the funeral procession two brothers, named Thomas and James Baron, of Newfield, Black-a-moor, Lower Darwen, who were noted old poachers. The coffin was being carried at the usual mournful speed along the road from Black-a-moor to Lower Chapel, when a hare was observed to flit across the path. Like a shot the two poachers darted after it, and were soon lost to view. The rest of the procession moved slowly on, and the service was being solemnly conducted in the Lower Chapel when in stalked the poachers to continue their mourning, having been disappointed in their sport. This ludicrous incident happened at the funeral of Henry Hunt, son of my cousin James. I believe there was yet another son, Robert, and two or three daughters whom I didn't know personally.

John, third son of my cousin Nathaniel, went off for a soldier and served seven years in Canada. He came over to Darwen to see my father on his return in 1814, and he said it was so cold in Canada that he had never heard the cuckoo during the whole seven years. The only one of John's family that I know is Jesse Hunt, shoemaker, of Lower Darwen, but Jesse has three sisters,—Betty, wife of John Baron; Ann, wife of Henry Longworth; both of Stopes brow, Lower Darwen; and Ellen, who resided about thirty years in Preston, and died there some years ago.

Mary, my cousin, sister of James and John, and half sister of Nathaniel, married Thomas Walkden and left a family. Nancy married Joseph Nuttall, and Betty married Thomas Bury. All Betty's family died young. I must say a little more about Nancy, who was a remarkably strong woman. When a young woman she could carry a pack of flour or a load of meal as well as a man, and she could walk across the kitchen floor with half a pack of flour in her teeth. She lived and died about Waterloo, Blackburn, and one Sunday afternoon I went over to see her. She was then about 80 years of age, and I had not seen her for a generation at least. During that generation—say thirty years,—she had grown a trifle older, as you may imagine, and one of the first things I said to her when I saw her was—"Eh, Nancy, tha couldn'd carry hafe a pack o' fleawr across th' flooar i' thi teeth, neaw." "Eh nowe," hoo says, laughing.

My uncle James went, when a young man, to live at Preston, and he was employed chiefly as a gardener in gentlemen's families. He was three times married, and had a family, I believe, each time. I cannot pretend to know them all, but he had sons named Robert and Nathaniel, and one of his last was James, whom I remember seeing about seventy years back, a lad about my own age. The family lived at Penwortham then. My uncle and his last wife came over to see us about that time, and brought their son James with them. I kept sight of the lad for about ten years longer, but have not heard of him since. Nathaniel came to see us many a time. He lived and died in Preston, but some of his family are still living in Blackburn. Robert went to Manchester sixty years ago, and I have not heard of him since. My uncle's eldest daughter, Mary, became the wife of Richard Ingham, tailor, Mellor, and her grandson, Joshua, kept the Eagle and Child Hotel, Blackburn, until a few years ago. Another daughter was Jane. When her mother—my uncle's first wife—died, she came to live with my uncle John, at Harwood Fold, and was married from there to William Entwisle, but died in her first confinement. There was another daughter, Rachael, who was never married.

My uncle Nicholas went as a farm servant to Samlesbury, when a young man, more than a hundred years ago. He had one son, Ralph. I have heard old folks at Samlesbury talk about them both. They said Ralph was a good singer. Hunt-like he could make a noise. Ralph left one son, who died and left one daughter, who will be an old woman, if she is living.

My uncle Robert married Ellen Livesey, of Sough. He enlisted for a soldier, and left his wife with one son and six daughters. This was the second time of his enlistment—he had been bought off once,—and he was so much affected when he began to take a sober view of the situation that he died of a broken heart at Woolwich, before ever he tried how a red coat suited his complexion. His son Nathaniel was married, but his family died young. His eldest daughter, Mary, married a man named James Harwood, better known as "Owd Dinner Bag." Such nicknames are common enough in Darwen to this day, and are often transmitted from father to son. It will be a hundred years since this particular nickname was invented, and it came about in this way:—James Harwood was a stonemason, and whenever he was working in the town he used to have his dinner brought to him "as regular as clock work" in a bag. There were not many clocks in Darwen in those days, for it was not everybody who could afford the large oak case clocks which were then made, so the primitive inhabitants of this valley hit upon the expedient of telling the time by the passing of the infallible dinner bag, and from this the owner of the bag got to be called "Owd Dinner Bag." What a thing it is to be noted for punctuality! As I

OLD DARWEN FAMILIES.

have said, Mary, daughter of my uncle Robert, married "Dinner Bag," and no doubt made his famous dinners. There was another daughter, Ann, who became the wife of Richard Waddicor, and left a family beyond Manchester. The eldest of Dinner Bag's family was Ralph Harwood, who has just died at St. Helens, aged about 87. Another daughter was Ellen, who married first John Eccles and afterwards Timothy Yates. "Lime Dick," previously mentioned, is her son. Esther married Thomas Watson, of Holden Fold, and has descendants living there. Rachael married George Whittaker, but died and left no family. The youngest, Pernall, who was married to John Hindle No. 2, mentioned in a former chapter, has left eight children.

Nathaniel, youngest son of Nathaniel, was my father, and brother to my above-mentioned uncles.[1] He was born on December 18th, 1757, and died on the 11th of September, 1844. He married my mother, Ellen, daughter of John Leach, on the 5th of November, 1786. She was not my mother then, nor did she become so until twenty years later. She was born on the 18th of June, 1762, and died on the 1st of June, 1839. My eldest brother, John, was born in May, 1789, and died unmarried in July, 1833. My second brother, Nathaniel, was born on the 18th of June, 1791, and died of brain fever, unmarried, in June, 1813. My third brother, James, was born on the 26th of June, 1799, and died on the 22nd of April, 1868; he was married, but never had a family. I was the next son, and my birthday was the 27th of February, 1806. I was married on the 4th of January, 1841, to Hannah Kirkham, who died on the 23rd of December, 1846, leaving me three lads—Nathaniel, John, and James. The youngest died at the age of eight months. Nathaniel and John are living yet, one of them a draper in Darwen, and the other a draper in Chorley. My eldest sister, Mary, was born on the 9th of August, 1787, and married on the first Monday in September, 1814, to Michael Shorrock, son of James Shorrock, of Chapels, as mentioned before. He died on the 2nd of April, 1817, and left her with two girls. I had another sister, Alice, who was drowned in a well a few yards from our door at Pickup Bank Mill, when she was about 2½ years of age. That was before I was born. My sister Ellen was born in March, 1796, and died in April, 1870. Her husband, Samuel Harwood, has been mentioned already. She left a family. Another of my sisters, Ann, died from measles, aged two years, before my time. I had another sister, Hannah, born on the 29th of June, 1803. She married John Jepson, and they went to America about 60 years ago. He went in 1826, and sent for his wife, who

[1] He was the youngest of five brothers, and Jeremy was his youngest child.

followed him in 1827. I have never seen her since. She died there on the 25th of March, 1885, aged nearly 82 years of age, leaving a family of three sons and one daughter. She and I were the youngest in our family, and we have lived the longest. We were the liveliest in the family when we were children, and I suppose our good spirits have kept us up.

My aunt Rachael, whom I have mentioned as having been born three weeks after her father's death, left one son, who is dead, and her family is extinct.

John Hunt, my grandfather's brother, died unmarried in 1759. Margaret, their eldest sister, married a man named Kenyon. Ellen, the second sister, was the second wife of Timothy Holden, son of the famous "Owd Timothy o' th' Looms." Ann, the third sister, the only one of my great-grandfather's children I ever knew, was married to James Nightingale, of Tockholes. She died at Wrangling, Blackburn, about 70 years ago. She had two sons and one daughter—Benjamin, James, and Rachael. Rachael became the wife of the Rev. John Crossley, Independent minister, of Horwich, near Bolton.

Robert Hunt, brother of John Hunt, who came into Darwen as a lad, with his father, from Samlesbury, is the head of another family of Hunts. I never knew whom he married, and the only son of his that I can trace is Nathaniel.

Nathaniel, son of Robert, married Ann Lowe, of Edgeworth, and had two sons and six daughters—Robert, James; Mary, Elizabeth, Ellen, Ann, Sarah, and another. To take the daughters first, Mary married Richard Eccles, of Walton-le-Dale; Elizabeth married George Jepson; Ellen married his brother, John Jepson; Ann married first a man named Livesey, and secondly a man named Haworth; Sarah married Jeremy Leach, my uncle; and the other girl, whose Christian name I do not know, married a man named Sharples. The Leaches and the Eccleses have already been dealt with, and the Jepsons I shall come to next. Ann by her first marriage had two daughters, Ann and Jane. The former became the wife of James Walsh, and mother of the late Nathaniel Walsh, of Orchard Mill; while Jane married John Holden, of Cotton Hall. By her second marriage Ann had several sons—John, Nathaniel, Robert, and others. Mrs. Sharples has some descendants. Old "Jack o' Isaac's," who keeps a public-house in Wellington Fold, is one of her grandsons. His mother was born on the same day as my sister Hannah, June 29th, 1803, and this makes me recollect her mother, Mrs. Sharples, whose Christian name I don't know.

Old Nathaniel died on November 16th, 1798, aged 64. His wife

OLD DARWEN FAMILIES.

survived him by twenty years, and died on October 24th, 1818. She was the same age as my grandmother, for she was born in the spring of 1735. The old woman had a notion for years that whenever one died the other would die. I recollect going to Harwood Fold, the morning my grandmother died, to tell my Aunt Ann the news. The old woman was there and heard me tell my Aunt Ann the fatal news. She was sitting with a hand-wheel, winding a bobbin, with a cop in her mouth. She put down her cop, looked up in a melancholy way, and said, "Then aw morn'd live lung." She never took her cop up again, but died about five weeks after (October 24th, 1818). So much for the influence of superstition on her mind. She had made up her mind that she and my grandmother were to die together, and the news of my grandmother's death was a shock which she could not withstand. She was $83\frac{1}{2}$ years of age, and my grandmother was the same. Her son, James, married my mother's sister, Ann, so my grandmother was mother-in-law to him, and she was mother-in-law to my Aunt Ann.

Robert, son of Nathaniel, was bitten by a mad dog, when about 14 years of age, and died of hydrophobia.

James, son of Nathaniel, as I have said, married Ann Leach, my mother's sister. He had three sons and two daughters—Nathaniel, John, and James; Alice and Ann. Nathaniel was born the same time as my sister, Hannah, and he lived until about two years ago, when he died, aged 82. His wife was a daughter of Jos. Walmsley—"Owd Joe o' Lawrence's"—a celebrated Darwen alto singer, and he had four sons and one daughter—Nathaniel, James, Joseph, Lawrence, and Ann. Ann is the wife of John Hacking. Nathaniel is dead. James and Joseph are living in Darwen, with families. Ann has one daughter, who married a man named Townend—grandson of "Owd Tummas o'th' Shaver's,"—and they are now living in the Isle of Wight, employed by Mr. Roylance, of Manchester, to manage some property there. John son of James, married Betty, daughter of the late John Lightbown, of Darwen. She was a widow when he married her. He left one son, Roger, who is living at Pendleton. James, son of James, married Miss Aspden, of Hoddlesden. She has died lately. He has five sons and six daughters. The sons are David, Nathaniel, James, William and Jeremy—all married except Jeremy. Alice, daughter of old James, married Joshua Duckworth. They are both dead, but they have left a family in the town. Ann, the other daughter of old James, married James Holden, of Chapels. Both are dead, but have left a family.

There is one prominent gentleman in the town whom I ought to have mentioned earlier—Richard Hunt. He has been engaged for

17 years in the Town Clerk's office, at Darwen, and from 1874 to 1878 was a sidesman at St. James's Church, Black-a-moor, Lower Darwen, and a churchwarden at St. James's Church, Chapels, Over Darwen, during the years 1879, 1880, and 1881. His great-great-grandfather was my father's brother, for he is the only son of Moses, who died in March, 1873, the grandson of George, the great-grandson of Nathaniel, and the great-great-grandson of my uncle John, of whom I have said so much.

I have received the following letter from an unknown relative. The Robert Hunt whom he mentions as having been born in 1775 could not be my cousin Robert, son of my uncle James, and I cannot find a clue to connect him to our family, but I believe he belongs to the same lot of Hunts. The letter is as follows :—

53, Billinge-street, Audley, Blackburn, April 11th, 1887.

Dear Jeremy,—Seeing you are giving the history of the Hunt family, I should very much like to hear you give the history of Robert's family. Believing, as I do, that I am a descendant of this man, I am somewhat interested in the remarks you have made about them. Would you kindly state if you know his descendants or any of them? My grandfather was in Samlesbury in 1826. His name was Robert Hunt, and I think he would be born about 1775. I have heard my father state that he had plenty of relatives in and near Blackburn.—Yours truly,

GEORGE HUNT.

The Jepsons.

The Jepsons of Cheshire—Samuel Jepson, of Waterside—" Sam o' Sam'l's—More Marriage Curiosities—Tychicus, Onisimus, Obed, Edom, and Barachias—Micah Jepson—Prevailing Family Names—Evan Jepson, of Tockholes—Henry Jepson, of Hoddlesden.

THOUGH a very old Darwen family, the Jepsons are only moderately numerous. There is an old tradition that they came from Cheshire, but if they did it must have been two or three hundred years ago. The tradition is held by all branches of the family, and one of the Darwen Jepsons tells me that there are Jepsons about Macclesfield to this day, who are supposed to be distant relatives of his. There are also Jepsons at Middlewich, in Cheshire. I will divide my account of the Jepsons into two chapters, and first I will deal with a pretty numerous branch descended from one Samuel Jepson, who, "once upon a time," kept a small farm in Waterside Lane, Eccleshill. He and his wife died within six weeks of each other in the winter, or early Spring, of the year 1791, leaving four sons and four daughters. Samuel's wife was formerly a Dewhurst—of the Darwen Dewhursts. I knew one of her brothers when I was quite a little lad. The present race of Dewhursts in the town are related to her.

Samuel the First, as I will call him, had four sons and four daughters—John, Edward, Samuel, and George ; Mary, Ann, Esther, and Betty. Let us deal with the daughters first ; we shall get rid of them sooner than the sons. Mary became the wife of Ebenezer Harwood, mentioned in a previous chapter. Ann was the wife of Thomas Walkden, of Waterside. Esther married Timothy Holden, of Wheathead, grandson of the old patriarch, " Owd Timothy o'th' Looms." Betty died unmarried.

John Jepson, son of Samuel, married Ellen, daughter of Nathaniel Hunt, of Harwood Fold, Eccleshill. He had three children—Nathaniel, Ann, and Lettice. Ann became the wife of young William Walkden, of Waterside, and left him with three children when she died. Lettice was the wife of James Hunt, of Black-a-Moor, my cousin. She lived to be 88 years of age. Nathaniel, John's son, married, as his first wife, Ellen, daughter of Thomas Duxbury, of Stand, near Hoddlesden, but she only lived four months afterwards. His second wife was Susan Baron, and by this marriage Nathaniel had seven sons—John, Nathaniel, Blake, Jabez, Samuel, Barachias, and Elihu; and there were also four daughters, two of whom died unmarried, while the other became the wife of John Duxbury, and one is unmarried. I will now dispose of the seven sons of Nathaniel, just mentioned. John married a daughter of Thomas Lightbown, of Lower Darwen. Thomas and Nathaniel Jepson, who hold good positions at Belgrave Paper Works, are his sons. Another, James, went to America, came back and married Miss Nuttall, and then went again. John Ely, another son, is now manager of the Star Paper Mill at Feniscowles. Yet another son of John is Robert Jepson, paper dealer, Blackburn. John had also four daughters; two are dead, and one is the wife of Joseph Haworth, of the Spring Vale Paper Works, and the other married a Nuttall—her brother James's wife's brother. Nathaniel, aon of Nathaniel, has a family in Darwen, but I don't know them particularly well. One of his daughters married Eccles Grime, cousin of our Mayor, and manager of a Co-operative Store at Rishton. Blake married a daughter of Joseph Walmsley, of Grimshaw, and he has a family in Darwen. Jabez is living, a widower. He married a Miss Bury, who left him five or six children, who are grown up and scattered about the town with their families. Samuel, I believe, is also living.

Edward, second son of Old Samuel, married Ann, daughter of Thomas Holden, and a granddaughter of the old patriarch. They both died within a period of six months, leaving three daughters. One of them, Lettice, I knew very well. She became the wife of the late James Briggs, of Blackburn, and the ex-M.P. for the borough, W. E. Briggs, is her grandson. Her sister, Jane, married Michael Holden, of Jack's Kay, and left three children—Michael, John, and Ann. All the three are dead. Ann was the mother of the late Joseph Slinger, organist at Belgrave Chapel. The third daughter of old Edward Jepson was Betty, who married James Beckett, and left sons—William, John, Edward, Robert, Eli, and James. She had also two daughters, but they died in infancy. W. E. Beckett and J. J. Beckett, both prominent men of the town to-day, are sons of John; and Christopher J. Beckett, secretary of the Industrial Co-Operative Society, is a son of Eli.

Samuel, third son of Samuel ("Sam o' Owd Sam'l's), married Betty, daughter of Thomas Holden, grand-daughter of Owd Timothy o' th' looms, and sister of his brother Edward's wife. He had sons—Timothy,

Samuel, Thomas, Edward, and John; daughters—Lettice and Jane. Lettice married a Thomas Ainsworth, of Pin Fold. Some of her descendants are living in Burnley, some in Darwen, and others I don't know where. Jane became the wife of John Kay, and mother of Alderman John Kay, J.P., of Burnley Wood, William Kay, Samuel Kay, and other Burnley men. Timothy, son of Sam o' Sam'l's, married, as his first wife, a Miss Walsh. He went to live in Stockport nearly sixty years ago, buried his wife, married another, went to America and died there. What family he had I never knew. Samuel, son of Sam o' Sam'l's, married Ann, daughter of John Eccles, of the Closes, Eccleshill. His family I never knew. Thomas, son of Sam o' Sam'l's, married a woman I did not know, and I have inquired of one of her granddaughters without being able to get any nearer. But whoever she was she left him four sons and five daughters. One of the daughters was the second wife of the late Richard Holden, grocer; another married a man named Holt, and one of her granddaughters keeps a shop in Greenstreet East. Two of his grandsons are living, one of them an overlooker named Thomas, residing in Sarah-street. He was a funny old chap was old Thomas. He used to tell a comical story of what he said to his wife when he courted her. It was as much the manner as the matter that made his story so funny. The sum and substance of his courting was contained in this injunction—"Neaw, lass, every word as aw say to thee, led id fo' o' thi he'rt like a peawnd weight!" Edward, son of Sam o' Sam'l's, went to America in 1827, taking with him my youngest sister to join her husband, his younger brother, there. He himself found a wife across the Atlantic, but she died there. He returned to England, and died in Burnley, without family, a few years ago. John, youngest son of Sam o' Sam'l's, married my youngest sister on January 1st, 1824, at the Blackburn Parish Church. He went to America in 1826, leaving his wife and one child at home. She followed him under the escort of her brother-in-law, Edward, in July, 1827, and I have never seen her since. John lived until the 25th of January, 1884, when he died, aged 89 years. My sister followed him home on March 25th, 1885, aged nearly 82. They had six of a family. The first child, born in Darwen, and the next, born in America, died young, within five days of each other, of scarlet fever. The other four are living—three sons and one daughter. The daughter is the eldest, and she is unmarried. The three sons are married. One is a silversmith in Washington, Illinois; another is a doctor in Weling, West Virginia; the third keeps a store in St. Clairsville, Ohio.

George, fourth and last son of old Samuel the First, married

N

Elizabeth, daughter of Nathaniel Hunt, of Harwood Fold, Eccleshill, and sister to his brother John's wife ; so that we have in old Samuel the First's family a curious instance of two brothers falling in love with two sisters, and two more brothers being captivated by two sisters out of another family, George's sons were John, Samuel, and Nathaniel, and his daughters were Lettice, Ann, Mary, Elizabeth, and Rachael. Lettice married Nicholas Entwisle. Both died, leaving one daughter, who became the wife of George Bury, of Cotton Hall. She died and left a daughter, who remarried into the Jepson family, her husband being John Jepson, of Charles-street. Ann became the wife of Thurston Fish— "Little Tot" and "Blackburn Times," as he was called. Mary, who is still living, aged 86, is the widow of James Cheetham, of Bank-street, Salford, Manchester. She had about seven girls, but some of them are dead. When I was over in Manchester about four years ago one of her daughters was keeping a school. The old woman and I had a rare time of it reaping up the incidents of our childhood. She has lived in her own house at Salford for a generation or more, but she has not forgotten her younger days in Darwen. Elizabeth and Rachael, her remaining sisters, died unmarried. John, son of George, married Nancy, daughter of Thomas Entwisle, of Slack, near Hoddlesden. He had two sons— George and James. George married Mary, daughter of John Beckett, of Pickup Bank. Both are dead, but they have left a family in Darwen. James married Jane Radcliffe, of Wood-street, Darwen. He has three daughters. One of them, Nancy Jane, went to New Zealand, last September. She was an alto singer at Belgrave Chapel, and the singers made her a present of all their photographs framed. Her sweetheart had gone three years before her, and last year [1886], by arrangement, she followed him to become his wife. The young man is a Grime, and a nephew of the Mayor's. James's eldest son, William, is the head-master of Blacksnape school, and James Edwin, the youngest son, is an assistant teacher, at Bolton-road School. There is a daughter called Mary, besides Nancy Jane, unmarried ; another, Elizabeth Ann, is the wife of J. J. Beckett, and there are two other sons employed like their father at Belgrave Works. The youngest of them is a very good organist, and he plays frequently at Belgrave Chapel pending the appointment of a new organist. John, son of George, had three daughters. One died unmarried ; another became the wife of James Kirkham, my wife's brother. She died and left two sons and a daughter. The daughter was married to George Harwood, of Pickup Bank, died, and left one child ; and the son is married, and has a family at Cotton Hall. Nancy, sister of George and James, the sons of John, married Samuel Kay, brother of Alderman Kay, of Burnley. Samuel, son of old George, was married three times. His first wife was Ann, daughter of William Jepson, of Bolton-road. She died without issue. He next married Grace Chambers, by whom he had five sons—Tychicus, Onisimus, Obed, Edom, and Barachias. He was a very eccentric character was Sam o' George's, as you may guess. His third wife was a daughter of John Walkden, of Sough, by whom he had two sons, christened plain George and John. George died a young man ten years ago; John is living at Edenfield, near Accrington. Nathaniel, third son of old George was married, but he went to Padiham, and I never heard any more of him.

The second main trunk of the Jepson family tree springs from one Micah Jepson, whose three sons I knew very well seventy years ago. They were named respectively, Micah, William, and Henry, and I believe they were near relatives of old Samuel Jepson, of Waterside.

Micah, the son of Micah, has a good number of descendants in Darwen whom I know, but I cannot piece up all the connecting links, as I did not know their fathers and their grandfathers sufficiently well. I do know, however, that Micah, the son of Micah, had himself a son called Micah, for at odd times in the course of my life I have come across Bob o' Micah's and Roger o' Micah's, who are grandsons of Micah the Second. Micah is the prevailing family name in this branch of the Jepsons, just as Samuel is in the branch I mentioned last, as Timothy is among the Holdens, Jeremy among the Leaches, and Nathaniel among the Hunts. Among the descendants of Micah the Second are Jabez Jepson, butcher, James Jepson, tripe dresser; and Mrs. Kay, mother of the Market Inspector, was another. I am told that old Micah (No. 2) has a daughter living yet, aged about 80, but I cannot find her, and he has a granddaughter, Rosannah Jepson, aged about 50, and living yet, single.

William, son of Micah the First, had two sons, William and Micah, whom I knew personally. The old man must have been dead I should think some sixty years. We never called him anything else but " Owd William o' Micah's." William, the son of William, had eleven children— four sons and seven daughters. One of the sons, and six of the daughters are living. Micah, the other son of William, had one son, John, who died and left a family. One of John's sons is Christopher Jepson, tape sizer. Old William o' Micah's had four daughters. One, Ann, became the wife of Samuel Jepson, mentioned before, and another married Thomas Riding, and became the mother of the present Thomas Riding, of Hindle-street. I don't know whom the other two married.

Henry, son of Micah the First, married Mary Watson, daughter of Jonathan Watson, of Waterside, whose family will come under review next. Henry had six sons and four daughters. The sons were Jonathan, Micah, Henry, Richard, Thomas, and William; the daughters—Mally, Jenny, Betty, and Ann. I believe the daughters all married and settled in Darwen. I will deal with the six sons in order. Jonathan had sons— William (twice married, family in Darwen); Henry (twice married, five children living; his first wife's father, a Blackburn man, was buried last Tuesday,[1] aged 86 years; his second wife was Elizabeth, daughter of Jeremy Grime, of Charles-street); John (married John Bury's daughter, has only one child, a young woman); Richard (married his cousin, Ann, daughter of Micah Jepson; she is dead, but has left two sons and two daughters); Jonathan (married a daughter of Hugh Whalley; he—Jonathan—was killed by a horse and buried last week[2]); Micah (twice married; has two daughters by his first wife; his second wife was a Sarah Ann Kershaw); and three daughters, one of whom is the wife of John Preston, of Darwen. Micah, son of old Henry, had a family as follows: Henry (died young, unmarried); Mary (died, nearly sixty years of age, unmarried); Sarah (wife of Alderman Howorth, of Blackburn; she is now dead); Ann (who married her cousin, Richard Jepson); Rachael (wife of Edward Marsden, tailor and draper); and Elizabeth (wife of Andrew Hollis, lodging-house keeper, Blackpool). Henry, third son of old Henry, went to Horwich and then settled in Halliwell. His family were colliers. Richard, fourth son of old Henry, has a family, I am told, about Lower Darwen, but I do not know them. Thomas, son of old Henry, died unmarried. William, last son of old Henry, is the only one of his generation left in the land of the living. He is over seventy years of age. He married a daughter of Mark Townley, of Bolton Road, and his eldest son is Mark Townley Jepson, of Hindle-street. Another son is Richard, who married a daughter of Robert Smalley, of Blackburn-road. A third was John William who married a woman I didn't know. She was not a Darwen woman. They kept the Brookside Hotel; both are dead, but they have left two children. Micah Thomas was a fourth son. He married a Miss Beswick, and both are living in the town. Old William has also had four daughters. He has buried three of them— upgrown young women,—and the youngest, unmarried, is living with him at Cotton Hall. Old William had also another son, called Thomas, who, when a lad of twelve, was killed, by having his arm torn off, at Hollins Paper Mill. This will be at least a generation ago, for it was before his brother Micah Thomas was born.

[1] April 26th, 1887.   [2] Week ending April 23rd, 1887.

OLD DARWEN FAMILIES.

There is a distinct lot of Jepsons in Darwen who seem to have come out of Tockholes. Old Evan Jepson, who died on the Lee, not long ago, was one of them.

Yet another distinct lot springs from one Henry Jepson, of Hoddlesden. I have no doubt that he was a relative of the Darwen Jepsons, but I cannot find the connection. He married Miss Harwood, cousin of Molly Harwood, a famous English prima donna more than a century ago. He had two sons that I knew. One of them, John, died at the end of 1812, or the beginning of 1813, and left a family. Mrs. Roger Lightbown is one of his descendants—a great-granddaughter, I believe. The other was Henry, who has been dead about twenty years. He lived at Turncroft, and we always called him "Owd Henry o' Harry's." He has left a family. His father, old Henry, of Hoddlesden, had also several daughters. One, Betty, died unmarried; another became the wife of Marsden Hindle, of Hoddlesden; and a third, Hannah, was the second wife of the Rev. Henry Townsend, minister of Pole Lane Chapel from 1793 to 1806.

The Watsons.

A Benefactor of St. James's Church—William Watson, my great-grandfather—"Owd Snuffy Timothy" —Jonathan Watson's Sad End in 1791—A Woman with 239 Living Descendants—" Long Tom," " Little Tom," and " Little Singing Tom."

IN the graveyard of the Higher Chapel there is a tombstone bearing the following inscription :—"Here lyeth the body of Thomas Watson, of this town, chapman, son of Edmund Watson, of Hague Hall, in the County of York, gentleman, who departed this life the nineteenth day of December, 1732. And gave for the congregation of this Chappel, the summ of three hundred eighty-five pounds. DEUS AMAT LÆTUM DATOREM." The first Watsons I ever heard my father speak of were three brothers, William, Jonathan, and John, and I think there was another. I will give a reason for my thought further on.

William, the first of the three brothers, was my great-grandfather, and his wife was a sister of Owd Timothy o' th' Looms. I think her name was Ellen. She died young, leaving only two daughters behind her—Mary and Grace. Mary married Nathaniel Hunt, and became my grandmother. Grace was married to a man named Henry Ainsworth, and had two sons and a daughter. The sons were William and John. Both died young, but one of them left a family, and I have known some of his descendants. The daughter was Jane. She became the wife of Timothy Marsden, of Oakenhurst, best known as "Owd Snuffy Timothy," because of his habit of taking snuff, which was not very common in those days. William Henry Marsden, Sanitary Inspector for the Borough of Darwen, is her grandson.

Jonathan, second of the three brothers, had a farm at Waterside, Eccleshill. His family were attacked with fever in the winter of 1790, and, after one or two had died, the old man himself was stricken down with the disease. One bitterly cold night, when the snow lay deep on the ground, he got out of bed in his feverish delirium, and, protected only by his nightshirt and nightcap, rushed across the fields to the brook. He flung himself down in a little pool in the brook, at a spot near where Mr. Bullough's Waterside Mill now stands, and drowned himself. A great outcry was raised in the dead of the night, and the neighbours turned out, telling one another the mysterious news, "Owd Jonathan's off," and began the search. The search was a very short one, for Jonathan's bare feet had left their tracks in the snow right down to the water's edge, and so shallow was the pool where his body lay that his shirt could be seen floating on the top of the water. My father was one of the first to get there, and he helped to get the body out. It happened on the second Tuesday in January, 1791, which is not far off a hundred years since, but the "hole" is there yet where the old man drowned himself, and I can testify to its shallowness myself, for I bathed in it many a time when I was a lad. I think Jonathan's wife was dead at the time when this tragedy disturbed the quietude of Waterside, and one or two of the children had just been carried off by the fever, but there were still three left. One of them, Nanny, died before my time, but I knew the other two. One was Richard, who married Sarah, daughter of old John Pickup, of Sunnyhurst; and the other was Mary, who became the wife of Henry Jepson, mentioned in the last chapter.

John Watson was the third of the original three brothers on whom this chapter depends. He had sons—Joshua, Thomas, and John—but whether he had any daughters or not I don't know. Joshua, the first son of John, married Ellen, another daughter of John Pickup, of Sunnyhurst, and had three sons whom I knew—John, Thomas, and Joshua, the last of whom died unmarried. Of the other two I fancy John would be the elder. He had four daughters, two of whom died young women, unmarried. One of the survivors married Timothy Marsden, grandson of Owd Timothy o' th' Oakenhurst; and the other became the wife of a man we always called Monk, though I believe his real name was Ellison. John's wife was a Miss Walsh. She was the daughter of a rather remarkable woman. I remember more than a quarter of a century ago, as I was walking to Blackburn on business, meeting, in Craven-brow, a funeral procession that was going from Ewood to Lower Chapel. I didn't lift up the pall as on the former occasion I have mentioned, because the coffin was in a hearse, and the mourners were walking behind it, but I asked whose the corpse was, and learned that it was that of an old woman who had had no fewer than 347 descendants in a direct line, of whom 239 were living, and might all have been following the hearse if circumstances had permitted. It is not every old woman who can have between 200 and 300 children, grandchildren, &c., to attend her funeral, so I have been at the pains to borrow, from one of the 239, an old funeral card giving particulars of this old woman's progeny. The card reads as follows :—

In memory of the late Sarah Walsh, who died March 30th, 1861, aged 85 years; and was interred at Lower Chapel, Over Darwen, April 3rd. She was the mother of 16 children, grandmother to 99, great-grandmother to 209, great-great-grandmother to 23 ; making a total of 347, of whom 239 were living at her death.

The voyage of life's at an end,
The mortal affliction is past ;
The age that in heaven I spend,
For ever and ever shall last.

I will just add that this Sarah Walsh was married at the age of 15, and so lived 70 years after her wedding day. It was one of her daughters that married John Watson. I have mentioned what became of John's own daughters—four in number—and now I will deal with his sons, of whom there were three. One of the three was Joshua, who died a young man, leaving a son bearing his name—Joshua Watson, grocer, Market-street. The second was James, who married Ann, daughter of George Briggs, of Chapels, and had a son Joshua, tape sizer, and another, John, manager at Mr. Robert Leach's, Barley Bank Mill. The tape sizer has three sons and three daughters (one of the sons married), and the manager has two sons and five daughters. He had also daughters, Susannah, wife of Thomas Mayoh ; Ann, widow of the late Joseph Briggs, bandmaster ; and Sarah, wife of Christopher Duxbury, on the Lee, who has a lad in my Sunday School class. The third son of John is Thomas, who had two children, a boy and a girl. The boy, John, grew up and married. He lives in London-terrace, and has four daughters, but no son. His sister married a man named Calvert, and she is living at Edgeworth. Thomas Watson, son of Joshua Watson, and grandson of old John, married Ann Briggs, daughter of James Briggs, Scotland Farm, near Hoddlesden. He had two sons and three daughters, Ann, Sarah, and Alice. Ann is the wife of Moses Scholes ; Sarah is the widow of William Bury, living at Manchester ; Alice is over 60 years old, unmarried. His son Joshua died unmarried. James married Alice, the daughter of John Fish, of Radford-street. He has one son, John, married, and three sons and one daughter unmarried.

Thomas, second son of the original John, I knew very well. He was my grandmother's cousin, and people always called him " Little Singing Tom." He was a remarkably good tenor singer, and folks used to say that he could make singing sound as well off the key as other men could on it. I remember meeting him more than fifty years since, when I was walking through the streets with my old " Messiah " under my arm. He was then over sixty years of age, but as good a singer as ever, and as soon as he saw the book he took it from under my arm and burst off with "Comfort ye," which he sang in a most delicious manner, "trolling in" bits of the accompaniment. When he had done it he said, "Eh! See yo'! Aw sung that at Kirkham Church." He was proud of his singing, I can tell you, especially when he was sent for all the way from Kirkham. He lived at Pothouse, in Eccleshill, and was a handloom weaver. At any time of the day or night he could be heard singing cheerily at his loom, beating time with the picking stick; and a cousin of mine once told me that he used to go and cower under " Little Singing Tom's " window to drink in the music. He came to a tragic end did "Little Singing Tom." When handloom weaving was going down he took to doing odd jobs of any kind for a living, and at the time of his death he was engaged repairing the gable end of a house at Catleach, in Pole-lane. Underneath the ladder was an old pit or a draw well, which had been covered over with timber. The timber had rotted, and down went Tom and the ladder into the pit. Whether he was killed or drowned I don't know, but I should think *both !*

There was another family of Watsons whose relationship with the foregoing I cannot trace, and this makes me think that the original three brothers whose history was handed down to me by my father had a fourth brother, from whom the family I am now dealing with are descended. "Long Tom Watson" belonged to this lot. He married my cousin Esther, of Chapels. He had two sisters—Susan, second wife of James Pickup, of Chapels; and Betty, wife of James Briggs, farmer, Ellison Fold.

There is still another unattached branch of the Watsons, among whom comes "Little Tom Watson." There were three Tom Watsons, all men living at the same time in Darwen, about two generations ago, and they were always distinguished by the nicknames of "Long Tom," "Little Tom," and "Little Singing Tom." This "Little Tom" was the son of a Thomas and also father to a Thomas,—the Thomases hereabouts being quite conflicting,—but I do know that he was not descended from one of the original three brothers, although both he and "Long Tom" was probably descended from a fourth brother of the old stock. I didn't know "Little Tom's" wife, but I knew two of her children, a son and a daughter. The son, John, married Miss Isherwood, of Hey Fold, and the daughter, Betty, became the wife of John Catlow, a country gentleman. She has left two sons and two daughters, who are living yet. Richard and Thomas are the sons; the daughters are Sarah, wife of Eli Leach (Lightbown, Leach, and Catlow, cotton manufacturers) and Nancy, wife of Henry Lightbown, of the same firm.

The Grimes.

A Fugitive from York Castle—Grime or Graham?—James Grime, of Bobbin Hall—Thomas and Mary —Thomas Grime, Mayor of Darwen, 1887—The "Black Grimes"—"Dick o' Jim's o' Jack's"— William Grime, cotton manufacturer—"Six Queens and never a King"—The Blackburn Grimes —Old Dr. Grime.

THEY are a considerable family in Darwen, are the Grimes, there are so many different branches of them. My great-grandmother, that is, my grandfather John Leach's mother, was a Grime. There is a tradition in the family that the first Grime that ever came into this district escaped out of York Castle with a chain to his foot, and settled on a lonely farm on the edge of Oswaldtwistle, just on the other side of Pickup Bank Height.[1] Three townships meet at that point— Oswaldtwistle, Haslingden, and Pickup Bank, and it might be the end of the world instead of the end of these townships merely, for it is a lonely place yet, and must have been very lonely three or four hundred years back, when the escaped prisoner hid himself in its seclusion. I have no authority whatever for saying what offence had caused the first Darwen Grime to be chained up at York. I will suppose that he was a political prisoner, but for aught I know to the contrary he was a sheep-stealer or a highwayman. Anyhow, it is to the circumstance of his escape from York Castle that we owe the fact of the Grimes settling in Darwen and one of them becoming our present Mayor. [1887].

Now, the name of the Grime family is sometimes spelt "G-r-i-m-e," and sometimes "G-r-a-h-a-m," and I judge from this that they come from the north country. I knew two cousins, one of whom spelt his name "Grime" and the other "Graham," and I am inclined to think that the name originally was "Graham." One of the cousins was no other than the late Doctor "Graham," of Woodside House, and the

[1] This farm, called Jackson House, is just above the Blackburn Waterworks, on the east side of the ridge separating Pickup Bank from Belthorn. There is a pretty little clough here now, and the place was probably covered with brushwood three or four hundred years ago, and so would afford a secluded retreat.

other was the late Jeremy "Grime," of Charles Street. Their fathers were brothers, whose father, I believe, was generally called "Grime." But they had a great uncle or a great-great uncle named Doctor "Graham." He lived at Blacksnape; I knew him very well, and he invariably spelt his name "Graham."

In the year 1812 there died at Harwood's Farm, near Hoddlesden, one Thomas Grime,[2] an old man of about three score years and ten, who had six sons and one daughter—James, Robert, Thomas, Benjamin, Eccles, John, and Alice—whose families will furnish me with an abundance of matter for this article. Before passing on to them, however, I will just mention that old Thomas the First's wife was a Miss Eccles, of the Greenlow Eccleses. The present Richard Eccles (Harwood and Eccles), cotton manufacturer, belongs to the same lot. She lived a long time after the old man had died, and I knew her very well.

James, the eldest son of Old Thomas, lived to be over 80. He married Mary, daughter of Jeremy Townend, of Hoddlesden, and had two sons—Thomas and James. He had also a daughter, Mary, who was drowned when between two and three years of age. Old James lived at "Bobbin Hall," up the New Road—I mean Bolton Road; all old folks call it the New Road yet. In fact he gave the name to the hall; he was a joiner, and he kept a lathe there for the purpose of turning bobbins for handloom weavers. There was a lodge close to the hall, and in this lodge his child was drowned. She was pushing open a gate on a gusty day, when a puff of wind swung it back and knocked her into the lodge. The old man lived until February, 1857. He was uncommonly attached to the chapel—Belgrave—and was always to be seen in his pew on one side of the singing pew. He died in the chapel, and I can picture the event as if I saw it happening now. It was during the afternoon service. We were just getting up to sing that hymn of Dr. Watts's—

    Raise your triumphant songs
    To an immortal tune—

when Old James got up from his seat, staggered back, and lay down dead before we had got through the first line. The singers were rather shocked, and nearly broke down, but I got them to keep on, and so avoid a commotion. When the hymn was sung, I went down, and found him laid back on a chair, dead, with a cloth thrown over him. Another man and I carried him to a cab which had been sent for. The doctor said he didn't think the old man had drawn a single breath after falling back in the pew. Old James had complained to his wife at noon that he felt starved, and she wanted to persuade him to stay at home,

    [2] A very eccentric character. He died in October, 1812.

but he would not. He had often expressed a wish to die in the chapel, and he said he would not stay away from chapel because he was a little starved. His son, Thomas, was married to Mary, daughter of Robert Eccles, of the Closes, Eccleshill, and never had a family. The other son, James, married Ellen Ainsworth. He is dead, but she is living. He had one son and seven daughters, all of whom are married. One of his daughters married a Frenchman named Voyez, who died in Blackburn, last week,[1] aged 70. I don't think she is more than 40 or 45. Another of the seven girls is the wife of Ashworth Higham, Darwen's principal basso, but they have no family. The youngest of the seven is the wife of Charles Wardley, son of John Wardley, printer.

Robert, second son of old Thomas, married Susan Walkden. He enlisted for a soldier, and left her with two children—Thomas and Mary—who became noted for their eccentricity. Susan could never get to know what became of her husband, though she applied to the War Office many a time. Thomas and Mary were a very simple-minded couple. When Mary died, and was buried at Lower Chapel, Thomas stipulated that he should be buried in the same grave. In 1861, however, the graveyard was closed, and Thomas then went to the sexton to bargain for a secret burial. He said in a whisper: "Ged a donkey an' cart, an' fotch me i'th' neet, an' lap th' donkey's feet i' rags, sooa as id cornd mek a din." In his old age, Thomas married an old woman who was a good match for him. They lived at a place called Cookstool, off Bridge-street, and kept a donkey in the house until the Local Board dislodged it. They are both dead now, but the wicked sexton didn't respect the old man's wish, for he is buried on a hill at one end off the town, and his sister on a hill at the other. I will pass over some of his eccentricities, but you will see what a curious old stick he was when I tell you that he used to come constantly to my father, who was well and hearty at the time, to try and get an order from him to make his coffin. Not that he could make coffins, but he thought he could.

Benjamin, third son of old Thomas the First, married a Miss Grimshaw, but they both died without family.

Eccles, fourth son of old Thomas the First, married a woman named Fish, daughter of William Fish, of Blacksnape, and sister of the well-known Fish Fish.

Thomas, fifth son of old Thomas the First, married Ann Grime, a distant relative. He had two sons and four daughters—John and Thomas; Mary, Alice, Ann, and Nancy. I will deal with the daughters first. Mary married James Briggs, son of James Briggs, of Blacksnape.

[1] May 2nd, 1887.

Alice married John Briggs, his cousin, who went off for a soldier, leaving her with two children, as you will remember. Ann died a young woman, unmarried. Nancy married the late Thomas Holden, but never had a family. She is living yet, aged 78, the only one of the family of Thomas Grime, the son of Thomas. Now for the two sons — her brothers. I believe John was the eldest. He was born in February, 1800, and lived to be about 78. He had no difficulty in reckoning his age, for it kept pace with the Nineteenth Century. Thomas Grime, the present Mayor of Darwen [1887], is a son of his, and the Mayor's mother was a Mary Harwood, and a relative of the famous prima donna, Miss Molly Harwood. The Mayor has no children of his own, but he has adopted a son of Alderman Carlisle, ex-Mayor of Clitheroe, and brought him up from childhood to manhood. Another son of John was George, who went to Australia, leaving a wife and family in Darwen. His wife was a Miss Jepson, daughter of Evan Jepson, of the Lee, and his family consisted of six sons and a daughter. George Johnson Grime, secretary of the Darwen Spinning Co.; John Bright Grime, a promising young man, who died a few years ago on his way home from Egypt; Herbert Seymour, and Ewart Leonard, who are in Australia (Herbert sent for his sweetheart, as already mentioned); Joseph Hague (deceased); Thomas Beecher; and May Grime, a teacher at Belgrave schools. Another brother of the Mayor is John Grime, now living in Blackburn; and yet another was called Joseph. He married a Miss Hindle, and died. The Mayor has another brother, Eccles, living in Darwen, and he has also had three sisters. One, Nancy, married a widower named Mallilue; another married a tailor named Davies (both are dead); and a third became the wife of a Mr. Forrest, cotton manufacturer, Nova Scotia, Blackburn. I now come to Thomas, the brother of John of 1800, and son of Thomas the Second. He married Nancy Eccles, another daughter of Robert Eccles, of the Closes. She died suddenly and he married again. He had five sons and some daughters. The sons were —John, Thomas, Eccles, Charles, and James. John was rather a noted singer. He married a Miss Howard, of Edgeworth, and has three sons and three daughters. Thomas is a druggist in Bolton-road. He married a Miss Holden, and has a son and two daughters. The son, Edwin, is an excellent violinist, and much sought after as an amateur solo player. Eccles is the manager of the Rishton Co-operative Society. He married a daughter of Nathaniel Jepson, of the Lee, and has a family. Charles is unmarried. James married a daughter of Roger Lightbown, and has a family. He is a grocer in Bolton-road. Ann died a young woman. Mary married David Ainsworth, grocer, Market-street. Elizabeth married Thurston Briggs, Rochdale-road, Manchester. Susan married a Lightbown. Anna Maria married a man named Kay; and Nancy, William Holden, son of John Holden, of Wheathead.

John, sixth son of old Thomas the First, married Sarah, daughter of William Fish, and sister of his brother Eccles's wife. He had two sons, Thomas and William. Thomas married Dorothy, daughter of Nicholas Walkden, singer and composer, and died without family. William, who was just six months younger than myself, married first a Miss Croft and secondly a Miss Harwood. His family, all told, consisted of two sons and nine daughters. Old John had also five daughters. Francis Walkden married two of them, and Joseph Bury, of Holden Fold, married another. The only one living is the wife of Jesse Kay, of Joseph-street.

Alice, the only daughter of old Thomas the First, became the wife of Richard Waddicor, of Height Side (Thorney Height), She had three children, but they are dead.

Another important branch of the Grime family was distinguished from the branch whose history I have given by the darkness of their complexion, which caused them to get the name of "The Black Grimes." The first of the Black Grimes that I recollect was Doctor Graham (or Grime), of Blacksnape, who died in November, 1823, aged 72, and was buried at Lower Chapel, where there is a gravestone giving a few particulars about him and his family. Who his wife was I don't know, but I know he had a good number of children, who mostly died in infancy. One of his sons grew up to manhood, enlisted for a soldier, and died in the East Indies ; and he had a daughter also, who grew up, and was spoken of as "Molly o' th' Doctor's." She became the wife of Richard Livesey, of Sough, commonly called "Dick o' Jim's o' Jack's," and she was mother of the late Thomas Livesey, town councillor. I was 17 years of age when old Doctor died, so I remember him very well. He was a very peculiar character, and, among other things, he was reckoned to be uncommonly fond of money. The son who 'listed once wrote to him, begging to be bought off, as he had rued of his bargain with the King's officer. A niece of the old man's—the wife of Thomas Grime, mentioned before—was living with him at the time, and, knowing that he was pretty well off in cottage and other property at Blacksnape, she pleaded with the father for his absent son, when the letter arrived, and reminded him that he had plenty of money. The lad in his letter also said, "Now, father, you have money and cannot take it with you," but the father replied, "No, but I'll take it as far as I can." He kept his word, for he died in November, 1823, on the day after the rent day, and it was said at the time that he was reckoning up his cash at the time of his death, and actually breathed his last with a number of £1 notes grasped in his hands. By the way, this was one of the Grimes who always spelled his name "Graham." He was great-uncle to the late Doctor Graham, on the Lee. I cannot trace his family through, but I remember "Black Bob" Grime, and Jeremy, his brother, and the late Doctor Graham's father, who were all closely related to old Doctor Graham.

Jeremy Grime, brother of "Black Bob," had four sons and a daughter—Jeremy, Robert, David, William, and Nancy. Young Jeremy married Martha Shaw, and had a son David (who died a young man), and four daughters—Jane Ann, Sarah, Elizabeth, and Sophia. Jane Ann became the wife of Thomas Bury. She is dead, but has left two sons. Sarah married John Duxbury. She is now a widow, with two sons and a daughter. Henry Jepson, already mentioned, married Elizabeth, who has two sons living; and my eldest son, Nathaniel Hunt, married Sophia, by whom he has one son, Ernest, who is in his 20th year. [1887.] Robert, second son of Jeremy the elder, married a woman who was not a "Darruner," and left the town. David did likewise. William married a Darwen woman, and removed to Ringley, where he died. Nancy married a man named Kay, removed to Rochdale-road, Manchester, and died there.

Once upon a time there was in Darwen a David Grime, of whom I personally know nothing, except that he had four sons and three daughters. One of his sons was David, whose widow is living yet, aged 78. I have been to her for information, but all she can tell me is that she thinks their family are old Darwen Grimes, and that her husband was the eldest son of his father. She was formerly a Miss Kay, daughter of "Owd Skriking Aleck." She has two sons—William Grime, cotton manufacturer, Springfield; and John Grime, paper bag manufacturer. William, the cotton manufacturer, married the only daughter of the late James Varley, clogger, and he has two children,—a son and a daughter. His brother John, the paper bag maker, married the daughter of William Beckett, and has four sons and two daughters. A second son of old David was John Grime. He died on the Lee a few years ago. His wife was a Miss Isherwood, of Hey Fold, and he had four sons and two daughters, who, I think, are all living. Another son of David the Unknown was called William, and the fourth was christened Briggs. There were also three daughters. The only near relation of their generation living is the old woman mentioned above, widow of their brother David, and she can only tell me what I know about them myself—nothing! I remember her from childhood. She was one of six girls, and she had no brothers. Her father used to go about remarking, "Aw've six queens and never a king."

The Blackburn Grimes, or, at any rate, some of them, spring from Darwen, and I have a notion that all the Grimes about here are descendants of the York Castle hero. Sixty years ago there was a Jeremy Grime, chapel keeper at Chapel Street Chapel, Blackburn, who came from Darwen. The name Jeremy cropping up again reminds me that it is very prevalent among the Grimes, and that it was from the Grimes that the Leaches inherited it. My great-grandfather, John Leach, married a Grime, and I trace my name, Jeremy, back through the Leaches to the Grimes.[1] In September, 1846, while enjoying the fresh air at Blackpool, I met with one of Jeremy the Chapel Keeper's daughters, an old woman of about 60. She told me that she was the wife of a reedmaker and heald knitter, in Blackburn, named Shorrock. Nearly thirty years later I was walking down Feilden Street, Blackburn, when one of her daughters, whom I didn't remember, spoke to me and proved her acquaintance by reminding me what I and her mother had talked about in Blackpool. She was a heald knitter, and lived in Feilden Street. Another family of Blackburn Grimes is that connected with the present old Dr. Grime, J.P., who has retired from practice after upwards of fifty years' labour. His uncle, the real *old* Dr. Grime, who established the well-known surgery which stands in a back yard off Water Street, was nephew of a certain Harry Grime, tape-sizer, who was one of the principal men to build Mount Street Chapel, and this Harry Grime, I know, sprang from Darwen, for he left some brothers behind him.

[1] Every family had its own distinguishing list of Christian names at one time, but with the increase of population and the intermarriages of families the custom is getting broken up, and Christian names cannot now be traced to their family origin, except in a few peculiar cases.—J.H.

The Walshes.

Walsh Fold, or Darwen Green—A Nonconformist Vicar of Blackburn—His Suspension and Death—The Vicar's Son a Parish Clerk—Roger Walsh, a Governor of Blackburn Grammar School—Baron and John Walsh—Nathaniel Walsh, of Orchard Mill—James Walsh, J.P., and George Walsh—Ted o' Baron's—Jack o' Ted's—John o' Baron's and his Spanish bride—The Sunnyhurst Walshes—Murder of Thomas Walsh—Hannah Walsh's encounter with the Bull—The Chapels Walshes—The Holden Fold Walshes—"Diddling Tom"—James Walsh, Methodist Preacher.

THAT portion of Darwen commonly known as "The Green," or "Darwen Green," was formerly Walsh Fold, the home of an ancient Darwen family of the name of Walsh. Before giving my own recollections of the Walshes of this century and the last, I will quote from Mr. Abram's "History of Blackburn" some interesting particulars of the Walshes who lived here in the sixteenth, seventeenth, and eighteenth centuries. I cannot connect the Walshes of my recollection with those who lived in the stormy days of the Revolution, but I believe there have been Walshes in the town ever since then, and that the various Walshes of to-day are mostly distant relations of that Vicar of Blackburn who was suspended for Nonconformity in the time of King James I. Mr. Abram's History gives the following particulars :—

At Walsh Fold, in this township, sometime was domiciled a family of Walshe descended from Edward Welshe, a Puritan Vicar of Blackburn, suspended in 1606 for nonconformity. In 1590, he being then Vicar, Mr. Edward Welshe was one of 17 Lancashire Preachers who signed an Address upon "The manifolde enormities of the Ecclesiasticall State in the most partes of the Countie of Lancaster," printed by the Chetham Society in 1875 from the original MS. in the Bodleian Library. Canon Raines, in a note to the Address, gives some facts about this Vicar of Blackburn, of which I cull the following :- Sept. 26th, 1596, he "appeared personally before the Commissioners at Chester, and said that he neither did nor would refuse to wear the surplice if the same was fit and tendered to him in good sort. He was enjoyned to wear it hereafter." Eight years later, Oct. 3rd, 1604, he "was cited to appear before the bishop, and was required to subscribe to the three Articles in the 36th Canon of 1603." He was deprived of his benefice about two years after, and retired to his little farm at Walsh Fold, Over Darwen. By Mary, his wife, he had a

P

son Thomas, and other issue. The deprived minister died at Walsh Fold, and was buried April 18th, 1628.

Thomas Walshe, son of Edward, occurs as Parish Clerk of Blackburn, in 1627. He had a son Edward, born in 1625, whose baptismal register runs :—1625-6. Feb. 12. "Edwarde, sonne of Thomas Walshe, filii vicarii." He had also sons, Thomas and John. Thomas Walsh, of Upper Darwen. was buried Dec. 2nd, 1657. John Walsh, son of Thomas, married July 18th, 1656, Mary, daughter of William Ellison, of Upper Darwen.

Thomas Walsh, of Upper Darwen, son of Thomas, had sons, Ralph, born in 1657; Richard, bapt. April 6th, 1662; John, bapt. Aug. 23rd, 16 4; and Roger; and a daughter Ann, born in 1667.

Ralph Walsh, of Upper Darwen, yeoman, eldest son of Thomas, died in 1703.

John Walsh, of Upper Darwen, chapman, another son, died Jan. 11th, 1732. His brother, Roger Walsh, of Upper Darwen, chapman (made a governor of Blackburn Grammar School in 1729), died, aged 65, Jan. 28th, 1739; his wife Elizabeth, died, aged 71, Oct. 16th, 1740.

The first Walshes of my own recollection were two brothers named Baron and John, and a sister of theirs who became the wife of John Eccles, son of old Sapling Bough. Baron married twice and had four sons and a daughter. The sons—James, Edward, John, and Ralph,—I will deal with one by one.

James ("Owd Jem o' Baron's") had sons—Baron (who was found dead in bed in their house in Back Duckworth-street); John (living now in his 84th year, a bachelor); James (died young); Ralph (married Mrs. Milner, and kept the George Inn, but died without family; Nathaniel (formerly a cotton manufacturer at Orchard Mill, married Miss Altom, and was father of James Walsh, J.P., and George Walsh, the cricketers, &c.); and Eli (married Miss Smalley, of the New Inn, died suddenly not long ago, leaving two sons and two daughters); daughters—Ann (married Seth Harwood, joiner and builder); Maria (wife of Thomas Fish, has two sons and four daughters); Miriam (died about fourteen years of age); and Mary (married Nicholas Fish, and had three sons and four daughters). The Nathaniel Walsh, of Orchard Mill, mentioned above, had a large family. His sons were James, George, Charles, and Joseph; and his daughters, Ann, Mary, Ellen, Frances, and Mabel. Two of the sons have married two of J. B. Deakin's daughters; the daughter Mary is the wife of Dr. Aspinall; and the daughter Ellen is the wife of the Rev. Mr. Berry, of Smallbridge, near Rochdale. Their father Nathaniel died at Blackpool, rather suddenly. Some of his descendants are living at Southport and some in Darwen.

Edward Walsh ("Ted o' Baron's") married Catherine Townend, of Hoddlesden. He had sons—Baron (who married a Miss Almond), Edward, and John ("Jack o' Ted's"), and daughters—Mary (married

John Kirkham, and died without family), Annas (married John Briggs), Amelia (married Philip Kershaw), Betty (married Philip Bury), Jane, and Nancy. John ("Jack o' Ted's") married Jemima Harwood, of Hoddlesden, and afterwards Miss Anderton. He is a well-known cotton spinner and manufacturer in the town. He had one daughter by his first wife, and she is now the wife of Mr. Hindley, cotton spinner, Darwen.

John of Old Baron's used to keep a private school at Lower Darwen. He was, however, allotted into the Militia, and taking kindly to his fate, he volunteered into the "reg'lars," no doubt thinking that if he had to gain glory by being shot at he would have better opportunities in the regular army. He went to Spain in the Peninsular War, but they made him a schoolmaster among the soldiers, as he could handle the birch quite as well as the musket, if not better. This was a clear case of the schoolmaster being abroad. During the campaign he was captivated by the charms of a Spanish lady, whom he married. He settled in the land of his bride, and has two sons living there now.

Ralph of Old Baron's I don't know anything about, nor do I know anything about old Baron's daughter, except that she sprang from a second marriage, and was half sister to the four brothers mentioned above.

Old Baron's brother John had sons Thomas and Baron. Of the latter (Baron) I know nothing, but I can give the history of Thomas's family. Thomas first married Nancy Harwood, a distant relative of Miss Molly, and by her he had sons Ralph and William, and a daughter Jane. Jane became the wife of John Isherwood, contractor. Ralph was married, but never had a family. William got married, and I cannot tell what became of his family. Thomas of old John's married as his second wife a Miss Houghton, of Belthorn, daughter of "Owd Ned o' Bill's." By her he had sons Thomas and Edward, and daughters Betty and Margaret. Betty is the wife of a butcher in Market-street, named Roberts. Thomas was never married; Edward has been married twice.

There is another branch of the Walshes, of Darwen, clustered about Sunnyhurst, and I judge by the common family names, such as Ralph, that they belong to the same old stock. Among the Sunnyhurst Walshes there were Ralph, Thomas, William, Henry, James, John, and Hannah. Their families are now scattered about Darwen, and the only one that I can trace distinctly is that of Ralph. Ralph married Hannah, daughter of old James Pickup, of Sough. His sons were James, John, and Ralph, the last-named being a young man who was killed at a coal pit, as narrated in connection with his mother's history.

Thomas Walsh, of Sunnyhurst, brother of old Ralph, was murdered. He was building some property in Market-street, Darwen, and after a dispute with his workmen, he was waylaid in Nova Scotia, Blackburn killed, and thrown into the canal. This happened nearly seventy years ago, and the murderers were never really discovered. There were three of the workmen suspected, two Irishmen and an Englishman. The Englishman, a long time afterwards, was reported to have made a confession on his deathbed that two of them seized old Thomas and the third killed him by a blow on the heart with a heavy mason's hammer. The wound over the heart had been discovered at the post-mortem examination. Of course the two other murderers had got away, and the affair blew over. I knew the Englishman well, and I know his descendants very well. They occupy good positions in the world, but I prefer not to give their names and addresses.

The other old Sunnyhurst Walshes named above were also brothers of Thomas, except Hannah, and she was his sister. I cannot find out the name of their father, but it runs in my mind that he must have been called John. Hannah, like her brother Thomas, met with a violent death. She was loosing the cattle on Sunnyhurst farm one day when a young bull attacked her. The brute had a ring in his nose, but no chain attached. Hannah courageously made a grab at the ring, but missed it, and the bull, more infuriated than ever, planted his feet upon her, and with his horns ripped her up to ribbons. This was rather more than seventy years ago, so it may be a sensational item of news for the newspapers of the present day.

Chapels is another part of Darwen where a branch of the old Darwen Walshes seems to flourish. I won't go into exact details, for there was one woman alone coming out of Chapels, old Sally Walsh, who had no fewer than 347 descendants.[1] You will remember that I encountered her funeral at Ewood. Anyon Walsh, newsagent, Chapels, and his brother William are representatives of the Chapels Walshes. They are both very good amateur singers. I have sung with them many a time.

The Holden Fold Walshes are another lot. There was an old John Walsh, of Holden Fold, who had a large family. One of his sons, William, best known as "Billy 'Cute," lived at Knowle Farm, and died without family. Two other sons, "Aleck" and "Dan," have families. Old John himself died fifty or sixty years ago, and we always called him "Old Jack King." Old Jack had a brother named Thomas, who was rather a noted character. His eyesight was very weak, and this infirmity

[1] See note under the head of the Watson family.

caused him to follow the occupation of a rag gatherer for a livelihood. He was nicknamed "Owd Diddling Tom," for he was a remarkably good diddler—not a prig, but a man who could diddle or fiddle, or chatter out musical sounds between his teeth,—and he used to be hired to "diddle" for dancing at wedding parties instead of having a fiddler. There was no fancy step-dancing in those days, but a sort of hornpipe, and Tom could "diddle" tunes for the dancers for hours together without getting tired. "Diddling Tom" used to follow his two-fold profession without hat or cap of any kind, and I have seen him in wet weather with his hair hanging down his back like mouse tails.

All the Walshes in the town do not belong to the old Darwen stock, but I believe the families I have mentioned do. There was an old Methodist preacher named James Walsh, living 60 years ago, and he is another "Darruner." The rest of the Walshes I will pass by.

The Fishes.

A Shoal of Fishes—The descendants of one man—Origin of the Fishes—"Old Nick"—A Prowl round Pole Lane graveyard—Three brothers marry three sisters—Trees Farm and Jubilee Park—"Skriking Nick"—William Fish, of Pasture Barn—Thomash Fish and his Seven Sons—The Blacksnape Fishes—The Press Gang—Bill o' Ann's, the singing cobbler—*Prestissimo !*—"Little Tot," *alias* "BLACKBURN TIMES"—The Chapels Fishes—Burgoyne Fish, the Wesleyan—Johanna Southcott, the fanatic—"Signs and Wonders"—John Fish inherits a fortune.

HALF-A-DOZEN more important families will about complete my list, and then I shall be able to bring this long series of articles to a summary conclusion, but two of the families I have yet to deal with—the Fishes and the Entwisles—are pretty numerous ones, so I will tackle them first. After that I will deal with the Burys and the Duxburys, the Kays and the Kirkhams, and wind up with a condensed account of the rest. The Fishes are one of the most numerous families in Darwen. I will first speak of the descendants of one man, Nicholas Fish, whom I may as well call "Old Nick," because he is the first Nicholas Fish I have heard of, and his name sticks to the family like glue down to the present day. I never could get at the origin of the Darwen Fishes, but, I suppose, like Topsy, they "grow'd." At the head of one important branch stand three brothers—Nicholas, Thomas, and William. The two latter I knew when I was a boy, but I fancy "Old Nick" died before my time. I know he lies comfortably buried beneath a gravestone in Pole-lane graveyard, and I have had a walk round that way to refresh my memory, but found the gate locked and the wall too high for me to climb at my time of life. But there he is, and it is about his descendants that I will tell you to-day. I will first mention, in passing, that "Old Nick" had a sister who married one Thomas Entwisle, and another who married John Harwood. Nicholas the First had five sons and three daughters—Thomas, James, George, William, and Nicholas; Alice, Hannah, and Kitty.

Thomas,[1] eldest son of Old Nicholas, married Ann, daughter of John Holden, and grand-daughter of Owd Timothy o' th' Looms. He had sons—Nicholas, Thomas, John, and James, and daughters—Catherine, Mary, Hannah, Phœbe, Alice, and Rachael Ann. Nicholas, eldest son of Thomas, married Susannah, daughter of James Briggs, of Ellison Fold, and had sons—Thomas, James, George, Nicholas, and John, and daughters—Ann, Sarah, and Susannah. Thomas married Maria, daughter of James Walsh. James, second son of the Nicholas who married Susannah Briggs, and great-grandson of "Old Nick," is living in Birmingham, married. George, his brother, married Betsy Briggs, and he is living at Ashton-under-Lyne, with a family. Nicholas, the next brother, married Hannah, daughter of Samuel Harwood, and died more than 20 years ago, leaving a family. John Fish, draper, of Bury, and Samuel Fish, draper, of Darwen, are his sons, and he has a daughter, Sarah Ann, living, unmarried. John, the last of these five brothers, sons of Nicholas, married a young woman in Blackburn, named Ellen Fish, no relation to the Darwen Fishes, so far as I am aware. He keeps a draper's shop at Southport, and has a family. Now for these men's sisters. Ann married William Green, and left a family. Sarah died a young woman, unmarried. Susannah married a distant relative of mine named Jacob Hunt, and has a family living in Blackburn, though her husband is dead. Turning back again to Thomas, eldest son of "Old Nick," you will see that his second son was called after himself. This son, Thomas, second son of Thomas, and grandson of "Old Nick," married Ann, daughter of John Briggs, of Cranberry Fold. He had sons—Thomas, who went to America, and died there; John, who died a young man, unmarried; Nicholas Fish, cabinet maker, who married Nancy Ellen, daughter of John Holden, and is living in Darwen with his family; and James, cabinet maker, of London, who married a widow in the great metropolis, and is living there with a family. Thomas, the son of Thomas, had also two daughters—Ann, widow of Philip Kershaw, who had one daughter, now dead; and Louise, wife of James Grime, of Lower Darwen. John, third son of Thomas, and grandson of "Old Nick," married another daughter of John Briggs, of Cranberry Fold—Alice. He died and left her with two sons and two daughters. The two sons are named Thomas and John. Both went to America, and Thomas is

[1] This Thomas Fish, eldest son of Old Nicholas the First was singing master at Pole Lane and Ebenezer Chapels for over fifty years. He never had any salary, not he; it wasn't the custom in those days to pay singing masters salaries; but in 1833 we made him a present of a silver cup, a Bible, and a hymn book in acknowledgment of his services for upwards of forty years, He continued the work as long as long as he was able, but died in February, 1846. He was singing master long before I can recollect the place, and I sang under him many a year.—J.H.

there now. John has come back, and is living in Darwen, and he says he'll live on sour milk and porridge before he'll go to America again. Of their two sisters, one, Phœbe, is dead, and the other, Mary Ann, is with her brother, in America, unmarried. James, the fourth son of Thomas, and grandson of "Old Nick," married yet another daughter of old John Briggs, of Cranberry Fold—Fanny; so that we have here another instance of three brothers marrying three sisters. Both he and his wife are dead, and their only descendant is an unmarried daughter. Catherine, daughter of Thomas, and grand-daughter of "Old Nick," married Edward Harwood—"Neddy o' Eben's." Mary married twice. Her first husband was Christopher Beckett, who died in the course of a few weeks, leaving her childless, and her second husband was Robert Hollis, by whom she had several children. Hannah married Robert Leach, and left one son, who was killed at Accrington, as already recorded. Phœbe married Richard Waddicor, and she is dead. Alice became the wife of Thomas Holden, and Rachael Ann the wife of John Hargreaves.

James, the second son of "Old Nick," married a woman I did not know, and left a son and a daughter. The daughter died a young woman, and the son 'listed for a soldier.

George, third son of "Old Nick," married a daughter of John Holden, of Jack's Kay. He had a family of fourteen—Nicholas, who married Hannah Hargreaves, went beyond Manchester, and died there; John, married Miss Eccles; George, married Miss Briggs; William, married Miss Nightingale; Thomas, died unmarried; James, died unmarried; Andrew, married Miss Dewhurst; Ralph; David, married Beulah Entwisle; Ebenezer; Seth; Ellen, married Walsh Hargreaves; Betty, married William Livesey, relieving officer for Darwen for many a year; Catherine, married a man named Kay. David, who married Beulah Entwisle, was born at Trees Farm seventy years ago, and he lives there yet, but he runs a great risk of having to flit in his old age, for Trees Farm is going to be converted into a public park in celebration of the Queen's Jubilee. He has three sons, married, and a daughter, unmarried. His eldest brother, Nicholas, son of George, had two children. The next, John, had sons—John, Andrew, Samuel, and George; daughters—Alice, Mary Ann, and Elizabeth. The fourth of the fourteen. William, had sons—William, Shepherd, Ralph, and George; daughters—Betty, Rachael, Nancy, and Alice. Nancy married Thomas Fish, and Alice became the wife of James Whittaker.

William, fourth son of "Old Nick," was twice married. His first wife was a daughter of Henry Briggs, of Cranberry Fold, and his second was the daughter of William Fish, of Blacksnape. He had a family of seven—Nicholas, who married Mary Walsh, as mentioned among the Walshes; William, married Miss Pilkington; John, married Miss Shorrock; James, died young; Catherine, died unmarried; Betty, married James Fish, who went to America; and Mary, who married, as her second husband, my cousin, James Pickup. Now, Nicholas, the eldest of these seven, had himself a family of nine, as follows:—James Walsh Fish, dead; William, died young; Baron, living, unmarried; Ralph, died young from typhoid fever, and was buried on the same day as his brother William; Nathaniel, living; Ann, wife of Richard Hitchen, has daughters—Mary, Elizabeth, Annie, and Miriam, and a son—Nathaniel; Mary, wife of Thomas Kay, has sons William, Thomas, and Edwin; Miriam, unmarried; and Betsy, unmarried. Nathaniel, one of the nine, first married Ellen, daughter of William Holden, of Cotton Hall, and had issue, Mary and Ellen. As his second wife he married Ann Jane, daughter of James Ainsworth, formerly registrar of births and deaths, and had four sons, of whom James, Edwin, and Frank are living.

Nicholas, fifth son of "Old Nick," was never called anything else but "Skriking Nick," not out of any disrespect for him, but simply to distinguish him from all the other "Nick" Fishes. He got his name from the circumstance that his voice was pitched in such a high key. He was married twice, and had fourteen children. His first wife was a daughter of Arthur Kay, of Cranberry Fold, and his second was a woman named Livesey. The following is a list of his fourteen children:—Arthur Fish, died young; Fish Fish, died a few years ago; Catherine, wife of Thurston Rostron; Hannah, married John Schofield, died lately; Mally, married James, son of Richard Eccles, died in America lately; Isabel, died a long time since; George, died young; James, died in Blackburn; Alice, living in America; Seth Harwood Fish, living at Mill Hill; Jane, died young; James Livesey Fish, died a young man; Levi Livesey Fish, rate collector; and another Isabel, living.

Lastly, I come to "Old Nick's" three daughters. Alice married George Wood, of Pickup Bank, and died, leaving seven sons and two daughters. Hannah married William Holden, of Jack's Kay, died, and left a family. Kitty married John Kirkham, of Pickup Bank, and became my mother-in-law.

The above-mentioned "Darruners" were all the descendants of one man, and there are many more of the same stock whom I cannot pretend to enumerate.

JEREMY HUNT'S RECOLLECTIONS OF

Old Nicholas Fish, whose history I have given above, had two brothers. One was called William Fish   He lived at Pasture Barn, across Darwen Moor. He had one son, Nicholas, who was married and had six sons called William, Thomas, Lawrence, John, Nicholas, and James, and three daughters, named Sarah, Mary, and Nanny. I thought he had a grandson who lived in Bolton Road, so I went to see him a few days since, but I found out that instead of being the grandson he was the great grandson of this William Fish. He could not recollect anything about Nicholas Fish or his family. The only representative of the family that I know of at the present time is this farmer who lives at a farm in Bolton Road, called Grainer's farm, near Jack's Kay Lodge. He is the great grandson of the William Fish who lived at Pasture Barn.

Thomas Fish was another of the three brothers. He married a Miss Hampson, sister of Thomas Hampson, the quack doctor. They had seven sons,—Nicholas, Roger, William, Thomas, John, James, and Arthur, and two daughters, Hannah and Mary. Nicholas, the oldest son, married a daughter of John Holden, of Jack's Kay. Roger was never married. He went to America and on his way home died on shipboard. William married Miss Rachael Holden, daughter of Briggs Holden, of Aushaw farm, near Entwistle. Thomas married Miss Peggy Holden, sister of his brother William's wife. John was never married, and I cannot say whether James was married or not, but I know that Arthur was married and had a family. Hannah Fish, the eldest daughter, married a Ralph Holden, of Jack's Kay. They went to live at Littleborough, and their descendants reside there at the present time. The other sister, Mary, was married to Edmund Bury, son of Andrew Bury, of Bury Fold. Their family reside in Darwen yet, but I cannot trace them.

William Fish, whom I have mentioned as having married a Miss Holden, was a farmer at Fdgeworth, and lived and died there. One of his sons, Briggs Fish, was in Darwen only a week or two ago. He is the representative of that branch of the family, and has never been married. There are a good many of Thomas Fish's family in Darwen, and the late Richard Fish was one of his sons. He married a Miss Green, who died about 25 or 26 years ago. He was thus a son of Thomas, and nephew of Roger. One of his sons is called Frederick Fish, and is secretary of the Mission School connected with Belgrave Chapel. He is one of the youngest representatives of Thomas Fish's family. Thomas Fish had a daughter called Hannah. She married Thomas Fish, and they are living yet with their family in London Terrace, Darwen. Another daughter married a George Haworth, of Blackburn.

William Fish, who was nicknamed "Bill o' Margaret's," was married, and had seven children, three of whom were sons and four daughters. Fish Fish, the eldest son, married Ellen Marsden; William Fish married a Miss Livesey; Thomas Fish married Jane Fish; Alice Fish married a man named Marsden; Betty Fish married William Fish, who had been married before; and Kitty Fish married Robert Eccles, brother of the late well-known James Eccles—"Old Squinting Jimmy" as he was called.

Fish Fish, who married Ellen Marsden, had four sons and four daughters. William, the eldest son, is now dead, but has left a family of two daughters and a son. The son married a Miss Ward, and Isaac, the second son, married a woman named Ellen Critchley. They had no family, and are now living at Eccleston, near Chorley. Lawrence Fish, the third son, died a number of years ago. He married a Miss Myers, of Darwen Street, Blackburn. They had one son, but he, and all the rest of the Lawrence branch are dead. Robert Blake Fish, fourth son, died at the age of sixteen. Of the five daughters Ann was the eldest. She was the wife, and is now the widow, of John Holden, grocer at the corner of Arch Street, Darwen. She is living yet, and is in her 89th year. Their family consists of one son and one daughter. The name of the son was John Fish Holden, and he married a woman called Roberts, but died nearly 20 years ago, and left his wife and one son also named John Fish Holden, who is the only living male representative of that branch of the family. The daughter was called Nancy Ellen, and she is now the wife of Nicholas Fish, the well-known cabinet maker, Darwen. They have four sons and one daughter. Alice was the second daughter of Fish Fish. She was married to William Holden, who was for many years collecting overseer for Darwen. He was a capital musician, and was for many years organist at both the chapel and the church, and the conductor of the Darwen Choral Society. They are both dead, but they left one daughter, who is unmarried, and lives in South Street. Her name is Elizabeth Ellen Holden. The next two daughters were Mary and Peggy, who were twins. Mary married her cousin, John Fish, and there are five of their sons and one daughter living, unmarried, at Baron's, near Blacksnape. Peggy, the other of the twin sisters, has died recently. She was the wife of William Kay, of Lower Barn, near Blacksnape. There is one son living, but I do not know of any daughters. Ellen was the fifth of the daughters of Fish Fish. She was married to William Pickup, of Marsh House, where she is living yet. They had only one daughter, and she was married to Robert Yates, land surveyor, of Blackburn.

There is another branch of the Fishes connected with the Blacksnape Fishes. I knew the old man from whom the stock springs, more than seventy years ago. His name was James Fish, and he lived at a place in Blacksnape called The Temple. He had been a soldier, and he preserved his military bearing in his old age, when I knew him. He had sons called George, William, Timothy, and James; daughters, Isabella, and Mary.

George, first son of old James, went on a pleasure visit to Liverpool at a time when the Great Napoleon had the world at fever heat. He didn't get much pleasure out of the visit, for when he got to Liverpool the King's officers took a fancy to him, and pressed him strongly to be a soldier. But George wouldn't. They kept him on board ship for seven years, but no inducement or threat could make him take the oath of allegiance, and he was practically a prisoner during the whole of that seven years. When the peace was signed in 1815, the King very kindly allowed George to come home, but George was not very grateful for his liberation, for he turned out a terrible Radical, if not a Republican, as well he might after his experience. I knew him very well after his return. He married the widow of Thomas Holden, of Hoddlesden (Tom o' Titus's), but never had any family except the son and three daughters that she brought with her into the family when she changed her name a second time.

William, second son of old James, was a very remarkable man. They sometimes called him "Bill o'th' Temple," but generally "Bill o' Ann's." I suppose his mother must have been called Ann, but she died before my time, and I never knew anything about her. William was one of the best singers Lancashire has ever produced. He had a fine tenor voice, as flexible as a fiddle, and he took a pride in over-singing everybody he came across. He always chose the most florid songs, if you know what that means—elaborate, brilliant; we always used to call them florid. I have heard him sing "Every Valley" with such power and flexibility as would nearly make one hold his breath with delight. Among his most popular airs were "Haste, Israel, haste," from "Joshua;" "Why does the God of Israel sleep," from "Samson;" "How vain is man," from "Judas;" and "So shall the lute and harp awake." You could have heard him on his cobbler's stool go through the famous runs of these songs just like a string of beads. He never took his breath in the longest run, but sustained it evenly to the end, and finished with a flourish. He could play the violin, and that helped him a good deal. He was a star in music; I never heard a man's voice so flexible in my life, though I have heard women excel him. For many a year William was singing master at Tockholes Independent Chapel, and for about six years he led the choir at Mount Street, Blackburn. That would be about fifty years ago, for William Riley succeeded him for a couple of years, and I went to Mount Street myself in 1843. This William Fish kept a farm at Stand, near Hoddlesden, and his wife was Lucy, daughter of Oliver Duxbury. He had four sons and about three daughters. Two of his sons are living yet—James, in his seventieth year, and John, the youngest. He went over to the religion of the Baptists, and became quite a high Calvinist before he died, though he was a very intelligent man. He was well read, and could cavil a good deal—argue, if you prefer the term; and he could plague folks, too, "gradely ill," but he never tried to plague me. I don't know how it was, but he never did. There used to be a butcher's shop at the corner of Fleming Square and Back Lane, Blackburn, kept by a man named Smith. Smith was a Catholic, and thought he could sing, and he would have been very much offended if he had been told that an Independent or a Calvinist could teach him how to tackle the great oratorios of Handel, much more one of his own particular Masses. This man was an ardent musician, and he used to pour over his music in the shop until William Fish, in passing by, became terribly anxious in his curiosity about it. So one day William stepped into the shop and discovered that the butcher was humming away at one of the Masses in which there was a very long florid passage—a "run" as we call them—with a curious change of key in the middle of it. William said, "Tha connot sing that, and aw con." "Can you?" says the other. "Yes," replied William, "and" (he added, when telling me of the incident) "aw geet howd o' thad book an aw sung id slap off, bud sitho id wer' as mich as ever aw could manage. He wanted to know who aw wor, bud aw would na tell him." The well-to-do butcher was astonished at a working man, in coarse clothing, being able to go through this passage so nimbly, and though William would not tell him his name he found it out before he saw him again. Whenever there was a company of singers in Blackburn William would get into their company and find out what state of proficiency they had attained, and then with a glory of pride he would show them how far he was superior to them. When he died, on the 4th of May, 1861, old William Fish was in his 75th year. He had lost the control of his voice long before then, and could not sing in tune. Now, I am in my 82nd year, and I can sing in tune yet. With all his ability and intelligence, he was very superstitious, for to his last day he was "feared o' boggarts." I have heard him tell how he felt when he had to walk over from Darwen to Hoddlesden alone in the evening. He used to say, "When aw geet up t' top o' Sudell Road gooin' o'er to'rt t' Princes it wur *prestissimo* wi me aw con tell thee." And I have heard one of his sons tell that, when the old man got home at night, if the rest of the family had gone to bed, he would rush headlong upstairs with his shoes on, never feeling safe alone.

Timothy was the next son of old James. He was never married, and, as he emigrated to America and settled there, I don't know much about him.

The fourth of the brothers was called James, after his father. For his first wife he married Jane, daughter of William Fish, better known as " Bill o' Nicholas's." What family he had by this marriage I don't know. His second wife was the daughter of Robert Eccles, who lived above Blacksnape. Like his elder brother, "Tim," he went to America. He wrote many a time to his cousin, William Holden, and we learnt that he became a chapel-keeper over there. But all at once his letters ceased coming, and it was supposed that he was dead.

Isabella, daughter of old James the First, became the wife of John Holden, of Blacksnape Fold, and mother of the late John Holden, grocer, Arch-street, and the late William Holden, overseer for Over Darwen, organist at the Higher Chapel and Trinity Church, &c. Isabella died many years ago, but her daughter Nancy is living yet. She is the widow of Joshua Baron, J.P. And the second John Holden's wife is living, in her 89th year.

Mary, another daughter of old James the First, married a man named John Whewell, and had a family, some of whom are now living at Blacksnape.

I now come across a family of Fishes that I could never make anything of. The foremost figure of the group is "Little Tot," otherwise called " Blackburn Times." Many a time have I tried to work out his relationship with the other little Fishes of Darwen, but I could not succeed, although he was evidently a genuine " Darrun Salmon." His father was a James Fish, of Darwen, who married a daughter of Thurston Briggs, of Blacksnape. one of the original four brothers who stand at the head of the Briggs family. She died and left her husband with two children—Mary, who married John Duxbury, of Hoddlesden, and " Little Tot." James married again and had another son called Ben, who would have been my age if he had lived until to day. "Little Tot" married Ann, daughter of George Jepson, and had a very large family. Altogether I should think he had more than a dozen children. but I can only reckon up four who are living now—Thomas, John, Benjamin, and Margaret. Tom and Maggie are twins. They were born in September, 1823. The latter is a second wife of Richard Kershaw, of Hob-lane, Edgeworth. Kershaw's first wife was Mary, another of "Little Tot's" daughters, who was formerly one of my singers.

There is another lot of Fishes, living about Chapels, that I never could quite read, and I have heard John Fish, late of Mill Hill, Blackburn, say he was one of that family. I once knew a man named Burgoyne Fish, who lived at Chapels, and I always had the impression that he had been a soldier. He had two sons and two daughters that I knew—Mark, Thomas, Betty, and Jane,—and more that I didn't know. Jane became the wife of Thomas Fish, one of old "Bill o' Margaret's" sons, and Betty married James Entwisle. Of course they are dead, but they have both left families. There was something remarkable about old Burgoyne. He was one of the followers of John Wesley who established Methodism in Darwen upwards of a century ago, and he could either fight or pray if necessary. The early Methodists were much persecuted in the town, pelted with stones, hooted and hustled. They had no place of worship for a while, but they held outdoor meetings and improvised platforms for the preacher and his assistants. At one of their meetings a little, noisy, mischievous fellow annoyed the Methodists terribly, but old Burgoyne Fish—a big powerful man with a soldierly bearing—leapt down from the platform, took his assailant up in his arms like a child, and, to the terror of both the little fellow and the bystanders, walked off with him to the brook side. There had been a good deal of rain, and most of my readers will know that in rainy weather the river Darwen is no longer a brook, but a mountain torrent, fierce enough and deep enough to drown a small army and to wash away houses and stone bridges. Over this torrent the powerful Wesleyan held his tormentor at arm's length, and vowed that if he would not make a solemn promise to annoy the Methodists no more he would drop him in the brook. The roar of the river and the power of his captor terrified the little mischievous fellow, and he was glad to enter into any sort of compact that Burgoyne liked to enforce. He never troubled the meetings again, for he had a wholesome dread of their leader ever after. This incident happened over a hundred years ago. I have heard not only my father but many an old Wesleyan tell the story, for as long as old Burgoyne lived his exploits used to be freely talked about; and I knew him very well in his old age and my own childhood. His son Tom—a great roaring basso—used to sing beside me in the Choral Society.

When I was a little lad, over 70 years ago, there was a shoemaker's

shop at the bottom of Darwen Street, Blackburn, kept by a man named Henry Wilkinson, and my father, who, as a handloom weaver, had to carry his work from Blackburn to Pickup Bank and back, used to leave his load here while he did his errands in the town. There was a certain John Fish, of Darwen, a Methodist, who worked at this shop, and my father had many a good cavil with him on the topics of the day. Now, in those days there was a great deal of fuss about a new sect that had arisen with a young woman named Johanna Southcott at its head, and I remember that my father gathered a good deal of his information about the progress of the new sect in Blackburn. Johanna pretended that she had been visited by the Holy Ghost, and that a Saviour was going to be born into the world. Her followers bought her a silver cradle and an embroidered quilt, The men began to grow long beards in imitation of the Jews of old, and to imagine that they were the elect people of God. There were a good many of the sect in Blackburn, but Ashton-under-Lyne was the greatest stronghold that I heard of. The earth was full of signs and wonders. A woman named Mary Bateman had a hen that laid an egg on which the full revelation of the new Saviour was written, and another woman named Ann Moore was said to be living without food in anticipation of Christ's coming. The printing press was a ricketty old thing at that time, but the doings of the new sect set it in motion; and I remember a rhyme being published which I read at the time. Two couplets in the rhyme " stick in my crop " until this very day. The first one was :—
   Mary Bateman's hen laid an egg in her nest
   On which Christ's coming was fully expressed.
The other couplet I will not quote because it is not couched in language suitable to the refined taste of the present generation, but it was a very forcible one, and it told how the doctors examined Ann Moore, who was pretending to live without food, and found her case to be a fraud. The hopes of the fanatics were never realised, for Miss Johanna, to her credit, died childless. Her disciples must have been more deluded than herself, for they lived in the hopes of her rising from the dead, until by degrees they all withered away. Old John Fish, the cobbler, was a strong opponent of the Southcott sect, and he and my father talked of scarcely anything else for many years. On one occasion, however, my father couldn't get a word out of John, and he said, " John, you're not for talking to-day. What's to do?" " Well, 'Thannel," said John, " I've something on my mind this morning." " What's that, John ?" For reply John suddenly asked, " Did you ever know aught of those Fishes who lived in Eccleshill ?" " Oh, yes," my father answered,

"I knew them very well." "Well," said John, "there's a piece of landed property here advertising for an owner, and I believe it's me!" Upon this my father told him all he knew about the Eccleshill Fishes, to which family he belonged, and old John, having satisfied himself that he was heir to the vacant property in the North which he had seen advertised, applied for it, and got it. It was worth about £600 a year, so John cobbled no longer, and my father teased him persistently by calling him "Mr. Fish" instead of plain "John." When I was a lad I used to go to Blackburn with my father, and I met old John several times. He was dressed like a well-to-do country gentleman, with good clothes and a white choker, and my father used to take off his hat to him and remark what a great man he had become. John couldn't stand this, and I heard him plead more than once, "Neaw, 'Thannel, do let me alooan," while my father laughed at him and "Mister"-ed him in a most aggravating fashion. This John Fish was twice married. By his first wife he had one son, who became a handloom weaver in Bolton, and by his second he had three daughters. The girls got a good education, and one of them married Thomas Armistead, commonly called "Tom o' Fisher's," after his uncle, I suppose, old James Fisher, handloom cutlooker. The last of John Fish's three girls that I ever heard of was a Mrs. Brierley, who lived in Richmond Terrace, Blackburn. Old John never looked as happy in his days of retirement as when he cobbled at Henry Wilkinson's, near the old House of Correction, at the bottom of Darwen Street, Blackburn.

There are other Fishes in and around Darwen, but I cannot pretend to reckon them up.

Three centuries back I trace tenants or freeholders of the name of Fish in Over Darwen. One of the earliest is Ralph ffishe, who is named in the Will of Edward Osbaldeston, made in 1588, as holding under the Osbaldestons, Lords of Darwen Manor, "one parcell of grounde lyinge between Soughe and Coubron tenement in Over Darwin."

About the same date lived John ffishe, whose wife died in 1604, and Lawrence ffishe, buried Aug. 8th, 1603.

William Fishe, of Over Darwen, is the first who appears as a landowner in the township. He died June 21st, 1616, and at an Inquisition as to his estate, taken at Chorley, the 9th Jan., 14 James I., it was attested that the deceased William Fishe had held of Richard Hoghton, Knt. and Bart., in free socage, one messuage, one garden, and 20 acres of land, meadow and pasture, in Over Darwen. Ellen Fishe, widow of William, was then living at Over Darwen; and James Fishe, aged one year, two months, and nineteen days, was William's son and heir.

James Fishe, of Upper Darwen, who died Dec., 1689, may perhaps have been the same with the infant heir, James Fishe, of 1616.

But there were others of the name, distinct from William Fishe's family, resident in Darwen in the reigns of the first two Stuarts. Ralph Fishe, possibly a son of the

R

Ralph of 1588, had an estate in the township up till his death, which happened about 1623. The after-death Inquisition, taken at Blackburn, 8th April, 21st James I., shewed that Ralph Fishe, deceased, possessed in Over Darwen, one messuage, one garden, 10 acres of land, 5 acres of meadow, 5 acres of pasture, and 4 acres of moss. He left no male heir, but two daughters, co-heiresses, viz., Augusta, the wife of James Cunliffe, and Margery Fish.

Next I note Thomas Fishe, of Over Darwen, also a small freeholder. He died June 2nd, 7th Charles I (1631) ; his wife—" Uxor Thomæ ffyshe de Upper Darwen," had been buried at Blackburn, Nov. 16th, 1623. The escheat, taken at Blackburn, April 24th, 9th Charles I., returned that Thomas Fishe had died seized of one barn, with 12 acres of land, meadow and pasture, in Over Darwen, and 6 acres of land, meadow and pasture, in Livesey, late improved from the waste of Livesey.

Thomas Fishe, aged 30 years and above in 1633, was son and heir of the above Thomas. He had a son John, born in 1634. The names of both Thomas Fish and John Fish are affixed to the petition on behalf of Vicar Clayton in 1660. The following notes of subsequent members are the sum of my information respecting the families of Fish in Darwen :—John Fish married Agnes Walsh, Aug. 21, 1632. William Fish, of Upper Darwen, was living in 1676. John Fish, of Upper Darwen, yeoman and chapman, conveyed in 1718, a plot of land to be the site for a new Nonconformist Meeting House, in Clarke's Field, on his estate. At Chapels, in Darwen, stands an old messuage, no doubt once the residence of this John Fish ; a stone in the wall having the initials " I F E" (John and Ellen or Elizabeth Fish) and the date "1725." John Fish, of Upper Darwen, chapman, had a son John, bapt. May 15th, 1702. This son was John Fish, of Upper Darwen, chapman, who by Jane his wife, had a son John, born in 1726. I also meet with a Ralph Fish, of Upper Darwen, afterwards of Blackburn, chapman, who married, Feb. 9th, 1697-8, Mary Wilkinson, of Blackburn, and had sons Richard, born in 1699, and Ralph born in 1701. Thomas Fish, of Upper Darwen, chapman, was living in 1704. Ralph Fish, of Over Darwen, whose wife Nanny died in March, 1790, was buried Feb. 16th, 1796, aged 62.—*History of Blackburn*, pp. 505-6.

Conclusion.

In the foregoing chapters I have omitted a great deal that I might have given, but I was afraid of getting tedious. It was originally agreed when Mr. Shaw began to jot down and arrange my "Recollections," that we should confine our attention to about twenty families and give them on an average one chapter each, dividing the numerous ones into two, and putting two of the smaller families into one chapter. But we have already given thirty-two chapters, and if I had not been taken ill we could certainly have made forty, if not more. I will, however, conclude for the present with a few words about the Entwisles, the Kirkham's, and the Kays, and if I am spared a little longer I shall be glad to put on record some more of my "Recollections" before I die.[1]

The first Entwisle that I knew was the grandfather of Robert Smalley Entwisle, of Sough. He was one of the original Darwen Methodists, along with old Burgoyne Fish, upwards of a hundred years ago, and he once had the honour of entertaining John Wesley, while that great divine was on a visit to the district. His name was Ralph Entwisle, and though I cannot recall his features or his personal appearance, I know so much about him that I think he must have been living when I was a lad. Most of the Entwisles spring from him and his brothers. I also knew a William Entwisle, of Catleach, who died about sixty years ago. He had sons, James, Ralph, Lawrence, Edward, Joseph, John, and William, and about four daughters. He married a woman I have previously mentioned under the nickname of "Old Nine Penn'orth."

The Kirkhams, to a great extent, are descended from two brothers, Richard and Benjamin Kirkham, whose mother was one of "Owd Timothy o' th' Looms's" sisters. Old Ben married my mother's sister. There is another branch about Hoddlesden, springing from the cousins

---

[1] Jeremy never recovered from this illness, and his life's work was never completed. What I can do to put on record his Recollectons has been done in this book.—J.G.S.

of Richard and Benjamin. Hoddlesden used to be a bleaching place, and I remember very well one old man, a labourer there, who had two sons, Thomas and Benjamin, and two or three daughters—Betsy, Mary, &c.

The principal Kays that I ever knew were old Arthur Kay's lot at Cranberry Fold. Three of his sons married three daughters of old James Briggs. He had a large family. Of his sons I knew Thomas, Alexander, William, Arthur, James, Joseph, and George. The two youngest were about my own age.

There are three other families I intended to include—the Burys (or Berrys), who date back four hundred years; the Duxburys a very old and very numerous Darwen family; and the Walmsleys. I have mentioned Joseph Walmsley, a famous alto singer sixty years ago. Alderman John Walmsley, cotton manufacturer, is his nephew.

ADDITIONAL FAMILIES.

When Jeremy Hunt ceased the publication of his "Recollections," owing to his illness, he stated that he intended giving the history of six more families, and then summing up the rest of the Old Darwen Families in a few sentences. It would therefore appear that if the history of these half dozen families could be written, my old friends' work would be completed. The families he intended telling about, as shown in the concluding chapter of his "Recollections," are the Entwisles, the Kirkhams, the Kays, the Burys, the Duxburys, and the Walmsleys. Now it happens that while dictating to me the history of one family, Jeremy would often run into that of another, and on searching my note-book I am able to transcribe in his own words some account of the history of these six remaining families, besides a pretty good history of the Lightbowns and something of the Thompsons, of whom I know he intended to speak, although he forgot them for the moment when winding up summarily his articles in *The Blackburn Times*. I am thus able to enlarge his "Recollections" by the addition here of the following eight chapters :—

The Entwisles.
The Kirkhams.
The Kays.
The Burys.

The Duxburys.
The Walmsleys.
The Lightbowns.
The Thompsons.

What Jeremy says of these families is printed hereafter in large type, just the same as the chapters that precede them, and I have subjoined, in smaller type, some fragmentary information which I have gleaned from my note-book without being able, on Jeremy's authority, to string it together in genealogical order.—J. G. S.

The Entwisles.

RALPH ENTWISLE, a Methodist, is the first Entwisle of whom I have any recollection. I know a lot about him, and I think he died when I was a lad, because I know so much about him, but I cannot remember whether he was tall or short, stout or thin, or anything about his personal appearance, as I can in the case of most of the old men living seventy or seventy-five years ago. John Wesley put up at his house when he came to Darwen to found a mission here more than a hundred years ago, and Ralph Entwisle, Burgoyne Fish, and two or three other old "Darruners" were the real founders of Methodism in this town. Old Ralph had several brothers, and most of the Entwisles of Darwen are descended from these men.

Old William Entwisle, of Sough, was son of Ralph. I knew him very well. He married Betty Smalley, grand-daughter of the Rev. Robert Smalley. Robert Smalley Entwisle, J.P., of Southport, and Alderman William Entwisle, J.P., an ex-Mayor of Darwen, are his sons. Robert Smalley Entwisle, J.P., married two cousins, the first being Sarah, only daughter of James Pickup No. 2, while the second was one of William Pickup's five daughters. By the first marriage he had an only son, James Pickup Entwisle.

A second important branch of the Entwisle family is descended from William Entwisle of Catleach, better known as "Owd Billy o' Ralphs."[1] Owd Billy died when I was a young man of twenty. His wife was Rachael Marsden—"Owd Nine Penn'orth"—daughter of old James Marsden. Her history has already been given in connection with the Marsden family. They had seven sons, and, I think, four daughters, and a good many of the Darwen Entwisles are their descendants. The seven sons were James, Ralph, Edward, Lawrence, Anyon, John, and William. One of the daughters married old James Hindle, of

[1] Jeremy never told me anything about Ralph, father of "Owd Billy," and I presume it would not be Ralph Entwisle, the Methodist, for he had a son William who is called "William Entwisle of Sough," to distinguish him from this William Entwisle of Catleach."—J.G.S.

Eccleshill (son of James and grandson of Christopher). I forget her name, but I remember her sister Hannah.

James, the eldest son of "Owd Billy o' Ralph's," married Ellen Holden, and his descendants now live near Guide. He used to farm at Mouse House, just above Putforth, a farmstead between Guide and Belthorn. Ralph married Ellen Holden's sister Mary. They were the daughters of old Thomas Holden, and sisters to the grandfather of George Pickup Holden.

Anyon[1] married a woman named Alice, commonly called "Owd Ailse o' Adam's." She had a sister Mary who married Thomas Cooper, of Pole-lane. Owd Ailse was a queer old stick. When she was a big young woman of about 16 or 17 years of age, she went to a school opened by the Methodists at a place called Crane Head. She could not tell one letter from another, and they had lots of fun in trying to teach her. The letter W was an especial stumbling block to her sharp but uneducated intellect. One day after the teacher had been trying to drive the letters into her head she went home and told her mother she would go to a school where they put them in the Bible Class first thing; she wasn't going to be learning her alphabet for ever.

About sixty years ago, there used to be gigantic musical festivals at Liverpool, in which a number of singers from Darwen took part—old Richard Entwisle, William Fish, Joseph Walmsley, John Peel, and others. Some particulars have been given in the account of the Marsden family. A man of the name of Entwisle is mentioned as having married Rachael Hindle, only daughter of James Hindle (son of old Christopher the First). She had three sons, if not more,—Anyon, Marsden, and Caleb. Anyon was a well-known local character 60 years ago, and particularly notable for composing peace-egg songs, and going about peace-egging. For his tragic history see page 84. "Money Ned's lot," mentioned in the history of the Briggses, introduces us to the important family of one Edmund Entwisle, which, in the early part of this century, "supplied half the country side with wives." One of the earliest of the Entwisles mentioned by Jeremy is Thomas Entwisle, who married a sister of old Nicholas Fish the First, sometime last century. Beulah Entwisle is an old woman of whom Jeremy often spoke. She was the wife of David Fish, who was born at the Trees Farm 70 years ago, and lives there yet. James Entwisle married Betty, daughter of old Burgoyne Fish the Methodist. William Entwisle married Jane Hunt, daughter of Jeremy's uncle James, who lived at Harwood Fold with Jeremy's uncle John. Joseph Entwisle, of Blacksnape, married a daughter of Ephraim Harwood. James Entwisle married Betty, daughter of old George Briggs, of Sunnyhurst. Nicholas Entwisle married Lettice, daughter of George Jepson. Thomas Entwisle, of Slack, near Hoddlesden, had a daughter, Nancy, who married John, son of George Jepson.

[1] Jeremy never told me anything about the families of Edward and Lawrence, or John and William, but I have an impression that he has told me they all grew up and married.—J.G.S.

The Kirkhams.

THE second sister of "Owd Timothy o' th' Looms" was named Mary, and she married a man named Kirkham. I remember three of their sons, Richard, Benjamin, and Christopher, and I can trace their descendants nearly all over Darwen. The principal Kirkhams of Darwen belong to this stock, but there is another race of the same name in the town. Benjamin Kirkham, mentioned above, married Catherine Leach (my mother's sister), eldest daughter of "Old John the First." She died in 1807, leaving him five sons and six daughters. Most of the Kirkhams of the present day are descendants of Old Dick and Ben., but but there is another important branch of the Kirkhams, living mainly about Hoddlesden, who are descended from their cousins. One of the first of this lot was a labourer at Hoddlesden Bleach Works, who had sons called Thomas and Benjamin; and daughters, Betsy, Mary, &c. John Kirkham, of Pickup Bank, a descendant [grandson?] of the Kirkham who married Mary Holden, sister of "Owd Timothy o' th' Looms," took for his wife Kitty Fish, daughter of "Old Nick" the First. His daughter Hannah became my wife.

An Alice Kirkham is mentioned as having become the second wife of Robert, second son of old Richard Eccles, of Walton-le-Dale. Richard Kirkham, alias "Dick o' Sally's," married Jane, only daughter of old Titus Holden, grandson of "Owd Timothy o' th' Looms." Peggy Kirkham, of Pickup Bank, became the wife of Briggs o' Titus's (Holden). Thos. Kirkham, of "Harrud's," near Hoddlesden, had a daughter, Elizabeth, who married successively John and Joseph Harwood, sons of Ephraim. She outlived both her husbands, but is now dead. By her first marriage she had a son, John, who keeps a shop in the Market House. Thomas had also a daughter, Martha, who married John, son of Marsden Hindle.

The Kays.

THE principal Kays that I ever knew were old Arthur Kay's lot at Cranberry Fold. Three of his sons married three daughters of old James Briggs. He had a large family. Of his sons I knew Thomas, Alexander, William, Arthur, James, Joseph, and George. The two youngest were about my own age.

Jeremy speaks of an old "Darruner" named Kay, as " Owd Skriking Aleck," one of whose daughters, the widow of David Grime, is living yet [1887], aged 78 years. Jeremy knew her nearly all her long life. She was one of six girls, and she never had a brother. Of her father "Owd Skriking Aleck," Jeremy relates that he used to go about saying " Aw've six queens an' never a king." One of the daughters of Arthur Kay, of Cranberry Fold, was the first wife of "Skriking Nick," the fifth son of the original " Old Nick " Fish.

The Burys.

THE Burys (or Berrys) are a very old and a very numerous Darwen family, dating back four hundred years. I shall take the account in Abram's History as a basis, and tell you about the old men I knew when we come to them.[1] One of the principal representatives of the family at the present day is John Bury, of Bolton-road, who married Nancy Hindle.

I think Andrew Bury, of Bury Fold, is one of the oldest members of the Bury family I have heard Jeremy mention. He had a son Edward who married Mary, daughter of Thomas Fish, one of the original three Fishes mentioned in Jeremy's "Recollections." The descendants of these Burys reside in Darwen yet, but Jeremy could not trace them. Andrew Bury, of Bury Fold, had a daughter who became the wife of John Eccles, son of " Thomas o' Owd Sapling Bough's." Two cousins of the name of Bury married two daughters of James Hindle (grandson of Christopher the First). One of them used to be spoken of by Jeremy as Jack Bury. Thomas Bury married Betty Hunt, daughter of Jeremy's uncle John. George Bury, of Cotton Hall, married the only daughter of Nicholas Entwisle.

[1] Jeremy did not live to reach this part of his work.

The Duxburys.

THE Duxburys are a very old Darwen family, and they are very numerous in the town. Old Christopher Duxbury, of Hoddlesden, is the first I know of. He married Jane, daughter of Thomas Holden, and grand-daughter of " Owd Timothy o' th' Loom's." He had a numerous family, and I knew them all. Tom was the eldest— "Skriking Tom"—great-grandfather of Thomas Duxbury, gas manager. The nickname descended from father to son, for "Skriking Tom's" son Christopher was called "Skriking Kess." "Kess" had a son William, and William had several sons, one of whom is Thomas Duxbury, gas manager, and another John Duxbury, who was goalkeeper for the Darwen Football Club in its best days. "Skriking Tom" got his nickname by his noisy and peculiar way of amusing himself as he walked along the country lanes when in a state of exhilaration seventy years ago. He had sons, Christopher and William. There are several branches of "Skriking Tom's" family in Darwen, but all the Duxburys are not of this stock. Moses Duxbury, town councillor, for instance, belongs to a different family altogether.

Another of Old Christopher the First's sons was Timothy, who married Betty Kirkham. He was killed one terrible winter's night near the Anchor Inn, in Blackburn-road. His cart began to slip along the hard, frosty road, and as he was trying to stop it, he slipped too, and, getting under the wheel, was killed.

Another son of Old Christopher was John, and the youngest was called Christopher, after his father. He fell down stairs and broke his neck, in Blackburn, where he had gone to live. A son of his yet lives towards Furthergate.

Christopher Duxbury, of Hoddlesden, had a daughter Betty, who was the first wife of John Hindle (son of James, and grandson of Old Christopher the First). "Peggy o' Owd Kester's" (Duxbury) married Marsden Hindle (uncle to John, who married Betty Duxbury).

John Duxbury, of the Knowle, Darwen Chapels, was a famous character at the end of last century. He was a cotton manufacturer after the manner of those days being a "putter-out" of pieces to hand-loom weavers. It was not, however, for his business connections that he was most noted, but for his sporting proclivities, and he became so famous as to receive the nickname of "Th' Duke o' Darrun." He lived into the nineteenth century, and Jeremy remembered him very well. Horse-racing and cock-fighting were his great hobbies, and though he was not a real duke he numbered such members of the old nobility as the then Earl of Derby among his associates, On the spot where Duckworth-street Congregational Church now stands he originated the Darwen Horse Races, and supported them by his personal patronage and his influence among sporting men. A pair of silver spoons won in these local races are still preserved in the family as a relic. Cock-fighting was a very popular sport in Darwen at the beginning of the present century, and the poultry fanciers of the town trained fighting cocks which became famous all over the county. Jeremy remembered a main being fought at Chapels, at which the Earl of Derby (grandfather of the present Earl) and other sporting characters from Preston were present.

John Duxbury, of the Knowle Farm (Th' Duke o' Darrun), had a daughter Betty, who married George Hindle (son of Thomas), farmer, of Sunnyhurst, and afterwards innkeeper at the Black Horse. Thomas Duxbury, of Hoddlesden (Tummas o' Owd Kester's), married Ann, daughter of old Henry Briggs, of Cranberry Fold, and had a large family. Thomas Duxbury, of Stand, near Hoddlesden, who flourished seventy years ago, married Rachael Leach (Rachael o' Owd Richard's). They had several sons whose history Jeremy intended giving in connection with the Duxburys if he had lived to complete his work. Their daughter Ellen became the wife of Nathaniel Jepson, son of John, but only lived four months after her marriage. Timothy Holden, fifth son of "Owd Timothy o' th' Looms," married a Miss Duxbury as his first wife, and had by her two sons and a daughter. Alice Duxbury was courted more than fifty years by John Pickup, but John died single at the age of seventy, and she never enjoyed the pleasures of matrimony. There was a George Duxbury, organist at the Higher Chapel, nearly a hundred years ago. He married Betty Hindle, only daughter of old John the First. Lucy, daughter of Oliver Duxbury, became the wife of William Fish, of Stand Farm, near Hoddlesden, a famous singer. One of her sons, James Fish, is living yet [1887], aged 70 years. John Duxbury, of Hoddlesden, married Mary, daughter of James Fish, a woman born before Jeremy Hunt's time. Richard Duxbury married a daughter of Nathaniel Jepson, the son of John. John Duxbury married Mary, daughter of Ebenezer Harwood ("Old Eben"). Alice Duxbury, of Hoddlesden, was the second wife of Thurston Briggs, of Hoddlesden, who dropped down dead. John Duxbury, of Hoddlesden, married Mary Fish, sister of "Little Tot," as his first wife. She died leaving him a son and a daughter. The daughter is dead, but the son is living at Ashton-under-Lyne, an old man over seventy,

The Walmsleys.

LAWRENCE WALMSLEY, who lived at the latter part of last century, had a son Joseph ("Owd Joe o' Lawrence's), whom I knew very well when I was a young man. This Joseph Walmsley was a famous Darwen alto singer sixty years ago, and was one of those "Darruners" who used to sing at the Liverpool festivals. On one occasion they were rehearsing "And the glory of the Lord," from the "Messiah," under the conductorship of Mr. Gratrix, when the whole body of the singers, except Joe Walmsley, started a passage a beat too soon. Joe would not be dragged wrong, but all alone he chimed in his solitary voice in the proper time, and did his best to pull the others right. Gratrix stopped the singing, went up to him, and said, "Young man, you stand here and lead these altos," and stand there Joe did, two inches taller than ever he stood before, every day of the festival. Joe died about 1861. One of his daughters became the wife of my cousin Nathaniel, who was born in 1805, and died in 1885, aged 80 years. Old Lawrence had also sons called John and David. John Walmsley, cotton manufacturer, and formerly an alderman of the borough of Over Darwen is a nephew of "Joe o' Lawrence's." There used to be a Joseph Walmsley, of Grimshaw, who had two sons, John and Abraham. Isaac Walmsley, who keeps the Manor House Inn, is a representative of this family, and another representative is the landlord of the White Lion.

The Lightbowns.

JAMES HOLDEN, the second son of "Owd Timothy o' th' Looms," went off to be a soldier, leaving a wife and two girls behind him. James Lightbown married one of the girls, and the late John Lightbown, who died recently, at the patriarchal age of 92, was his youngest son. James had four sons, Thomas, Henry, James, and John, and two or three daughters.

Thomas Lightbown had a son named James, who married Betty, daughter of Richard Smalley, of Darwen, and he is living near Manchester with his family. He went into partnership in the paper-staining trade at Pendleton with his cousin Henry (son of Old John). He has one daughter married, living in Blackburn, and another unmarried, living with her father near Manchester.

Henry Lightbown was a schoolmaster in Blackburn, and I never knew his family. He kept a private adventure school of the better class, and many boys who have since become the gentry of Darwen went to Blackburn to attend it. Among them I remember was Mr. Joshua Baron, one of our oldest and most respected magistrates, who died a few years ago.

James Lightbown has sons named William, Henry, Timothy, Robert, and James. James the Third, as I must call him, was about my age. He died many years ago, but his widow is living in Blackburn to-day. Henry (of Chapels) is a member of the Darwen Town Council [1884], a prominent teetotaller, and a Guardian for the township of Eccleshill.

John (the fourth son of old James the First) was the oldest man in Darwen when he died last year [1883], and his youngest son, Timothy, is at the present time [1884] the Mayor and Chief Magistrate of our borough. Everybody in Darwen knew old John Lightbown, for it is not much more than twelve months since he died, and when he did die he was without doubt the "oldest inhabitant" in a town containing

30,000 people. The fact of the "oldest inhabitant" being the great-grandson of "Owd Timothy.o' th' Looms," and the great-great-great-great-grandson [six generations] of the first Holden of Darwen of whom I have told you, shows more than anything else I can think of how far back the traditional history of these, our ancestors, takes us.

Old John Lightbown, who died in 1883, and was buried on his 92nd birthday, had three sons and one daughter by his first wife—James, Henry, Roger, and Betty; and one son and one daughter by his second. The son, Timothy, is now Mayor of Darwen [1884]; the daughter died while a young woman. Roger lives in Darwen to-day, and is well-known; Henry is the head of a wealthy paper-staining concern at Pendleton, near Manchester; Betty married twice, her second husband being John Hunt, son of James. They had a son Roger, who lives at Pendleton. The Mayor's grandfather was a very old man when I knew him. He lived at Shaw Fold, Eccleshill, and before that he lived in Pickering Fold, on this side of Black-a-Moor. His son John was born at Pleasington, on the 27th of January, 1791.

"Owd Harry Dep" was the familiar name of a collier named Henry Lightbown, who lived in Dandy Row last century. He had two sons, who married two daughters of James Hindle (grandson of old Christopher the First). Thomas Lightbown, of Lower Darwen, had a daughter who married John Jepson, son of Nathaniel. Mrs. Roger Lightbown is a descendant or Henry Jepson, of Hoddlesden, a great-grand-daughter, Jeremy believed. Henry Lightbown, of the firm of Lightbown, Leach, and Catlow, cotton manufacturers, Darwen, married Nancy, daughter of John Catlow.

The Thompsons.

THOMPSON is not a name that has flourished greatly on Darwen soil, but there are a few yet, descendants of a man who married Owd Timothy o' th' Looms's eldest sister, about 150 years ago. My brother James married a woman named Ann Thompson, who was the great-grand-daughter of Owd Timothy's sister. Her father's name was Thomas, and his father's name James, but the Christian names of her great-grandfather (the first of the Thompsons) or her great-grandmother (Owd Timothy's sister) I never knew. One of the Thompsons of three or four generations back, James, brother of the Thomas named above, removed to Harwood, and within the last ten years a branch of the same family of the Thompsons has emigrated to America.

My brother's wife had four brothers—James, Thomas, John, and Benjamin. James lived and died at Baxenden, a block printer, but he has some descendants living. Thomas had twelve children, but there is only one left out of the lot; he keeps a farm belonging to "Jack o' Ted's" (John Walsh), on the edge of Tockholes. John is living in Blackburn. He had thirteen of a family, but there is only one (a daughter) living now; he buried two children in one day. Benjamin never had a family, but he died last December [1884], leaving a widow. He was born in March, 1818, and was 66 years of age when he died. His death occurred very suddenly. He had got up in the morning, lit the fire, and tied the lace of one of his clogs, but while in the act of tying the other clog he rolled over dead.

There are not many Thompsons of this family in Darwen, but the Thompsons, cotton manufacturers of Blackburn, are related to them. The Thompsons of Harwood are related to the Old Darwen stock.

William Thompson married Kate Holden, daughter of Briggs o' Titus's.

THE END.

Other exciting titles available from
Heritage Publications

Bygone Blackburn by Geo. Miller	£14.99
Lancashire and Cheshire Past & Present by Thomas Baines	£23.99
History of the Fylde of Lancashire by John Porter	£17.99
Life is What You Make It, John Fairclough	£5.99
The Four Blackburn V.C.s	£7.99
Drummer Spencer John Bent V.C	£7.99
Andrew Moynihan V.C	£7.99
Presentation of New Colours to the First Battalion The Queen's Lancashire Regiment	£7.99
Prints of Baines maps from 1862 of Blackburn, Bolton, Burnley and Lancaster	£12.99